Companion

to

The Divine Comedy

Portrait of Dante in the Bargello, Florence

Companion

to

The Divine Comedy

Commentary by C. H. Grandgent
as edited by Charles S. Singleton

Harvard University Press
Cambridge, Massachusetts
1975

Library of Congress Catalog Card Number 73-92714
ISBN 0-674-15175-5

Printed in the United States of America

Preface

This little volume is designed to serve as a commentary to Dante's *Divine Comedy*, and primarily as a "Companion" for those students of the poem who are obliged to read their Dante in English. What it offers is essentially a generous extract of those parts of Grandgent's well-known edition of the poem which can be understood by a reader who has little or no Italian (and quite possibly no Latin). Thus, no matter which of the many available English translations of the great poem may be chosen for solitary study or classroom use, Grandgent's general essays on Inferno, Purgatory, and Paradise, his charts and diagrams so helpful toward an understanding of the world picture that the poem bears within itself and presupposes, his introductions (termed Arguments) to each of the hundred Cantos, together with selected notes from the running commentary on each: all this and more is here offered to the modern reader who seeks to understand a poem in proper historical focus and in detail.

Most current editions of translations into English of the *Comedy*, whether in prose or in verse, are notoriously chary in the kind of aids toward that fuller historical understanding of Dante's poem which Grandgent's edition so readily provides. Many translators, it would seem, have published their work in editions designed for classroom use, and their feeling seems to have been that a commentary too lengthy and too detailed would "frighten away" the student. But this teacher of Dante can report, from his own teaching of Dante in translation, that the serious student is, more often than not, left truly hungry by such meager presentations. Time and again he finds no note whatsoever on this or that historical personage or mythological allusion or all the rest that comes to mind, wherein *every* reader needs help—on first reading at least.

The *Companion* represents an attempt to remedy this regrettable situation in the study and teaching of Dante *in translation* throughout the English-speaking world. The original edition of which it is the offspring is the revised Grandgent of recent publication: Dante Alighieri, *La Divina Commedia*, edited and annotated by C. H. Grandgent, revised by Charles S. Singleton (Harvard University Press, 1972).

May such an offspring serve well that companionable purpose for which it has been specifically brought into print, and thus cast on a great poem that fuller light which every modern reader requires. One of the main themes of the *Divine Comedy* is precisely the theme of "light"; and the poet himself would be the first to deplore the reading of his poem in "darkness": the darkness of scanty commentaries.

Charles S. Singleton

Contents

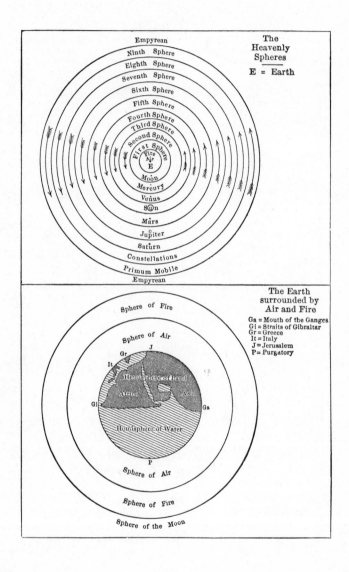

The
Heavenly
Spheres

E = Earth

Empyrean
Ninth Sphere
Eighth Sphere
Seventh Sphere
Sixth Sphere
Fifth Sphere
Fourth Sphere
Third Sphere
Second Sphere
First Sphere
Fire
Air
E
Moon
Mercury
Venus
Sun
Mars
Jupiter
Saturn
Constellations
Primum Mobile
Empyrean

The Earth
surrounded by
Air and Fire

Ga = Mouth of the Ganges
Gi = Straits of Gibraltar
Gr = Greece
It = Italy
J = Jerusalem
P = Purgatory

Sphere of Fire

Sphere of Air

Gr
J
It
Hemisphere of Land
Africa
Asia
Gi
Ga
Hemisphere of Water
P

Sphere of Air

Sphere of Fire

Sphere of the Moon

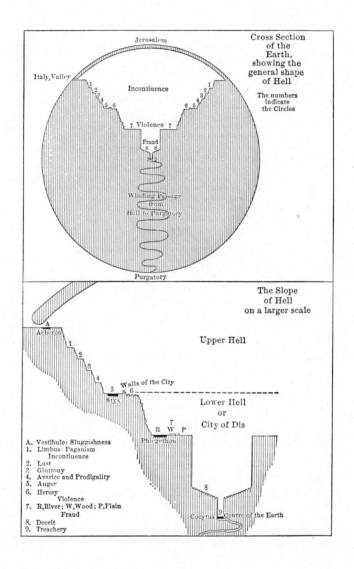

Cross Section
of the
Earth,
showing the
general shape
of Hell

The numbers
indicate
the Circles

Jerusalem

Italy, Valley

Incontinence

Violence

Fraud

Winding Passage
from
Hell to Purgatory

Purgatory

The Slope
of Hell
on a larger scale

Acheron

Upper Hell

Walls of the City

Styx

Lower Hell
or
City of Dis

R W P
Phlegethon

A. Vestibule: Sluggishness
1. Limbus: Paganism
    Incontinence
2. Lust
3. Gluttony
4. Avarice and Prodigality
5. Anger
6. Heresy
    Violence
7. R, River; W, Wood; P, Plain
    Fraud
8. Deceit
9. Treachery

Cocytus Centre of the Earth

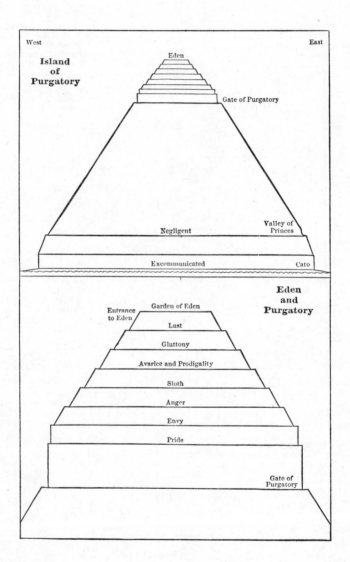

Bibliographical Abbreviations

Acts: The Acts of the Apostles

Aen.: Virgil's *Aeneid*

Arist.: Aristotle

Austin: H. D. Austin, "Dante Notes," *Modern Language Notes* XXXVII (1922): 36–39

Britt: Matthew Britt, O.S.B. (ed.), *The Hymns of the Breviary and Missal*, rev. ed., 1955

Cons.: Boethius's *Consolatio Philosophiae*

Cons. Phil.: see *Cons.*

Cor.: The Epistles of Paul the Apostle to the Corinthians

Deut.: Deuteronomy

Eccles.: Ecclesiastes

Ecclus.: Ecclesiasticus

Ep.: Dante's *Epistles*

Exod.: Exodus

Freccero (1959): John Freccero, "Dante's Firm Foot and the Journey without a Guide," *The Harvard Theological Review* LII (1959)

Gardner: E. G. Gardner, *Dante and the Mystics*, 1912

Gen.: Genesis

Holbrook: Richard Thayer Holbrook, *Dante and the Animal Kingdom*, 1902

Inf.: Dante's *Inferno*

Isidore: Isidore of Seville, *Etymologiarum sive Originum libri xx*, ed. W. M. Lindsay, 2 vols., 1911

Jer.: Jeremiah

Levit.: Leviticus

Macc.: Maccabees

Mat.: The Gospel according to St. Matthew

Met.: Ovid's *Metamorphoses*

Migne: *Patrologiae cursus completus: Series Latina*, ed. J.-P. Migne, 1844–1864 (with later printings)

Mon.: Dante's *Monarchia*

Moore: E. Moore, *Studies in Dante*, 4 vols., 1896–1916. There is a more recent edition.

Novati: F. Novati, *Freschi e Minii del Dugento*, 1908

Olschki (1949): Leonardo Olschki, *The Myth of Felt*, 1949

Par.: Dante's *Paradiso*

Phars.: Lucan's *Pharsalia*

Phil.: The Epistle of Paul the Apostle to the Philippians

Pr.: Proverbs

Ps.: Psalms

Purg.: Dante's *Purgatorio*

Rev.: The Revelation of St. John the Divine

Singleton (1949): Charles S. Singleton, *An Essay on the Vita Nuova*, 1949. There is a later edition.

Singleton (1954): Charles S. Singleton, *Dante Studies no. 1: Commedia: Elements of Structure*, 1954. There are later reprintings.

Singleton (1958): Charles S. Singleton, *Dante Studies no. 2: Journey to Beatrice,* 1958. There are later reprintings.

Singleton (1965b): Charles S. Singleton, "Inferno XIX: O Simon Mago!" *Modern Language Notes* LXXX (1965): 92–99

Singleton (1970): Charles S. Singleton, *Dante Alighieri, The Divine Comedy,* translated with a commentary: *Inferno,*
2 vols. (complete edition to be 6 vols. in the Bollingen Series), 1970

Theb.: Statius's *Thebaid*

Toynbee: P. Toynbee, *Dante Studies and Researches,* 1902

V.N.: Dante's *Vita Nuova*

Vulg.: the Vulgate

Vulg. El.: Dante's *De Vulgari Eloquentia*

Wisdom: the Wisdom of Solomon

Companion

to

The Divine Comedy

Introduction

1. The Florence in which Dante lived was virtually an independent municipality controlled by trade unions. Intense local pride, multifarious energy and enterprise, zest for politics, and partisan rivalry kept the blood of her citizens hot. The town was rapidly coming to the front rank among European cities; in manufactures and commerce she was a leader; inrushing wealth and increasing magnificence made her a pleasant abode. And all these interests — self-government, business, luxurious living — had the charm of novelty. So it was with painting, which was undergoing transformation at the hands of Giotto, the successor of Cimabue; so with sculpture and architecture; so with literature in the vulgar tongue, first introduced into Tuscany in the generation preceding Dante. Yet all these innovations were developing, not in a traditionless new settlement, but in a very ancient community, the home of countless generations of civilization. This, no doubt, is the reason why all her creative activities, material and intellectual, naturally assumed an artistic form in which delicacy and sobriety are allied to a dominant sense of harmony. It was a fit place for the breeding of genius: the swiftly growing town was big enough to afford a field for all kinds of talent, and yet so little that all were neighbors and merit could scarcely go unrecognized. The public offices, too, were numerous and the terms of service short, so that many citizens had a direct share in the management of affairs. On the other hand, the community was rent by party strife. The middle class, with its accumulating wealth and strength, was hated by the old military aristocracy, largely of Germanic origin, which lurked entrenched

in castles within and without the city, surrounded by armed retainers, ready to seize upon any pretext to make trouble; and the burghers were bent on reducing the feudal lords to political impotence. The old quarrel between Guelfs and Ghibellines had ceased with the defeat of the latter party at Benevento in 1266, but new factions, as irreconcilable as the old, carried on the internal war. The Whites, under the leadership of the Cerchi family, represented the new power of industry and money; the Donati, with their Blacks, stood for the old nobility, with which the unaffiliated lowest class was inclined to side. In 1300 the most active leaders of both parties were sentenced to banishment. The Blacks, unsuccessful at home, sought aid abroad. Pope Boniface VIII, who had an old claim on Tuscany, sent to the city that royal adventurer, Charles of Valois, ostensibly as a peacemaker. He entered Florence with an army, and straightway turned it over to the Blacks. The Whites were driven out, among them Dante, who never returned. This was in 1302.

2. In such a community Dante was born in 1265, probably in the last days of May. We know little of his career. His works afford some bits of information, and there are a few scraps of documentary evidence; his neighbor Giovanni Villani inserted a brief sketch of him in his Chronicle; Boccaccio prepared a short, eulogistic account of him after his death, and his life was written in the next century by Leonardo Bruni. These are our principal sources. The mass of legend that has grown up about him makes the truth all the more difficult to ascertain. He came of a family ennobled several generations back, but neither rich nor particularly conspicuous. Their name was originally Alagherius, or Alaghieri. His own name, Dante, is a shortened form of Durante. His mother died during his childhood, and his father, after marrying again, died in 1283. A half-brother, Francesco, and a half-sister, Tana, were the fruit of this new marriage. Concerning another sister we do not know whether she was the child of the first wife or the second. As far as we can judge from the *Commedia*, the lad's early impressions of family life were happy. He doubtless received a careful education; it is likely enough that, after learning the rudiments from the Dominicans, he attended the Franciscan school of Santa Croce. Close familiarity with country as well as city life is shown in his writings. His imagination was cultivated by much reading of Provençal and Italian poets, from whom he learned unaided the science of metrics. He was deeply influenced, too, by contemporary art, and himself practiced drawing. Early he distinguished himself as a poet, in a town where poetry and music were just acquiring an unprecedented vogue; and through his verse he made valuable acquaintances. His "first friend" was the famous poet Guido, considerably his senior and his literary adviser, of the rich Cavalcanti family. Brunetto Latini,

Casa di Dante
House of the Alighieri, near the center of Florence.

a great scholar, secretary of the Republic, aided him with counsel.   Other poets, the notary Lapo Gianni and later the youthful Cino da Pistoia, as well as the musician Casella, were his associates.   A comrade of less desirable character was Forese Donati, brother of Corso, the leader of the Blacks; Forese, a high liver of shady reputation, exchanged with Dante a series of scurrilous sonnets. Dante mingled in the pastimes of his city and did not hold aloof from more serious civic matters: in 1289 he took part in an important military campaign, probably not his first.   He may have been in Bologna in 1287 or thereabouts; he must have visited Lombardy before 1300.   Between 1293 and 1300 he got deeply into debt.   At some time between 1283 and 1285 he married Gemma Donati, a fourth cousin of Corso and Forese, to whom he had probably been affianced since boyhood (the dowry having been fixed in 1277); she bore him two sons, Pietro and Jacopo, and (in all likelihood) one daughter.[1]   The family did not follow him in his exile, although three of the children later joined him in Ravenna.   Gemma remained in Florence, where she continued to live until her death, sometime before 1343.   In 1295 Dante entered public life and a few years later became an important figure in local politics.   He strove for the independence of Florence and repeatedly opposed the projects of the Pope.   After going on a successful embassy to San Gimignano, he was for two months, in the summer of 1300, one of the six Priors of Florence.   In 1301 he was commissioned

---

[1] We have two daughters' names, Antonia and Beatrice, but they appear to refer to the same person, the second, Beatrice, being a monastic name.   Of a mysterious Giovanni, "son of Dante Alighieri of Florence," we know nothing except that his signature appears as a witness to a business document (in Lucca in 1308), recently discovered.

to supervise the widening and improvement of a street. At the critical moment of the advent of Charles of Valois, or shortly before, Dante is said, on good authority, to have been absent on a mission to Rome. On trumped-up charges he was condemned, first to fine and exclusion, later to death by fire; subsequently, perhaps in 1315, he refused to purchase pardon by submission. For a little while after his banishment, in 1302, he conspired with his fellow exiles; then, disgusted with their policy, perhaps in danger of his life from their violence, he turned his back on them and "formed a party by himself." The story of his wanderings is fragmentary. His first refuge was with the Scala family in Verona. On the death of his generous patron, Bartolommeo or Alboino, in 1304, he is supposed to have visited the university at Bologna, where he was known by 1287. There is reason to believe that he traveled widely in Italy, especially in the North. He appears to have been in Padua in 1306. In the same year he was in Lunigiana with the Malaspina, for whom, on October 6, he acted as attorney in concluding a peace with the bishop of Luni. Thence he probably went to the mountains of the Casentino, on the upper Arno; and it is believed, on the authority of Boccaccio and Villani, that he journeyed between 1307 and 1309 to Paris. In 1308 Henry of Luxembourg, a noble idealist, was elected Emperor; crowned the next year at Aix as Henry VII, he descended in 1310 into Italy, to reunite Church and State, restore order, and reduce rebellious cities to submission. His coming aroused wild excitement and conflicting passions. Florence from the first offered sturdy and successful opposition. Dante, who firmly believed that the woes of Florence and all Italy — in fact, most of the evils in the world — were due to lack of Imperial guidance, greeted Henry as a savior and hastened to pay him homage. Three letters written in 1310 and 1311 show him in a state of feverish exaltation. He was probably in Pisa in 1312. Henry's invasion, however, was fruitless: he was involved in a turmoil of party strife; the Pope who had summoned him turned against him; and just as his prospects were brightening, he died ingloriously near Siena in 1313. With him perished Dante's immediate hopes of peace, the regeneration of his country, and his own restoration. Possibly he took refuge with the Imperial champion Can Grande della Scala in Verona in 1314. If, as we may infer from a passage in the *Commedia*, Dante went to Lucca, this visit may well have occurred shortly after Henry's death, possibly in 1315; in that year or the next he doubtless returned to Verona. Later — we do not know when — the poet, already famous through his lyrics, his *Convivio*, *Inferno*, and *Purgatorio*, was offered an asylum in Ravenna by Guido Novello da Polenta, a nephew of Francesca da Rimini. His daughter Antonia, who had taken the monastic name Beatrice, was a nun in that city; his son Pietro held a benefice there. This was his home until his death on September 13 or 14, 1321. Shortly before the end he was sent on a mission to

Venice. His last years seem to have been peaceful and happy. In Ravenna, where he was greatly esteemed, he had congenial society and eager pupils. He maintained friendly relations with Can Grande della Scala, captain of the Ghibelline league, on whom he built great hopes. Though Florence still repudiated him, Bologna desired his presence.

3. The foregoing biography of Dante omits the most significant feature of his life, the love for Beatrice. The chivalric amorous service of ladies, which had sprung up among the poets of southern France, developed with some of the later troubadours, under the influence of the growing cult of Mary in the 13th century, into an idealization of woman and a spiritual devotion. But it remained for the school of Bologna and its Florentine disciples to transform this sentiment into a transcendental passion, a combination of religious mysticism and instinctive desire with the Averroistic doctrine of a passive individual soul and an active oversoul. In the verse of Guido Guinizzelli, who lived just before Dante, woman becomès the visible symbol of the angelic nature; the lover worships in his lady the Heavenly Intelligence, which reveals itself in her; only the noble heart is capable of love, and without a fitting object to arouse its inborn love to activity even such a heart is powerless to manifest its latent goodness. These ideas are set forth in a beautiful *canzone* beginning "Al cor gentil rempaira sempre amore," to which Dante continually reverts. Guinizzelli he calls his master, and master of all those who write sweet rhymes of love. Dante, dreamer that he was, and profoundly religious, naturally fell under the sway of this teaching. Critics have hotly debated the question whether his Beatrice was a real woman. Boccaccio asserts that she was Beatrice Portinari, daughter of Folco Portinari, a wealthy and public-spirited Florentine who died in 1289; before that date she was married to a rich banker of good family, Simone dei Bardi. There is no valid ground for rejecting this statement. But after all it makes little difference who she was: the living woman merely furnished the impression that aroused the poet's creative fancy. All imaginative lovers idealize their mistresses beyond recognition. The Beatrice that Dante presents to us, real as she was to him, is almost wholly the product of his own mind. With the flesh-and-blood Beatrice he seems to have had little more than a bowing acquaintance, and there is no reason to believe that she returned or even understood his affection. He first met her when he was nine and she was eight, and even then — at least so it seemed when he looked back upon the episode — she appeared to him as a revelation of the heavenly. Nine years later they exchanged a greeting. When, led to think ill of him by his excessive attentions to another lady, she refused to recognize him, he was profoundly hurt; and his pain was redoubled on one occasion when, with other ladies, she

laughed at his show of emotion.   He grieved with her sorrow at the loss of a friend and again when her father was taken from her; he was tormented by a foreboding of her death.   Stirred by feminine criticism, he determined to exclude supplication from his verse and make all his love poetry a hymn of praise. So much he tells us, in the *Vita Nuova*, of his relations with the living Beatrice. After her death, in 1290, her image seems to have become clearer and more fixed; but her influence could not preserve him from morbid dejection and unworthy pursuits.   Book learning and worldliness engrossed him for a while, in spite of the recurring prick of conscience.   Even in early youth his fancy had strayed to other women, and his comradeship with the disreputable Forese Donati is perhaps to be ascribed to a boyish period.   After the passing of Beatrice he was, as he thought, unduly moved by the pity of an unnamed lady, who soon, however, became in his mind a mere visible picture of the object of his great passion, Philosophy.   At some time, perhaps later, in the Casentino, he apparently became violently enamored of a young woman to whom he addressed the most wildly beautiful lyrics in all amatory literature; but even these poems are not beyond the suspicion of allegorical intent.

4. When we ask ourselves why we are so strangely stirred by the words of a man of whom we know so little, one so remote in date and in thought, we find that it is because, on the one hand, he knew how to present universal emotions, stripping his experiences of all that is peculiar to time or place; and, secondly, because he felt more intensely than other men: his joy, his anguish, his love, his hate, his hope, his faith were so keen that they come quivering down through the ages and set our hearts in responsive vibration.   This intensity seems to distinguish him from other poets of the Middle Ages, perhaps, in part, because he alone had the art to express it.   His mastery of language far transcends that of any other medieval poet and surpasses that of all but the few very foremost in the world's history.   In his close observation and apparent enjoyment of the varying, even the sternest, aspects of nature, he seems nearer to our generation than to his own.   His study of human nature is no less close.   Though the title *Commedia* contained, in its author's mind, no suggestion of the stage, the poem exhibits a command of dramatic situation, a skill in characterization by means of dialogue, not to be found in any playwright between Euripides and Shakespeare.   One other gift he possessed that belongs to no period, but is bestowed upon the greatest artists of all times — the power of visualization, the ability to see distinctly in his mind's eye and to place before the mental vision of the reader not only such things as men have seen but also the creations of a grandiose imagination and even bodiless abstractions.   In most other respects he belonged to his age: in his submission to authority in all matters of science

and philosophy; in his unquestioning acceptance of Christian dogma; in his subordination of beauty to truth and his relegation of it to the position of handmaid to utility; in his conception of the individual, not as an independent unit, but as a part of humanity, and his consequent desire to suppress all reference to the events and characteristics that differentiate himself from other men. Medieval, too, was his mysticism: in him we see a man with the most acute perception of reality, the most eager interest in the doings of his fellows, yet imbued with the idea that the world of fact is all a shadowy image of the world of spirit; his feet were firmly planted on earth, while his head was in the clouds.

5. Visionary as he was, saddened by his own misfortunes, and exasperated by human wickedness, he had a fundamentally healthy disposition. In his character fierce passion was mated with equally vigorous self-control; vehemence was balanced by introspection and self-judgment; imagination was yoked with logic. He admired simplicity, even asceticism, but he was far from being a foe to culture or to the usages of polite society. He was fond of courtly pursuits, and erudite even to pedantry. In the great writings of pagan times he found a source of endless delight, and he did not hesitate to put them on a par with his Christian authorities. His admiration was less excited by Christian martyrs than by heroic pagan suicides. His Christ is always sublime, a part of the triune God, never the meek lamb nor the humble preacher of Galilee. His outlook upon life was persistently hopeful. Bad as the world was, there could be no doubt of ultimate reform. The Lord, in his unfathomable wisdom, might allow evil to triumph for a while, but his kingdom was sure to come. Dante's political views were entirely abstract and theoretical, and reactionary even for his own day. He had always before him the general principle rather than the particular case. Man being naturally a social creature, political organization is necessary, both in order to supply the manifold needs of the community, assigning different functions to different members, and in order to check greed and ensure justice and peace, so that every citizen may have an opportunity to attain his highest development. The State, then, is as necessary — though not so venerable — as the Church. God ordained both, and decreed that Caesar should found the one, Christ the other. Empire and Papacy are coordinate powers, neither subservient to the other, but both responsible directly to God. The goodness and happiness of the world depend on the balance of the temporal and the spiritual authorities. The rapacity of the clergy and the negligence of sovereigns have disturbed this equilibrium by transferring to the Papacy what belongs to the Empire. Mankind cannot thrive until the adjustment is restored. In his treatment of civics, and in the importance given to

avarice as a disturber of society, Dante follows Aristotle (*Ethics*, V). From the same master he derived vast stores of physical information, as well as a philosophical method and terminology. His general classification of sins and his definition of moral virtues are Aristotelian, but his essential conception of sin and virtue is quite different, being thoroughly Christian. One can only guess what Dante would have been had he really known Plato, to whom he was temperamentally so much more akin. On the ethical side Dante was an eclectic, as were his ancient masters, Cicero and Boethius; Senecan stoicism and Franciscan mysticism dwelt in him side by side. St. Thomas, the interpreter of Aristotle, the learned and ingenious expounder of moral philosophy and Christian dogma, furnished Dante with an abundance of religious doctrine and a host of subtle observations and arguments (not always devoid of inconsistency), and reinforced his inborn fondness for intricate reasoning. To St. Thomas's teacher, Albertus Magnus, the "Universal Doctor," perhaps the greatest scholar and philosopher of the Middle Ages, Dante was directly indebted for not a few of his physical and ethical ideas. Like St. Augustine, Dante takes as his starting point the Pauline doctrine of predestination and grace; but he draws from it very different consequences. In Dante, as in St. Paul, love is supreme. It is the moving force of the universe and of God himself. Through love God was impelled to create, that there might be others to share his happiness. Everything created is filled with love of the Creator. Animals, plants, lifeless things express their love by being what he made them: the stone, by its hardness and its magic power; the star, by its light and its influence upon earth; the beast, by following its instinct. They cannot do wrong, having no choice. It was God's purpose, however, that there should be creatures with an individual consciousness, a real life of their own; this could not be without freedom of the will, and such freedom implies the possibility of sin. Angels and men alone were given ability to sin, because they alone were created free. But almost instantly after their creation the angels were endowed with such overwhelming grace of vision that their will was identical with that of their Maker. The revolt of Lucifer and his fellows occurred in the moment between creation and the acceptance of this grace. The power of vision bestowed on the Heavenly Intelligences is not the same for all: no two angels see God alike, and consequently their natures and functions are diverse, though entirely good. So it is with men. God, in his grace, gives to different men, as he shapes their souls, different degrees of vision. On this vision all their knowledge and all their love depend. According to its clearness, the love of God is more or less intense, wisdom is greater or less, the choice of good and evil is easier or harder, and the eternal state of the soul, if Heaven be attained, is a higher or lower degree of blessedness. Every soul has sight enough to win salvation, and is therefore fully responsible; but some are capable of greater beatitude than others. Pre-destination becomes, then, in Dante, a mysterious manifestation of God's love: he loves all men, but he fashions them for different ends, on earth and in Heaven, and his love for all is not identical. The natural instinct of man is to return to his Creator and to love all that is like him. But through inexperience and lack of guidance he may at first mistake evil for good. He possesses, how-ever, the grace of vision, which enables him to discriminate; if he persists in wrongdoing, he rejects grace and sins. If he dies unrepentant, he loses grace forever; if he repents before death, he regains grace and innocence by discipline. Had mankind from the beginning made the proper use of the free will, there would have been no death; all human beings would have lived happily on earth until the Judgment Day, and would then have been taken up to Heaven in the flesh. Adam's disobedience brought death and sin into the world, and sus-pended salvation until atonement was made by Christ. Only by faith in Christ, before or after his coming, can man be saved; but this faith is (theoreti-cally, at least) within the reach of all. We have seen that man's path is made unduly hard by the lack of temporal direction, for which the impotence of the State is to blame. Men's talents and dispositions differ, too, being the product of the stars — governed by Heavenly Intelligences — that presided over their birth; but every human creature has power to overcome his natural defects so far as to make himself worthy of Heaven. The origin of imperfection in the universe is a difficult (not to say insoluble) problem — one to which Dante often reverted, without ever finding a satisfactory answer. His main argument is that whatsoever is directly shaped by God is perfect, what is fashioned by nature (that is, by the influence of the stars) is faulty. God created brute matter, the heavens, the angels, and creates human souls as they are born. All the rest is the work of nature. Why nature, itself the work of God, should operate de-fectively, we are not told. Elsewhere Dante says that God, in making material things, has to work with matter, which being imperfect, the divine plan is not realized; but inasmuch as God created matter, this statement can be reconciled with the other only by the supposition that Dante here means, not brute matter, but matter already differentiated and compounded by nature. His whole ex-planation reduces itself to this: the angels, having an incomplete vision of the divine mind, cannot execute its intent so well as God himself. If we ask why — this being the case — the angels were given this ministry, or, having the charge, were not endowed with complete sight, no reply is offered. The theory that evil was introduced into the world that man might have exercise for his free will is not formulated in the *Divine Comedy*.

6. Outside of the *Divine Comedy*, Dante's ideas are to be found, first of all, in the *Convivio*, an unfinished encyclopedic work, in Italian, in the projected form

of a discursive prose commentary on fourteen of the author's *canzoni;* of this projected fifteen books, only four were written, and only three *canzoni* are included.   The logically constructed but purely idealistic and theoretical *Monarchia*, a Latin treatise in three books, contains his political views.   Another Latin treatise, the uncompleted *De Vulgari Eloquentia*, gives us his opinions on language in general, the use of the modern idiom as a literary medium, the relative merits of the various Italian dialects, and the principles of poetic composition in the vulgar tongue; he believed that an ideal, universal Italian, different from any of the actually spoken dialects, was fit, not only for amatory verse, but for martial and moral themes as well.   A third Latin work ascribed to him, the *De Aqua et Terra*, is a controversial lecture delivered in Verona in 1320, debating technically the question whether the water of the sea rises in any part higher than the land.   Some fourteen Latin letters, written at different periods, are attributed to him in manuscripts, and there is record of others, now lost; the authenticity of all the fourteen has been doubted, but it is probable that at least ten are his.   Of a political character are the epistles to the princes and peoples of Italy, to the Emperor, to the Florentines, to the Italian cardinals, to a Florentine friend, and an early one to Niccolò da Prato.   The most important from a literary standpoint, if he really wrote it, is the later, ponderously exegetical *Epistola ad Canem Grandem*, accompanying the first canto of the *Paradiso* with a minute comment on its opening lines and a general discussion of allegory.   Many letters and many poems have doubtless perished.   On the other hand, some pieces of verse that have gone under his name are, in all likelihood, not his.   There seems to be no sufficient reason to ascribe to him the long sonnet sequence called *Il Fiore*, an abridged paraphrase of the *Roman de la Rose*. Among the miscellaneous poems, not contained in his longer works, that are attached to him, we may reckon as his a dozen *canzoni*, a half dozen or more *ballate*, two *sestine*, and some twenty-five or thirty sonnets; they were composed at various times, and treat of love, philosophy, ethics, and sundry occasional topics.   Some of them are similar in tone to those comprised in the *Convivio*; others are in the same vein as the thirty-one (mostly sonnets) that form the skeleton of the *Vita Nuova*.   This "little book" consists of a carefully selected and artistically arranged series of amatory poems, surrounded by a dainty prose commentary telling of the poet's early love for Beatrice.   There is reason to believe that the prose was written in 1292.   Now the final chapter of the *Vita Nuova* speaks of a wondrous vision which determined the lover to write no more of his lady until he should be worthier of the theme; to prepare himself, he was studying with might and main, and he hoped, if his life were spared a few years, to say of her what never had been said of woman.   This study, begun for comfort's sake in the darkest hour of mourning for his dead love, as he declares in the *Convivio*, soon became an object in itself, and aroused a new passion that threatened to quench the memory of the old.   Beginning with Cicero's *De Amicitia* and the *Consolatio Philosophiae* of Boethius, he plunged deep into philosophy and theology.   Of the vast knowledge thus accumulated the scholar was naturally proud, and he planned to set it before his fellow men in the *Convivio*, which was to be a guide to others and a defense of himself. This treatise doubtless occupied him between 1305 and 1308.   Only when vast hopes were awakened and then temporarily blighted by the advent and death of his Imperial hero did Dante forsake this project; then, leaving it two-thirds unrealized — leaving unfinished, too, it would seem, his *De Vulgari Eloquentia* — he returned to the fulfillment of his earlier purpose, which, in all probability, he had never quite abandoned.   Conceived, then, it appears, as early as 1292, the plan of the *Divina Commedia* was probably not fully matured until after the death of Henry VII, the Emperor whose advent in 1310 had aroused such wild expectations in Dante's breast.   As Henry died in 1313 and the poet in 1321, we may ascribe the composition of the work, in the main, to the years that lie between these dates.   Some critics, however, put the *Inferno* much earlier.   Both the *Inferno* and the *Purgatorio* were made public, either singly or together, considerably before the *Paradiso*.   If report is to be trusted, this last *cantica* busied the author until the very end of his life.   Yet he found time, in his last years, to write two graceful Latin eclogues and (if they are his) the letter to Can Grande and the *Quaestio de Aqua et Terra*.   There is no external and no definite internal evidence to fix the date of the *Monarchia*; its general style and maturity point to the latest possible period.

7. In making his preparation, what books had he studied?   The *Aeneid*, that cornerstone of medieval education, must have confronted him from childhood; he tells us that he knew it all by heart.   There is no proof, however, that he read the *Georgics* or any of the *Eclogues* except the fourth.   The Latin Bible he had at his fingertips.   Cicero's ethical writings — especially *De Amicitia* and *De Officiis* — and the great work of Boethius introduced him to philosophy.   Much of Aristotle (but not the *Poetics*) and perhaps Plato's *Timaeus* he mastered later, in Latin translation.   He seems to have seen something of Seneca's prose.   Of the Christian scholars and theologians, first of all St. Thomas, then Albertus Magnus, St. Augustine, Hugh and Richard of St. Victor, St. Bonaventure, St. Bernard, Peter Lombard, and apparently St. Gregory the Great, St. Isidore of Seville, and Peter Damian were assiduously consulted; and his works show traces of many others.   His principal historians were Livy and the Christian Paulus Orosius, author of the *Historia adversus Paganos;* he knew also several compendiums, notably the anecdotical compilation of Valerius Maximus.   The

treatises of Aegidius Romanus and John of Paris probably came under his inspection. He doubtless was acquainted with the elder Pliny and Solinus; he certainly read the *Trésor* of Brunetto Latini and probably the *Composizione del mondo* of Ristoro d'Arezzo. Astronomy he pursued with characteristic thoroughness, first, perhaps, in the *Elementa Astronomica* of Alfraganus. Some strange words and a deal of curious misinformation he got from the *Magnae Derivationes* of Uguccione da Pisa, who lived in the second half of the 12th century. Among the Latin poets, besides Virgil, he was intimate with Ovid, Lucan, and Statius, from whom he derived most of his classical mythology and much of his ancient history. He knew Horace's *Ars Poetica*. Many classical authors whom he had not read were known to him by name and reputation — among them, Homer. Greek and Hebrew he never learned, save a few isolated words. Latin, of the rhetorical, medieval sort, he wrote well, but with less ease and brilliance than Italian. He could read and write Provençal and assuredly knew French. He was deeply versed in the lyric poetry of southern France and was familiar, directly or indirectly, with the epics of the north. He had critically examined the work of the Italian poets who had preceded him in Sicily, Tuscany, and Bologna; his estimates are to be found not only in his *De Vulgari Eloquentia* but also incidentally in the *Vita Nuova* and the *Divina Commedia*. His own lyrics, by the way, reveal a skill far excelling that of any of his forebears. The learning acquired by all this study was not wasted: it reappears in the *Divine Comedy*. This great poem, unrivaled as it is for sustained grandeur of thought and symmetry of form, resolves itself, upon careful analysis, into at least six diverse elements, fused by genius into a single masterpiece (*Par.* XXXIII, 89, 90). Six literary types are blended into one: the Encyclopedia, the Journey, the Vision, the Autobiography, the Praise of Woman, the Allegory.

8. The idea of a practical compendium of human knowledge was not unknown to the old Romans: Pliny, for instance, composed the *Historia Naturalis*, Celsus the *De Artibus*. To the borderland of ancient and medieval times belongs that famous compilation, the *Origines* or *Etymologiae* of St. Isidore of Seville. Others followed not only in Latin but also in the vulgar tongues; and then came the attempt to give such works poetic form: witness, for example, the French *Image du monde* and the Provençal *Breviari d'Amors*, a huge allegorized treatise, written and widely diffused in Dante's lifetime. In Dante's own city lived Brunetto Latini, author of the French *Trésor* and also of the Italian *Tesoretto*, a versified guide to learning in the semblance of a mystic journey. The *Commedia* contains the essentials of the vital science, theology, with a full discussion of difficult problems — also the principles of the ancillary discipline, philosophy. It offers, furthermore, a complete course in astronomy and cosmography, with

occasional lessons in physics, and much incidental instruction in history and mythology. And this solid doctrine is not to be regarded as intrusive; it forms, so to speak, the nucleus of the whole work.

9. Among the travelers' tales that delighted the wonder-loving public none were better liked than those which told of journeys to the Garden of Eden; and of these the most famous was the *Voyage of St. Brendan*, the narrative of an Irish monk who sailed out into the Atlantic and after marvelous adventures discovered the Isles of the Blest. It is in Dante's *Purgatorio*, and especially in his description of the Earthly Paradise, that the influence of such stories is most evident. The inaccessibility, the wall of fire, the birds, the flowers, the streams, the eternal springtime are traditional features; even the lovely youthful figure of Matilda, genius of the place, has a counterpart in the *St. Brendan*. Some authorities put the Garden on a remote mountaintop; others consigned it to a distant island. Dante combined these locations and made his Eden the summit of a lone peak rising sky-high from the midst of the great ocean. The spot where man first sinned is directly opposite Jerusalem, where he was redeemed.

10. In 2 Corinthians xii, St. Paul declares that "he was caught up into paradise, and heard unspeakable words, which it is not lawful for a man to utter." What he saw and heard he refused to tell, but posterity was less discreet. Toward the end of the 4th century there appeared a Greek document, found, it was said, in the apostle's house in Tarsus — the *Apocalypse of St. Paul*. Though denounced by St. Augustine and never accepted by the Church, it enjoyed an immense vogue and was turned into Syriac and Latin. The Latin *Visio Sancti Pauli* — which tells how the Chosen Vessel, led by an angel, visited the realms of the dead — formed the basis of several versions in the vulgar tongues of Europe. But it stood by no means alone. Visions too numerous to tell were seen and invented for many centuries; conspicuous among them are those described in two Irish tales, the *Tundal* and *St. Patrick's Purgatory*; in Dante's own country there was recorded the *Visio Alberici*. Most of these treat of the lower world, in which Hell and Purgatory lie side by side. A large part of the punishments portrayed by Dante were commonplaces of vision literature, but he avoided the extremes of coarseness and grotesqueness and introduced system and fitness where all had been chaotic. It was his happy idea, moreover, to lift Purgatory to the earth's surface, place it far from Hell, next to the Garden of Eden, and surround it with an atmosphere of light and hope. Meanwhile St. Paul's reticence had borne other fruit. A Neoplatonic treatise, not earlier than the 5th century, *On the Celestial Hierarchy*, dealing with the heavens and the Heavenly Intelligences, had been ascribed to Dionysius the Areopagite, the

apostle's convert in Athens, and was supposed to contain an authentic record of revelation confided by the master to his disciple. Dante's classification of heavens and angels is founded on this work. But heathen as well as Christian could dream dreams of the hereafter. The *Somnium Scipionis* in Cicero's *De Re Publica* depicts good souls rising to the stars and the petty earth in the center of nine revolving spheres. If Homer's account of a descent into the world of the departed was unknown in the Middle Ages, those of Ovid, Lucan, and Statius were familiar to scholars, and Virgil's was before every schoolboy's eyes. Dante's Hell is full of Virgilian names; Christian and pagan figures are strangely commingled. This must have seemed less incongruous to the author than to us, for in his day the gods of classic mythology were regarded as demons, fallen angels who had seduced mankind to worship them. Furthermore, Dante thought of the ancient poets as seers, who had some inkling of the truth, and in veiled language told of things that became fully known only through the word of God: for instance, when Ovid sang of the Golden Age, or the battle of the giants, he was dimly conscious of the state of man before the fall, and the revolt of the angels against their Maker.

11. The *Divine Comedy* is not only an Encyclopedia, a Journey, a Vision — it is the Autobiography of a soul. The events of his external life Dante scrupulously excluded from his works: he never mentions his parents, his children, nor, in all probability, his wife; an apparent reference to his sister, in the *Vita Nuova*, is couched in the vaguest terms; only incidentally and rarely does he afford a passing glimpse of his material affairs. His *Vita Nuova*, professedly the story of his youth, is the most baffling record ever penned. In his opinion, it is not meet to speak of oneself: "parlare alcuno di sé medesimo pare non licito," he declares in the *Convivio*. This maxim evidently does not apply, however, to the inner self, provided that self be generalized into a type of mankind, and provided the recounting of its experiences be helpful to other erring souls. Like St. Paul and Aeneas, Dante had a mission, a vital message for humanity. The *Divine Comedy* is the epic of remorse, repentance, purification, and final uplifting. Incidentally it depicts the depravity of the world and points the way to social regeneration. For a work of this kind Dante had a great example in the *Confessions* of St. Augustine, and another, allegorically conceived, in Boethius's *Consolatio Philosophiae*.

12. From the dawn of amorous poetry in Provence it was the habit of the bard to vaunt the charms of his mistress and her superiority to the rest of her sex, attributing to her influence all credit for such gifts as he himself might possess. His life, he alleged, was given to her service, his verse was a tribute

to her power. Such a tribute, but a loftier, more enduring one, Dante determined to pay to his lady. The *Divine Comedy* is a monument to Beatrice, and, in truth, such a monument as never was erected, before nor after, to any woman.

13. "Sciendum est," declares the letter to Can Grande, referring to the *Divina Commedia*, "quod istius operis non est simplex sensus, ymo dici potest polisemos, hoc est plurium sensuum; nam primus sensus est qui habetur per litteram, alius est qui habetur per significata per litteram. Et primus dicitur litteralis, secundus vero allegoricus ..." (that the sense of this work is not simple, but on the contrary it may be called polysemous, that is to say, "of more senses than one"; for it is one sense which we get through the letter, and another which we get through the thing the letter signifies; and the first is called literal, but the second allegorical [or mystic] ...). Allegorical interpretation had been applied by the ancient Hebrews to the prophecies of the Old Testament, and by the Greeks — in late, sophisticated times — to the Homeric poems. It was early applied also to some of the Latin poets. The *Aeneid* was regularly so expounded; a commentary of this kind was surely known to Dante. The method reached its highest development, however, in the explanation of the Bible by the Church fathers. In the second book of the *Convivio* Dante discusses it at length, and there he differentiates theological from poetic allegory. In the former the literal as well as the mystic sense is true, while in poetry the letter is fiction and truth resides in the allegory alone. The Old Testament is an accurate record of fact but at the same time a prophecy of the New, whereas the fable of Orpheus is literally false and only metaphorically true. Furthermore, Dante distinguishes, in addition to the literal and the allegorical, a moral and an anagogical meaning: the one is merely the useful inference that the reader may draw from a story, for the guidance of his own life; the other, which is obscurely defined, seems to be a revelation of spiritual truth, hidden in the words of the text. Dante himself, in the interpretation of his *canzoni* in the *Convivio*, confines his attention to the literal and the allegorical senses. Allegorical composition was to Dante, not an artificial, but a natural process. He lived in a world of mystic correspondences. Numbers, stars, stones, and beasts had a mysterious significance; even the events of history were fraught with symbolic meaning. The relation of fact to symbol was not arbitrary nor fortuitous; it was real and predestined; for Dante combined mystic symbolism with formal allegory. Thus in his poem the outer and the inner narratives seem indissolubly bound; neither obstructs the other, neither is complete without the other, and to the intelligent reader the two are of equal interest. The *Divine Comedy* is perhaps the only great allegory of which this can be said today. In Bunyan's *Pilgrim's Progress*, for example, the literal story is too crude

and fantastic to please any but a child, and the symbolism appeals only to the adult.   In the *Roman de la Rose* the allegory is ingenious and artistically attractive, but the literal fable is insignificant, while the converse is true of Spenser's *Faerie Queene.*

14. In exposition, says Dante, "always the literal must come first"; and he adds, describing his interpretation of his own *canzoni,* "I shall discourse first of the literal meaning, and after that shall treat of the allegorical, that is, the hidden truth."   We may pursue the same course.   Literally, then, the *Divina Commedia* is the narrative of a journey through Hell, Purgatory, and Heaven. The poet, in the middle of his life, finds himself astray at night in a dark wood. He tries to save himself by climbing a mountain whose top is lit by the rays of the rising sun; but three beasts, besetting his path, are about to drive him back, when Virgil, summoned to Dante's help by Beatrice, at the bidding of Mary and St. Lucia, appears and offers to guide him.   They can escape from the wood only by going through the earth from side to side.   This path leads them through the whole of Hell, where Dante sees the punishment of every kind of sin and converses with the damned.   Hell ends at the earth's center, and from that point the poets climb out by a dark, undescribed channel to the opposite hemisphere.   They emerge in the middle of the ocean, on the shore of an island which consists mainly of a colossal mountain.   Cato of Utica, the guardian of the place, meets and directs them.   Up the steep mountain-side Dante drags himself, still accompanied by Virgil.   On the ledges are repentant souls preparing themselves by discipline for the heavenly life.   As Dante and Virgil are approaching the summit, they are joined by Statius, who has just completed his penance.   The three mount together to the top, where they find the Garden of Eden, and in it a fair, happy, amorous young maiden, Matelda, who seems to embody the spirit of the place.   Amid the trees and flowers they witness a pageant of the Church, or Triumph of Revelation, whose culmination is the appearance of Beatrice in a shower of lilies thrown by angels.   Now Virgil vanishes, and presently Statius is mentioned for the last time.   Beatrice it is who leads Dante up from earth through the revolving heavens into the real Paradise, which is the presence of the Almighty, and consigns him to St. Bernard, the great mystic.   There has been unrolled before us a picture of mankind, past and present, and a view of the universe.   Dante's conception of the world is essentially symmetrical and organic; there is exact correspondence between the physical, the intellectual, and the spiritual.   The poem ends with the vision of God.

15. In its "allegorical and true sense" the *Divine Comedy* is the history of a soul

struggling with sin and, with celestial help, winning peace. The wood typifies the worldly life; the sunlit mountain, righteousness; the three beasts, evil habits, which make reform impossible for the unaided soul. But divine Mercy and Grace send Revelation to direct it — that heavenly enlightenment or super-human Wisdom which *Beatrix*, the Bestower of Blessings, had always personified in Dante's eyes. For direct Revelation the sinner is not yet fit; he must approach it through Reason. So Virgil, who typifies human understanding, discloses to Dante the true nature of sin in all its hideousness and folly: for the punishments of Hell, so minutely described, are but the image of the sins themselves. When Reason has probed sinfulness to the bottom, Dante, horrified, turns his back upon it and painfully wrests his soul from its clutches; such is the signifi-cance of the laborious but uneventful journey from the center of the earth to the Island of Purgatory. As yet, however, Dante has merely weaned himself from evil practices; he has still to cleanse his soul so that wrongdoing shall no longer attract it — to purify it and prepare it for the sight of God. This can be accomplished only by discipline, under the guidance of the Church. Then, as the shackles of sin are removed, the soul once more enjoys its inborn liberty; it regains the Free Will, God's most precious gift to man. Of all the doctrines that Dante expounds, that of Free Will is closest to his heart — the wholesome doctrine of individual responsibility. And Cato, Dante's favorite character in all history — Cato, who gave up life to assert his independence — is made its exponent. The torments on the terraces of Purgatory represent the penances that the soul, under proper direction, must undergo before it can return to its first freedom and innocence. As Dante approaches the top, some questions confront him which Reason alone cannot quite solve; and to answer them, apparently, comes Statius, or human understanding illumined by Christianity. When the soul has regained its original purity — has climbed to its Garden of Eden — and is restored to the primeval life of innocence and activity (which Matelda seems to symbolize), it has no more need of Reason, for all its instincts are unerring. Then, after the true glories of the Church are unfolded before its eyes, it can follow Revelation through heaven after heaven, ever nearer and nearer to the real Paradise, until at last it stands before its Maker. In the presence of the Source of all knowledge, even Revelation is superfluous; Beatrice resigns her great office, leaving Dante in the charge of St. Bernard, the type of Intuition. "Blessed are the pure in heart, for they shall see God."

16. If to the literal and the allegorical we must add a moral and an anagogical interpretation, we may assume that morally the poem is a warning against sin, an exhortation and guide to repentance, and an incentive to religious contem-

plation. Anagogically, the poet may be said to portray in Hell the wicked world as he knows it, in Purgatory the rescue of the elect, and in Paradise the kingdom which is to come.

17. The epithet "Divine" became attached to the poem in the 16th century through its use in the edition of 1555. The title which Dante gave his work is *Commedia* (or, as he pronounced it, *Comedía*), meaning a poetic composition in a style intermediate between the sustained nobility of tragedy and the popular tone of elegy; according to the letter to Can Grande, the name indicates also a sad beginning and a happy end. The author, in fact, does not scruple, on occasion, to sacrifice elegance and even clearness to brevity, vigor, and pictorial effect. He expected to be minutely studied and weighed, not cursorily read. The characteristic detail, the specific term, the appropriate coloring were worth more to him, when he wrote the *Commedia*, than any absolute standard of poetic propriety. His imagery stamps on the reader's mind an unbroken sequence of visual impressions. An inexhaustible inventiveness, a compact style, a richly varied and picturesque vocabulary make the perusal of the *Commedia* a series of literary surprises. Especially when we consider the poverty of the poetic idiom before Dante, does the master's creative power seem almost beyond belief. His literary medium was virtually his own handiwork. And this nervous strength, this irrepressible originality do not preclude a haunting melodic beauty and a triumphant rhythm that remind one of the tramp of many feet marching to sweet music. Vowel harmonies, pervasive but seldom obtrusive alliteration, skillful distribution of stress are the elements that combine to work the spell. His language is, in the main, the Florentine speech of his day, as it sounded in the mouths of cultivated people. Mingled with this are a few Gallicisms, some archaisms, some words borrowed from other Italian dialects, and a great many Latinisms. The foreign and unusual words and those employed in a strange sense occur for the most part in the rhyme. Dante was generally averse to periphrasis or deviation from his idea, and was loath to end a verse with an insignificant word; so he was sometimes forced to do violence to usage in his rhymes.

18. Of the external attributes of the *Divine Comedy*, the most wonderful is its symmetry. With all its huge bulk and bewilderingly multifarious detail, it is as sharply planned as a Gothic cathedral. Dante had the very uncommon power of fixing his attention upon the part without losing sight of the whole: every incident, every character receives its peculiar development, but at the same time is made to contribute its exact share to the total effect. The more one studies the poem, the clearer become its general lines, the more intricate

its correspondences, the more elaborate its climaxes. At the end of each *cantica* is one of these great culminating points — the sight of Lucifer, the appearance of Beatrice, the vision of God; and for each of them the reader is insensibly prepared by a series of gradations whose structure reveals itself only after long repeated readings. The arrangement of the *Commedia* is based on the number three, the "mystic" number, the symbol of the Trinity. Dante shared with most philosophers of his day a profound belief in the significance of numbers. The *Divine Comedy* falls into three books, or *cantiche*, of nearly equal length; each of these has thirty-three cantos, except that the *Inferno* has an additional first canto which serves as an introduction to the whole. The total number of cantos is therefore 100, or the "perfect" number, ten, multiplied by itself. The verse, invented by Dante for this use, is what is called *terza rima*, a succession of tiercets in which the first and third lines rhyme together while the middle line rhymes with the first and third of the next *terzina*. The meter is the *endecasillabo*, which had developed long before Dante's time. It is really the same verse, essentially, as the French ten-syllable line; but the French take the "masculine," or oxytonic, verse as the standard, while the Italians take the "feminine," or paroxytonic. The Italian line has normally, then, eleven syllables, with an accent on the tenth: see, for instance, *Inf.* I, 1. Occasionally the final unstressed syllable is dropped, and the verse becomes "masculine," or *tronco*: for example, *Inf.* IV, 60. Sometimes, on the other hand, an extra unaccented syllable is added, making a dactyllic ending, and the line is called *sdrucciolo*: e.g., *Inf.* XXIV, 66. In counting syllables, contiguous vowels, whether in the same word or in adjacent words, are generally reckoned as one, being blended together, as in *Inf.* I, 25–26:

> "co-sì — l' a-ni-mo — mio — ch' an-cor — fug-gi-va
> si — vol-se a-re-tro a — ri-mi-rar — lo — pas-so."

But often two vowels which in prose may make separate syllables are allowed to count as two in verse; this is regularly done at the end of a line; so *Inf.* I, 12:

> "che — la — ve-ra-ce — vi-a ab-ban-do-na-i."

It is done also in Latin words, as in *Inf.* XXXIV, 1:

> "Vexilla regis prode-unt inferni."

Besides the fixed accent on the tenth syllable of every line, there must be a stress either on the fourth or on the sixth, as in *Inf.* I, 1–2:

> "Nel mezzo del cammín di nostra víta
> mi ritrovái per una selva oscúra."

In point of fact, however, Dante almost always has a more regular alternation of strong and weak syllables — a movement more nearly approaching that of English poetry — than this theoretical scheme would indicate; see, for instance, *Inf.* V, 106:

> "Amór condússe nói ad úna mórte."

19. The *Divina Commedia* has come down to us in nearly 600 manuscripts, none of them in the author's hand and none taken directly from the original; upwards of 200 are in Florence, the others are collected in Italy or scattered over Europe. Many are beautifully illuminated.[2] Although some of the manuscripts go back to a time within fifteen or twenty years of Dante's death, these copies are by no means in full agreement with one another; furthermore, the early commentators cite variants: it is evident that the corruption of the text set in as soon as the poet died, perhaps even before his decease. The poem was first printed in 1472. In 1502 appeared the Aldo Manuzio edition, in 1595 that of the Accademia della Crusca; these were for centuries regarded as authoritative. There was no critical edition until 1862, when K. Witte published one based on four good manuscripts; for one canto he also collated over 400 manuscripts. Three years later A. Mussafia brought out a collation of two manuscripts. After a long interval came editions by P. Toynbee and G. Vandelli. A fruitless attempt to establish a genealogical sequence of manuscripts was made by G. A. Scartazzini. No satisfactory classification of manuscripts has been made; but it is certain that no existing manuscript or group of manuscripts can be regarded as authoritative throughout. In 1894 appeared the "Oxford Dante," *Tutte le opere di Dante Alighieri,* edited by E. Moore (3rd ed., 1904); the *Divine Comedy* in this volume is based primarily on Witte's text, but Dr. Moore has examined for crucial passages some 200 manuscripts and has made use of the investigations of other scholars. The text published in 1921 by the Società Dantesca Italiana (Bemporad, Florence) is due to G. Vandelli, who from year to year had revised the Scartazzini edition. This has now been superseded by the text published by Giorgio Petrocchi, based on the earliest MSS and entitled *La Commedia secondo l'antica vulgata,* 4 vols., Milan, 1965–1967. His first volume includes an account of the early manuscripts.

20. Countless allusions, some of them purposely blind, vast accumulations of learning, conciseness and originality of phrase, symbolism, and not infrequent obscurity combine to obstruct the understanding of the poem. Some of the

---

2 See *Illuminated Manuscripts of the Divine Comedy,* by Peter Brieger, Millard Meiss, and Charles S. Singleton, Princeton, N.J., 1969.

difficulties we encounter are due to our remoteness from Dante's world, our different habits of thought, the archaic character of his language. Many of them, however, were as great in his day as in ours, and the need of interpretation was immediately felt. At least eleven commentaries on the whole or a part of the work were composed in the 14th century; from the 15th century we have five. The first commentator certainly known to us by name is Graziolo de' Bambaglioli, who goes back as early as 1324. Within sixteen years after him were written the expositions of Jacopo della Lana, those of Dante's sons Jacopo, who expounded the *Inferno* in Italian, and Pietro, who expounded the whole poem in Latin, and the work known as the "Ottimo Commento," probably made in 1328. To the latter part of the 14th century belong the exegeses of Boccaccio, who was appointed to expound the *Commedia* in Florence but carried his explanation no further than the 17th line of canto 17, of Benvenuto da Imola, and of Buti. The best informed of all these are perhaps Pietro and Benvenuto. All, however, must be used with caution, as they were deficient in poetic insight, and in historical matters did not always discriminate between fact and invention. The task of interpretation has been carried on, with greater or less intelligence and erudition, down to our own day. To keep well abreast of the Dante literature that now appears from year to year would require more than a man's whole time.

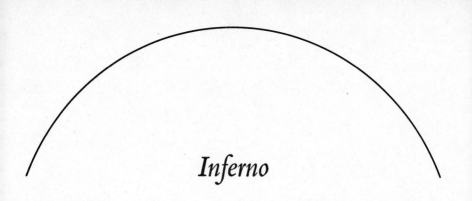

Inferno

Preliminary Note

According to the Ptolemaic system, which was accepted from antiquity down to the time of Copernicus, the earth is a solid, motionless sphere in the center of the universe. Around it revolve nine transparent hollow spheres, each within its outside neighbor up to the ninth, the Primum Mobile; this imparts its movement to the others and constitutes the frontier of the material world. The eighth heaven carries with it all the fixed stars. Each of those below it contains one heavenly body: the seventh, Saturn; the sixth, Jupiter; the fifth, Mars; the fourth, the Sun; the third, Venus; the second, Mercury; the first, the Moon. They all circle around the earth together, from east to west, once in twenty-four hours. But each heaven except the ninth has, besides, an independent motion of its own, so that it is really moving in a compound curve, made up of two or more different circular revolutions; for instance, the special revolution of the moon is accomplished in a month; that of the sun, in a year. By these sets of motions, and an elaborate system of computation by epicycles, the shifting positions of the sun, moon, and stars were accurately accounted for. Outside the whole universe of matter is the spiritual Paradise, the Empyrean, the true abode of God, the angels, and the blest. The earth is surrounded by air, and between this air and the heaven of the moon is a sphere of fire, toward which all the fire on earth is striving to return. All natural operations on earth are controlled by the movements of the spheres, which are directed by nine orders of angels, or Heavenly Intelligences, created by God for this office.[1]

[1] See diagrams on p. viii. Cf. Moore, III, 1 ff.

We have seen that two of the four elements, fire and air, are between the moon and our globe; this body itself consists of the other two, water and earth. The four are arranged in the order of their lightness and their purity. Dante believed the earth to be perfectly spherical and about 20,000 miles in circumference. The continents are all grouped on one side, the Hemisphere of Land, which contains not only Europe, Asia, Africa, and some islands but also the Mediterranean and a part of the great ocean; at the exact center of this hemisphere is Jerusalem. On the other side is the Hemisphere of Water, in which is no land, except (according to Dante's idea) the mountainous Island of Purgatory, situated precisely opposite Jerusalem. At the top of the mountain of Purgatory is the Garden of Eden. The greater part of the land on the earth's surface is north of the equator, the greater part of the water is south; but the Hemispheres of Land and Water by no means coincide with the northern and southern hemispheres. At the eastern extremity of the Hemisphere of Land is the River Ganges; at the western edge are the Straits of Gibraltar. The Mediterranean was thought to extend over 90°, or a quarter of the earth's circumference; Italy, midway between Gibraltar and Jerusalem, is therefore 45°, or three hours, from each.[2]

Hell is a vast cavity in the form of an inverted cone, whose apex is at the center of the earth and whose circular base lies beneath the Hemisphere of Land, from which it is shut off by a crust; it extends, apparently, from Italy to mid-Asia. The round declivity of the cavern is broken into nine steps, each of which runs all the way around it; they are of unequal width and separated by cliffs of varying height and steepness. Two enormous precipices divide it roughly into three horizontal sections. A huge wall, circling around one of the terraces, severs the outermost section from the other two, making an Upper and a Lower Hell; the latter is called the City of Dis. On each of the steps is punished some particular kind of sin: in the Upper Hell, the sins of Incontinence, due to lack of self-control; in the Lower Hell, the sins of Violence and Fraud, due respectively to Bestiality (or rather *bestialis malitia*)[3] and Malice (or *malitia humana*). Violence occupies the middle section, Fraud the lowest. Four steps, or circles,[4] are devoted to the four kinds of Incontinence — lust, gluttony, avarice (and prodigality), anger. One circle suffices for Bestiality, but it is

---

[2] See diagrams on p. viii. Cf. Moore, III, 109.

[3] The term "Bestiality" is taken from Aristotle but is not used in the Aristotelian sense: its meaning is extended and generalized, and it is combined with the violence mentioned by Aristotle and Cicero.

[4] From the 4th century on, Virgil's lower world was regarded as made up of *novem circuli*. Servius in *Aen.* VI, 426, says: "Novem circulis inferi cincti esse dicuntur." In the nine circles are nine classes of souls.

divided into three parts, according to the object of the violence: that object may be one's neighbor, oneself, or God.   Malice occupies two circles: in the first are the fraudulent, those who deceived persons not bound to them by any special ties; in the second are the traitors, destroyers of their kinsfolk, their countrymen, their guests, or their benefactors.   This last circle forms the very floor of Hell; it is a lake of ice at the bottom of a pit; embedded in the middle, at the center of the earth, is Satan, in whose three mouths are the three archtraitors Judas, Brutus, and Cassius.   Outside of this general scheme, but within Hell, are three regions inhabited respectively by the souls of sluggards and timeservers, those who were neither good nor bad; the souls of unbaptized children and virtuous pagans; and the souls of heretics.   All three are circles, like those mentioned.   The first, sometimes called the *Antinferno,* is a vestibule, just inside the entrance, but outside the River Acheron.   The second, the Limbus, is within the encircling Acheron, at a lower level than the Vestibule, and forms the first of the nine steps.   The third, which constitutes the sixth circle, lies close within the walls of the City of Dis, but is separated from the rest of the Lower Hell by a mighty precipice.   The souls in the netherworld are, then, arranged in this order: sluggish; *unbaptized;* lustful, gluttonous, avaricious (and prodigal), wrathful; *heretical;* violent; fraudulent, treacherous.   The sluggish, the unbaptized, and the heretical lie outside the three great classes — Incontinence, Violence, Fraud.   The sluggish are in the Vestibule; all the others are in the nine circles. The punishments vary according to the sins, each being a retaliation for the offence.   It must not be forgotten, however, that allegorically the torments represent the sins themselves.   "Wherewith a man sinneth, by the same also shall he be punished" (Wisdom xi, 16).   Dante, under the guidance of Reason, ransacks the human heart and learns to know wickedness as it really is, stripped of the false semblance of good.   Thus, for instance, the furious blast that eternally wafts the carnal sinners symbolizes irresistible passion; the ice in which traitors are buried is the coldness of the heart from which all love has been expelled.5

In Dante's Purgatory the sinners are arranged as follows: lustful, gluttonous, avaricious (and prodigal), *slothful,* wrathful, *envious, proud.*   Sloth intervenes between avarice and anger; envy and pride correspond to the violence, deceit, and treachery of Hell; there is no place for paganism or heresy.   The difference is a natural one.   Hell is the eternal abode of those who die unrepentant; Purgatory is a place of passage for those who, whatever their crimes may have been, die penitent within the Church.   In Purgatory we have to do only with man's fundamental evil dispositions, of which the soul is to be cleansed; in Hell

5 See diagram on p. ix.

souls are tortured for specific acts or states of the will, the multifarious fruit of these dispositions. The seven capital vices had long been defined by Church writers, and their order, in the main, was pretty well established; the relative positions of sloth and wrath were the most doubtful. In the *Moralia* of Gregory the Great (XXXI, Cap. 45) and in one passage in St. Thomas (*De Malo*, VIII, i) they are all arranged as in Dante, but St. Thomas has them in three other orders and apparently regards their sequence as unimportant; he prefers *inanis gloria* to *superbia* as a designation of Pride. All the sins in the Lower Hell are directed against justice, and are due to some kind of malice, originally caused, perhaps, by Envy and Pride. Pride, indeed, is the foundation of all sin, inasmuch as sin consists in defying God's law; this doctrine is laid down by St. Cyprian and recurs in Gregory and St. Thomas. Sloth, or lukewarmness in love of the Lord and his creatures, corresponds to the philosophical *ignavia* and *pusillanimitas;* insofar as it belongs in the netherworld at all, it has its proper place in the Vestibule. The unbaptized are beyond redemption, and therefore Purgatory is denied them. Heresy belongs to the speculative intellect, not to the lower appetite nor to the will; it is neither incontinence nor malice, and therefore has no manifestly appropriate place in Dante's system, nor in St. Thomas's. What becomes of repentant heretics we are not told, but we may assume that their penance must be paid in the circle of pride.

The mystic journey occurs in 1300, the year of the great papal jubilee proclaimed by Boniface VIII. It was a time of general religious enthusiasm, an appropriate moment for a moral awakening. The date is given vaguely in the opening line of the poem, definitely in *Inf.* XXI, 112–114. This latter passage tells us also that the descent was begun on the anniversary of the crucifixion. This may mean March 25, the real date, or Good Friday, the movable Church anniversary. Good Friday in 1300 fell on April 8, and several references in the poem seem to fit that day better than March 25. *Inf.* XX, 127, and *Purg.* XXIII, 119, inform us that the moon was full the night before; in reality the full moon occurred in 1300 on April 5, but in the ecclesiastical calendar for that year the Paschal full moon was set down for the night of April 7. *Purg.* I, 19–20, represents Venus as the morning star two days later; this was the case in 1301, not in 1300, but here again it was surely the almanac that led Dante astray. There is a peculiar fitness in starting on the downward journey on the evening of Good Friday, when day and hour are conducive to gloom. The ascent of Purgatory, on the other hand, begins at a time when everything suggests hope, the morning of Easter Sunday. Throughout the poem we are apparently to think of sunrise and sunset as occurring at six o'clock. It is, then, on the night of April 7, 1300, that Dante comes to his senses in the dark wood of sin. The next day he spends in trying to struggle out, directing his steps toward the sunlit mountain of righteousness; but three beasts — evil habits or sinful inclinations (the character Dante here functions in the role of Everyman) — impede his progress.   When all seems lost, Virgil, or Reason, appears and offers to lead him out by another way.   They enter Hell at sunset on April 8, and spend the night and the next day in their spiral course, turning always to the left as they descend.   In Hell they go by the time of Jerusalem, which is directly over the bottom of the pit.   When they reach the center of the earth, they pass beyond, climbing along the shaggy side of Satan, who is planted there; then, of course, they are under the opposite hemisphere, whose middle point is Purgatory, between which and Jerusalem there is a difference of twelve hours.   Dante represents Virgil and himself, therefore, as gaining twelve hours when they pass the earth's center: they have a new Saturday before them, and they use all that and the following night in climbing out, by a dark, difficult cavern, to the other side of the earth, where they emerge on the Island of Purgatory on Sunday morning.   Dante has turned his back on sin, has laboriously weaned himself from it, and is now ready to cleanse his soul by penance.

Virgil evidently represents Reason, human understanding, as opposed to Revelation, heavenly intelligence, embodied in Beatrice.   One may ask why he was chosen for this function, rather than Aristotle, "il filosofo," "maestro di color che sanno."   For many centuries the *Aeneid* had been the best of school-books, the one from which pupils learned grammar, rhetoric, history, mythology.   It was expounded literally and allegorically.   Its author, at least until Aristotle was discovered in the 12th century, was universally regarded as the wisest man of antiquity, the personification of the best that humanity, without superhuman enlightenment, could achieve; and even in 1300 his fame was scarcely dimmed by the greater glory of the Greek philosopher.   Moreover, he had already proved, in the sixth book of the *Aeneid*, his competence as a guide to the other world.   People generally believed, too, that in his fourth Eclogue he had unconsciously prophesied the coming of Christ.   Furthermore, Aristotle was to Dante only a book, while Virgil had been so long a figure in popular and scholarly legend that he had become a distinct personality, one with whom it was a joy to travel and from whom it was anguish to part.   Dante thought of himself as in reality a disciple and successor of Virgil.   The Mantuan was the bard of imperial Rome, its beginnings in history, and its future greatness as ruler of the world.   The Florentine was the prophet of the second advent of Rome, now the seat of both temporal and spiritual authority.   The *Commedia* is, then, as it were, a second *Aeneid*.

Canto I

Argument

This canto, which serves as a general introduction to the poem, is more formal in its allegory than those which follow; it affords, in some measure, a key to the whole interpretation. This announcement and summary of the whole *Commedia* may be compared to the opening lines of the *Aeneid*, the *Pharsalia*, and the *Thebaid*. The author has purposely enveloped its incidents in a veil of mystery, which enhances its impressiveness.

It is the night of April 7, the night before Good Friday in the great jubilee year 1300. Dante, at the age of thirty-five, suddenly becomes aware that he is astray in the dark wood of worldliness. In terror he seeks refuge at the foot of the mountain of rectitude, whose summit is lit by the rising sun. The sun, here and elsewhere, typifies enlightenment, perhaps more specifically, as Flamini suggests, righteous choice, the intelligent use of the free will. When Dante tries to scale the hill, three beasts beset his path: a leopard, a lion, and a wolf — the same creatures that appear in Jer. v, 6: "Wherefore a lion out of the forest shall slay them, and a wolf of the evenings shall spoil them, a leopard shall watch over their cities: every one that goeth out thence shall be torn in pieces." Apparently he has a fair prospect of passing the first two, at least the leopard, but the wolf drives him back. These animals evidently stand for man's vicious habits, which prevent his reform. The old commentators interpreted them respectively as luxury, pride, and avarice; this would imply (unless we understand the poet's whole experience to be generic, not individual) that Dante's dominant sin was avarice, which is scarcely believable. A more modern view is, in spite of some grave objections, far more satisfactory in itself and more in harmony with the whole structure of the poem. Inasmuch as the sins of Hell fall under the three heads, Incontinence, Violence, and Fraud, it is natural that the beasts should stand for corresponding practices: the ravening wolf is Incontinence of any kind, the raging lion is Violence, the swift and stealthy leopard is Fraud. St. Thomas and Richard of St. Victor, two of Dante's favorite authors, saw in the spotted pard a fit symbol of fraudulence.

At this crisis Reason, personified in Virgil, comes, at divine bidding, to the sinner's rescue. He declares that escape is possible only by another route, which will lead them through Hell: we cannot run away from evil before we know what it really is; a rational understanding of human wickedness must precede reformation. The wolf, he says, is ravaging the world, and will continue to do so until a Hound shall appear and drive it back into Hell, whence it first came. This Hound is obviously a redeemer who shall set the world

aright. If we compare this passage with another prophecy in *Purg.* XXXIII,
40–45, it is tolerably clear that he is to be a temporal rather than a spiritual
savior — a great Emperor whose mission it shall be to establish the balance of
power, restore justice, and guide erring humanity. Such an Emperor, destined
to come at the end of the world, was not unknown to legend; his advent appears
to have been sometimes associated with the *annus canicularis*, the period of
Sirius, the Dog Star. As the prediction was still unfulfilled at the time of writing,
Dante naturally made it vague; in fact, he rendered Delphic obscurity doubly
obscure by adding the mysterious words 'tra feltro e feltro': *e sua nazion sarà tra
feltro e feltro.* The prophecy is deliberately obscure. If *nazion* means 'birth,'
which seems probable, the phrase *tra feltro e feltro* could well indicate that the
time of the expected advent will be under the constellation of Gemini — i.e.,
the twins Castor and Pollux, the Dioscuri, who were commonly represented as
wearing felt caps and were, accordingly, known as the *pilleati fratres*. To be
sure, such an indication does not actually make the oracular pronouncement
much clearer in its meaning. Dante thought Gemini one of the best constellations to be born under, however, — it was his own.

*I.
Cf. Ps. xc (Vulg. lxxxix), 10: "The days of our years are threescore years and ten." Compare
also *Thebaid*, I, 390–391:

Medio de limite vitae
in senium vergens.

(... verging now toward old age from life's mid-course.)
    7. Cf. Ecclus. xli, 1: "O death, how bitter is the remembrance of thee!" Cf. also Eccles.
vii, 27: "amariorem morte" (more bitter than death.)
    11. According to St. Augustine, "The soul's sleep is forgetfulness of God": Flam., II, 204.
    16. Cf. Ps. cxxi (Vulg. cxx), 1: "I will lift up mine eyes unto the hills, from whence cometh
my help."
    30. This famously obscure verse is given
its sufficient gloss by J. Freccero (1959). A long tradition applied the metaphor of feet to
faculties of the soul. As this metaphor merged with Aristotle's dictum that all motion
originates from the right, it was said that the first step is taken by the right foot while the left
remains stationary. The left foot was seen as the *pes firmior*, the firmer or less "agile."
Later, in a Christian tradition, there came about a more specific identification of the "two feet
of the soul." According to Bonaventura and others, the "foot" or power that moves first is
the *apprehensivus*, or the intellect, and therefore is the right. The other, or left, "foot" is the
affectus or *appetitivus* — i.e., the will. In Adam's sin, wherein all men sinned, it was the intellect or right "foot" that suffered the wound of ignorance, while the left "foot," the *affectus*
or will — the *pes firmior* — suffered the wound of concupiscence. As a result, postlapsarian
man is a limping creature (*homo claudus*). He limps especially in his *left* foot, because it is
wounded by concupiscence, the chief *vulneratio* of original sin.
    In this opening scene of the poem, the wayfarer, as he strives to climb toward the light at

* All line numbers refer to *La Divina Commedia*, ed. C. H. Grandgent, rev. Charles
Singleton (Cambridge, Mass., 1972).

the summit, has to discover that he bears within him the weaknesses of *homo claudus*. He can see the light at the summit (seeing, in this case, is a function of the intellect or right "foot"). At best, however, he can only limp toward the light he sees because in his other power, his will — the left "foot" or *pes firmior* — he bears the wound of concupiscence. Thus, the *piè fermo* is the *pes infirmior*, as Freccero fully documents.

In this whole figure of conversion, or turning toward the light, as it is staged here in Canto I, the wayfarer learns that he is wounded in the power of his will and cannot advance effectively toward the apprehended goal. In fact, the sinful dispositions he thought he had left behind him in the darkness now appear before him in the form of the three beasts blocking his way.

32. *Lonza* is etymologically connected with *ounce* and perhaps with *lynx*. The animal portrayed, however, is evidently the leopardess, which Dante probably regarded as identical with the panther; it appears, in fact, that the panther, in Dante's day, was thought to be the female of the leopard (cf. *Giorn. dant.*, XV, 1). See K. McKenzie, "The Problem of the Lonza," in *Romanic Review*, I, 18. Cf. J. Camus in *Giorn. stor.*, LIII, 1. According to A. Levi, in *Giorn. stor.*, LXIV, 190, *lonza* is the same as French *once* (English 'ounce'), which meant 'hunting leopard.'

38. The sun was in the constellation of Aries, the Ram.

40. It was believed that when the universe was created, the heavenly bodies were placed in their vernal positions. The sun is in the sign of Aries from March 21 to April 20 inclusive.

42. Cf. Ovid, *Met.*, III, 669: "Pictarumque iacent fera corpora pantherarum" (lie the forms of fierce spotted panthers).

48. Cf. Ovid, *Met.*, XIII, 406: "Externasque novo latratu terruit auras" (and with strange barking affrighted the alien air).

60. For this transference of sense notation, cf. *Inf.* V, 28.

63. The voice of Reason has not been heeded for so long that it comes faintly to the sinner's ear; so the figure of Virgil appears dim.

65. *Miserere*, 'have mercy upon me': beginning of Ps. li (Vulg. l).

70. Virgil was barely twenty-six when Caesar perished.

72. Repeatedly Virgil makes pathetic but always dignified and reticent allusion to his lack of Christianity and his consequent eternal exclusion from the presence of God.

73. *Aen.* I, 544–545:

> Rex erat Aeneas nobis, quo iustior alter,
> Nec pietate fuit, nec bello maior et armis.

(Our king was Aeneas: none more righteous than he in goodness, or greater in war and deeds of arms.)

75. *Aen.*, III, 2–3: "Ceciditque superbum Ilium" (after proud Ilium fell). *Met.*, XIII, 408: 'Ilion ardebat.' (Ilium was in flames.)

84. We learn from *Inf.* XX, 114 that Dante knew the *Aeneid* by heart.

100. Rev. xviii, 3: "For all nations have drunk of the wine of the wrath of her fornication, and the kings of the earth have committed fornication with her."

103. It was a common belief that wolves eat dirt.

105. This line is intentionally obscure. See Argument above.

106. *Aen.*, III, 522–523: "Humilemque videmus Italiam." (We see low-lying Italy). Virgil meant 'low-lying,' but Dante took the word in a moral sense.

107. Camilla, a warrior virgin who fought against the Trojans: *Aen.*, XI.

108. *Aen.*, IX, XII.

111. Cf. Wisdom ii, 24: "through envy of the devil came death into the world."

117. The phrase was often used in this sense by theologians. Cf. Rev. xxi, 8: "the lake which burneth with fire and brimstone: which is the second death"; also Rev. xx, 14. Cf. Dante, *Epistola* VI, ii, 5: "Vos autem divina iura et humana transgredientes ..., nonne terror secunde mortis exagitat ...?" (But you, who transgress divine and human law, — doth not the dread of the second death pursue you?)

Canto II

Argument

As this canto opens, twelve hours have been consumed in the attempt to scale the mountain, the encounter with the beasts, and the conversation with Virgil. The world is going to rest, and Dante, "all alone" among the creatures of this earth, is preparing for a stern and fearful task. At this point — really the beginning of the *Inferno*, inasmuch as the first canto is a general introduction to the poem — Dante invokes the Muses, following the example of the great poets of old. Dante probably believed that the Muses, even to the ancients, were only a figure of speech, a metaphor for poetic inspiration or art.

Doubting his fitness for the proposed journey, Dante recalls his two great predecessors Aeneas and St. Paul, to whom the realms of the departed were revealed. The former, as the sixth book of the *Aeneid* relates, visited the lower world; the latter "was caught up into Paradise," as he tells us in 2 Cor. xii. The one listened to prophecies of Rome's future greatness; the other "heard unspeakable words, which it is not lawful for a man to utter." The experience of Aeneas prepared the way for the Empire, the *alto effetto* or "mighty result" of his vision; the rapture of St. Paul strengthened the faith which sustains the Church. Dante has no such mission — he merely represents the ordinary run of humanity: why should such a revelation be made to him?

It is worth noting that in introducing the example of Aeneas, Dante begins with "you say that ...," and a few lines further on he uses the phrase "this journey which you claim he made"; so in *Par.* XV, 26, referring to the same episode, he adds "if our greater Muse deserves belief," meaning Virgil. These expressions seem to imply a mental reservation with regard to the literal veracity of Aeneas's adventure. In *Conv.*, II, i, he makes it clear that in poetry truth is to be sought not in the letter but in the allegory, which he calls "a truth hidden under a beautiful fiction." The sixth book of the *Aeneid*, then, is allegorically true, in that it records revelations made to the hero, but in its material details it may be regarded as fiction. In *Aen.*, VI, 893–898, Anchises lets his son out through the ivory gate of deceptive dreams; and Servius, in his commentary, explains this incident as an indication that the whole story is an invention.

To strengthen Dante's wavering courage, Virgil assures him that the experience vouchsafed him is a fruit of the Divine Care, which watches lovingly over erring man as long as hope is left. In dramatic fashion he tells how Mary, pitying Dante's plight, called upon Lucia (presumably St. Lucia of Syracuse), who, in turn, summoned Beatrice to his aid; she sought out Virgil in the Limbus and sent him to rescue the struggling sinner. On hearing this, Dante takes heart again and follows his master into the earth. The three ladies form a counterpart to the three beasts. The Virgin, here as generally in Christian thought, symbolizes divine Mercy. Lucia has by almost all interpreters been regarded as the emblem of Grace — probably, as her name suggests, Illuminating Grace; inasmuch as Mary describes Dante to Lucia as "il tuo fedele," it would seem that our poet, for reasons unknown to us, had held this saint in particular veneration. Beatrice, as we have seen, stands for Revelation, for which Dante's distorted mind must be prepared by Reason. God in his mercy sends forth his illuminating grace to prepare the way for complete revelation, which will ensue as soon as the reawakened voice of reason shall have made the sinner ready to receive it.

There was another St. Lucy, Lucia degli Ubaldini (sister of the Cardinal), nun in the convent of Monticelli, where was Piccarda, sister of Dante's friend, Forese Donati (*Purg.* XXIV, 13-15; *Par.* III, 34-120). Her day was May 30, which may have been Dante's birthday. Perhaps this coincidence was a cause of the poet's devotion to the great St. Lucia of Syracuse. See Moore, IV, 235.

18. Father Aeneas, founder of Rome. Cf. *Mon.*, II, iii, 7-10. Aeneas had nobility both of birth and of character: see E. H. Wilkins in *Annual Report of the Dante Society of Cambridge, Mass.*, 1918, 1.

21. The Empyrean, the spiritual Heaven, outside the confines of space and time.

24. St. Peter, greatest of Peters or Popes.

28. 'The Chosen Vessel,' St. Paul: Acts ix, 15.

58. Virgil was born near Mantua.

77. Mankind surpasses everything contained within the sphere of the moon (everything perishable) only through divine revelation, embodied in Beatrice.

92. The happiness of the blest is not marred by compassion for the damned. It is perhaps to enforce this doctrine that Virgil's dilatory question has been introduced. Cf. *Purg.* I, 89-90.

94. The Virgin is not expressly named anywhere in the *Inferno*, Hell being a place where mercy does not enter.

102. Beatrice's seat in Heaven is described in *Par.* XXXII, 8-9. Rachel symbolized the contemplative life.

108. The river is perhaps the Acheron, the river of death, which flows beneath Dante's feet. Most commentators understand it as a mere metaphor, signifying the same thing as the wood. For a different explanation, see Singleton (1970).

Canto III

Argument

A solemn inscription over the open gate of Hell arouses Dante's apprehensions, but he is led on by his master into a place full of darkness and the confused wail of countless tortured souls.

The part of the lower world on which they enter is the abode of the lukewarm, who were neither good nor bad and contributed nothing to society. Here, presumably, are to be found those who were given over to acedia, or sloth, one of the seven capital sins. To one of Dante's intense activity and positiveness of judgment these are the most contemptible of all creatures. To him they are as the Laodiceans, "neither cold nor hot." "So then," says Rev. iii, 16, "because thou art lukewarm, and neither cold nor hot, I will spue thee out of my mouth." Both Heaven and Hell reject them. Not one of them does Dante mention by name. Their punishment describes them: as he who will attach himself to neither party must be continually shifting sides, the lukewarm are depicted eternally rushing to and fro after an aimlessly dodging banner; as he who loves his ease is more annoyed by trifles than is the magnanimous man by severe trials, we see the sluggards tormented by flies and wasps, which seem to them worse than any other punishment.

Between this vestibule and the real Hell flows the Acheron, whose bank is crowded with lost souls ready to be ferried over by Charon, the ancient boatman. The personages of ancient mythology had come to be regarded as demons in the Christian scheme; similarly, Christianity, at an earlier date, had taken over such figures as Beelzebub and Lucifer. By Charon, as by most of the spirits whom he meets in Hell, Dante is immediately recognized as a living man; although these incorporeal creatures have all the appearance of bodies, can be seen, heard, and (in Hell) even touched, and possess the same senses as those in the flesh, there are certain tokens by which a genuine live body can be distinguished from them. Charon, moreover, discerns — perhaps by virtue of his office — that Dante is one of the elect, and therefore refuses to carry him in his boat. Divine intervention mysteriously helps the poet on his way. A sudden earthquake, similar to that which preceded the descent of Christ, frightens Dante into a swoon; and when he recovers consciousness, he is on the other side of Acheron, at the edge of the abyss. Thus the sinner who is trying to better himself and meets apparently insuperable obstacles is carried past them, he knows not how, by a higher power.

5. Hell was made by the triune God — Father, Son, and Holy Ghost, or Power, Wisdom, and Love.

7. "In the beginning God created the heaven and the earth. And the earth was without form, and void" (Gen. i, 1–2). At this point, apparently, Hell was created for the rebellious angels, who sinned almost as soon as they were made. Cf. Mat. xxv, 41: "... everlasting fire, prepared for the devil and his angels." The story of the revolt and fall of the angels belongs to very early Christian and even to pre-Christian tradition. It is recorded distinctly in 2 Peter, ii, 4 and Jude 6, more obscurely in Rev. xii, 9. Tertullian and St Augustine refer to it, and it is narrated in full by Cassian (4th and 5th centuries) in his *Collationes*, ch. viii–xi.

8. On the Judgment Day, when all the wicked shall have been consigned to Hell, it will be sealed up and will remain unchanged forever.

14. Cf. *Aen.*, VI, 26: "Nunc animis opus, Aenea, nunc pectore firmo." (Now, Aeneas, thou needest thy courage, now thy stout heart!)

18. The vision of God.

22. Cf. *Aen.*, VI, 557–558:

Hinc exaudiri gemitus, et saeva sonare
Verbera; tum stridor ferri tractaeque catenae.

(Therefrom are heard groans and the sound of the savage lash; withal, the clank of iron and dragging of chains.)

37. Such neutral angels are mentioned in a Syriac version of the *Apocalypse of St. Paul*, and they appear again, in the form of birds, on one of the islands visited by St. Brendan.

42. The guilty might derive some satisfaction from comparing themselves with these.

60. Without much doubt this is Celestine V, a pious hermit, who, after a long vacancy of the papal office, was elected Pope in July, 1294, but abdicated five months later, feeling himself physically and mentally unfit. Through his renunciation Boniface VIII, Dante's chief enemy, became Pope. According to Torraca, Celestine (then called Pietro) was in Tuscany in 1280, when Dante may have seen him. He was canonized in 1313. Gardner, 326–328, suggests that *conobbi* may refer to a legend found in the life of Celestine by Tommaso da Sulmona (written between 1303 and 1306): after his abdication, Celestine sought solitude, hoping to hide his shame; but everywhere he was recognized, even by people who had never seen him before.

64. Cf. Rev. iii, 1: "I know thy works, that thou hast a name that thou livest, and art dead."

72. Cf. *Aen.*, VI, 318–319:

Dic, ait, o virgo, quid volt concursus ad amnem?
Quidve petunt animae?

([Aeneas] cries: "Tell me, O maiden, what means the crowding to the river? What seek the spirits?")

78. Cf. *Aen.*, VI, 295: "Hinc via Tartarei quae fert Acherontis ad undas." (Hence a road leads to the waters of Tartarean Acheron.) Virgil checks Dante's impatience to know everything at once; as they proceed, Dante's questions will find their due answer.

93. Charon sees that Dante is destined to be carried, after death, to Purgatory in the angel's boat described in *Purg.* II, 10–51.

95. Virgil makes use of this formula on other occasions; cf. *Inf.* V, 23.

97. Cf. *Aen.*, VI, 298–300:

Portitor has horrendus aquas et flumina servat
Terribili squalore Charon, cui plurima mento
Canities inculta iacet, stant lumina flamma.

(A grim warden guards these waters and streams, terrible in his squalor — Charon, on whose chin lies a mass of unkempt, hoary hair; his eyes are staring orbs of flame.)

Charon, like most of the classical guardians retained in Dante's Hell, becomes a demonic figure; his "fiery eyes" become "encircled with wheels of flame."

112. Cf. *Aen.*, VI, 309–310:

> Quam multa in silvis autumni frigore primo
> Lapsa cadunt folia ...

(... thick as the leaves of the forest that at autumn's first frost dropping fall ....)
The simile is evidently suggested by Virgil, but Dante adds the descriptive "one after another" and the pathetic touch of the last clause. Nearly always, when Dante borrows a simile, he makes it more vivid or more human.

117. The poem is full of figures taken from bird hunting, the favorite sport of the nobility in the Middle Ages.

126. Any reality seems to them less intolerable than the apprehension.

127. Cf. *Aen.*, VI, 563: "Nulli fas casto sceleratum insistere limen." (No pure soul may tread the accursed threshold.)

129. See note on l. 93.

Canto IV

Argument

A thunderclap announces the consummation of the miracle. Dante finds himself on the brink of the cliff that surrounds the dark abyss. A "roar of countless wails" greets his ear. At this sound, Virgil, who later in the journey sternly rebukes Dante for his sympathy with the damned, himself turns pale with pity: while Reason, face to face with sin, can feel only abhorrence, it may well be moved to anguish by contemplation of sin's consequences.

The descent of the bank brings the poets to the first circle of Hell, the Limbus. The Church fathers defined the Limbus as an underground place, near Hell and Purgatory, the abode of the souls of unbaptized children and, until the Harrowing of Hell, of the virtuous members of the Old Church; the only punishment is exile from God's presence; the patriarchs were cheered by hope of ultimate rescue. Salvation can be won only through faith in Christ: the ancient Hebrews believed in Christ to come; Christians believe in Christ already descended and arisen. Admission to community with Christ, which redeems man from original sin, must be sanctified by prescribed rites — in Christian times by baptism.

After the crucifixion Christ went down into Hell — breaking the gates, which have ever since remained open — and took from Limbus the souls of the worthy people of the Old Testament. The doctrine of the Harrowing of Hell is foreshadowed in Messianic tradition. In the Bible only passing references to it are to be found: as in Ephesians iv, 9; 1 Epistle of Peter iii, 19, and iv, 6; also, according to St. Augustine, in Ps. cvii (Vulgate cvi), 14. It is mentioned in the apocryphal Gospel of Peter and described in the apocryphal Gospel of Nicodemus.

It remained for Dante to place in his Limbus the souls of virtuous pagans. These, as they had never believed in Christ, were not saved, but remained with the unbaptized infants. Only Cato of Utica, who appears in the first canto of the *Purgatorio*, was apparently released and is working out his salvation on the Island of Purgatory; how his entrance into the Church is to be effected, we are not told. It is interesting to note that in the *Aeneid*, VI, 426–429, the children are on the outer edge of the lower world — "infantumque animae flentes in limine primo" (souls of infants weeping on the very threshold).

Dante's Limbus is shrouded in darkness, and the air quivers with sighs. Such is the life of those devoid of true knowledge of God: their minds are enveloped in ignorance, and their hearts are full of a vague longing forever unsatisfied. But those among them who combine wisdom with virtue are illumined by mortal intelligence — a light dim compared with the vision of God, but bright beside the obscurity in which their less gifted fellows dwell. The state of the heathen sages of old is symbolized by the "nobile castello," the Palace of Wisdom (or, as some understand it, of Fame), where the great souls congregate, "neither happy nor sad," enjoying the companionship of their peers and the light of human knowledge. In the noble castle are the "Magnanimi," as opposed to the "Pusillanimi" of the Antinferno. Cf. *Conv.*, I, xi, 19–21. Dante's description of them is reminiscent of Virgil's Elysian Fields in *Aen.*, VI, 637 ff.

2. Inasmuch as lines 2 and 3 point to a sudden noise, this "thunder" can hardly be identical with that of l. 9.

9. In the *Visio S. Pauli* there is a "tonitruum" of groans and sighs.

33. Virgil will not have Dante suppose for a moment that his companions in Limbus have been evildoers.

48. As soon as Dante learns that Virgil's soul dwells in Limbus, he is eager to receive from this witness corroboration of the doctrine of the descent of Christ into Hell.

52. Virgil died in the year 19 B.C.

53. Christ is never named in the *Inferno*.

54. Doubtless a cruciform nimbus.

58. Cf. Gen. xvii, 5: "thy name shall be Abraham, for a father of many nations have I made thee."

60. To win Rachel, Jacob served Laban twice seven years: Gen. xxix, 18–28.

63. Before the descent of Christ all human souls went, if bad, to Hell, if good, to Limbus. Since that time Christian souls penitent at the moment of death have gone to Purgatory.

69. A light radiates up in all directions from the Castle, forming a hemisphere of brightness over and about it.

76. God allows the intelligence, by the good use of which they won such renown on earth, to remain with them in the other world.

79. We are not told which of the spirits utters the greeting to Virgil.

86. Homer is depicted with a sword because he sang of arms. According to *Vulg. El.*, II, ii, the three best themes of poetry are arms, love, and righteousness.

88. Dante did not know Homer directly. The reputation of the latter as 'sovereign poet' must have survived in school tradition. In the *Ars Poetica*, 73–74, Horace says:

> Res gestae regumque ducumque et tristia bella
> quo scribi possent numero, monstravit Homerus.

(In what measure the exploits of kings and captains and the sorrows of war may be written Homer has shown.) A passage in *Vita Nuova*, XXV, 9, suggests that Dante may have formed his impression of Homer, in part, through Horace. It is noteworthy that the ancient poets thus grouped in the *Inferno* are cited together in the same chapter of the *Vita Nuova*. Dante was thoroughly familiar with Virgil, Ovid, and Lucan. Another ancient poet whom he had read much, Statius, appears in Purgatory.

89. The *Odes* and *Epodes* were probably unknown to Dante. In the *Ars Poetica*, 235, Horace speaks of himself as a writer of satire.

104. Things appropriate to that time and place, but not to the present poem.

107. The Palace of Wisdom is surrounded by seven walls possibly representing the four moral virtues (prudence, temperance, fortitude, and justice) and the three intellectual virtues (understanding, knowledge, and wisdom). The stream may well stand for eloquence.

110. The gates probably symbolize the seven liberal arts of the *trivium* (grammar, logic, rhetoric) and the *quadrivium* (music, arithmetic, geometry, astronomy), which afford access to knowledge.

121. Electra, daughter of Atlas, and mother of Dardanus who was the founder of Troy: *Aen.*, VIII, 134–135. Cf. *Mon.*, II, iii, 11: "avia vetustissima, Electra" (most ancient ancestress, Electra).

123. Caesar, the founder of the Empire, is briefly described as 'in arms, with hawklike eyes.' Nowhere in the poem do we find a long description or discussion of him. While he deserved, by virtue of his great political act, a place in history beside that of Christ, he was probably, as a tyrant and the opponent of Cato, distasteful to Dante.

124. Camilla, a warrior maiden: *Aen.*, XI, 498 ff. Penthesilēa, queen of the Amazons: *Aen.*, I, 490 ff.

125. Cf. *Aen.*, VII, 45 ff.

127. The other Brutus is in the center of Hell.

128. Lucretia, wife of Collatinus; Julia, daughter of Caesar, wife of Pompey; Marcia, wife of Cato of Utica (cf. *Purg.* I, 79; *Conv.*, IV, xxviii, 13); Cornelia, mother of the Gracchi.

129. Saladin, the model of chivalry, was sultan of Egypt and Syria in the 12th century. He is different in race and religion from those mentioned hitherto.

131. Aristotle, whom Dante often calls simply "il Filosofo," and to whom he repeatedly refers in terms of the deepest admiration. Aristotle was known to Dante in Latin translations, one of which had been made for St. Thomas.

136. Democritus, known to Dante probably through Cicero.

137. Anaxagoras, cited by Aristotle. Thales, one of the seven wise men of Greece: *Conv.*, III, xi, 4.

138. Empedocles, to whose doctrine reference is made in *Inf.* XII, 42. Heraclitus, mentioned by Aristotle. Zeno, Stoic philosopher: *Conv.*, IV, vi, 9.

139. Dioscorides wrote a treatise on plants and their properties.

140. Orpheus, considered as a philosopher: *Conv.*, II, i, 3.

141. Tully, or Cicero, was one of the first philosophers that Dante studied: *Conv.*, II, xii, 3; see also *Inf.* XI, 22–24. Livy wrote philosophical works, mentioned in a letter of Seneca to Lucilius; most texts have Lino, i.e., Linus, an imaginary Greek poet. Seneca the moralist was thought to be a different person from the dramatist.

142. Ptolemy, the great geographer and astronomer of Alexandria, who lived in the 2nd century B.C.

143. Hippocrates, Avicenna, Galen: three famous physicians of Greece, Turkestan, and Mysia.

144. Averroës, a Spanish Moor of the 12th century, was a celebrated scholar and philosopher. Having read the works of Aristotle in ancient Syriac translations, he composed three commentaries on them; one of these, the 'gran commento,' was followed by St. Thomas and by many other philosophers and theologians of Dante's day.

148. The company of six dwindles to two — Virgil and Dante.
150. Out of the peaceful atmosphere of the Palace into the air that quivers with sighs: cf. ll. 26–27.

Canto V

Argument

In this canto are found several striking similes drawn from birdlife, which Dante loved to depict. The second circle, with its wind-wafted spirits, offers fit opportunity for these portrayals of starlings, cranes, and doves. Cranes are put to a like use by Virgil in *Aen.*, X, 264–266:

> Quales sub nubibus atris
> Strymoniae dant signa grues atque aethera tranant
> Cum sonitu, fugiuntque Notos clamore secundo.

(Even as amid black clouds Strymonian cranes give signal, while clamorously they skim the air, and flee before the south winds with joyous cries.)

The descent from Limbus to the second circle is not described; we have no means of conjecturing the size or the steepness of the cliff. The journey through Hell being physically impossible, Dante purposely refrains from furnishing particulars that might destroy the illusion, while abounding in such details as serve to heighten it. As the pit narrows progressively toward the bottom, the terraces correspondingly decrease in circumference, but the penalties become more and more severe. At one point in the round of this shelf is a break, where the rock has fallen. When Dante mentions this *ruina*, in l. 34, he offers no explanation: shrieks and curses are redoubled here, but we know not why. Our suspense lasts until we reach Canto XII, ll. 31–45. There we are told that when Christ descended into Hell, his coming was preceded by an earthquake, which shook down the walls of the abyss in three spots. Mat. xxvii, 51: "And behold, the veil of the temple was rent in twain from the top to the bottom; and the earth did quake, and the rocks rent." Those broken places lie beside the circle of the pagans, just beyond the enclosure of the heretics, and over the hypocrites by whom Christ had been condemned (XXI, 112–114; XXIII, 133–138) — all close to the abodes of those who had offended the Savior by disbelief in his mission. In each case the word 'ruin' is used. The sight of the first *ruina* moves the souls of the second circle to lamentation, because it reminds them of the time when the neighboring Hebrew spirits in the Limbus were rescued, while all the other souls in Hell were left to eternal torment.

Most of the fallen angels, or fiends, are in the lower Hell; a few, however, appear as presiding genii outside the City of Dis: so Charon, Cerberus, Plutus,

Phlegyas, and, at the threshold of the second circle, Minos, the judge. Both theologians and simple folk were prone to look upon the heathen gods as demons who had beguiled men into their worship. It is not strange, therefore, to find in a Christian Hell many classic personages, especially such as were already associated with the lower world. Dante did not treat all the pagan divinities alike; if he depicted Plutus as a devil, the Muses and Apollo were to him simply allegorical figures, while Jove apparently represented the ancient poets' dim conception of the Supreme Being. Minos, the great king and legislator of Crete, holds in the 11th book of the *Odyssey* the noble office of judge of the dead. In the *Aeneid*, VI, 432–433, though briefly sketched, he retains the same honorable function:

> Quaesitor Minos urnam movet; ille silentum
> Conciliumque vocat, vitasque et crimina discit.

(Minos, presiding, shakes the urn; 'tis he calls a court of the silent, and learns men's lives and misdeeds.)

In Dante he has become a hideous demon, arbiter of the damned — the symbol, it would seem, of the guilty conscience.

The second circle punishes *lussuria*, or lust, the first of the sins of Incontinence. The luxurious are forever blown about in the darkness by stormy blasts, typifying the blind fury of passion. In some previous tales of Hell a wind torments evildoers, notably in the *Visio Alberici*, XIV, where souls are driven by the fiery breath of a dog and a lion. Dante divests the torment of all grotesqueness, and, indeed, treats sinners of this class with special consideration. This may be due in part to sympathy, and partly, no doubt, to a sense that their fault is the result of a mistaken following of love, the noblest of human emotions. Theologically speaking, the fate of lost souls should arouse no pity, as the sight of sin should excite only repugnance. But we must remember that the Dante who is visiting Hell is himself still a sinner. Moreover, allegorically interpreted, these harassed souls are men and women loving and suffering on earth; and even the most sinful, as long as they live, are fit objects of compassion.

Compassion, tenderness, sympathetic curiosity, and anguish reach their climax when Dante meets and converses with Francesca da Rimini. This unhappy lady was the daughter of Guido Minore da Polenta, a powerful citizen of Ravenna, and was married to Giovanni di Malatesta da Verrucchio (called Sciancato, or Gian Ciotto), master of Rimini. Of her love for Paolo, her husband's brother, and the murder of the two by Giovanni, we have no record before Dante, although the event must have been well known. It probably occurred about 1285. When Dante was eighteen, in 1282–83, Paolo was for five months in Florence as Capitano del Popolo; he is not mentioned among Malatesta's sons in 1287; and in 1288 there is evidence of a child born to Giovanni by a second wife. In 1285 Paolo was some 35 years old, had been married sixteen years, and had two children; Francesca had one child. Paolo's daughter married a son of Aghinolfo of Romena. After Francesca's adventure had been made eternally famous by Dante's poem, many fables grew up about it; her fate is still a favorite theme for artists and authors. Of all the episodes in the *Commedia*, this has always been the most popular.

It is not alone the undying passion of Francesca that moves us, but even more her gentleness and modest reticence. In her narrative she names none of the participants; not even her city is called by name. Her identity is revealed by Dante, who, recognizing her, addresses her as "Francesca." Everything in her story that could mar our pity is set aside, and nothing remains but the quintessence of love. Amid the tortures of Hell, where all is hatred, her love does not forsake her, and she glories in the thought that she and Paolo shall never be parted.

Should we be inclined to question whether mere impersonal sympathy, however natural and profound, could have sufficed to lead a religious poet, a stern moralist, thus to idealize an adulteress and mitigate her punishment, we might feel ourselves justified in seeking some special reason for his kindliness. As we look through the *Commedia*, we find that in one place or another the exiled poet contrived to pay an appropriate tribute to all those who had befriended him in his need: it was the only return his grateful heart could make. His last and probably his happiest years were spent in Ravenna under the protection of Guido Novello da Polenta, himself a poet, a nephew of our Francesca. Now, we do not know exactly when Dante went to that city, but in any case it was almost certainly at a period later than the time when the *Inferno* was composed. His son Pietro, however, established himself in Ravenna, perhaps as early as 1317, receiving a benefice from Guido's wife; and his daughter Beatrice entered a convent there. It is possible that previous courtesies, of which we have no record, were extended to Dante or his kindred before this *cantica* was completed. Guido Minore da Polenta, Francesca's father, was *podestà* of Florence in 1290, when Dante was 25. There is, then, some slight ground for the supposition that this passage was intended as an incidental homage to Guido's family (there being no other tribute to it in the poem), a rehabilitation of Francesca's memory. Love, she says, comes to gentle hearts with irresistible force — "a nullo amato amar perdona." Had she lived, she would have repented; it was her sudden taking off that damned her. Her fate is contrasted with that of her husband: her soul is one of the highest in Hell; his, one of the lowest.

This canto is an excellent example of Dante's creative imagination. His emotion once stirred, he conjured up a whole scene in all its details. So he did with the story of Count Ugolino in *Inf.* XXXIII.

20. Cf. Mat. vii, 13: "wide is the gate, and broad is the way, that leadeth to destruction." Also *Aen.*, VI, 126–127:

> facilis descensus Averno:
> noctes atque dies patet atri ianua Ditis;

(Easy is the descent to Avernus: night and day the door of gloomy Dis stands open.)

23. The same formula was used in III, 95–96.

54. Semiramis, queen of Assyria, of whom Dante had read in the *Historia* of Paulus Orosius, I, iv. In *Mon.*, II, viii, 3, Dante says that Ninus, her husband, "Asiam totam sibi subegerit" (subdued all Asia to himself).

56. To excuse her own unnatural passion, "praecepit ... quod cuique libitum esset, licitum fieret" (she prescribed ... that each should be free to do as he pleased), i.e., she made every one's pleasure lawful.

60. The lands in Egypt and Syria which the Sultan now rules. Two Babylons were distinguished in the Middle Ages: "Babylonia antiqua a Nembroth gygante (Nimrod) fundata" and "Babylonia altera, id est Memfis (i.e. Cairo) super Nilum." Dante perhaps made the Sultan ruler of both.

61. The story of Dido's fatal love for Aeneas (and her infidelity to the memory of her dead husband, Sichaeus) is told in *Aen.*, IV.

62. Note *Aen.*, IV, 552: "non servata fides cineri promissa Sichaeo." (The faith vowed to the ashes of Sychaeus I have not kept!)

64. Helen, 'on whose account so many evil years were spent' in the Trojan war.

66. The Old French poet, Benoît de Sainte More, in his *Roman de Troie*, developing an allusion in Dares's *Excidium Trojae*, narrates that Achilles, madly in love with Polyxena, was lured into an ambush, where he perished. See also Servius's Commentary on *Aen.*, III, 322.

67. *Paris*, son of Priam. *Tristano*, Tristam, hero of the most famous medieval love romance.

81. God is never named to the damned, nor by them, save in blasphemy.

82. This beautiful simile was doubtless suggested by *Aen.*, V, 213–217:

> qualis spelunca subito commota columba,
> cui domus et dulces latebroso in pumice nidi,
> fertur in arva volans plausumque exterrita pinnis
> dat tecto ingentem, mox aëre lapsa quieto
> radit iter liquidum celeris neque commovet alas.

(Even as, if startled suddenly from her cave, a dove whose home and sweet nestlings are in the rocky coverts, wings her flight to the fields and, frightened from her home, flaps loudly with her wings; soon, gliding in the peaceful air, she skims her liquid way and stirs not her swift pinions.)

Dante, however, while keeping a part of the general picture and a few of the expressions ("sweet nest" and "motionless wings"), alters the situation, making the dove fly to her nest instead of flying away from it; furthermore, he infuses an entirely new spirit into the figure by his conception of love as the sole power that sustains the mother bird in her flight.

92. 'Peace' is what Francesca most desires; and she imagines that everyone else must crave peace — even the rivers running to the sea, as in l. 99.

96. In l. 31 the poet tells us that the "bufera infernal" never rests. But the "bufera" seems to indicate the whole storm of conflicting blasts: in a single spot the gust may die down for a moment — 'as it now does.'

97. Ravenna, then only one mile from the sea and connected with the Po by canals.

99. 'To have peace with its pursuers': the tributaries are conceived as chasing the Po down to the sea.

101. Love seized him, Paolo, 'for the fair body that was taken from me'; and 'the way (in which it was taken from me) is still harmful to me,' because, murdered as she was without a chance to repent, she incurred eternal punishment.

103. 'Love, which exempts no loved one from loving in return, seized me for his charms with such might ...'

107. *Caïna*, the abode of traitors to kindred, at the bottom of Hell, awaits Francesca's husband, Gian Ciotto.

112. Evidently there is a pause between question and answer.

127. The French prose romance of Lancelot of the Lake, which tells of the love of the hero for Guinevere, wife of King Arthur.

129. In the romance, Lancelot and Guinevere were not alone, as Paolo and Francesca were.

137. Gallehaut was the intermediary who brought Lancelot and Guinevere together; Paolo and Francesca had no such go-between — the book was their Gallehaut, their guide to love. Gallehaut in the French *Lancelot* was a model prince and knight, type of the faithful friend and discreet helper in love. Dante was strongly influenced by the beautiful romance, with its idea of courtly love.

Canto VI

Argument

For the reason already mentioned, Dante likes to pass lightly over the transitions from one step to another. Thus, when he awakens from his second swoon, he finds himself once more mysteriously transported, this time to the third terrace. Gluttony, the next of the sins of Incontinence, is essentially foul and selfish, and so is fitly symbolized by the cold, slimy filth which constitutes the punishment of the third circle. It is a sin that robs men of their humanity, making them unrecognizable to their friends. Its perfect embodiment is Cerberus, the tormenting genius of the place. This beast, opposing the poets' passage, is offered a double handful of mud, which it eagerly devours. So in the *Aeneid*, VI, 417–423, Cerberus is pacified by the Sibyl with a honey cake:

> Cerberus haec ingens latratu regna trifauci
> personat, adverso recubans immanis in antro.
> cui vates, horrere videns iam colla colubris,
> melle soporatam et medicatis frugibus offam
> obicit. ille fame rabida tria guttura pandens
> corripit obiectam, atque immania terga resolvit
> fusus humi totoque ingens extenditur antro.

(These realms huge Cerberus makes ring with his triple-throated baying, his monstrous bulk crouching in a cavern opposite. To him, seeing the snakes now bristling on his necks, the seer flung a morsel drowsy with honey and drugged meal. He, opening his triple throat in ravenous hunger, catches it when thrown and, with monstrous frame relaxed, sinks to earth and stretches his bulk over all the den.)

The substitution of dirt for medicated sweets serves still further to debase greediness.

With one of the souls here confined Dante holds converse. This is Ciacco, a Florentine renowned both for his gluttony and for his cleverness, who figures also in one of Boccaccio's tales, *Decameron*, IX, 8. It is not certain whether *Ciacco* was his real name — perhaps a synonym of Jacopo — or a nickname meaning "pig"; nor is it known whether he is to be identified with a poet called Ciacco dell' Anguillaia. In response to a question by Dante, this spirit prophesies the approaching victory of the Whites — the *selvaggia* or 'rustic' party — over their opponents and the ensuing triumph of the Blacks through the connivance of Boniface VIII. In Florence, he further declares, there are only two just men, and they have no influence. Who these two are, we are not told. A comparison with the close of Canzone IX (*Rime* CVI) — in which Dante sends his song 'to the three least guilty of our city' — and with *Purg.* XVI, 124-126 (where the only three good men now left in Lombardy are named), makes it likely that the poet had in mind two specific persons; but it is impossible to guess whom he meant.

In ll. 35-36 Dante speaks of walking over the empty shades which look like real people. Throughout Hell the souls, though without weight, are not only visible and audible but tangible. On the lower slopes of the mountain of Purgatory, however, Dante cannot touch a shade (*Purg.* II, 79 ff.), although two spirits can still embrace (*Purg.* VI, 75); and near the summit one soul apparently cannot clasp another (*Purg.* XXI, 130 ff.). In *Purg.* XXV, 79 ff., we are informed that after death the atmosphere collects around the departed spirit, forming an aerial body, which reflects all the emotions of the soul itself. Although Dante nowhere says so explicitly, it would seem that he chose to regard this airy shape as more substantial in proportion to its proximity to the center of gravity of the universe (which is also the center of sin), and more ethereal as it rises above the earth's surface. This conception of the shade appears to be Dante's own, although we find that St. Thomas mentions the power of angels and devils to assume aerial forms.

21. *Profani*, the impious gluttons, 'whose God is their belly': Phil. iii, 19.

48. Dante, who has not yet seen the rest of Hell, assumes that no punishment can be more disgusting than this.

51. To the lost souls the earthly life appears, by contrast, clear and beautiful.

65. After long strife between the adherents of the Donati, representing the old aristocracy,

and the followers of the Cerchi, who had come to Florence from the country and enriched themselves by commerce, blood was shed in an encounter on May 1, 1300. In June, 1301 the leaders of the Black or Donati party conspired against their opponents, and in consequence were exiled. — G. Villani says that the Cerchi were *di bizzarra salvatichezza,* or 'curiously rustic.'

67. The Blacks having gained the upper hand through the cunning of Boniface VIII and his pretended 'peacemaker,' Charles of Valois, banished, between January 1 and October 1, 1302, some 600 Whites. Dante was sentenced on January 27, and again on March 10. — *Tre soli* means three solar years, beginning January 1; the Florentine year began on March 25.

69. Here the reference is to Pope Boniface VIII. The Pope in 1300 was acting ambiguously and was also engaged in litigation with Florence.

85. Farinata degli Uberti is among the heretics, X, 32; Tegghiaio Aldobrandi and Jacopo Rusticucci are with the sodomites, XVI, 41, 44; Mosca dei Lamberti is one of the sowers of discord, XXVIII, 106. Arrigo, who cannot be identified with certainty, is not mentioned again.

96. Christ; cf. John v, 27: "And [the Father] hath given him authority (*potestatem*) to execute judgment also, because he is the Son of man." On the Day of Judgment, at the sound of the last trumpet, all souls in Heaven and Hell will return to earth, resume their bodies, gather in the Valley of Jehoshaphat, and listen to their eternal sentence, after which they will go back to their respective places.

106. Torraca quotes from St. Thomas: "The soul separated from the body, is, in a way, imperfect, like any part existing outside of its whole, since the soul is naturally a part of human nature. Man, then, cannot attain the utmost felicity until it is reunited to the body." If the bodiless soul cannot attain the utmost happiness, we may infer that it cannot attain the utmost misery. It follows that the pains of Hell will be severer after the Judgment, because, although the word "perfection" cannot be fitly applied to "these accursed people," they expect to be more complete after the Great Day than before it.

115. Plutus, the god of wealth, who was not always distinguished, even by the ancients, from Pluto.

Canto VII

Argument

Plutus, the symbol of wealth, an inflated, puffy-faced monster, is as unsubstantial as he seems gigantic; when thwarted, he collapses and falls in a heap. Virgil addresses him, in l. 8, as "maladetto lupo." Similarly in *Purg.* XX, 10, Dante exclaims, in the circle of avarice and prodigality: "Maladetta sie tu, antica lupa!" These two passages afford strong support for the interpretation of the wolf in Canto I as avarice. The arguments on the other side seem, however, conclusive; it is probably safe to assume that the wolf, in Dante's mind, always signified Incontinence, either in the abstract or in some one of its forms — and of these avarice is by far the most important and injurious. The swarm of the money-lovers is greater than any other in Dante's Hell, as it was in Virgil's (*Aen.,* VI, 610–611):

> Aut qui divitiis soli incubuere repertis
> Nec partem posuere suis (quae maxima turba est).

(... or who brooded in solitude over wealth they had won, nor set aside a portion for their kin — the largest number this.)

The fourth circle contains both misers and spendthrifts — those who showed no moderation in the use of worldly goods, but handled them so "undiscerningly" that they are themselves made indistinguishable, "darkened beyond discernment," their individuality being sunk in their vice. The insulting cries which they exchange — "Why hoard?" "Why squander?" — proclaim, or "bark," their sin clearly enough. So the usurers, in Canto XVII, are altered beyond recognition and can be picked out only by their moneybags. As Dante comes down among the sinners of the fourth shelf, the avaricious, as the more despicable, are on his left, the prodigal on his right. The "clenched fist" is the sign of greed; the "cropped hair," of lavishness. Clerics form a large part of the miserly host; Dante was by no means alone in regarding avarice as the besetting fault of the clergy. In this canto we find none of the gentleness with which our poet treats the amorous; even the gluttonous receive more consideration. The verses bristle with derisive terms: *cozzi, zuffa, ontoso metro, rabbuffa*. As in *Aen.*, VI, 616, "saxum ingens volvunt alii" (some roll a huge stone), so these two classes of sinners, each traversing one-half the ring, roll huge weights, pushing with might and main "by strength of chest," the misers moving toward the right, the spendthrifts toward the left. When they reach a spot in front of Dante, they clash together; then, with mutual execration, they turn about and laboriously work their way to the opposite side of the ring, where the encounter is repeated. And so the weary, futile round goes on to all eternity, a fit image of the incessant and useless efforts of humanity to transfer worldly possessions.

For this transfer God created a special minister, Fortune, a power similar to the celestial intelligences that move the heavens. She may be called the Angel of Earth. It is her mission to shift prosperity to and fro, without apparent plan, seeing that it remain not too long with one person, family, or nation. In many of his utterances about Fortune, Dante evidently follows Boethius, in whom, as later in Albertus Magnus, there appears not only the pagan but also a distinctly Christian conception of her as God's instrument; but her rank as an angelic intelligence is bestowed by Dante himself.

Cutting across this circle, the poets find a stream that pours down over the edge to the terrace below; they keep close to this torrent, and so descend to the fifth shelf. Here the brook feeds a vast swamp, filled with muddy figures, all intent on mangling one another. Thus foul wrath pictures itself. These souls fare no better, at Dante's hands, than their immediate predecessors: their marsh is a "puddle," they "gurgle in their gullets" and "guzzle mud." Aristotle, in his *Ethics*, IV, v — and, after him, St. Thomas, both in his commentary on

Aristotle and in his *Summa Theologiae*, Prima Secundae, Qu. xlvi, Art. 8, and Secunda Secundae, Qu. clviii, Art. 5 — divided the wrathful into three classes: the *acuti*, or quick-tempered; the *amari*, or sullen; the *difficiles* (also called *graves*), or vindictive.   The *acuti* are evidently the sinners on the top of the pool; but below in the mire, so we are told, are others, whose presence is indicated only by the bubbles they send to the surface.   These are the *amari*, and not improbably the *difficiles* as well.   Inasmuch as these sunken spirits are said to harbor "sluggish fumes" or the "fumes of sloth" (*accidioso fummo*), some commentators regard this marsh bottom as the regular abode of acedia or sloth, one of the seven capital sins, which in Purgatory has a circle to itself.   But acedia is a disposition, not an act: insofar as it leads to cowardice or indifference, it belongs to the *Antinferno;* when it manifests itself as sullenness, that sullenness is punished in the bog.

2. Plutus clucks like a hen.   The first line is evidently intended to produce the effect of an unintelligible jargon.   If (as is scarcely probable) Dante meant the words to signify anything, they may perhaps be interpreted: 'Oh! Satan! Oh! Satan! Alas!'   *Pape* looks like the Greek exclamation *papae*; and *aleppe* has suggested to some the Hebrew *aleph*, which is said to have been used as an interjection of grief.

12. For the story of the revolt of the angels, through pride, and their ejection from Heaven, see III, 7, and the argument to XXXIV.

74. The angels, or heavenly intelligences, who govern the revolutions of the spheres.

84. Cf. Virgil, Eclogue III. 93: "latet anguis in herba."   (A snake lurks in the grass.)

88. Cf. Boethius, *De Cons. Phil.*, II, Pr. i.

99. The stars which were rising in the east when they started have now crossed the meridian and begun to descend toward the west: it is past midnight.   Virgil usually states the hour in astronomical terms — in Hell by the positions of the moon and stars, which, of course, he cannot see, except with his mind's eye. — Cf. the words of the Sibyl in *Aen.*, VI, 539: "Nox ruit Aenea; nos flendo ducimus horas."   (Night is coming, Aeneas; we waste the hours in weeping.)

106. The Styx was the most famous of the rivers of the classical lower world.   Virgil uses the phrase "Stygiamque paludem" (Stygian marsh) in *Aen.*, VI, 323. — The four rivers of Dante's Hell — Acheron, Styx, Phlegethon, Cocytus — are all connected, forming one stream. Lethe is not in Hell, but in the Garden of Eden.

121. Cf. *Summa Theologiae*, Secunda Secundae, Qu. clviii, Art. 5: "Amari habent iram permanentem, propter permanentiam tristitiae quam inter viscera tenent clausam."   (For a *sullen* person has an abiding anger on account of an abiding displeasure, which he holds locked in his breast.)   So he declares also in his Commentary on Aristotle's *Ethics*, IV, xiii.

130. Here, as frequently, Dante breaks his narrative at an interesting point, using suspense as a means of heightening effect.

Canto VIII

Argument

The guardian of the fifth circle is the swift Phlegyas, who seems to impersonate both *furor* and *rancor*.   On earth he was a king of the Lapithae, who, in a frenzy of rage against Apollo for the violation of his daughter, set fire to the temple at Delphi, and was slain by the god.   He is mentioned, without specific punishment, in the *Aeneid*, VI, 618–620:

> Phlegyasque miserrimus omnis
> admonet et magna testatur voce per umbras:
> ' discite iustitiam moniti et non temnere divos.'

(And Phlegyas, most unblest, gives warning to all and with loud voice bears witness amid the gloom: "Be warned; learn ye to be just and not to slight the gods!")

"Learn moderation from my example" is his warning.   In the *Commedia* he is a boatman on the Styx.   It can hardly be his duty to ferry over all the spirits that are to go beyond: his tiny skiff would not suffice; and, besides, we are given to understand that each lost soul, after hearing its sentence, falls — as it were by the weight of its own sin — to the depth that befits it.   His function seems to be to carry the wrathful spirits to their proper places in the Stygian pool.

St. Thomas, in the *Summa Theologiae*, Secunda Secundae, Qu. clviii, Art. 1, distinguishes from sinful rage the righteous indignation that is aroused by the sight of wickedness.   This justifiable anger is illustrated, in an exciting scene, by the attitude of Dante toward one of the violently wrathful — an attitude which Reason heartily approves.   The furious soul that so incenses Dante is Filippo Argenti degli Adimari of Florence, who "in the world was a haughty person."

To the shores of the swamp an air of mystery is lent by two signal lights which are kindled, we know not how, at the top of a tower, and another light which responds from afar.   When at last the poets arrive with Phlegyas at the other side, they are confronted by a vast wall that encircles the City of Dis, or Lower Hell, the abiding place of those whose sins were due, not to Incontinence of desire or temper, but to permanent evil dispositions, Bestiality and Malice. Their crimes are the fruit of envy and pride.   In Ps. lxxxvi, 13, we read: "thou hast delivered my soul from the lowest hell" (eruisti animam meam ex inferno inferiore); and from the word *inferiore* St. Augustine and others argued a division of Hell into two parts.

Before landing, the boat has to make a long circuit about the fortifications. When the gate is reached, hosts of demons appear upon the ramparts — "più di mille da ciel piovuti" — who successfully oppose Dante's entrance. They lend a deaf ear to Virgil and shut the doors in his face. The discomfited guide and his terrorstricken follower are obliged to wait for heavenly aid. The erring soul, which, seeking enlightenment, is trying to probe the recesses of human wickedness, comes to a stage where further advance seems impossible. Fear and remorse seize it at the aspect of the worst iniquities; reason can direct it no longer; it is on the verge of despair. To the horrified searcher it appears that reason is about to forsake him, that he is to be left without its guidance, while sin besets him on every hand. But in the hour of need divine help is not lacking. A special grace descends upon the distracted spirit, and opens a way where all seemed hopeless. Such, apparently, is the allegory of this dramatic episode.

According to a story transmitted by Boccaccio, Dante, excluded from Florence, left behind him the first seven cantos of his poem, which, found subsequently by his wife, Gemma, were sent to him at the home of Moroello Malaspina, where he was visiting. The poet then resumed his task with the word *seguitando*. Although this anecdote is generally regarded with doubt, its authenticity has been defended by some scholars.

7. The 'Sea of all wisdom' is of course Virgil.

18. Phlegyas, in his blind wrath, seems not to have noticed that there are two newcomers.

27. Cf. *Aen.*, VI, 412–414:

> simul accipit alveo
> ingentem Aeneam.   gemuit sub pondere cumba
> sutilis et multam accepit rimosa paludem.

(The while he takes aboard giant Aeneas. The seamy craft groaned under the weight, and through its chinks took in a marshy flood.)

68. Cf. *Aen.*, VI, 127: "atri ianua Ditis" (the door of gloomy Dis). Dante transfers the name from the god to the city.

70. In the distance the wall, with its towers, looks like great buildings, which Dante appropriately calls "mosques," or places of demon-worship.

71. The sixth circle is apparently on the same level as the fifth. The boat passes presently (l. 76) from the swamp into the moat.

72. Cf. *Aen.*, VI, 630–631:

> Cyclopum educta caminis
> Moenia conspicio.

(I descry the ramparts reared by Cyclopean forges.)

78. Cf. *Aen.*, VI, 554: "stat ferrea turris." (There stands the iron tower.)

97. 'Seven' is often used to indicate an indeterminate number in the Bible (as in Prov. xxiv, 16) and elsewhere.

120. Cf. *Aen.*, VI, 534: "tristes ... domos" (sad dwellings).

125. The demons are still possessed by the pride that caused their original fall. Their "insolence" was shown at the outer gate of Hell, when they tried to oppose the descent of Christ.

126. Cf. Ps. cvii (Vulgate cvi), 16: "For he hath broken the gates of brass, and cut the bars of iron in sunder."

130. The one who is descending from the gate to open the city is an angel.

Canto IX

Argument

Dante in his terror begins to doubt whether Reason is a safe guide. Without venturing a direct question, he tries to ascertain whether his companion has full knowledge of the road they are to travel. The sage assures him that he has gone down to the very bottom of Hell. Even so the Sibyl, in the *Aeneid*, VI, 564–565, tells Aeneas:[1]

> sed me cum lucis Hecate praefecit Avernis,
> ipsa deum poenas docuit perque omnia duxit.

(But when Hecate set me over the groves of Avernus, she taught me the gods' penalties and guided me through all.)

It was the Thessalian sorceress Erichtho, Virgil declares, who sent him, shortly after his death, to fetch a soul from the pit of treachery. Why she should have made him her messenger, instead of directly conjuring up the traitor, we are not told; perhaps Virgil's soul, being nearer the earth's surface, was more easily reached by her incantations. This same Erichtho, long before Virgil's adventure, had summoned for Sextus, the son of Pompey, on the eve of Pharsalus, the shade of a soldier to foretell the outcome of the battle: Lucan relates the incident at length in *Pharsalia*, VI, 413 ff. That witches had such power over the departed was firmly believed not merely by the ancients but in Christian times down almost to our day. Did not the woman of Endor, in 1 Samuel xxviii, call up Samuel to prophesy to Saul?

While the poets are awaiting heavenly aid, suddenly at the top of a tower appear the threatening forms of three Furies, who presently summon Medusa to turn Dante to stone. Virgil quickly covers his disciple's eyes with his own hands. "Shouldst thou see the Gorgon," he says, "there would be no returning to earth." At this point our author expressly bids us ponder the allegory. Many solutions have been proposed. The most natural and appropriate interpretation makes the Furies symbols of remorseful terror and Medusa the emblem of despair. *Desperatio*, or despair of the mercy of God, though not so wicked as hate and unbelief, is, according to St. Thomas, incurable and therefore

---

[1] It may be noted that in *Aen.*, VI, Aeneas does not enter the gate (552, 563) that leads to the region of punishment (628–631); it is described to him by the Sibyl (564–628).

more dangerous. In the *Summa Theologiae*, Secunda Secundae, Qu, xx, Art. 3, he also quotes from St. Isidore, 'To despair is to descend into Hell.' St. Gregory, in his *Moralia*, Book VIII, chap. xviii, § 34, declares that by *desperatio* 'the way of return is cut off.' Fear and hopelessness lead to insanity. So, in Ovid's *Metamorphoses*, IV, 481 ff., Tisiphone brings madness in her train:

> Nec mora, Tisiphone madefactam sanguine sumit
> Inportuna facem, fluidoque cruore rubentem
> Induitur pallam, tortoque incingitur angue,
> Egrediturque domo. Luctus comitatur euntem
> Et Pavor et Terror trepidoque Insania vultu.

(Straightway the fell Tisiphone seized a torch which had been steeped in gore, put on a robe red with dripping blood, girt round her waist a writhing snake, and started forth. Grief went along with her, Terror and Dread and Madness, too, with quivering face.)

Help comes in the shape of an angel, the bearer of divine grace. He moves through Hell like a storm wind, scattering the damned before him and opens the gate with a touch of his wand. The only obstacle to God's grace is the dense atmosphere of ignorance and spiritual blindness that it must penetrate.

Inside the walls are the archheretics and their followers, those who willfully defied their Maker and renounced his truth. Their existence is a living death, an invocation of divine anger: hence their souls appear to us as buried in tombs, consumed by that fire which, in the *Inferno*, seems to be a constant symbol of God's wrath. Those who denied a future life are eternally buried. Their sin, though not a manifestation of Violence nor of Fraud, is due essentially to pride rather than to weakness; it indicates a disposition of the spirit, not an impulse of flesh or temper: their place, then, is within the City of Dis, but above the first great precipice that separates the upper from the lower circles. Heresy belongs to the speculative intellect. It is not incontinence nor malice, not a sin of the lower appetite nor of the will. Both St. Thomas and Dante are apparently doubtful as to how it should be classed. Here Aristotle, who furnishes the general plan of Dante's Hell, offers no help.

8. Beatrice. Cf. XII, 88.
17. Limbus.
27. Giudecca, the innermost part of the ninth and last circle of Hell.
29. The Primum Mobile, the outermost of the revolving heavens.
38. Cf. Statius, *Thebaid*, I, 103 ff.; Ovid, *Met.*, IV, 490 ff.
43. The Furies are coupled with Hecate in *Aen.*, IV, 609–610:

> Nocturnisque Hecate triviis ululata per urbes,
> Et Dirae ultrices.

(... and Hecate, whose name is shrieked by night at the cross-roads of cities, and avenging Furies.)

45. The Erinyes, or Furies, were named Alecto, Tisiphone, and Megaera.

48. Cf. *Aen.*, X, 761: "Pallida Tisiphone media inter milia saevit." (Pale Tisiphone rages amid the thousands of men.)

54. Theseus, who had attempted to rescue Persephone from the lower world, was himself rescued by Hercules. Cf. *Aen.*, VI, 392 ff.

94. Cf. Acts ix, 5: "it is hard for thee to kick against the pricks."

99. Cerberus, having tried to obstruct Hercules, was chained by him and dragged outside of Hell. Cf. *Aen.*, VI, 395–396:

> Tartareum ille manu custodem in vincla petivit,
> Ipsius a solio regis, traxitque trementem.

(The one by force sought to drag into chains, even from the monarch's throne, the warder of Tartarus, and tore him off trembling.)

102. Cf. *Aen.*, IX, 294: "Atque animum patriae *strinxit* pietatis imago" (and the picture of filial love touched his soul), and VII, 402: "si iuris materni *cura remordet*" (if care for a mother's rights stings your souls).

112. At Arles, near the delta of the Rhone, and at Pola, in the south of Istria, were ancient burying grounds. The graves at Arles, of Roman origin, were thought to be filled with the bodies of Christian heroes who had fallen in battle with the Saracens. Just outside the city, on that side, the current of the Rhone turns to an eddy.

114. The Bay of Quarnero bathes the northeastern confines of Italy.

132. Usually, in the descent through Hell, the poets turn to the left in each circle, this course symbolizing the direction taken by the sinner. The turn to the right, in this particular place, was perhaps suggested by *Aen.*, VI, 540 ff.:

> Hic locus est, partis ubi se via findit in ambas:
> Dextera, quae Ditis magni sub moenia tendit;
> Hac iter Elysium nobis.

(Here is the place, where the road parts in twain: there to the right, as it runs under the walls of great Dis, is our way to Elysium.)

For the symbolical meaning of a right turn here, see Singleton (1970).

Canto X

Argument

In this canto allegory yields to dramatic realism.   Startling is the first call of Farinata as he stands upright in his tomb; not less effective Cavalcante's sudden interruption of the colloquy, and Farinata's prompt continuation of it, as soon as Calvalcante has sunk out of sight.   A curious impression of verity is given by the little word 'credo' in line 54:

(I think he had risen on his knees.)

We now learn that the damned, while aware of the past and indistinctly cognizant of the future, have no knowledge of present events on earth. Just how much time the "present" embraces we are not told. This idea, which seems to be original with our poet, opens the way to an intensely pathetic situation in this canto; and throughout the *Inferno* it provides opportunity for varied narrative, the things of 1300 being told by Dante to the shades, while later events are prophesied by them to him. After the Judgment Day, when earthly life shall cease and the foresight of lost souls shall thus come to an end, their blindness will be unrelieved. Ignorance of the present (*sensibilia*) is in accord with St. Thomas and other theologians. Prophecy of the future (intellectual deduction from past facts) is, according to St. Augustine and St. Thomas, easier for spirits unencumbered with flesh. St. Bonaventure tells us that, after the Judgment, the damned shall know only what can torment them.

Although all heresies are punished in this circle, the only one that concerns Dante is that called "Epicurean," a name bestowed, in his day, upon materialistic freethinking which denied the immortality of the soul and regarded a comfortable life as the highest good. There is grim irony in the eternal burial of sinners who affirmed that the spirit perishes with the body. Epicurus himself, pagan though he was, is with them. According to Dante, all philosophies, ancient and modern, admit the existence and the afterlife of the soul, which Epicurus alone denied; he, then, was a heretic toward the truth that prevailed in his own time. Many of the best minds of the 13th century were led by intellectual pride into this false belief. Their excellence makes their example the more terrible.

Among them was Cavalcante de' Cavalcanti, a noble and wealthy Florentine, the father of that Guido whom Dante calls his "first friend." This Guido, a little older than Dante, was a famous poet and student, an ardent partisan, hostile to the Donati. In June, 1300, while Dante was a prior, Guido was banished with the other leaders of the two factions. He was soon taken ill and recalled, and died in the same year. Several passages in the *Vita Nuova* point to discussions of literary principles by the two poets; Guido, we know, advised Dante to write his early work in Italian rather than in Latin. He seems to have been an independent thinker and probably was inclined to skepticism. When Cavalcante sees Dante traversing Hell in the flesh, imagining that "altezza d' ingegno" enables the young man to perform this miracle, he wonders why his son, Dante's companion and likewise endowed with "lofty genius," is not with him. Dante hastens to explain Guido's absence by the assurance that it is not his own wit but Virgil's which directs him, adding that Guido may not have duly esteemed the ancient sage —

> forse cui Guido vostro ebbe a disdegno.

This may mean that Guido's pride would not submit to the guidance of true Reason; or it may refer to some difference of literary opinion — possibly concerning the mystical significance of the *Aeneid* or the fourth *Eclogue* — to which we have no other clue. Dante's use of the past tense, "ebbe," suggests to the father that his son is dead, that he is past repentance and salvation; and this supposition being confirmed by the bewildered silence of the poet (who does not yet know that lost souls are ignorant of the present), he falls back in despair.

Another famous heretic is Manente degli Uberti, called Farinata, chief of the Florentine Ghibellines, a wise and valiant leader, who died in 1264, a year before Dante's birth. In 1260 he had taken part in the battle of Montaperti, where the Guelfs of Florence suffered a fearful defeat from the Sienese, the exiled Ghibellines, and King Manfred's Germans. Some 10,000 of the Florentines were killed, 5000 wounded, and 15,000 taken as prisoners to Siena; the battlefield, we are told, was all red with blood, as if it had been covered with scarlet cloth. After this rout, the neighboring towns and barons held a council at Empoli, and all but Farinata were in favor of destroying Florence; he, however, opposed the project so stoutly that it was abandoned. In 1283 the inquisitor, Salmone da Lucca, condemned him (nearly twenty years dead), his wife, his sons, and his grandsons, as heretics; his bones were cast out, his property confiscated and sold. His brave and haughty spirit is not quelled even by his fiery punishment: he appears with head and chest erect, 'as if he held Hell in great contempt.' Dante approaches him with deference; only when goaded beyond endurance by Farinata's taunts does he show resentment. To him, as to Cavalcante, he uses the respectful *voi*, a form of address that he applies to no other of the damned, save Brunetto Latini.

1. Cf. *Aen.*, VI, 443: "secreti celant calles" (are hidden in walks withdrawn).

11. On the Day of Judgment all souls, having recovered their bodies, will gather in the Valley of Jehoshaphat, whence, after hearing their sentence, they will return to Heaven or Hell.   See Joel iii, 2: "I will also gather all nations, and will bring them down into the valley of Jehoshaphat ..."   Also Joel iii, 12: "Let the heathen be wakened, and come up to the valley of Jehoshaphat; for there will I sit to judge all the heathen round about."   The Vulgate has *gentes* in both passages. Cf. Mat. xxv, 31 ff.

21. Cf. III, 80.   The unspoken desire is perhaps the wish to see Farinata: cf. VI, 79.

48. Farinata scattered the Guelfs in 1248 and 1260.

49. The Guelfs returned to Florence in 1251, after the death of Frederick II, and in 1266, after the battle of Benevento; they then expelled the Ghibellines, who never "learned the art" of returning.

51. This would have been Dante's natural reaction in 1300.

69. Cf. Eccles. xi, 7: "Truly the light is sweet (*dulce lumen*), and a pleasant thing it is for the eyes to behold the sun."

73. Had Farinata overheard the conversation with Cavalcante? Guido was Farinata's son-in-law.

80. 'The queen who rules here' is Hecate, who in the sky appears as the moon. Before fifty months have passed, Dante is to learn how hard is the art of returning from exile.   The unsuccessful mission of Cardinal Niccolò da Prato, sent by Benedict XI to Florence to secure peace and the restoration of the exiles, began on March 10, 1304.   The 50th new moon after Dante's visit to Hell was about April 4, 1304.   See Moore, III, 372.

84. In 1280, when most of the Ghibellines were allowed to come back, several of the Uberti were expressly excluded.

85. 'The rout and great slaughter' of Montaperti, beside the Arbia, not far from Siena, in 1260.

87. The Florentine councils usually assembled in the Baptistery of S. Giovanni.

91. At the Diet of Empoli, just after the battle.

111. Guido died on August 29, 1300.

119. The great Emperor Frederick II (1194–1250), who was long engaged in strife against the Papacy, was generally regarded as an Epicurean.

120. Cardinal Ottaviano degli Ubaldini, apostolic legate in Lombardy and Romagna against Frederick, in the Kingdom of Naples against Manfred, was accused of unbelief and of sympathy with the Imperial cause. Several of the early commentators report him as saying: "If there is a soul, I have lost it for the Ghibellines."

129. 'He lifted his finger' in the usual didactic attitude.

131. Beatrice. In fact it is Cacciaguida who supplies the prophecies (*Par.* XVII, 94).

Canto XI

Argument

On the rough edge of the circular precipice leading to the seventh circle we meet the most shocking example of unbelief, a heretical Pope — the more gruesome because he does not appear, his presence being indicated only by an inscription on his tomb. This is Anastasius II, who for many centuries was generally but unjustly thought to have been induced by Photinus, deacon of Thessalonica, to deny the divinity of Christ; it is likely that he had been confused with the Byzantine emperor Anastasius I.

At this point the master explains to his follower the general plan of the lower world. In Purgatory, too, the exposition occurs in the middle of the journey. The arrangement of punishments has been described in the preliminary note to the *Inferno*. In Virgil's account, based on the teaching of ancient philosophers, there is no mention of the sluggards, the unbaptized, or the heretics. Cicero wrote in his *De Officiis*, I, 13: "Cum autem duobus modis, id est aut vi aut fraude, fiat iniuria, fraus quasi vulpeculae, vis leonis videtur, utrumque homine alienissimum, sed fraus odio digna maiore. Totius autem iniustitiae nulla capitalior quam eorum qui, cum maxime fallunt, id agunt ut viri boni esse videantur." (While wrong may be done, then, in either of two ways, that is, by force or by fraud [both are bestial], fraud seems to belong to the cunning fox, force to the lion; both are wholly unworthy of man, but fraud is the more contemptible. But of all forms of injustice, none is more flagrant than that of the hypocrite who, at the very moment when he is most false, makes it his business to appear virtuous.) Aristotle makes the same distinction. These two kinds of sin, *vis*, or violence, and *fraus*, fraud, are chastised in the Lower Hell.   Outside the City of Dis, in the second, third, fourth, and fifth circles, are those who erred through Incontinence.   In Aristotle's *Ethics*, VII, i, are specified three sorts of conduct to be shunned, κακία, ἀκρασία, θηριότης; the Latin translation used by St. Thomas calls them (Flam., I, 146) "malitia, incontinentia, et bestialitas," and we are told further (Flam., I, 151), "minus autem bestialis malitia, terribilius autem." "Maior infamia, minor culpa," says Gregory.   St. Thomas often uses the term *bestialitas*, as well as *bestialis incontinentia* and *bestialis malitia*.   Incontinence is treated in the *Ethics*, VII, iii–x.   Although Bestiality, as Aristotle defines it (VII, v), is something more inhuman than common violence, it seems probable that Dante roughly equated it with Cicero's *vis;* while malice corresponds well enough to the Ciceronian *fraus*.   At any rate, Incontinence, Violence, and Fraud are the three great groups under which evil acts are classified.

Expounding the sins of the Lower Hell, Virgil declares that every wrongdoing hateful to God has harm for its object, and this harm is inflicted either by force or by deceit.   Of these two methods the latter is the worse.   The former is punished in the seventh circle.   But inasmuch as force may be done to our fellowman, to ourselves, or to our Maker, this circle is divided into three concentric rings: the first contains assassins, robbers, and tyrants; the second, suicides; the third, blasphemers, sodomites, and usurers.   Sodomites do violence to Nature, the minister of God.   Usurers — that is, moneylenders — do violence to human industry, the offspring of Nature, and thus offend the Creator.   This view of the practice of letting money at interest was usual in the Middle Ages. "Thou shalt not lend upon usury to thy brother," says Deut. xxiii, 19.   At the beginning of the *Ethics*, IV, i, Aristotle declares that "the waste of property seems to be a sort of self-ruin, since life is maintained by property."   In accordance with this idea, Dante puts with the suicides, in the second ring, those who wasted their goods so recklessly that their death resulted; they are distinguished, in the *Inferno*, from the ordinary prodigals, whose fault was one of Incontinence.

Fraud may be perpetrated upon those who have no special cause to trust us, in which case only the common tie of humanity is broken; or upon those who have a particular ground for confidence, and then outrage is done not only to this universal fellowship, but also to the bond of family, country, hospitality, or gratitude.   Deceivers of the former sort are tormented, according to the nature of their fraud, in the ten circular, concentric ditches of the eighth circle: eight of the ten types are rapidly enumerated in this canto; the other two — evil counselors and sowers of discord — are dismissed with the epithet "similar filth." Traitors to kindred, fatherland, guests, or benefactors find their eternal abode in the icy plain of the ninth circle.

Dante inverts St. Thomas's order of *vis* and *fraus*.   Aristotle expresses no opinion as to their comparative wickedness. On this point Dante runs counter to most of his authorities, combining *vis* with *bestialis malitia*. He goes beyond St. Thomas in making bestiality a third distinct state of the will, opposing bestial sin to justice, while St. Thomas opposes it to temperance. In fact, Dante's 'bestiality' corresponds to St. Thomas's *bestialis malitia* rather than to his *bestialis incontinentia*. Into his 7th circle he puts the only kinds of bestiality seriously discussed by St. Thomas: ferocity (tyranny) and sodomy. Bestiality is worse than sins of *infirmitas*, less bad than sins of *malitia humana*. Fraud is 'de l'uom proprio male,' therefore *malitia humana*.

17. The 7th, 8th, and 9th circles of Hell, called *cerchietti* because they are smaller in circumference than those above.

22. Cf. Ps. v, 5: "thou hatest all workers of iniquity."

23. Sins of malice, punished in the last 3 circles, are directed against justice. Incontinence has no purpose of *iniuria*.

28. The first of the three *cerchietti* mentioned in l. 17: the 7th circle of Hell.

47. Cf. Ps. xiv, 1: "The fool hath said in his heart, There is no God."

49. 'The smallest round [the innermost of the three rings into which the 7th circle is divided] stamps with its mark' the sodomites and the usurers and the blasphemers.

50. Sodom: see Gen. xix. *Caorsa*, Cahors, a town in southern France, a notorious nest of usurers.

57. The 8th circle, the second of the *cerchietti* of l. 17.

64. The smallest of the *cerchietti*, the 9th and last of the circles of Hell. — 'The center' of the whole material universe, where Dis, or Lucifer, is confined.

70. The wrathful (5th circle).

71. The lustful and the gluttonous (2nd and 3rd circles).

72. The avaricious and the prodigal, who taunt each other when they meet (4th circle).

73. 'The ruddy city,' i.e., the City of Dis, or Lower Hell.

80. The *Ethics* (VII i) of thy master, Aristotle, who enumerates three evils to be avoided: malice (κακία), incontinence (ἀκρασία), bestiality (θηριότης).

84. In the *Ethics*, VII, x, incontinence is compared with malice.

101. Aristotle, *Physics*, II, ii.

108. See Gen. ii, 15, and iii, 19: "And the Lord God took the man, and put him into the Garden of Eden to dress it and keep it"; "In the sweat of thy face shalt thou eat bread ..."

110. He despises nature both directly and indirectly (through its follower, human industry).

111. The moneylender sets his hope on gain derived neither from nature nor from toil.

113. Virgil, as usual, indicates the hour (in Jerusalem) by a description of the sky, which of course, is not visible from Hell. The Fishes are wriggling on the horizon, i.e., the constellation of Pisces, which precedes Aries, is just rising; the wain, or Great Bear, lies wholly in the quarter of Caurus, the northwest wind. The time is three hours or more after midnight.

Canto XII

Argument

Throughout this episode, either by accident or by design, Dante does not speak.

The canto deals with the descent into the seventh circle — the abode of the violent — and the description of the first of the three concentric rings that

compose it. This first *girone* consists of a river of hot blood, a picture of san-
guinary relations to one's fellowmen. The *Visio Alberici* also tells of homicides
in a lake of boiling blood; and the *Visio Sancti Pauli* shows different kinds of
sinners immersed to varying depths in a fiery stream. In the *Inferno*, too, the
degree of immersion varies between eyebrows and feet, according to the wickedness of the offense.

Along the narrow bank run centaurs, whose business it is to keep the other
souls in their proper place. These half-human guardians are not depicted as
hateful or repulsive: they do not seem to be demons, although their function is
similar to that of the devils beside the ditch of barrators in the eighth circle; they
appear to be rather the spirits of real centaurs, creatures whose semi-equine
character made their excesses more natural and consequently less blameworthy.
They may be intended also to serve as illustrations of Aristotle's doctrine of
bestiality.

A still stronger suggestion of bestiality is conveyed by the presiding genius of
the whole seventh circle, the Minotaur, half man and half bull, whose blind fury
("quell' ira *bestial*") defeats its own end and affords the travelers a chance to pass
him. The monster — "bestia," Virgil calls him — was the offspring of a bull
and Pasiphae, wife of King Minos of Crete, who satisfied her abnormal passion
(inflicted by Venus as a curse) by enclosing herself in a wooden cow —

colei
che s'imbestiò ne le 'mbestiate schegge,

as Dante says in *Purg.* XXVI, 86–87.

The Athenian hero Theseus slew the Minotaur in the Labyrinth, guided by
Ariadne, the daughter of Pasiphae and Minos. Dante, to avoid placing this
monster in any one of the three *gironi*, puts him on the cliff that overlooks them
all. In the same way Geryon, the image of Fraud, is represented as hovering
over the eighth circle.

The poets' way down the precipice lies in a huge landslide made by the earthquake which, when Christ died and descended into Hell, shook also a part of
the wall between the unbaptized and the lustful (V, 34) and likewise damaged
the hypocrites' valley in the eighth circle. In each case Dante uses the word *ruina*.
This vast slide our poet compares with one in northeastern Italy, the Slavini di
Marco, described by Albertus Magnus.

2. The Minotaur.
17. Theseus: so called by Boccaccio, Chaucer, and Shakespeare.
20. Ariadne.
22. Cf. *Aen.*, II, 223–224.

Qualis mugitus, fugit cum saucius aram
Taurus et incertam excussit cervice securim.

(... like the bellowings of a wounded bull that has fled from the altar and shaken from its neck the ill-aimed axe.)

40. Cf. Mat. xxvii, 50–51: "Jesus, when he had cried again with a loud voice, yielded up the ghost. And, behold, the veil of the temple was rent in twain from the top to the bottom; and earth did quake, and the rocks rent."

42. According to Empedocles, the four elements, mixed together, produced chaos; hate, separating the seeds, brought forth from chaos all the things of the universe; love, by drawing the seeds together, can restore chaos. Dante probably got his idea of Empedocles (whom he mentioned in *Inf*. IV, 138) from Aristotle.

45. In the circle of the lustful, V, 34. The same earthquake shook down the bridges over the ditch of the hypocrites in the eight circle, but of this Virgil is not yet aware; cf. XXI, 106, and XXIII, 136.

49. The motives of violence to our fellowman are greed and wrath.

53. 'As if encircling all the plain.' So it does, but of course Dante can see only a small section, or arc, of it at once.

60. Cf. Lucan, *Pharsalia*, VII, 142: "Cura fuit lectis pharetras implere sagittis." (Care was taken to fill the quivers with picked arrows.)

63. Cf. *Aen.*, VI, 389: "Fare age, quid venias, iam istinc et comprime gressum." (O tell me, even from there, why thou comest, and check thy step.)

65. Chiron, son of Saturn, skilled in surgery, was the preceptor of Achilles.

67. Nessus, while trying to carry off Dejanira through the water, was struck by an arrow from Hercules, her husband. To avenge himself, he left with Dejanira his bloody shirt, which afterward caused the death of Hercules. Cf. *Met.*, IX.

72. Pholus figured in the battle between the Centaurs and the Lapithae: Statius, *Thebaid*, II, 563–564.

88. Beatrice.

107. It is not known whether Dante meant Alexander the Great (described as bloodthirsty by Paulus Orosius) or Alexander of Pherae, who was coupled with Dionysius as a typical tyrant by Valerius Maximus, and by Cicero in *De Officiis*, II, vii, 25. Dionysius ruled Syracuse from 407 to 367 B.C. *Cicilia* for *Sicilia* was common in medieval times and is still in use.

110. Azzolino or Ezzelino da Romano, who held extensive dominions in northeastern Italy in the first half of the 13th century, a notoriously cruel tyrant; he was called a son of Satan.

111. Òbizzo or Òpizzo da Este, Marquis of Ferrara in the second half of the 13th century, was a hard ruler. Line 112 seems to refer to an incident little known, or disputed, in Dante's day, so that the poet hears it with incredulity. Virgil, to whom he turns in doubt, tells him that in this matter the centaur is the best authority.

119. The solitary soul, apparently shunned by all the others, is that of Guy of Montfort, who, in church at Viterbo, during mass, to avenge the death of his father (Simon, Earl of Leicester), stabbed Prince Henry, the son of Richard Plantagenet (Earl of Cornwall). Both were grandsons of King John. Guy was vicar of Charles of Anjou in Tuscany in 1270. Henry's heart was placed, according to Villani, in a cup in the hand of a statue by the Thames, or (as others say) in a golden urn in Westminster Abbey.

134. Attila, King of the Huns, was called the "Scourge of God."

135. Pyrrhus, King of Epirus, a fearful enemy of the Romans. — For Sextus, son of Pompey, see Lucan, *Pharsalia*, VI, 420–422:

> Sextus erat, magno proles indigna parente,
> Cui mox Scyllaeis exul grassatus in undis
> Polluit aequoreos Siculus pirata triumphos.

(He was Sextus, the unworthy son of Magnus, he who later as an exile infested the waters of Scylla, and stained by piracy in Sicily the glory his father had gained from the sea.)

136. A figure which Dante uses again in *Purg*. XIII, 57.

137. Two highwaymen apparently famous in the 13th century. Rinieri de' Pazzi, a powerful lord and head of a Ghibelline company, declared himself an independent sovereign.

Canto XIII

Argument

The Church Fathers, from St. Augustine down, put suicide on a par with murder. Each is an attempt to cut short the term of life allotted by God, a crime of insubordination against the Creator. Neither can be justified by any excuse save the direct command of Heaven: thus Abraham was divinely bidden to sacrifice Isaac, and Samson destroyed himself in accordance with the Lord's will. It is perhaps worth noting that Dante mentions no pagan in this place; but as he cites only two examples, a Capuan and an unnamed Florentine, the significance of the omission is small — or would be so, had he not assigned several heathen suicides (Lucretia, Dido, Cato, Seneca) to different parts of the other world.

The Capuan is Pier delle Vigne, who, after studying, in all probability, at Bologna, entered the court of Frederick II as a notary, and so won the confidence and affection of his sovereign that for over twenty years he was entrusted with the most important affairs of the realm. He was one of the foremost poets of the Sicilian school; many of his verses, as well as some of his Latin letters, are preserved. In 1248 or 1249 he was accused and convicted of treason; his eyes were put out, and according to one account he was condemned by the Emperor to be led in derision, on an ass, from town to town. To escape dishonor, he killed himself by dashing his head against a wall. It was no doubt with a view of emphasizing the inexorableness of God's canon that Dante selected the most sympathetic case he could find, one in which cruel injustice might seem to condone the offense. Piero, as Dante conceived him, is loyal, magnanimous, courtly, and most pathetic in his unshaken devotion to the master who wronged him.

The style of this canto abounds in curious conceits, such as the

Cred' ïo ch'ei credette ch'io credesse

of l. 25, the "infiammati infiammar" of l. 68, the double antithesis of l. 69, and the involved paradoxes of the following tiercet. It would seem that meditation over Pier delle Vigne, who dominates the canto, had filled our poet with the spirit of the older school, so that, either purposely or unconsciously, he imitated its artistic processes. Pier delle Vigne's epistolary style is highly artificial and flowery.

The suicide uses his freedom of bodily movement only to deprive himself of it, robbing himself, by his own act, of that which corporeally distinguishes him from a plant. Such a sinner, then, his wicked deed eternalized, may aptly be figured as a tree or bush. Dante's self-slaughterers form a thick, wild forest in the second ring of the seventh circle. There, upon hearing their sentence from Minos, they fall at random, in no predestined spot: they have put themselves outside of God's law, rebelling against his eternal plan. On the Day of Judgment they will return, with the rest, for their earthly remains; but, instead of putting on the flesh again, they will drag their corpses through Hell and hang them on their boughs, where the poor bodies will dangle forever, a torment to the souls that slew them. The pent-up agony of these spirits finds no means of expression until they are broken in leaf or branch; then the voice issues forth, with tears of blood.

The like had been seen and heard by Aeneas in a Thracian grove, when, to deck an altar, he unwittingly plucked shrubs from the grave of Polydorus: blood trickled from the severed roots, and a voice came forth — not from the tree, as in Dante, but from the mound (*Aen.*, III, 39 ff.):

> gemitus lacrimabilis imo
> auditur tumulo, et vox reddita fertur ad auris:
> "quid miserum, Aenea, laceras? iam parce sepulto,
> parce pias scelerare manus. non me tibi Troia
> externum tulit, aut cruor hic de stipite manat."

(A piteous groan is heard from the depth of the mound, and an answering voice comes to my ears. "Woe is me! why, Aeneas, dost thou tear me? Spare me in the tomb at last; spare the pollution of thy pure hands! I, born of Troy, am no stranger to thee; not from a lifeless stock oozes this blood.")

In the suicides' wood, an outlet for the mournful voice is afforded by harpies, voracious, filthy birds with maidens' faces, which rend the foliage. They may well represent misgiving or fear of the hereafter — "tristo annunzio di futuro danno." Virgil describes them in the *Aeneid*, III, 216–218:

> virginei volucrum voltus, foedissima ventris
> proluvies, uncaeque manus, et pallida semper
> ora fame.

(Maiden faces have these birds, foulest filth they drop, clawed hands are theirs, and faces ever gaunt with hunger.)

Their appearance in the same book of the *Aeneid* with Polydorus may have led Dante to associate them with his speaking trees. On the Strophades islands, off Messenia, where they dwelt, their foul presence repeatedly interrupted the Trojans' repast; and finally one of them, Celaeno, perched on a high rock, uttered so threatening a prophecy that the warriors hastily departed.

> Dixit, et in silvam pinnis ablata refugit.

(She spake and, borne away on her wings, fled back to the forest.)
Thus in Virgil, as in Dante, the harpy is connected with a wood.

With the suicides are the reckless squanderers, those who rush madly through life pursued by the black hounds of Ruin and Death. Their sudden irruption is the more effective for its brevity and unexpectedness. The episode reminds one of legends of the Wild Hunt, and of the ghostly chase described by Boccaccio in his *Decameron*, V, 8. It resembles also the story of Actaeon, torn to pieces by his own dogs, in Ovid's *Metamorphoses*, III, 138 ff.; this tale, furthermore, had been rationistically explained by Fulgentius as meaning that the luckless hunter spent all his substance upon dogs.

1. On his return trip.

9. Cècina, a town near Volterra, and Corneto, now renamed Tarquinia, a town close to Civitavecchia, denote the northern and southern limits of the woody, swampy district known as the Maremma. In Dante's time it was covered with dense forest. Rinier da Corneto has just been mentioned.

19. The third *girone* consists of a waste of sand, upon which falls a rain of fire.

48. The story of Polydorus in *Aen.*, III, 22–43.

57. 'I am constrained,' like a bird caught in lime. 'Lime,' in this sense, continues the bird-hunting figure.

58. Cf. Isaiah xxii, 22: "And the key of the house of David will I lay upon his shoulder; so that he shall open, and none shall shut; and he shall shut, and none shall open."

64. The harlot is Envy, and the house of Caesar is the Imperial court.

96. The seventh circle.

102. By breaking the leaves, they provide an outlet.

120. The spendthrift Lano of Siena perished in the battle of Pieve del Toppo, where the Sienese in 1289 were defeated by the Aretines.

121. The speaker is Jacopo da Sant' Andrea.

133. The bush addresses the second of the two runners, a mad prodigal, who, it is said, was put to death by Ezzelino IV da Romano in 1239. Who the soul in the bush was, is not known for certain; Jacopo della Lana, one of the earliest commentators, declares that it was a certain Lotto degli Agli, a prior of Florence in 1285.

142. In accordance with the law of retaliation, these sinners, who ruthlessly destroyed their fleshly bodies on earth, care tenderly for their wooden bodies in Hell.

143. According to tradition, the first patron of Florence was Mars; the lower part of an old stone statue, supposed to represent the God of War, stood at the head of the Ponte Vecchio until 1333, when it was carried away by a flood. The new patron was John the Baptist, whose image adorned the florin. The Florentines gave up martial valor for moneymaking.

149. It was believed that Attila, King of the Huns, or Totila, King of the Ostrogoths, had destroyed Florence. Attila and Totila were often confounded. The latter was in Tuscany in the 6th century.

151. Two of the earliest commentators say that Lotto hanged himself with a girdle in his house.

Canto XIV

Argument

The third and innermost ring of the seventh circle consists of a sandy plain upon which falls a rain of fire.   It stands for the experience of those who directly and wittingly defy God and live in his wrath, of which fire is the symbol.   "Then the Lord rained upon Sodom and upon Gomorrah brimstone and fire from the Lord out of heaven," says Gen. xix, 24.   And in Ezekiel xxxviii, 22, we read: "I will rain upon him, and upon his bands, and upon the many people that are with him, an overflowing rain, and great hailstones, fire, and brimstone."   The blasphemers, who did violence to God himself, lie prostrate; the sodomites, sinners against God's minister, Nature, run incessantly; the usurers, outragers of human industry, the child of Nature, sit crouching.   Of these classes, the second is largest.

Rather curiously, the first class is represented by a pagan, the tall Capaneus, who, "scornful and twisted," maintains his arrogant pose and "seems not to be ripened by the rain."   His futile pride is more shocking to Reason than any offense yet encountered; his own rage is his worst punishment.   The story of Capaneus is told by Statius in the *Thebaid*, X, 870–939: he was one of the seven kings who attacked Thebes; scaling the walls, whence his gigantic shadow frightened the city, he mocked at the gods and challenged Jove, who thereupon slew him with a thunderbolt.

> Ille iacet lacerae complexus fragmina turris,
> Torvus adhuc visu. [*Thebaid*, XI, 9–10.]

(Grasping the fragment of a shattered tower the hero lies, with a scowl yet upon his face.)

So he lies in Hell, taunting Jove with his labors at the battle against the giants. Statius, too, recalls this conflict, saying that at the downfall of Capaneus the other gods rejoiced with Jupiter, 'as if he were wearily toiling in the fight at Phlegra.'

Traversing the plain, from the wood to the great precipice, is a raised channel built like a dike, through which runs a torrent of boiling blood.   This brook issues from the river of the first ring and falls over the cliff into the circle below. All the rivers of Hell, in fact, are connected, forming a single stream, which assumes different shapes in the various circles.   Its source is now described.   In the island of Crete, midway between the old world and the new, is the figure of an aged man, fashioned like the 'great image' in the dream of Nebuchadnezzar in Daniel ii, 32–33: 'This image's head was of fine gold, his breast and his arms of silver, his belly and his thighs of brass, his legs of iron, his feet part of iron and part of clay.'   Daniel interprets the image as a prophecy of four kingdoms.   But

Dante's statue evidently represents humanity in its successive ages, as they are depicted, for instance, in Ovid's *Metamorphoses*, I, 89 ff. The clay foot signifies the weak and unstable condition of man. Ever since the Golden Age (the state of Adam and Eve before the fall) mankind has been·imperfect; therefore all the statue except the head is split by a crack, St. Thomas's "vulneratio naturae." From this fissure flow the tears of the sinful generations of men; descending into Hell, they make the infernal streams. The torments of the human soul, in whatsoever form they appear, really consist in sorrow over its own imperfections. It should be remembered that Crete is a halfway station between the Old World and the New. Aeneas stopped there on his way from Troy to Latium; St. Paul, lost in a storm, stopped there, going from Jerusalem to Rome. But Aeneas, representing Empire, and St. Paul, representing the Cross, did not come together. Therefore humanity is still imperfect, the conjunction of Eagle and Cross being needed for its redemption. The Old Man looks forward to their union in Rome.

The bed of the connecting brook is all of stone, bottom and sides; and so are the high, flat, narrow banks on either hand. On one of these — the nearer, right-hand one — the poets mount to pursue their way across the desert; for no fire falls upon the duct. With great solemnity Virgil directs his disciple's attention to the stream, "which deadens all the flamelets above it." Nothing so noteworthy has been seen, he declares, since they entered the open gate of Hades. The unclosed door seems to figure our predisposition to sin. Does the quenching of the fire by boiling blood signify the appeasing of God's anger by human suffering? A symbol of atonement is manifestly out of place in the literal Hell, but allegorically Dante's lower world stands for the sinful life of man. Christian tradition had come to derive the four rivers of Paradise from the tears of Christ, and one branch of the story traced to the same source even the rivers of the lower world.

15. Cato led the remnants of Pompey's army across the Libyan desert in 47 B.C. Cf. Lucan, *Pharsalia*, IX, 371 ff., particularly 378 and 394–396:

> Atque ingressurus steriles sic fatur, arenas:
> ... Dum primus arenas
> Ingrediar, primusque gradus in pulvere ponam,
> Me calor aetherius feriat.

(And before he set foot upon the barren desert, Cato made them this speech: ... Foremost I shall tread the desert, and foremost set foot upon the sand; let the heat of the sky then beat upon me.)

31. Dante apparently got this story from Albertus Magnus. It is a fusion of two episodes from the so-called Epistle of Alexander to Aristotle, where we find a heavy fall of snow, trampled down by the soldiers, and later a rain of fire.

52. Even though Jove should labor as he did in the battle against the giants, in the valley of Phlegra in Thessaly, he could not subdue the spirit of Capaneus.

56. *Mongibello* is a Sicilian name for Etna.

79. *Bulicame*: a hot spring near Viterbo, frequented as a bath. The stream issuing from it was divided into separate baths for prostitutes, who were compelled to stay apart from the others.

96. In the golden age, under Saturn.

100. Rhea, wife of Saturn, to save the infant Jupiter from his father, who devoured his sons, entrusted him to the Curetes, or Corybantes, in Crete; and when he cried, she had them drown the sound with noise. Cf. Virgil, *Georgics*, IV, 150–152; Ovid, *Fasti*, IV, 197–210.

104. Damietta, an important city on the Egyptian shore, represents the East, the ancient, pagan world; Rome stands for the modern, Christian world.

116. Acheron, Styx, Phlegethon, and Cocytus all belong to the classic underworld. The *Visio Sancti Pauli* gives the four rivers as 'Cochiton, Styx, Acheron, Flegeton.'

119. The frozen Cocytus forms the bottom of Dante's Hell, beyond which 'there is no descending,' because it is at the earth's center.

123. 'Why do we see it only at this edge?': that is, why have we not crossed it in our spiral descent? Virgil replies that they have not made the whole circuit of the circumference of Hell.

135. The heat of this stream proves that it is Phlegethon. See *Aen.*, VI, 550–551:

> Quae rapidus flammis ambit torrentibus amnis,
> Tartareus Phlegethon

(and encircled with a rushing flood of torrent flames — Tartarean Phlegethon); and Statius, *Thebaid*, IV, 523:

> Fumidus atra vadis Phlegethon incendia volvit.

(Smoky Phlegethon rolls down his streams of murky flame.)

136. Lethe is in the lower world of the ancients; but Dante puts it in the Garden of Eden, at the top of the mountain of Purgatory.

Canto XV

Argument

Brunetto Latini, who fills this canto, was one of the leading figures in the Florence of the generation just before Dante. Born about 1220, of an illustrious family, he distinguished himself for ability, culture, and vast erudition. His profession of notary gave him the title of *Ser*. In 1260 he was sent as ambassador to the court of Alfonso X of Castile. On his way back he learned of the overthrow of the Guelf party, to which he belonged, at Montaperti and deemed it best to stay in France. There he wrote in French his great encyclopedia, *Li livres dou Trésor;* he composed also in Italian verse a shorter didactic work, allegorical in form, known as the *Tesoretto*. In 1266, after the overthrow of the Ghibellines at Benevento, he returned to Florence, where he filled various public offices and was held in great honor until his death in 1294. Dante addresses him with respectful *voi*.

Two motives, in all probability, induced our author to give Brunetto so conspicuous a place in his poem.   The first was gratitude.   To the *Tesoretto* Dante owed perhaps his first conception of a grand didactic poem clad in allegory. But there must have been, besides, a warm personal attachment between the gifted youth and the great scholar and statesman who, by his counsel, taught the lad "how man can make himself eternal."

Of their friendship we have no knowledge save the touching picture suggested by this canto.   It is by no means impossible that Brunetto lectured in Florence and that Dante was among his hearers.   Some have supposed that Latini had cast Dante's horoscope; this is unlikely, as both the *Trésor* and the *Tesoretto* ascribe little influence to the stars.   The word *stella*, as he uses it in l. 55, signifies no more than destiny or natural disposition.

Another reason for giving prominence to Latini was that which we noted in the case of Pier delle Vigne — the desire to furnish an extreme example.   In Brunetto we have a man endowed with fine intellectual and most endearing moral qualities, yet tainted with one vice, which destroys his soul.   It is only through Dante that we know of his sin, but there can be no doubt of its reality; in his day assuredly many were aware of it.   Thus the doctrine is again enforced that a single deadly fault, unexpiated, will damn a man otherwise noble.   The contrast between his general dignity and his fatal weakness is emphasized at the end of the canto, when the elderly sage is suddenly forced to put aside his gravity and run like a racer to rejoin his fellows.

Few episodes are more startling than the first encounter of Dante and his old friend in Hell; few are more pathetic than their walk together, the younger poet on the dike, the older on the plain below, beside his companion's skirt, his shoulders reaching perhaps to the level of Dante's feet.   No nearer approach is lawful.   The dusky setting is described (in ll. 18–21) with a couple of swift similes, which it is interesting to compare with the more leisurely style of Virgil in the *Aeneid*, VI, 268–272 and 450–454:

> Ibant obscuri sola sub nocte per umbram
> perque domos Ditis vacuas et inania regna,
> quale per incertam lunam sub luce maligna
> est iter in silvis, ubi caelum condidit umbra
> Iuppiter, et rebus nox abstulit atra colorem.

(On they went dimly, beneath the lonely night amid the gloom, through the empty halls of Dis and his phantom realm, even as under the grudging light of an inconstant moon lies a path in the forest, when Jupiter has buried the sky in shade, and black Night has stolen from the world her hues.)

> inter quas Phoenissa recens a volnere Dido
> errabat silva in magna.   quam Troius heros

ut primum iuxta stetit adgnovitque per umbras
obscuram, qualem primo qui surgere mense
aut videt aut vidisse putat per nubila lunam.

(Among them, with wound still fresh, Phoenician Dido was wandering in the great forest, and soon as the Trojan hero stood nigh and knew her, a dim form amid the shadows — even as, in the early month, one sees or fancies he has seen the moon rise amid the clouds.)

7. The Brenta is a stream in northeastern Italy.

9. *Carentana*, or Carinzia, is a mountainous region north of the Brenta. Its melting snows swell the river.

53. Dante avoids mentioning Virgil by name in Hell.

61–62. The Florentines. *Fiesole*, Latin *Faesulae*, is at the top of a steep hill near Florence. Catiline, driven from Rome, took refuge there with his followers. When the place was finally taken, tradition has it that the surviving inhabitants, combining with a Roman colony, founded Florence, 'which still smacks of the mountain and the rock.'

65. Cf. Mat. vii, 16: "Do men gather grapes of thorns, or figs of thistles?"

67. Various stories were told to account for the 'old report.' One has it that Florence accepted two damaged porphyry columns as a recompense from the Pisans, whom she had protected from Lucca. The columns still stand on either side of the Baptistery.

72. See Ps. xxvii, 2: "When the wicked, even mine enemies and my foes came upon me to eat up my flesh, they stumbled and fell."

78. Dante believed that his own family belonged to the old Roman stock of Florence.

82. Cf. *Aen.*, IV, 4: "haerent infixi pectore vultus" (his looks ... cling fast within her bosom).

88. Cf. Prov. vii, 3: "write them upon the table of thine heart."

89. The 'other texts' are the prophecies of Ciacco and Farinata: VI, 64 ff.; X, 79 ff. Cf. X, 127 ff.; also *Par.* XVII, 19–27.

96. Let fate and men pursue their thoughtless course: this sounds like a proverbial phrase.

97. Virgil, who evidently was walking ahead, turned his head back to the right. Dante was following Virgil, with Brunetto walking below him on the plain at his right.

99. 'He who takes heed is a good listener.' Dante's words to Brunetto prove that he still remembers Virgil's speech at the end of X. Cf. Rev. i, 3: "Beatus qui legit et audit verba prophetiae hujus, et servat ea quae in ea scripta sunt." (Blessed is he that readeth, and they that hear the words of this prophecy, and keep those things which are written therein.)

109. Priscian, the great Latin grammarian of the 6th century. Francesco d'Accorso, son of a still more famous father, was renowned as a jurist; he lived in Bologna and in England, in the 13th century.

112. Andrea di Mozzi was deposed in 1295 from the bishopric of Florence and transferred to the less important one of Vicenza, through which town the Bacchiglione runs. The Pope (or 'servus servorum Dei') who removed him was Boniface VIII.

122. In the annual games held in Verona in the 13th century the first prize in the footrace was a green cloth.

Canto XVI

Argument

At the close of this canto poetic ingenuity does its utmost to intensify the effect
of mystery and suspense.   Virgil's reading of his companion's unspoken thought,
the eager expectancy of both travelers, the strange and unexplained casting of a
girdle into the abyss, Dante's reluctance to impart to us an event too marvelous
for our belief — all this leads up to the final shadow of a weird form looming
into sight, with which the narrative stops.

Arriving at the edge of the cliff, the boundary of the seventh circle, Dante,
who hitherto has worn "una corda intorno cinta," takes off this girdle and hands
it, 'knotted and coiled,' to his guide.   Virgil throws it out into the darkness —
a signal (so we afterward learn) for the huge flying monster Geryon, the embodiment of Fraud and keeper of the eighth circle, who is to carry them down on his
back.   With this cord, we are told, Dante had once thought 'to catch the leopard
with the painted hide,' which in the first canto represented the habit of Fraud.
Henceforth Dante goes ungirded until he is about to begin the ascent of the
mountain of Purgatory; then, at the bidding of Cato, he is girt with a rush, the
emblem of humility.   It should be remembered that in the Bible a girdle
symbolizes strength.

The significance of the cord has been variously interpreted, and there is now
no agreement among commentators.   This rope must stand for something
upon which Dante at one time built false hopes, but now, at the command of
Reason, discards; something, moreover, to be appropriately replaced by humility; and, lastly, something that will attract Geryon and bring him to view.
This something may well be self-confidence, the opposite of humility; a seeming
strength, which the poet formerly deemed adequate for the mastery of his faults
— a delusion and therefore a lure to the genius of Deceit.   The coiled and
knotted rope itself suggests a snare; in *Par.* XXVIII, 12, indeed, Dante uses the
word *corda* in this sense — 'a pigliarmi fece Amor la corda.'   Geryon, when he
appears, has his breast and sides decorated with 'knots and rings,' corresponding
to the shape of the cast-off belt.   While girt with self-confidence, Dante con-
tended vainly against Fraud; but no sooner is this deceptive girdle put aside than
Fraud becomes amenable to Reason.

2. The 'next circle' is the eighth, separated from the seventh by a mighty precipice.
25. The three circled around and around in front of Dante, as if they were dancing in a ring.
All kept their faces turned toward him.
37. Gualdrada, renowned for her beauty and modesty, was the daughter of the Bellincion
Berti of *Par.* XV, 112.   Her grandson, Guido Guerra (or Guidoguerra), was a distinguished
Florentine soldier, who died in 1272.   He was the principal supporter of the Guelf party in
Florence.

41. Tegghiaio, of the Adimari family, was an illustrious citizen of Florence in the middle part of the 13th century.   If his counsel had been heeded, his countrymen would have escaped the defeat of Montaperti in 1260; that is why "his voice should be welcome." Dante had inquired of Ciacco (VI, 79–80) concerning Tegghiaio and Rusticucci.

44. Of Rusticucci, a contemporary of the other two, comparatively little is recorded. Nothing is known of his wife.

63. First I must descend, or 'fall,' to the center of the earth.

64. We have here, as in l. 66, the familiar formula of adjuration: 'as thou hopest that ...' or 'so may ...': cf. X, 82.

70. The newly arrived Guglielmo Borsiere is known to us only through a story in Boccaccio's *Decameron*, I, 8.

73. Dante ascribes the degeneracy of Florence to sudden prosperity and to deterioration of the stock through immigration from the country.   Instead of replying directly to his questioner, he lifts up his face toward the city and apostrophizes it.   The three listeners look at one another, nodding, as people do when they hear the manifest truth.

81. The spirits admire not only Dante's knowledge of the present, which they have lost, but his clear understanding and freedom of utterance.   Perhaps they dimly foresee a time when it will not be so easy for him to "satisfy another."

84. Cf. *Aen.*, I, 203: "forsan et haec olim meminisse iuvabit."   (Perchance even this distress it will some day be a joy to recall.)

94. The roaring cataract in Hell is compared to the noisy falls of the Montone, the first river on the left of the Apennines (as one descends into Italy) that has a course of its own to the Adriatic; the other streams run into the Po.

95. *Monte Viso*, the Latin *Mons Vesulus*, is Monviso.   One of the three upper branches of the Montone is the Acquacheta; at Forlì, Dante says, it gives up that name and merges into the Montone.

100. S. Benedetto dell'Alpe is a little village, named after an ancient Benedictine abbey. The river roars because it falls over a single ledge, when it ought to be caught (*recetto*) by a thousand.   In dry weather the water trickles over a long series of steps at the side; when the stream is full, it pours straight down in the center.

112. Virgil swings to the right, as one does to make a long throw.

126. It causes one to be unjustly suspected of falsehood.

127. Dante speaks of his poem as if it were a song.   The names *comedia* and *tragedia* (which Dante accented on the *i*) were applied to non-dramatic poems composed respectively in a lowly or a grand style; *tragedia*, according to the Letter to Can Grande, also has an unhappy ending.

136. To the observer above, a diver, returning to the surface, is foreshortened and magnified by the intervening water.

Canto XVII

Argument

In the description of the usurers, squatting on the edge of the chasm, now brushing off the flakes of fire, now lifting themselves on their hands from the hot sand, we are shown guilty souls in a state of abominable degradation.   Their faces have lost all human likeness; they can be recognized only by their moneybags, decked out with their coats of arms.   To such a pass man can be brought by inordinate love of gold, which consumes his humanity and his very individuality. Doglike, bovine, disgusting as these creatures are, they came of noble stock.

No poor Jews, but illustrious Italian Christians are selected by the poet to point his moral.

The descent into the darkness, on Geryon's back, is suggestively pictured in quick, realistic touches. At first nothing but the monster himself is visible, and Dante's only consciousness of motion comes from the upward rush of the air. Gradually, at various points below, the fires of the eighth circle begin to glimmer, and lamentations reach his ear; but all is dim and mysterious.

In classical mythology Geryon, son of Chrysaor and Callirrhoë, was a three-headed giant king in Spain, who was killed by Hercules; according to *Aen*, VIII, 202–203:

> tergemini nece Geryonae spoliisque superbus,
> Alcides aderat.

(For there came even Alcides, glorying in the slaughter and spoils of triple Geryon.)

A passing reference to his shade, as a "forma tricorporis umbrae," (the shape of the three-bodied shade) is made in *Aen.*, VI, 289. To the medieval scholar this triple nature apparently symbolized deceit. Boccaccio says, in his *Genealogia Deorum Gentilium*, I, 21, speaking of Dante's Fraud: "Et inde Gerion dicta est, quia regnans apud Baleares insulas Gerion miti vultu blandisque verbis et omni comitate consueverit hospites suscipere et demum sub hac benignitate sopitos occidere." (It is named after Geryon, who reigned near the Balearic Islands. With a mild face, with sweet words, using every politeness, he used to attract strangers to him; and then, having lulled them with his benignity, he would slay them.) He discusses the classic Geryon in XIII, 1.

The monstrous form ascribed to him by Dante was doubtless suggested in part by the locusts of Rev. ix, 7–11: "And the shapes of the locusts were like unto horses prepared unto battle ... and their faces were as the faces of men ... And they had tails like unto scorpions, and there were stings in their tails ... And they had a king over them, which is the angel of the bottomless pit ...' St. Thomas, in his commentary on this passage, tells us that the scorpion has a smooth and gentle countenance, to induce people to touch it. The belief that scorpions have attractive faces seems to have been prevalent. Dante's image was profoundly modified, however, by Pliny's description — followed by Solinus — of a strange beast called Mantichora (*Historia Naturalis*, VIII, 30), which has the face of a man, the body of a lion, and a tail ending in a sting like a scorpion's. Similar creatures are portrayed by Albertus Magnus (*De Animalibus*, Lib. XXII, Tr. ii, Cap. 1) and Brunetto Latini (*Trésor*, V, Ch. 59); all of these eat human flesh, and of one of them it is said that "deceptos homines devorat." In the Old French

Image du monde, of the first half of the 13th century, "Manticare" attracts men by song and devours them. On the appropriateness of an upright human face combined with a scorpion's sting, as an emblem of fraud, there is no need to dwell.

6. Near the end of the stony edge of the dike, upon which the poets had walked.

12. Cf. Gen. iii, 1, 'Now the serpent was more subtile than any beast of the field.'

15. In medieval pictures, dragons often have their whole bodies covered with little rings: cf. R. T. Holbrook, *Dante and the Animal Kingdom*, 63, 65.

17. The Tartars and Turks were famous for their cloths. At this line Boccaccio's commentary ends.

18. Arachne was the famous weaver who challenged Minerva to a contest, and was turned into a spider: *Met.*, VI, 5 ff.

22. It was believed that the beaver caught fish with its tail by dangling it in the water. In the Middle Ages the beaver was associated with Germany.

24. The sandy desert has an edge of rock, along the top of the cliff.

31. The poets, on leaving the wood, had mounted the nearer or right side of the embankment and had walked on the right side of the stream; now, therefore, they must come down on the right side, else they would have to cross the boiling blood.

36. The usurers, who did violence to human industry, are seated on the sand, close to the abyss.

60. A lion *azure* in *or* (gold): the arms of the Gianfigliazzi of Florence.

63. A goose *argent* ('whiter than butter') in *gules* (red): the arms of the Ubriachi of Florence.

64. A sow in brood *azure* in *argent*: the arms of the Scrovegni of Padua.

68. Of Vitaliano, the only one of the usurers mentioned by name, we have no certain information.

73. Three bucks were the arms of the Becchi family of Florence. It is thought that the 'sovereign knight' of usurers is Gianni Buiamonte, who was of some prominence in the second half of the 13th century. He belonged to a money-lending company. In 1297 or 1298 he was made Cavaliere. By 1308, however, he was bankrupt and a fugitive from justice. He compounded with his creditors, and died in 1310.

74. Cf. Isaiah lvii, 4: "against whom make ye a wide mouth and draw out the tongue?"

107. Phaëthon, son of Phoebus, was carried away by the horses of the chariot of the sun, which he tried to drive: *Met.*, II, 150 ff., especially l. 200:

> Mentis inops gelida formidine lora remisit.

(Bereft of wits from chilling fear, down he dropped the reins.)

108. The sky, scorched by the runaway chariot, still shows traces of it in the Milky Way.

109. Daedalus, to escape from Crete, fashioned wings for his son Icarus and himself and fastened them on with wax. In spite of his father's warning, the boy flew so high that the sun melted the wax, and, losing his wings, he fell into the sea. See *Met.*, VIII, 183 ff.

118. The water of Phlegethon, at the foot of the cataract.

Canto XVIII

Argument

To form an idea of the general structure of the eighth and ninth circles, one may think of a funnel with a shallow mouth and a thick spout. The upper part will represent the eighth circle, sloping down to the edge of a central hole ("un pozzo assai largo e profondo"), at the bottom of which is the ninth circle. Now let one imagine this upper part, the mouth of the funnel, horizontally corrugated, so that ten deep grooves run around it, one below the other. These are the ditches (*bolge* or *valli*) in which the various types of Fraud are punished. Furthermore, let one picture a number of strips running down the inside of the funnel from the outer edge to the beginning of the neck, like spokes converging upon a hub; and these strips should be conceived, not as flat, but as undulating, arching up over the grooves. The strips will correspond to certain sharp ridges of natural rock that traverse the circle, at intervals, from top to bottom, rising into high, steep bridges over the valleys, and resting on the intervening banks. These *scogli*, as they are called, form a set of embankments on which wayfarers — if such there be — may cross the circle without descending into the ditches. Dante gives to this circle the fantastic name of *Malebolge*, or "Evil Pouches." He compares the *bolge* and the *scogli* to a series of moats, with drawbridges, surrounding a castle in concentric rings.

In describing the double march of the lost souls in the first *bolgia*, Dante recalls a scene witnessed by many thousands in Rome in the Jubilee year of 1299–1300. The following account is borrowed from C. E. Norton's translation of the *Hell*, pp. 112–113: 'The Jubilee was instituted by Boniface VIII, who issued a Bull granting plenary indulgence for a year from Christmas, 1299, to all pilgrims to Rome who should spend fifteen days in the city, visit the churches of St. Peter and St. Paul, and should confess and repent their sins. The throng of pilgrims from all parts of Europe was enormous, and among other precautions for their safety was that here alluded to, a barrier erected lengthwise along the bridge of Sant' Angelo, in order that the crowd going to and coming from St. Peter's might pass in opposite directions without interference.'

The fraudulent are divided into ten categories, and some of these are subdivided. In the first *bolgia* are betrayers of women, who fall into two classes, panders (*ruffiani*) and seducers. They walk ceaselessly around the bottom of their ditch, in two files, moving in opposite directions (like the pilgrims on the bridge), the panders on the outer, the seducers on the inner side. Horned devils scourge them with whips as they pass. In Malebolge demons abound — not mere guardians, similar to those of the classic underworld, but malignant, tormenting fiends. There are no such spirits, however, in the second valley, where the punishment is simply nauseous filth and stench, a symbol of the unclean life of flatterers. To portray their abject vileness, the author deems no terms too gross.

3. The *cerchia* is the circular precipice between the 7th circle and the 8th.

18. They all converge, like the spokes of a wheel, upon the "well,", at the edge of which they stop.

26. On the nearer side of the bottom of the ditch, the sinners, in their circling course, were coming toward us; on the further side, they were going with us but faster than we walked.

32. *Castello*: Sant' Angelo.

33. *Monte*: Monte Giordano, a slight eminence on the left of the river.

50. Venèdico Caccianemico, of a prominent family of Bologna, was Podestà of Milan in 1275, of Pistoia in 1283. He was actually alive in 1300, although clearly Dante believed him to be dead by 1300.

51. 'What brings thee to such sharp sauce?' Probably there is a play upon *Salse*, the name of a ravine, three miles from Bologna, where bodies of criminals were thrown.

53. Dante shows himself well informed. The 'clear speech' restores clear recollection to the sinner.

55. Ghisolabella was Venèdico's sister, married to Niccolò Fontana of Ferrara.

56. *Marchese*: Òbizzo da Este of Ferrara.

57. We know the incident only from Dante's words.

61. *Sipa* is an old Bolognese word for *sia*, often used for 'yes.' Bologna lies between the two rivers Sàvena and Reno. The number of Bolognese panders in this ditch exceeds the number of all the living people who speak Bolognese.

71. Up to this point the poets have been walking to the left of the bank between the high precipice and the first *bolgia*; they now turn to the right to cross this ditch.

72. They now turn their backs upon the upper terraces; and Dante, as he leaves them, reflects that these circles will remain forever unchanged.

75. Dante is now to look down, at the right, on the seducers, whose faces he has not been able to see from the bank.

87. The 'tall' Jason despoiled the Colchians of the golden fleece: *Met.*, VII, 1–158.

90. The women of Lemnos, forsaken by their husbands on account of a curse put upon them by Venus, agreed to murder all the males on the island.

93. Hypsipyle had saved her father, King Thoas, by pretending to have killed him. See Statius, *Thebiad*, IV, V, VI; Ovid, *Heroides*, VI.

96. For the story of Medea, beguiled by Jason, the leader of the Argonauts, see *Met.*, VII.

100. The narrow ridge crosses the second bank (the further bank of the first ditch) and makes of this bank a buttress for a second arch. The ridge arches up over each ditch.

109. 'There is not room enough to see,' because the bank overhangs.

111. From the middle of the bridge they can see better into the ditch.

122. Alessio Interminei (or Interminelli) belonged to a noble family of Lucca; we know nothing in particular about him, although his name occurs in several documents of the second half of the 13th century.

133. Thais, the harlot, is a character in Terence's *Eunuchus*, to whom her lover Thraso, has sent a present (III, 1). Dante, however, who presumably had not read Terence, got the incident from Cicero's *De Amicitia*, XXVI: "Nulla est igitur haec amicitia, cum alter verum audire non volt, alter ad mentiendum paratus est. Nec parasitorum in comoediis assentatio faceta nobis videretur, nisi essent milites gloriosi. 'Magnas vero agere gratias Thais mihi?' Satis erat respondere 'magnas.' 'Ingentis,' inquit. Semper auget assentator id, quod is, cuius ad voluntatem dicitur, volt esse magnum." (There is nothing, therefore, in a friendship in

which one of the parties to it does not wish to hear the truth and the other is ready to lie. Nor should we see any humor in the fawning parasites in comedies if there were no braggart soldiers. "In truth did Thais send me many thanks?" It would have been enough to answer, "Many." "Millions of them," said the parasite. The flatterer always magnifies that which the one for whose gratification he speaks wishes to be large.) In reality it was the parasite, Gnatho, who said "ingentes"; but Dante from this passage evidently supposed that it was Thais.

Canto XIX

Argument

The sin punished in the third *bolgia* is simony, the use of ecclesiastical office for private gain. Dante classifies it as Fraud, but it was generally regarded as an offense against the Holy Ghost. It derives its name from the Simon Magus of Acts viii, 9–24: "But there was a certain man, called Simon, which beforetime in the same city used sorcery. ... And when Simon saw that through laying on of the apostles' hands the Holy Ghost was given, he offered them money, saying, Give me also this power. ... But Peter said unto him, Thy money perish with thee, because thou hast thought that the gift of God may be purchased with money." Inasmuch as this offense is one of perversion, it is symbolized by the culprit being turned upside-down; and as the perverted trust is a holy one, God's anger falls upon the incumbent in the shape of fire, which, owing to his distorted attitude, burns not his head but his feet. The bottom and sides of this ditch are perforated with little round holes, from each of which project the writhing feet and ankles of a sinner. Somewhat similarly, in the *Visio Alberici*, XI, simonists are confined in a fiery well. Dante's flame, however, merely plays upon the surface of the soles, from which it seems to suck its food. This grotesque penalty is inflicted even upon mercenary Popes, all of whom appear to be sunk in one hole. The latest comer is at the top, "planted like a stake," with his feet in the air; the others, with each new arrival, are pushed further and further down, to flatten in the crevices of the rock. Dante and Virgil descend into this *bolgia* to converse with Pope Nicholas III. To him our traveler addresses, with the approval of Reason, though with some misgiving, a stinging rebuke, made all the more impressive by Dante's professed reluctance to show disrespect to a former wearer of the papal mantle.

The burrows of the simonists are compared to the *pozzetti*, or smaller fonts for the *baptizings* (such is the more probable meaning of *battezzatori* (l. 18). The medieval font to which Dante refers was destroyed in the 16th century, and its exact form remains a mystery. However, it seems reasonable to think that it resembled in general style, and in respect to the *pozzetti* in particular, the extant font in the Baptistery of Pisa (see illustration, p. 75).

Baptismal Font, built by Guido Bigarelli da Como in 1246, in the Baptistery of Pisa.

We really know nothing about the curious incident here referred to, and it is hard to understand how Dante could break a stone structure such as one of the *pozzetti* must have been. The most plausible suggestion has been that he broke a sort of wooden cover that was commonly kept over the smaller font containing the holy water. But how did anyone fall in and thus need to be rescued in this way? The mystery is complete.

It should be noted, however, that Baptism as such is symbolically connected with simony. The whole reference is therefore relevant on that level of meaning; on this point and on the legend of Simon Magus and his headlong fall which caused him to be represented in medieval art as "upside-down," see Singleton (1965b).

5. Judicial sentences were proclaimed with a trumpet.

35. Inasmuch as all Malebolge slopes toward the central well, and the floors of the *bolge* are level, the inner bank of each ditch must be lower than the outer. There are several indications that the inner bank is also less steep than the other.

41. After crossing the third *bolgia*, they went down into it from its inner bank.

50. Murderers were planted, head downward, in a hole, and buried alive. Dante probably recalls some scene actually witnessed, in which the murderer, to put off his death a few minutes, called back the priest, pretending that he had something more to confess.

53. The speaker, Nicholas III, thinks that his successor in simony, Boniface VIII, has arrived. But as Boniface was not to die until 1303, the book of destiny seems to have lied.

56. He was charged with having induced Celestine V to renounce the papacy (cf. III, 60).

70. Giovanni Gaetano Orsini, Pope Nicholas III from 1277 to 1280, was notorious for his nepotism. Because of the fact that the she-bear, *orsa*, was the cognizance in his family arms, Dante refers to his relatives as *orsatti*, or 'cubs.'

73-75. See Apocalypse of St. Paul: M. James, *Apocryphal New Testament*, 1924, p. 543a.

79. Nicholas has been there nearly twenty years, from August, 1280, to April, 1300. Boniface's feet will burn only about eleven years, from October, 1303, to April, 1314, when Clement V will die. This passage must, it would seem, have been written after the latter date.

82. After the brief pontificate of the good Benedict XI, Bertrand de Goth of Gascony became Pope in 1305 with the name of Clement V. He was noted for his greed and licentiousness, and became the unscrupulous tool of Philip the Fair of France. In 1309 he transferred the papal see to Avignon; he deceived the Emperor Henry VII and aided Philip in the suppression of the Templars.

85. Clement is compared to the Jason of 2 Macc. iv and v, who bought the high priesthood of King Antiochus. As Antiochus favored Jason, Philip will have Clement made Pope.

92. Mat. xvi, 19.

93. John xxi, 19.

94. Matthias was chosen apostle to fill the place of Judas: Acts i, 23-26.

99. From the beginning of his papacy, Nicholas was hostile to Charles of Anjou.

106. See Rev. xvii: "I will shew unto thee the judgment of the great whore that sitteth upon many waters: with whom the kings of the earth have committed fornication, ... and I saw a woman sit upon a scarlet coloured beast, full of names of blasphemy, having seven heads and ten horns." Dante, dealing freely with this passage, combines the woman with the beast (the Latin text, indeed, might be so read) and makes her the symbol of the corrupt Church. She was born with seven heads, the Sacraments, and had as her defense ten horns, the Commandments, as long as her husband, the Papacy, loved virtue. Cf., for the beast, Rev. xii, 5.

112. Cf. Hosea viii, 4: "of their silver and gold they have made them idols."

113. The idolater (for instance, those who made the golden calf) worships only one idol, but you worship everything that is of gold.

115. The Emperor Constantine was thought to have donated the Western Empire to St. Sylvester, the first Pope to hold temporal possessions. The document of this donation was preserved, and was generally considered authentic until the middle of the 15th century. Dante did not doubt its genuineness, but disputed the right of Constantine to give and of Sylvester to receive.

Canto XX

Argument

In the fourth *bolgia* we have another instance of perversion — this time perversion of mental sight — symbolized by bodily distortion. The souls of soothsayers, who misused their great gift of intelligence to beguile their credulous fellows, have their heads twisted to the rear, so that they are obliged to walk backwards. They suffer constantly all the agony one would feel in the instant of neck wringing; unable to make a sound, they pour forth their anguish in tears that flow down their backs. The aspect of this strange affliction makes Dante weep, before he recognizes any of the sinners; in other words, he is sorry for the penalty itself, and insofar rebels against God's will. For this, Reason chides him. 'The righteous shall rejoice when he seeth the vengeance,' says Ps. lviii, 10; and theologians aver that the fate of the damned should be contemplated, not with pain, but with satisfaction, as a manifestation of divine justice. In the *Visio S. Pauli* (ed. H. Brandes, p. 66), when St. Paul weeps at the sight of the infernal torments, his angelic guide remonstrates: "Quid ploras? Vis plus esse misericors filio Dei?" (Why do you weep? Would you be more compassionate than the Son of God?) So Virgil finds it necessary to rebuke Dante, declaring:

Qui vive la pietà quand' è ben morta,

which probably means: "Here, in thy grief, pity shows life when by rights it is dead"; that is, in Hell there should be no such thing as compassion for punishment, and there is none, save for thy silly tears.

A meeting with the prophetess Manto, daughter of the Theban Tiresias, leads Virgil to launch forth into a lengthy account of the founding of Mantua, his native place. The town, he affirms, was named after this same woman, who, leaving Thebes, ended her long wanderings on the spot where it was afterwards built. Dante represents himself as listening respectfully but with only indifferent interest to the narrative, at the close of which he eagerly asks about the other souls. Now, the peculiar feature of this incident is that Dante here ascribes to Virgil quite another story from that indicated in the *Aeneid*, X, 198–200:

> Ille etiam patriis agmen ciet Ocnus ab oris,
> Fatidicae Mantus et Tusci filius amnis,
> Qui muros matrisque dedit tibi, Mantua, nomen.

(Yonder, too, Ocnus summons a host from his native shores, son of prophetic Manto and the Tuscan river, who gave thee, O Mantua, ramparts and his mother's name.)

According to this passage, then, it was Ocnus, son of a river-god and a presumably different Manto, who built and named Mantua. Dante knew of the Theban Manto from Statius; and he may have read in St. Isidore's *Origines*, XV, i, 59, or heard from local tradition, that it was she who founded Mantua. At any rate, he apparently was convinced that the version of the tale in the *Aeneid* was wrong and should be corrected; the correction he courteously put into the mouth of Virgil himself. But that is not all: the "cruel virgin" involves us in a problem still more perplexing. In *Purg.* XXII, 113, Virgil assigns "la figlia di Tiresia" to the Limbus, where he himself dwells. It is incredible that our poet should have forgotten where he had put Manto, after all the talk about her. We are almost forced to the conclusion that the passage in *Inf.* XX was written after the line in *Purg.* XXII and that Dante neglected to alter the latter in accordance with the former. It is likely that in his first draft of *Inf.* XX he introduced the Etruscan Manto and attributed to her the name of Mantua, as the *Aeneid* does; but later, changing his view, substituted the Theban Manto, and wrote the verses as we have them.

It is clear that in this canto Dante wishes to exonerate of any imputation of sympathy with magic his master, Virgil, who in Naples had and still has the reputation of sorcery, and perhaps incidentally himself. Virgil's city was not founded by (only named after) the sorceress Manto and was named without augury; in its inheritance, then, is no taint of magic. Virgil's indignation is aroused by the thought of the part played by sorcery and soothsaying in the ancient poets. Indeed, his present tale of Mantua may be merely an allegorical interpretation of the passage in the *Aeneid* (to wit, the city was founded by men who followed Manto and the river), designed as a showing-up of old fables.

19. A formula of adjuration: cf. X, 82.

33. *Thebaid*, VIII, 84–85, "Qui ... praeceps ... per inane ruis" (who rushest headlong through the empty realm).

34. The story of Amphiaraus, the augur, one of the seven kings who besieged Thebes, is told by Statius in the *Thebiad*, VII, 815 ff., and VIII, 1 ff.

40. Tiresias was a famous soothsayer of Thebes. The incident here referred to is related in *Met.*, III, 324–331: having struck with his stick two snakes that were together, he became a woman; seven years later, striking the same snakes again, he regained his male form.

46. Aruns was an Etruscan soothsayer of Caesar's time, of whom Lucan says, in *Phars.*, I, 586: "Aruns incoluit desertae moenia Lunae" (Arruns, who dwelt in the deserted city of Luna). Some texts have Lucae. The mountain cave seems to be an invention of Dante.

59. Bacchus was the son of the Theban Semele. Thebes came under the rule of the tyrant Creon.

63. 'Tyrol'; or more probably the name refers to the castle of Tiralli, which gave its name to the region. — *Benaco* is Lake Garda; Garda rises on the east of it; Val Camonica is a long valley some distance west of it.

67. There is a point in or near the lake where the dioceses of Trent, Brescia, and Verona meet, so that any one of the three bishops might *segnar*, make the sign of the cross, in that spot. Lines connecting the towns would make a triangle around the lake.

70. *Peschiera* is on the south side of the lake, where the shore is low.

78. At Governo, or Govèrnolo, the river Mincio empties into the Po.

95. The Ghibelline Pinamonte Bonaccorsi treacherously advised the Guelf Count Alberto da Casalodi, lord of Mantua, to exile the nobles so as to win the favor of the people. Following this counsel and thus losing support, Casalodi was driven from the city, with much slaughter and banishment of the Guelfs.

108. All the men of Greece had gone to the Trojan war.

113. *Tragedia*: cf. XVI, 127. The *Aeneid*, which, according to l. 114, Dante knew by heart, "sings" of this man, with the name Eurypÿlus, in II, 114–115:

> Suspensi Eurypylum scitantem oracula Phoebi
> Mittimus.

(Perplexed, we send Eurypylus to ask the oracle of Phoebus.)

The Greeks, in their doubt, send him to consult the oracle of Phoebus. In ll. 122–124 the augur Calchas is questioned about the will of the Gods. The two characters being thus associated in the poem, Dante inferred that Eurypylus, like Calchas, was a soothsayer and that he assisted Calchas in determining "the right moment for cutting the first cable at Aulis," when the Greeks set sail for Troy.

116. Michael Scot, the Scotch scholar, who lived many years at the court of Frederick II, had great repute as a sorcerer. Where Dante learned that he was 'spare in the flanks,' we do not know.

118. Guido Bonatti of Forlì, a famous astrologer of the 13th century, was at the court of Frederick II and several other princes. Asdente, a poor cobbler of Parma, of simple and modest disposition, was known far and wide as a prophet.

123. Wax or silver images of people were melted, to bring about their death. Torraca cites two trials for this crime in 1317 and 1319; in the latter (an attempt on the life of John XXII) it was asserted that one of the Visconti had sought, for the working of this spell, the aid of "Master Dante Alighieri of Florence."

124. The Man in the Moon, in Italian folklore, is Cain, who carries a bundle of thorns, "the fruit of the ground." The moon is directly over the dividing line between the Hemisphere of Land and the Hemisphere of Water; this circle passes close to Seville on the west and the Ganges on the east. For an observer in Jerusalem, the moon, which is nearly over Seville, is just setting; it is about 6 A.M. To indicate the time of day more precisely, Virgil adds that the moon is one night past the full — "yesternight the moon was round," when its light was of some use to Dante in the 'deep wood'; it sets, then, somewhat after sunrise.

Canto XXI

Argument

In nearly all medieval portrayals of the lower world the grotesque runs riot. Dante, while not discarding this element, has brought it within narrow bounds. In the fifth *bolgia*, however, he gives free rein to the comic spirit, which dominates this canto and the next. Here, too, he reflects, as nowhere else, the popular Christian conception of Hell. As in the *Visio Sancti Pauli*, a devil arrives carrying a lost soul, although the damned, according to Dante's regular plan, should sink unaided to their proper place by the weight of their own sin. The guardians of this ditch are the roguish fiends of folklore; they are more or less individualized, receiving fantastic names. Their generic designation is *Malebranche*, 'Badpaws'; *Alichino* is perhaps the French *Hallequin*, leader of the Wild Hunt; *Farfarello* seems to be a traditional demon name; *Barbariccia*, *Cagnazzo*, *Graffiacane*, *Malacoda*, *Rubicante* mean, respectively, 'Curlybeard,' 'Mean Dog,' 'Dogscratcher,' 'Badtail,' 'Rubicund.' Some of the appellations appear to be ludicrous distortions of the names of real people: there was a prominent Malabranca family in Rome; the Raffacani were numerous in Florence; a Pietro di Malacoda is attested; and Torraca cites, among others, Canasso, Scaldabrina, Ciriolo, Dragonetto, Biccicocco, Scormiglio, which are not unlike *Cagnazzo*, *Calcabrina*, *Ciriatto*, *Draghignazzo*, *Libicocco*, *Scarmiglione*. The whole humorous interlude, characterized by coarseness of incident and language, serves both to express contempt for the sinners and their earthly judges and to afford a relief from the horrors that precede and follow.

The peculiarity of swindlers is that they do dirty work in the dark; and unless they remain under cover, they are seized by the officers of the law. So Dante's barrators, or grafters, pursue their eternal career beneath the surface of a ditch full of boiling pitch, and demons stand ready to snatch them with hooks if they attempt to "air themselves." Cunning as they were on earth, they still incessantly scheme to cheat and elude their watchers; and these, just as tricky and far more vile and mischievous, are as eager to catch the innocent as the guilty. The mention of the pitch leads to a lifelike description of the great arsenal, or shipyard, in Venice, famous during and after the Middle Ages, where the sailors, as is the habit of seafaring folk the world over, utilize the enforced idleness of winter to repair their damaged craft.

To entrap Dante and his too confiding guide, the leader of the Malebranche informs them that though the nearest bridge over the following valley is broken, the next ridge will afford them a safe passage. This arch was shattered, he says, when Christ descended into Hell, 1266 years ago yesterday, and five hours later in the day. Now Dante, in *Conv.*, IV, xxiii, 9–11, after expressing the opinion that the age of thirty-five is the culminating point of the perfect human life, continues: "E muovemi questa ragione: che ottimamente naturato fue lo nostro salvatore Cristo, lo quale volle morire nel trentaquattresimo anno de la sua etade; ché non era convenevole la divinitade stare [in] cos[a] in discresc[er]e, né da credere è ch'elli non volesse dimorare in questa nostra vita al sommo, poi che stato c'era nel basso stato de la puerizia. E ciò manifesta l'ora del giorno de la sua morte, ché volle quella consimigliare con la vita sua; onde dice Luca che era quasi ora sesta quando morio, che è a dire lo colmo del die. Onde si può comprendere per quello 'quasi' che al trentacinquesimo anno di Cristo era lo colmo de la sua etade."

(And I am moved thereto by this argument that our Saviour Christ was of perfect nature, and it was his will to die in the thirty-fourth year of his age; for it was not fitting that the Divinity should thus abide in decrease. Nor is it to be believed that he would not abide in this our life up to the apex, inasmuch as he had been therein in the low estate of infancy. And this is manifested by the hour of the day of his death, for he desired to conform this to his life; wherefore Luke tells us that it was about the sixth hour when he died, which is to say the apex of the day. Wherefore we may understand by this that about the thirty-fifth year of Christ was the apex of his age.)

Not only is this argument curiously lame, but its very foundation is false, for Luke does not state that "era quasi ora sesta" when Christ died. What he does say (xxiii, 44–45), after recording the conversation between Jesus and the thief, is: "And it was about the sixth hour, and there was a darkness over all the earth until the ninth hour. And the sun was darkened, and the veil of the temple was rent in the midst." Matthew (xxvii, 45, 46, 51) and Mark (xv, 33, 34, 38) agree in putting the crucifixion and the beginning of the darkness at the sixth hour (noon), the death and the rending of the veil of the temple at the ninth (3 P.M.); and there is nothing in Luke's vaguer statement that is inconsistent with this. If Dante, when he wrote Canto XXI, still adhered to the opinion set forth in the *Convivio*, the colloquy between Virgil and the fiend occurred at 7 A.M., five hours before noon; if, on the other hand, he had rejected this untenable view, the hour was 10 A.M. It was, in any case, the morning of Saturday, April 9, the day following Good Friday, in the year 1300, counting from the Conception — 1266 years after the death of Christ, who expired, according to Dante's belief, at the age of thirty-three, just thirty-four years after the Conception.

38. The chief magistrates of Lucca were called Ancients. Santa Zita, who lived in the 13th century, was the special patron saint of Lucca.

41. Bonturo Dati, boss of Lucca, was the worst grafter of all; in 1300 he was at the height of his power. In 1308 he was leader of a triumvirate that controlled Lucca. That is the year in which a document in Lucca was witnessed by "Johannes filius Dantis Alagherii de Florentia." Possibly Dante was there that year under the protection of Moroello Malaspina. Of this "Johannes" nothing more is known.

42. The Latin *ita* was used in clerical language for 'yes.'

46. His shape suggests to the humorous demons the attitude of prayer.   But the meaning of *convolto*, in this context, may well be 'rump up' — and in this case it would be a rump covered with blackest pitch.   Now the most striking feature of the *Holy Face* is that it is ebony black.   The thrust, then, and the devilish taunting humor are therefore the more pungent. See Singleton (1970) for an illustration of the black Volto Santo.

49. The Serchio is a stream near Lucca.

69. He stops and begs where he is, instead of going up to the house.

95. Caprona, a castle on the Arno, surrendered in 1289 to the troops of Lucca and Florence. It is evident from these lines that Dante was serving with the Florentines.

136. They proceed along the bank, at the left of the bridge.

Canto XXII

Argument

Opening in mock-heroic continuation of the gross theme immediately preceding, this canto goes on to describe the ways of grafters — who, it would seem, are especially rife in remote dependencies.   It relates the capture of one of them by the infernal sleuth hounds, and his clever escape from the domineering Barbariccia, the suspicious Cagnazzo, the overconfident Alichino, the quarrelsome Calcabrina, and their fierce comrades.

4. Dante was present at the battle of Campaldino, in 1289, when the forces of Arezzo (the 'Aretines') were defeated by those of Florence and Lucca.

15. This sounds like a popular proverb.   Cf. Ps. xviii, 26: "With the pure thou wilt shew thyself pure; and with the froward thou wilt shew thyself froward"; see also 2 Sam. xii, 26.

21. The belief that dolphins warn sailors of an approaching storm was very common.

37. Dante explains how it is that he knows the name of this demon.

48. Some of the early commentators ascribe to this man from Navarre the name of Ciampolo or Giampolo, but we really know of him only what Dante tells us.

52. Thibaut II, count of Champagne, son-in-law of Louis IX of France, was king of Navarre in the middle of the 13th century.

67. From an island near Italy.

82. The Pisans, who conquered Sardinia, divided it into four provinces, or *giudicati*, Gallura, Logudoro, Arborea, and Cagliari, each of which was governed by a *giudice*.   The early commentators say that the governor of Gallura, at the time of this Friar Gomita, was Nino Visconti, who appears in *Purg.* VIII, 53.   It is said that Gomita was hanged.

88. Michel Zanche is not mentioned in any document; he is said to have been vicar of King Enzo of Sardinia, son of Frederick II.   From XXXIII, 144, we learn that he was murdered by Branca Doria.

104. He says it is the custom, among these souls, that one shall peep out and whistle if the coast is clear.

111. He tries to put the demons off the scent: 'To be sure, I am pretty tricky, when I get my fellows into worse trouble.'

116. The 'collo' is the high edge of the inner bank of the 5th *bolgia*.   The demons are to go a little way down the slope toward the 6th valley, so that the bank shall hide them from the sinners in the pitch.

119. They turned their backs on the 5th *bolgia*, to go toward the slope of the 6th.

123. Barbariccia, their leader or 'provost.' Cf. l. 94.
129. Alichino, who plunged after the fugitive and barely threw back his head and chest in time to escape going under with him.
134. 'Eager' that the sinner should escape, so that he might have a 'scuffle' with Alichino.
139. 'Full grown': the term was applied to hawks caught toward the beginning of winter.
142. The heat was an 'ungrappler.'

Canto XXIII

Argument

The scene just witnessed reminds Dante of a "favola d' Isopo," the story of the frog and the mouse. The tale exists in Greek; but the name *Ysopus* was given in the Middle Ages to any fable collection, and the story in question occurs in several. A frog, having offered to tow a mouse across a stream, ties itself to the animal, jumps in with it, and then treacherously tries to dive to the bottom, expecting to drown its companion. While the mouse is struggling to keep afloat, a kite, seeing the disturbance, swoops down and carries off both creatures. The beginning and the end of the fable, Dante says, are exactly like the recent episode: that is, the fall of the two grappling fiends into the pitch is a reproduction of the plunge of the tethered quadrupeds into the water; and their rescue, as they are hooked out by their mates, is a counterpart of the seizure of the frog and the mouse by the kite.*

Our travelers have a narrow escape from the angry devils. Virgil, taking Dante in his arms, slides on his back down the precipitous bank into the sixth *bolgia*, where they are safe from pursuit. They find themselves in the valley of the hypocrites. "Woe unto you, scribes and Pharisees, hypocrites!" says Mat. xxiii, 27, "for ye are like unto whited sepulchres, which indeed appear beautiful outward but are within full of dead men's bones, and of all uncleanness." Such is Dante's conception of hypocrisy. In slow and solemn file the souls march by — "gente dipinta," painted people, beautiful outward with bright gold. They are clad in cloaks of the cut affected by the monks of Cluny; and these garments, gilded on the outside, are made of crushing lead. Their cowls hang massive and heavy over their eyes, their heads are bowed down by the weight, they can scarcely drag themselves along. Their enforced decorum, measured pace, and sidelong glances are all in character; and so is the pious platitude which one of them sententiously volunteers when Virgil discovers how he has been tricked by the Malebranche. The exact form of their punishment

---

* For a different interpretation, see Singleton (1970).

was probably suggested to Dante by the *Magnae Derivationes* of Uguccione da Pisa, who defines *ypocrita* as 'superauratus,' taking it from ὑπέρ and χρυσός.

On the floor of the ditch, pegged down at intervals in the pathway, where the heavy procession tramples on them as it passes, are Caiaphas, Annas, and the other false councillors who favored the sacrifice of Christ.   Thinking to destroy him, they really crucified their own souls, exposing themselves to the perpetual obloquy of mankind and assuming the burden of blame for all subsequent hypocrisy.   Over their *bolgia* the bridges are broken down, shattered by the great earthquake that accompanied the Savior's death on the Cross.   Here again, in l. 137, the word *ruina* is used.   An impressive picture is that of Virgil "marveling" over Caiaphas, who was not there at the time of his previous journey through Hell.

For the "favola d' Isopo," see K. McKenzie in *The Seventeenth Annual Report of the Dante Society of Cambridge, Massachusetts* (1898), pp. 6–13.

For the lead cape punishment, in tradition and in vision, see G. L. Hamilton in *Romanic Review*, XII, 335.   A similar punishment (not for hypocrisy, but for an angry oath) is related by Helinand of Froidmont, as recorded by Vincent de Beauvais, *Speculum Historiale* (Venice, 1494), XXIX, cxviii: the soul of a clerk appears to a friend, clad in a beautiful lead-colored cape, heavier than a tower. — For hypocrites, see St. Thomas, *Summa Theologiae*, Secunda Secundae, Qu. vi, Art. 5: "they steal a reputation among men."

3. Franciscans.

25. If I were a mirror ('leaded glass'), I should not catch thy bodily reflection more swiftly than I now receive the reflection of thy thought (thine inner image).   Cf. Prov. xxvii, 19.

31. The 'right bank' is the declivity leading to the 6th *bolgia*.

44. He lay on his back and let himself go.

45. The cliff encloses the valley on the outer side.

47. A 'land mill,' is one situated at a distance from the water as opposed to one built on a boat or raft in a river.   The latter were common in the Arno.

48. At the moment when the water pours down on the paddles of the mill-wheel.

66. That those which Frederick II put upon criminals were, in comparison with these, as light as straw.   The old commentators say that Frederick had offenders against the throne dressed in leaden cloaks, which were then melted upon them; this statement is not corroborated by any documentary evidence.

83. Their 'haste of spirit' could be manifested only by the expression of their faces.

84. Some of the *bolge* are evidently very much narrower than others: cf. XXX, 87.

85. Their heavy, lowered hoods prevented them from looking directly.

92. Cf. Mat. vi, 16: "be not, as the hypocrites, of a sad countenance' — 'sicut *hypocritae tristes*."

102. The heavily burdened sinners, as they moan, are compared to scales so overweighted that they creak.

103. The brethren of the lay order of Beata Maria, defenders of the faith and of justice, were not required to lead an ascetic life and were nicknamed "Jolly Friars."

104. Catalano de' Malavolti was a Guelf, Loderingo degli Andalò was a Ghibelline.   Both were men of great authority, very successful mayors of several cities.   The second was one of the founders of the order of Beata Maria.

106. It was customary in Florence, as in many other cities, to choose as mayor for a term of one year some distinguished outsider, who was called *podestà* or *conservator pacis*.   In 1266, however, instead of "a single man," two mayors, one from each party, were elected as a compromise, the Ghibellines, in control since 1260, having consented to the arrangement, hoping to make peace, before it was too late, with the reviving Guelfs.   It was believed that they conspired to advance their own interests and to favor the Guelfs, who were returning to power after the battle of Benevento.   It is now known that they were placed in office and controlled by Pope Clement IV.

108. *Gardingo* was the name of an old Longobard fortress in Florence.   Near it were the houses of the Uberti, which were destroyed in 1266, when the Ghibellines left the city and their site was turned into a public square.

109. The movement of this line is exactly like that of V, 116, and VI, 58, in which Dante voices his compassion for Francesca and Ciacco.   We may infer that he was about to express pity, probably ironical, for the *Frati godenti*.

112. He writhed with shame at being seen by a living man.

114. Catalano, who could not see so far ahead, 'took notice from that,' i.e., from the puffing.

117. John xi, 49, 50: "And one of them, named Caiaphas, being the high priest that same year, said unto them, Ye know nothing at all, nor consider that it is expedient for us, that one man should die for the people, and that the whole nation perish not." Also xviii, 14.

121. Annas: John xviii, 13, 24.

122. John xi, 47–53.

123. "Seed of ill for the Jews," in accordance with what Jesus had prophesied: Luke xxiii, 27–31.

134. A ridge, similar to the one they have followed as far as this *bolgia*. — 'The great belt': the circular precipice that encloses all Malebolge.

141. Malacoda.

144. John viii, 44.

Canto XXIV

Argument

For a moment, thanks to the dainty simile of the frost with which this canto opens, we are lifted out beneath the open sky into the bracing air of winter. Then the horrors redouble.   In this seventh *bolgia* we are shown the most weird and bloodcurdling sights that Hell affords.   The thief, when he plies his trade, abdicates his human nature and transforms himself into a sly, creeping snake. The serpent, then, is the symbol of thievery; and so this sin is depicted, through two cantos, with an astounding variety of gruesome detail.

2. The sun is in Aquarius (cooling his locks in the spray) approximately from January 21 to February 21.

3. From December 21 (the winter solstice) to June 21 (the summer solstice) the nights grow shorter in the northern hemisphere, longer in the southern.   In January and February, then, the nights are beginning to 'pass to the south.'   As the sun moves northward, the night moves southward.   I. Del Lungo proposes that they 'are dwindling toward half a day'; at the vernal equinox they become just twelve hours.

4. Cf. *V. N.*, I, I.   The 'white sister' of the hoar frost is the snow.

6. 'The temper of her pen lasts but a little while,' i.e., she cannot long continue her copying: in other words, the frost soon melts.

9. Smiting the thigh was a common expression of grief in ancient times (*percutere femur*) and in the Middle Ages.

28. These are pieces of the broken bridge.

34. They are climbing up the inner bank, which is lower than the outer.

42. Where the top of the heap of fragments joins the solid rock of the ridge.

51. Cf. Wisdom v, 14.

54. Cf. *Aen.*, VI, 731: "*quantum non noxia corpora tardant*" (so far as harmful bodies clog them not).

55. The climb from the center of the earth to the top of Purgatory. It is not enough to quit sin: we must attain virtue.

63. This ridge is much higher than the one they followed as far as the 5th *bolgia*.

73. 'Belt': the inner bank of the *bolgia* just crossed. — 'Wall': the descent from the ridge to the top of the bank. Because of the fact that this inner bank is quite low, they will be comparatively near the bottom of the ditch.

85. The Libyan sands were familiar to Dante through Lucan and Ovid: *Phars.*, I, 367; II, 417; IX, 705; *Met.*, IV, 617. The following snakes, and others, are mentioned by Lucan in his account of Cato's march through the desert: *Phars.*, IX, 700 ff. The *jaculi* and *cenchres* are described by Pliny and Solinus. The *chelȳdri* make their path smoke, the *jaculi* are swift as darts, the *phareae* furrow the ground with their tails, the *cenchres* never follow a straight course, the *amphisbaena* has two heads.

90. Not all Libya, Ethiopia, and Arabia can show so many serpents as the 7th *bolgia*.

93. The heliotrope is a precious stone that makes its bearer invisible. Cf. Boccaccio, *Decameron*, VIII, 3.

96. The snakes that bound the hands behind had their heads and tails thrust right through the bodies (from back to front) and tied in front.

97. Just below the bank on which we stood.

100. *O* and undotted *i* are written with a single stroke. Lucan, *Phars.*, IX, 761 ff., tells of a soldier who, bitten by a snake, melts entirely away. Cf. XXV, 95.

106. See particularly Ovid, *Met.*, XV, 392 ff. The phoenix was described also by Pliny and Brunetto Latini.

113. Epileptics were thought to be possessed by devils. See Mark ix, 17–26.

114. 'Stoppage' of the passages between heart and brain.

125. Vanni Fucci was a bastard, a natural son of one of the Lazzari family of Pistoia. He was a notorious ruffian, robber, and a party leader.

129. Dante — who, it appears from this line, had known Vanni — is surprised to find him here rather than in the first ring of the 7th circle, among the violent. In 1295 Vanni was condemned for theft and murder by a judge who was later one of Dante's fellow exiles.

138. In January, 1293, or a little earlier, some silver statues were stolen from the altar of a chapel in the cathedral of Pistoia. According to Chiappelli, the theft occurred probably in March, 1295.

139. The crime was attributed to several, especially to a certain Rampino Ranucci, who came near being hanged for it. Probably the truth had come out not long before April, 1300. It is probable that Vanni died shortly before 1300, having eluded justice until then. Vanni had been condemned for theft and murder in 1295, by Manetto degli Scali, subsequently a fellow exile of Dante. The poet may have learned the truth from this judge.

142. The following prophecy, couched in oracular style, is purposely obscure, and no perfectly satisfactory interpretation has been found. That of Torraca, the most consistent, is as follows: Pistoia was thinned of Blacks (adherents of the Black party) after May, 1301; Florence renewed her people (banishing the Whites and restoring the Blacks) and changed her government after the entry of Charles of Valois, November 4, 1301; in 1302, Moroello Malaspina, chosen captain of an expedition of Lucchese and Florentines against Pistoia, while

besieging the neighboring stronghold of Serravalle, was suddenly attacked by the Pistoiese, but, tearing down the palisades of his camp, issued forth and dispersed the enemy. Note the meteorological style.

145. The 'vapor,' or 'flame,' that Mars draws forth is Moroello Malaspina, lord of Lunigiana in the valley of the Magra. Dante was his guest in 1306 and was believed to have dedicated the *Purgatorio* to him.

148. It seems that the name *Campo Piceno* was applied to the territory of Pistoia. It was also an old name for Pistoia itself. Serravalle is four miles from the city, and higher, being on the south slope of the Apennines, at the foot of which Pistoia lies.

150. Serravalle surrendered soon after. This insignificant incident was probably of great importance to the White party, and therefore looked big to Dante. Had Pistoia been successful, the exiles might perhaps have been restored to Florence.

Canto XXV

Argument

In a lair on Mt. Aventine dwelt the bloody monster Cacus, son of Vulcan, whose story Virgil tells in the *Aeneid*, VIII, 193–267. When Hercules returned from the west with Geryon's herd, Cacus stole a part of it, dragging the cattle by their tails, that their footprints might point away from his den. Warned by their bellowing, Hercules followed them; and although the fire-belching Cacus filled the cave with flame and smoke, the hero boldly entered and strangled him — according to Dante's version, which follows Ovid's, slew him with his club. Virgil nowhere calls Cacus a centaur, but he does use the phrase (VIII, 194): "Semihominis Caci facies" (shape of half-human Cacus). A centaur Dante makes him, and puts upon his neck a mane of serpents and on his back a fiery dragon. Inasmuch as he was guilty of theft, he is separated from the centaurs of the Circle of Violence and incarcerated in the seventh *bolgia* of the Circle of Fraud. Presumably he is, like his fellows, a sort of guardian as well as a culprit.

Five other thieves claim our attention — Agnello, Buoso, Puccio, Cianfa, Guercio, all Florentines of whom we know little or nothing. The first three are introduced in the aspect of human beings. Cianfa darts in as a snake, twists himself about Agnello, and combines with him into an indescribable monster — "e tal sen giò con lento passo." Guercio then appears in serpent form, bites Buoso, and gradually exchanges shapes with him, the one becoming a man, the other a snake. Puccio remains intact.

Some strange effects of snakebites Dante learned from Lucan's *Pharsalia*, IX, 761 ff. Certain details of his transformations he evidently drew from Ovid's *Metamorphoses*: in IV, 576 ff., Cadmus is turned into a serpent; in V, 451 ff., a boy who laughs at Ceres becomes a lizard; in IV, 356 ff., a youth and a naiad are fused into a Hermaphrodite. But the sustained realism, the atmosphere of deep mystery and horror, the uncanny yawn, stare, and smoke are Dante's own.

For Ovid's version of the Cacus story, see *Fasti*, I, 569. It is possible that in this canto, Dante, convinced that Ovid is right, makes Virgil correct himself.

2. *La fica* (the fig) is a coarse, insulting gesture made by holding out the fist with the thumb between the fore and middle finger. It is said that the Pistoians had a stone hand in this gesture carved on their Castello di Carmignano to insult the Florentines: Chiappelli, 229.

12. Pistoia, according to tradition, was founded by the remnants of Catiline's army. However, inasmuch as 'seed' may signify either 'source' or 'product,' the reference is possibly to the party strife in Florence, which originated in Pistoia.

15. Capaneus: XIV, 63.

18. Vanni Fucci. On the special sense of 'unripeness' in connection with pride, see Singleton (1970). Ironically the centaur with his 'blowtorch' of a dragon means now to 'ripen' this proud one. Note that *pride*, with the reference in ll. 14–15, not *thievery*, is here to the fore.

19. *Maremma*: a wild and swampy part of Tuscany: cf. XIII, 8–9, XXIX, 46–49.

23. The dragon of folklore breathes fire.

28. The other centaurs are in the first ring of the 7th circle.

33. Hercules kept on striking him long after he was dead.

35. Virgil and Dante are looking down from the bank. The three spirits turn out to be Agnolo Brunelleschi, Buoso de' Donati (or degli Abati), and Puccio Sciancato. Two more come presently in the form of snakes.

43. Cianfa Donati was a Florentine who had attained some distinction; we have no information concerning his thefts. He appears, in l. 50, in the guise of a serpent.

51. Named, in l. 68, Agnello. The old commentators call him Agnolo Brunelleschi; we know nothing more of him.

54. The snake spreads its open mouth over Agnello's face.

60. Cf. *Met.*, IV, 365: "Utve solent hederae longos intexere truncos" (or as the ivy ofttimes embraces great trunks of trees).

64. The figure is that of a piece of cotton paper burning on the lower edge; a streak of brown precedes the advancing flame.

72. Cf. *Met.*, IV, 373–375 (Hermaphroditus and Salmacis):

> Nam mixta duorum
> Corpora iunguntur, faciesque inducitur illis
> Una.

(For their two bodies, joined together as they were, were merged in one, with one face and form for both.)

79. *Fersa*, 'scourge', i.e., the hot summer sun.

85. The navel.

95. *Phars.*, IX, 763 ff. and 790 ff. Sabellus as the result of being bitten by a little snake in the desert, melts away like snow. Nasidius, who has been poisoned by another serpent, swells into a shapeless globe and bursts his armor.

97. *Met.*, IV, 576 ff.; V, 572 ff.

101. Two individuals, in Dante's narrative, exchange their substance.

107. The legs grow together into a tail.

133. Cf. *Met.*, IV, 586–589 (Cadmus changed into a serpent):

> Ille quidem vult plura loqui, sed lingua repente
> In partes est fissa duas, nec verba volenti
> Sufficiunt, quotiensque aliquos parat edere questus,
> Sibilat: hanc illi vocem natura reliquit.

(He wanted to say much more, but his tongue was of a sudden cleft in two; words failed him, and whenever he tried to utter some sad complaint, it was a hiss; this was the only voice which Nature left him.)

Cf. *Met.*, I, 233, 637–638; II, 667–669; IV, 412–413.

135. 'The smoke stops,' bringing the transformation to an abrupt close. With similar abruptness the preceding metamorphosis ended, in l. 78.

138. The one, trying to speak, produces a hiss; the other tries to hiss, but can only spit and speak. Human saliva was thought to be poisonous to snakes.

140. The man turns his "new back" upon the serpent and addresses *l' altro*, the third of the original three and the only one that has not been transformed. *Buoso* is the new snake: according to some of the old commentators he is the nephew of Buoso Donati (cf. XXX, 44); according to others, Buoso degli Abati.

142. The transmutation of shapes in this 7th hollow reminds the poet of the shifting of ballast to and fro in the hold of a ship.

144. Cf. XXXI, 24; the meaning is obscure. But see Singleton (1970) for a possible interpretation.

148. As the two run away, Dante recognizes the unchanged one as Puccio Sciancato de' Galigai, a Ghibelline, banished from Florence in 1268.

151. "The other," originally the second snake, was Francesco, nicknamed Guercio de' Cavalcanti, killed for his misdeeds by the people of Gaville, a village on the upper Arno. Gaville mourns because of the vengeance taken for his death.

Canto XXVI

Argument

Once more a respite is afforded from the oppressiveness of Malebolge. Ulysses tells of his last journey, and his sea story breaks in upon the grim nightmare like a whiff of fresh breeze. This "mad flight" of the Ithacan out into the great waters seems to be essentially an invention of our poet. Although Solinus records an old tradition that Ulysses sailed into the Atlantic and founded Lisbon, and Claudian mentions a voyage to a land of shades in that part of Gaul which projects farthest into the ocean, their tales have almost nothing in common with his. Dante's imagination must have been stirred by the adventures of St. Brendan in his search for the Isles of the Blest, and by other yarns of wondrous voyages and expeditions to the Earthly Paradise; but he imitates none of them in this narrative. Homer he had not read.

Ulysses is found in the eighth *bolgia*, among evil counselors, those who applied their burning eloquence to the concealment of their real mind. They are completely enveloped in tongues of fire, which "steal" them from sight, just as in life their flaming speech cunningly hid their thought. Fire, the symbol of divine anger, is an appropriate punishment, because their sin consists in the misuse of superior mental power, the direct gift of God, who breathes into men at birth the intellective soul endowed with greater or less keenness of intelligence according to his grace. Dante, one of the most favored in this respect, manifests particular interest in the fate of his intellectual compeers and warns himself against falling into the error that wrought their destruction.

7. It was an ancient and popular belief that dreams occurring just before dawn would come true: cf. *Purg.* IX, 16–18. The poet seems to regard the present time of depravity as a dark night, to be followed ere long (as he repeatedly attests) by a better day. His prophecy is conceived just as the new morrow is about to dawn. According to Parodi the new light is to dawn with Henry VII.

9. *Prato* is a little town near Florence: thou shalt feel the grief which even thy nearest neighbors wish thee, not to mention thine enemies. Parodi thinks the reference must be to a recent event: on April 6, 1309, Prato expelled the Neri, and, shortly after, was punished for it.

12. The poet's mood changes from vindictiveness to tenderness.

13. The 'stairs' lead from the bank to the top of the ridge; they consist of 'bourns,' or rocky projections. Having climbed the ridge, the travelers pursue their way over the 8th arch.

23. The 'something better' is divine grace.

25. In this pretty simile of the fireflies, the season that is indicated (ll. 26–27) is the summer solstice, the hour (l. 28) is dusk.

34. Elisha (2 Kings ii, 23–24).

35. 'Elijah': 2 Kings ii, 9–12.

42. Dante conceives of these flames as stealing, i.e., secreting, the sinners contained within them.

54. Eteŏcles and Polynīces, the rival sons of Oedipus, contending for the possession of Thebes, killed each other. When their bodies were burned on the same pyre, the flames divided into two peaks. *Theb.*, XII, 420 ff. Cf. *Phars.*, I, 551–552:

> Scinditur in partes, geminoque cacumine surgit,
> Thebanos imitata rogos.

(... split into two and rose, like the pyre of the Thebans, with double crest).

57. Ulysses and Diomed, two of the leading heroes of the Trojan war, go together in their punishment, as they went together to expose themselves to divine wrath.

59. 'The ambush of the horse': the wooden horse full of Greek warriors, which the Trojans were persuaded to take into the city. By this means Troy was destroyed, and Aeneas and his followers, who afterward founded the Roman stock, had to flee: *Aen.*, II, 13 ff. In Virgil's account, Diomed has no share in this enterprise.

61. Thetis, to save her son Achilles from the war, disguised him as a girl and entrusted him to King Lycomedes of Scyros; there he won the love of the king's daughter Deidamīa and promised that he would be true to her. Discovered by Ulysses and Diomed, he departed with them to the war and forgot his promise. Deidamīa now mourns in the Limbus: *Purg.* XXII, 114. The story is related by Statius in the *Achilleid*, II, 15 ff.

63. Ulysses and Diomed stole the Palladium, an image of Pallas, on which the fate of Troy depended: *Aen.*, II, 162 ff.

74. From these lines and XXVII, 33, it may be inferred that Virgil thought himself less remote than Dante from the ancient Greeks, and more likely to influence them. Moreover, Dante thought of himself as by remote descent a Trojan, while Virgil came from a city of Greek origin.

80. Virgil assumes that he has immortalized Ulysses and Diomed in his *Aeneid*.

91. Circe, daughter of the sun, was a sorceress who turned men into beasts: *Aen.*, VII, 10 ff. Ulysses visited her and compelled her to restore her victims to human form: *Met.*, XIV, 245 ff.

92. *Aeneas* named the place in memory of his nurse Caieta, who had died there: *Aen.*, VII, 1 ff.; *Met.*, XIV, 441 ff.

103. Ulysses explores both shores of the Mediterranean, and its islands.

108. The pillars of Hercules, on either side of the Strait of Gibraltar.

112. Cf. the speech of Aeneas beginning 'O socii': *Aen.*, I, 198 ff.

117. 'The world without men' is the Hemisphere of Water.

124. They turn their stern to the morning and sail forth, constantly gaining on the left; that is, their course is not due west, but southwest.

128. Our northern pole; when they pass the equator, the North Star sinks below the 'sea level.'

130. They have sailed five months.

131. 'The light beneath the moon' may mean the moonlight on the water or the light which is on the underside of the moon (i.e., the side turned toward the earth).

133. Doubtless the mountain of Purgatory, directly opposite Jerusalem, in the middle of the Hemisphere of Water, but this will be known only later. For the moment the very fact that there *is* such a mountain in the so-called "Hemisphere of Water" should be as much a surprise to the reader as it is to Ulysses!

140. For the description of the shipwreck, cf. *Aen.*, I, 113–117:

> Unam, quae Lycios fidumque vehebat Oronten,
> Ipsius ante oculos ingens a vertice pontus
> In puppim ferit; excutitur pronusque magister
> Volvitur in caput; ast illam ter fluctus ibidem
> Torquet agens circum, et rapidus vorat aequore vertex.

(One, which bore the Lycians and loyal Orontes, before the eyes of Aeneas a mighty toppling wave strikes astern. The helmsman is dashed out and hurled head foremost, but the ship is thrice on the same spot whirled round and round by the wave and engulfed in the sea's devouring eddy.)

Canto XXVII

Argument

Guido da Montefeltro, the great Ghibelline general, was one of the foremost Italians of the 13th century. He was famous for his valor, wisdom, courtesy, and especially for his skill in strategy, which won for him the name of "fox." Dante's story of his final seduction by Boniface VIII, to whom he was induced, by promise of absolution, to give the evil counsel of taking Palestrina by false pledges, is corroborated by the chronicle of Pipino, written in 1314. The discovery of this early account would seem to settle the much debated question whether the incident was invented by the poet.

What Dante probably did invent was the struggle between Heaven and Hell for the possession of Guido's soul. St. Francis of Assisi, to whose order Guido belonged, claims the departing spirit; but he is opposed by "one of the black cherubim," who, after a brief discussion, is victorious. Such a conflict occurs in the *Commedia* in only one other case, that of Guido's son Buonconte, whose tale is told in *Purg.* V, 88 ff. In both instances the theme is introduced to emphasize an important doctrine, namely, that the eternal fate of a soul depends on its intrinsic condition at the moment of death. Though absolved by a Pope, Guido had not genuinely repented of his last misdeed, and therefore the absolution was invalid.   Buonconte, on the other hand, though neglectful of his religious duties during life, has, when mortally wounded, an instant of true repentance and love of God, and thus wins salvation.   The two contrasted examples are as extreme as the poet could contrive them, and they are the more striking in that the two men are father and son.

3. The words of the permission are given in l. 21.

7. The brazen Sicilian bull, made by Perillus of Athens for Phalăris, tyrant of Agrigentum, was so constructed that the shrieks of victims burned within it sounded like the bellowing of a real beast.   Phalaris tried it first on its maker, Perillus.   The story is told by Paulus Orosius; it is mentioned also by Pliny, Valerius Maximus, Cicero, and Ovid.

13. This line and the next are obscure.   Perhaps they mean: "Thus, having no outlet nor escape from their source in the fire (i.e., the soul, from which they emanate), the dreary words were converted into its language (the language of the fire).'   The vibrations of the soul's tongue are imparted to the fire, and little by little set the whole flame to oscillating like a great tongue.

21. There is nothing peculiarly "Lombard" in this sentence, unless it is *istra* for *issa = mo*; perhaps Dante meant to give only the Tuscan equivalent of what Virgil really said, or perhaps the suggestion of Lombardy lay in his accent.   Dante believed that the popular dialects, though constantly changing, reached far back into antiquity and that they had always existed side by side with the "grammatical language," or Latin; so Virgil, being of Lombard parentage, might appropriately enough speak in his local dialect.   Possibly, as Del Lungo suggests, *Lombardo* here means only 'Italian.'

28. Romagna is the region lying between the Po, the Apennines, the Adriatic, and the Reno.

30. 'The range from which the Tiber springs' is Monte Coronaro.   The county of Monte-feltro lies between Urbino and the Tuscan Apennines.

39. In April, 1299, the parties, townships, and usurping tyrants of Romagna, after 25 years' strife, concluded a peace.

41. The Polenta family had ruled Ravenna since 1275, when Guido (father of Francesca da Rimini) returned there with his Guelfs.   The family arms contained an eagle.

42. Cervia, a small but important town on the Adriatic near Ravenna was subject to the Polenta family for several years.

43. 'The city' is Forlì, head of the Ghibelline league in Romagna.   In 1281–1282 it resisted a long siege by the French and the Guelfs sent by Pope Martin IV.   In May, 1282, the in-habitants, led by Guido da Montefeltro, issued forth and defeated the besiegers with great slaughter.   In 1300 it was ruled by the Ordelaffi, who had in their arms a lion, green in the upper half.   Dante is thought to have been in Forlì in 1303 and 1310.

46. The 'old mastiff' is Malatesta da Verrucchio, lord of Rimini, father of Gian Ciotto and Paolo.   The 'young mastiff' is Malatestino, another son of Malatesta.

47. In 1296 Malatesta defeated the Ghibelline forces of Rimini and captured their leader Montagna.   At the instigation of his father, Malatestino murdered the prisoner.

48. Cf. Pr. xxx, 14: "There is a generation, whose teeth are as swords, and their jaw teeth as knives, to devour the poor from off the earth."

49. Faenza, on the Lamone, and Imola, near the Santerno, were ruled by Maghinardo di Pagano da Susinana, who bore a blue lion on a white field.   He was known as "the lion" and "the demon" (*Purg.* XIV, 118), and was notorious for his many changes of party, being Guelf on the south side of the Apennines, Ghibelline on the north side.

52. Cesena, on the Savio, preserved the forms of municipal self-government, but was ruled, from 1296 to 1300, by a boss, Galasso da Montefeltro, a cousin of Guido.

67. In his old age Guido became a 'cord wearer,' i.e., a Franciscan friar.

75. Cf. Cicero, *De Officiis*, I, 13 (also *Inf.* XI, 23–27).

78. Cf. Ps. xix, 4: 'and their words to the end of the world.'

83. 'I gave myself to God,' I became a friar.

85. Boniface VIII, who was waging war at home, close to his Lateran palace, with the Colonna family. In 1297 he excommunicated them and summoned them to surrender, but they entrenched themselves in their strongholds of Palestrina and Zagarolo. Palestrina, about 24 miles from Rome and visible from the Lateran hill, was surrendered to Boniface on false promises and then demolished. The Colonna family — among them two cardinals — had refused to recognize Boniface's election.

89. Not one of them had been a renegade to help the Saracens take Acre in 1291. The fall of Acre, the last bulwark of Christendom in the East, filled Europe with consternation; and Pope Nicholas IV exhorted the coast towns not to traffic with the lands of the Sultan. Six years later, Boniface was proclaiming a crusade against Christians.

92. The Franciscan girdle, 'which used (in the good old times) to make its wearers lean.'

94. Pope Sylvester I, who had taken refuge on Mt. Soracte, near Rome, was sought out, according to the legend, to cure the Emperor Constantine of leprosy; this he did by baptism. In return for this cure the donation of Constantine was made.

101. This is the important point, for the Pope promises that he gives absolution in advance. *Finor* also anticipates that the counsel requested will be fraudulent, and therefore sinful. — The formal words of absolution in Latin are *Ego te absolvo*.

102. *Penestrino = Palestrina* (birthplace of the famous composer).

105. Celestine V, who renounced the papacy (III, 60; XIX, 56), for which Boniface worked so hard. These words are spoken in bitter mockery.

119. One cannot repent without renunciation of the will.

125. Cf. V, 11–12.

127. Cf. XXVI, 41–42.

136. 'To those who make a load by separating': usually a load is made by putting together; but the sowers of discord, who occupy the next *bolgia*, make up their burden of sin by putting asunder those who were united.

Canto XXVIII

Argument

An involved simile, at the beginning of this canto, calls up the picture of a vast accumulation of maimed bodies gathered, through the centuries, from the many battlefields of southern Italy. Even this mangled host conveys but a faint idea of the ninth *bolgia*. Creators of strife are here hacked by the sword of a fiend as they pass by; their horribly dissevered state represents the life of bloodshed and dissension which they loved. Conspicuous among them are Mahomet, the Roman Curio, Mosca de' Lamberti of Florence, and the Provençal warrior-poet Bertran de Born.

Some of Dante's contemporaries believed Mahomet to have been originally not only a Christian, but a cardinal and an aspirant to the papacy. The poet, then, was justified in regarding him and his son-in-law Alì as the leaders of a great schism in the Christian Church.

The tribune Curio, banished from Rome, fled to Caesar, who was hesitating on the bank of the Rubicon, and "sunk the doubt" within him by urging him to march on the capital. The event is narrated by Lucan in *Pharsalia*, I, 266 ff. He now wishes he had never seen Rimini, near which town the Rubicon empties into the Adriatic.

In 1215 a Buondelmonte, who was betrothed to a lady of the Amidei family, was induced to jilt her and appear on his wedding day with a bride from the house of the Donati. The Amidei came together to discuss the best way to avenge this affront. Some advised inflicting on Buondelmonte a beating or a wound in the face. Mosca, however, affirmed that such an attack would result in more harm to the aggressors than to the victim. "Cosa fatta capo ha," he declared — "a thing once done has an end": if we do him a hurt, let it be a final one. The Amidei followed his counsel and murdered the offender. Hence arose the feud between the families and, according to local tradition, the first conflict between Guelfs and Ghibellines in Florence. The Lamberti, to whom Mosca belonged, were afterward banished from the city and never allowed to return.

Bertran de Born was a Provençal poet of the latter part of the 12th century. To further his private ends, he took advantage of the disputes and wars of Henry II of England and his two elder sons, Henry and Richard, who had extensive possessions in southern France. According to his old Provençal biography, which considerably exaggerates his political importance, Bertran was active in fomenting their quarrels, and formed a close friendship with the younger Henry. This prince was crowned in his father's lifetime and was consequently known as 'the young English king.' His early death in 1183 was mourned by Bertran in verse that gained wide renown.

9. The name Apulia was often given to all the continental part of the Kingdom of Naples.

10. 'On account of the Trojans,' i.e., the Romans, whose ancestors came from Troy: the allusion is to the conquest of the Samnites by the Romans, perhaps also to the defeat of Pyrrhus. The 'long war' is the Second Punic War, led by Hannibal against Rome. Livy in XXV, xii, records an old prophecy: "Amnem, Troiugena, fuge Cannam" (Flee the river Canna, thou descendant of Troy.)

11. It was said that after the battle of Cannae Hannibal's troops took from the dead Romans more than three bushels of rings — or (the 'unerring Livy' adds, XXXIII, 12), according to a report nearer the truth, about one bushel.

14. Robert Guiscard, the Norman conqueror who overran southern Italy in the 11th century and became Duke of Apulia.

15. Those slain in the battle of Benevento, in 1266, where Manfred, son of Frederick II, was defeated by Charles of Anjou and killed. In reality there was no fight at Ceprano; the first encounter was at S. Germano. Dante apparently followed, with several chroniclers, a false report. Manfred was deserted by the Apulian troops at Benevento; but the Apulian reputation for inconstancy antedates the battle. Giacomino Pugliese, before this, had conspired against Frederick II.

17. At Tagliacozzo, in 1268, the Imperial forces were again defeated by Charles of Anjou,

and Conradin, nephew of Manfred and grandson of Frederick, was captured. The victory was due to the strategy of an elderly French general, Érard de Valéry; he won by his wit rather than by his sword.

24. Cleft from chin to anus.

32. 'Ali': the husband of Mahomet's favorite daughter, and one of his most zealous followers.

55. Fra Dolcino, as he was generally called (though not a friar), became the leader of the heretical sect called the Apostolic Brethren, whose aim was to bring the Church and mankind back to a state of primitive simplicity. He made many converts in northern Italy. A crusade having been proclaimed against him by Clement V, he took refuge, in the winter of 1306, in the stronghold of Zebello, where he was besieged for three months and finally taken, after three days' fighting. He was put to death in Novara. According to Dante's version, he was obliged by snow and famine to surrender.

59. The people of Novara.

61. Mahomet is so eager to give this warning that he speaks while his foot is partly up-lifted to depart.

73. Of this acquaintance of the poet, little is known. Medicina is a little town near Bologna. The *dolce piano* is the plain of the Po, sloping from Vercelli to the stronghold of Marcabò, near Ravenna.

77. Guido del Cassero and Agnolello di Carignano belonged to opposing factions in the town of Fano; almost nothing else is known of them, nor have we any other information about the crime here predicted. The date is put conjecturally at 1312.

80. *Mazzera* means a bunch of stones fastened to a tunny net and suggests the precise manner of their drowning, i.e., in a sack weighted with stones. — *Cattolica*: a place on the Adriatic between Rimini and Pesaro.

82. From one end of the Mediterranean to the other.

84. 'Argolic people,' i.e., Greeks, famous of old as sea robbers.

85. Malatestino (XXVII, 46) had only one eye.

86. *Terra*: Rimini. — *Tale*: Curio (cf. l. 102).

87. Wishes he had never seen: cf. XVIII, 42.

90. They need offer no vow or prayer to the wind of Focara, i.e., they need have no fear of being shipwrecked, because they will be already drowned. The squalls which blew from Focara (near 'la Cattolica') were dangerous to sailors.

93. That is, the one who wishes he had never seen Rimini: cf. l. 87.

98. 'The man prepared has always lost by delay (endured waiting to his loss)' is a paraphrase of the words of Curio in *Phars.*, I, 281: "semper nocuit differre paratis" (delay is ever fatal to those who are prepared).

132. Cf. Lamentations i, 12: "behold, and see if there be any sorrow like unto my sorrow."

135. The great weight of manuscript evidence is in favor of the reading *re Giovanni*, instead of *re giovane*, and it must be confessed that *Giovanni* makes a much smoother line. But Bertran's relations were with Henry II and his oldest son, also named Henry, and commonly called "the young king"; he had dealings also with Richard (afterward Richard I), but none with John (subsequently King John). Either Dante or his first copyists must have made a blunder: inasmuch as there is every reason to believe that Dante was familiar with Bertran's poems and the Provençal biography of him, we may confidently ascribe the mistake to the copyists. At that time *giovane* and *Giovanni* might be spelled exactly alike. In the north Italian versions of the story the young king is referred to as "Roi Johans."

138. For the story of Absalom and Ahithophel, see Samuel xiv–xviii.

141. The "source" of the brain is the spinal column.

142. The law of retaliation, according to which the penalties are meted out in Hell. Cf. Exod. xxi, 24; Levit. xxiv, 20; Deut. xix, 21; Mat. v. 38.

Canto XXIX

Argument

The sight of the sowers of discord exercises a curious fascination on the beholder, who gazes on their "strange wounds" with "drunken eyes" until he is brought to his senses by a reproof from Virgil.   In other words, Dante, who was himself prone to strife, in his contemplation of this sin is beginning to feel more satisfaction than abhorrence, and needs to be warned by Reason that he is not meditating in the proper spirit.   A similar lapse is described at the end of the next canto. Dante attempts to justify his eagerness by the statement that he was searching for the shade of Geri del Bello, a first cousin of his father, who is punished in this ditch.   The early commentators give Geri a black character; but we really know little of him except that his house was damaged by the Ghibellines in 1260, that he received compensation for it from the Guelfs in 1269, and that he was killed by one of the Sacchetti.   The resulting feud between the families was ended by a reconciliation in 1342.   In 1300 his death, to Dante's shame, was still unavenged. Vengeance for a relative's murder was regarded, in spite of Christian teaching, as a part of a gentleman's duty.   This doctrine is explicitly laid down by Brunetto Latini in his *Tesoretto*, XVIII.

The 10th valley — the last of Malebolge — contains falsifiers of all kinds. Those described fall into four classes: falsifiers of metals, or alchemists; falsifiers of persons, or impersonators; falsifiers of coin, or counterfeiters; falsifiers of words, or liars.   It is to be noted that the alchemists here confined are damned as cheats, not as disturbers of God's creation.   The sin of all these culprits is symbolized by devastating disease, which alters their appearance: as they tried to change the aspect of things, so are they transformed by loathsome maladies.

9. We learn from XXX, 86, that the 10th and last *bolgia* is 11 miles in circumference.   These figures do not afford a clue for any further computations; they give, however, an impression of exactness, and they indicate a near approach to the center of the earth; furthermore, they suggest by contrast the vast dimensions of the upper circles.   The number 22 was one that would naturally occur to Dante in speaking of a circle, because the relation of circumference to diameter was expressed by the ratio of 22 to 7.

10. The moon being under their feet, the sun must be over their heads: it is about noon in Jerusalem.

22. 'Let not thy thought shatter itself upon him,' like a missile hurled violently at something hard.

29. *Altaforte*, or Hautefort (Provençal *Autafort*), was the castle of Bertran de Born.

33. By any of his relatives.

36. The thought of Geri's just grievance against him makes Dante more compassionate.

38. The 10th *bolgia*.

39. '(And) if there were more light, (would reveal it) quite to the bottom.'

40. *Chiostra* means 'enclosure' and also 'cloister'; the latter sense suggests the 'lay brothers' (*conversi*) of l. 41.

46. The swampy Valdichiana and Maremma (in eastern and western Tuscany) and the fens of Sardinia were noted haunts of malaria in the hot season.

52. The farther, inner bank of the 10th and last *bolgia*. The poets climb down, on the left, from the ridge to the bank itself, they do not mount the ridge again.

57. On earth.

58–59. A pest sent by Juno carried off the inhabitants and even the animals that occupied the island of Aegina; afterward, at the prayer of Aeacus, the sole survivor, Jupiter restored the population by turning ants into men: *Met.* VII, 518 ff.

66. 'Stacks,' 'shocks,' as of sheaves of grain piled one on another in the field. Cf. IX, 78.

78. One who is in a hurry to get to bed.

89. Evidently this constitutes a formula of adjuration: cf. X, 82.

97. 'Support,' of the two invalids who are propped against each other, like pans propped against each other, that is, on top of a stove, to dry (ll. 73–74).

99. 'On the rebound': who caught the words that were directed at the two lepers.

109. Most of the early commentators give the name of the speaker as Griffolino; a "Maestro Griffolino da Arezzo" is attested in Bologna in 1259. Albero da Siena belonged to a rich and noble family and was alive as late as 1294; nothing more is known of him.

111. One of the early commentators, Jacopo della Lana, says that Griffolino was burned for heresy. But what brings him here is alchemy.

116. Because I did not teach him to fly like Daedalus. Cf. XVII, 109.

117. 'By a certain man': the early commentators say it was the bishop of Siena. The latter part of the line probably means: 'who loved him (Albero) as a son.'

122. The foolishness of the Sienese was a standing joke in the rival city of Florence. A headless nail is there called a *chiodo senese*.

124. We learn in l. 136 that 'the other leper' is Capocchio. *Intese*, 'heard.'

125. *Stricca*: probably Giovanni Stricca de' Salimbeni, mayor of Bologna in 1276 and 1286.

127. *Niccolò*, said to be a brother of Stricca. Capocchio calls him the inventor of the 'costly fashion of the clove,' that is, apparently, the one who introduced into Siena the use of cloves as a spice. Cloves, which were imported from the East, paid a heavy duty.

129. 'The garden where such seed takes root' is Siena, where a foolish custom, once started, is bound to thrive.

130. Excepting also the *brigata spendereccia*, or Spendthrifts' Club, recorded from 1260 to 1275, a group of young men who vied with one another in extravagance.

131. *Caccia d'Ascian* is perhaps the poet known as Caccia da Siena.

132. *L'Abbagliato*: a nickname of Bartolommeo Folcacchieri, a brother of the poet Folcacchiero. He held important offices, and lived as late as 1300. — This line may be ironical, as it is generally taken, or it may be that Bartolommeo vainly tried to suppress the Club.

136. Capocchio was burned alive in Siena in 1293.

138. If thou art really the man I think.

Canto XXX

Argument

False impersonation is represented by Myrrha of Cyprus and Gianni Schicchi of Florence; counterfeiting, by the counts of Romena and their agent, Master Adam; lying, by Potiphar's wife and Sinon the Greek. Before leaving this valley, Dante, listening to a vulgar altercation, shows the same weakness for which he was rebuked in the preceding canto.

1. Juno was enraged at the royal family of Thebes on account of the love of Jupiter and Semĕle, daughter of Cadmus, the founder and king of that city. Cf. *Met.*, III, 253 ff.

3. The two instances are the destruction of Semele and the tragic incident that follows (*Met.*, IV, 512 ff).

5. Ino, sister of Semele and nurse of Bacchus, Semele's child by Jupiter. Ino and Athămas had two children, Learchus and Melicerta.

15. Cf. *Met.*, XIII, 404: "Troia simul Priamusque cadunt." (Troy fell and Priam with it.)

16. After the fall of Troy, Hecuba and her daughter Polyxĕna were carried away as slaves. On the way to Greece Polyxĕna was slain as a victim on the tomb of Achilles, to whom she had been promised. Hecuba's son, Polydorus, who had been entrusted to Polymestor, king of Thrace, was murdered by him and thrown into the sea. As the unhappy mother went to wash from her hands the blood of Polyxĕna, she saw the corpse of her son on the shore. In her frenzy she tore out Polymestor's eyes, and, when she tried to speak, began to bark. Cf. *Met.*, XIII, 399–575.

22. No furies (such as possessed Athamas and Hecuba) were ever beheld possessing anyone, beast or man, equal in cruelty to the furies that possessed two pallid shades in the 10th *bolgia*.

34. Formula of adjuration: cf. X, 82.

38. Myrrha was the daughter of Cinyras, king of Cyprus, mentioned in Ep. VII. Cf. *Met.*, X, 298 ff.

42. Schicchi, a famous mimic, belonged to the house of Cavalcanti. According to the story, Buoso Donati, a wealthy Guelf, bequeathed a small part of his property to churches and monasteries. To prevent the execution of this will, his nephew Simone concealed his death and engaged Gianni to impersonate the dying Buoso. This he did successfully, dictating a new will ("and giving it due form") and bequeathing to himself, Gianni Schicchi, a fine mare (or, as others say, a mule) — "the queen of the herd."

49. This dropsical spirit, if he had had his legs cut off at the groin, would have looked, with his monstrous belly and small head and neck, like a lute set on the ground.

61. This 'Master Adam' was a follower of the counts of Romena. In 1281 he was burned as a counterfeiter in Florence.

63. Cf. the "rich man" in Luke xvi, 24.

65. The Casentino is a district in the mountains at the head of the Arno. Dante was there in 1289 and in 1311. The ruins of the Castle of Romena are still to be seen on a hill beside the river.

74. This coin, first minted in 1253, had on one side the image of John the Baptist, who was the patron of Florence, on the other the lily flower from which it derived its name.

77. The counts of Romena, at whose instigation he committed the crime. They were head over ears in debt. Guido died in 1292; Alessandro and two other brothers, Aghinolfo and Ildebrando, were still alive in 1300. A rather perfunctory letter attributed to Dante (Epistle II) consoles the sons of Aghinolfo for the death of Alessandro.

78. *Fonte Branda*: Perhaps the reference here is to the celebrated fountain at Siena (mention of which occurs as early as 1081), situated at the foot of the hill upon which the church of San Domenico stands; the fountain was so called after the Brandi family, to whom the site at one time belonged. However, another fountain of the same name (now almost dry, but the existence of which is attested to by its mention in ancient documents), near the castle of Romena and thus much closer than Siena to the scene of Master Adam's crime, may be the one alluded to. The early commentators take the reference to be to the Fonte Branda at Siena, but this may be because it was better known.

87. The valley is not less than half a mile across; it must be very much wider than some of the *bolge*, perhaps in compensation for its small circumference.

90. His florins were 21 carats fine, instead of 24.

93. Dante speaks of the huge belly as if it were a territory.

97. For the story of Joseph and Potiphar's wife, see Gen. xxxix, 6–20.

98. Sinon, pretending to be a fugitive from the Greeks, persuaded the Trojans to take the wooden horse into the city: cf. *Aen.*, II, 57 ff.   Priam said to him (*Aen.*, II, 148–149):

> Quisquis es, amissos hinc iam obliviscere Graios;
> Noster eris.

(Whoever thou art, from henceforth forget the Greeks thou hast lost; thou shalt be ours.) So he is called derisively "of Troy."

114. Cf. *Aen.*, II, 149–152.

128. 'Narcissus's glass' is water, in which he saw himself mirrored: *Met.*, III, 407 ff.

140–141. Virgil here, as elsewhere, can read Dante's thoughts, so that Dante, in his dumbness, is "excusing himself" by his unexpressed remorse.

Canto XXXI

Argument

As the poets cross the broad bank that intervenes between the tenth *bolgia* and the great central pit of Hell, Dante sees looming through the dusk, like the towers of a city, the forms of giants, visible from the waist up all around the mouth of the well.   As far as we can judge, they are from sixty to eighty feet in total height.   But the apparently precise dimensions given are vague to us, because of the variability of standards: one creature measures from neck to middle thirty palms, probably something like twenty feet; another, five ells, perhaps some thirty feet.   One of these monsters, Antaeus, picks up the travelers and sets them on the ice at the bottom of the hole.   Dante speaks as if he did so without quitting his post; nothing but the giant's stoop is described, as he lifts them up, and his straightening when he has put them down.   We are told, however, that, unlike his mates, he is not bound.   Now, inasmuch as the last *bolgia* is eleven miles in circumference, and inasmuch as the poets walk for some time over the plain of ice before seeing, in the middle of it, the enormous figure of Lucifer, we must think of this pit as at least a mile wide; and since it is described in XVIII, 5, as "un pozzo assai largo e *profondo*," it can hardly be less than twice as deep as it is broad.   It is obvious, then, that the giants, the upper half of whose bodies appear above the edge, cannot be standing on the bottom: their feet must rest on a ledge or shelf near the top of the wall; in fact, in XXXII, 16–17, we are told that, when Dante and Virgil were on the bottom of the "pozzo scuro," they were, "sotto i piè del gigante assai più bassi."   Antaeus, therefore, carrying the poets, must have left his place and climbed down the precipice; but of this descent our author, for reasons of his own, says not a word.   Perhaps he conceived of himself as so terrified that he could recall nothing of the adventure but its awful beginning and end.   It is likely, too, that he preferred to leave a gap for the reason set forth in the argument to Canto V.

We do not know how many giants there are in all.   Those named are Nimrod, Ephialtes, Briareus, and Antaeus — all, except the last, damned for their presumption in attempting to scale Heaven.   Ephialtes and Briareus were among the most active at Phlegra, when the giants piled mountain upon mountain and threatened the Gods.   This combat is mentioned by Ovid (*Met.*, I, 151–155), Statius (*Theb.*, II, 595–596), and Lucan (*Phars.*, IV, 593–597); and the two latter authorities speak of Briareus.   Ephialtes is not named by any of the ancient poets that Dante seems to have known, but he is to be found in Servius's commentary on the *Georgics*, I, 180.   Antaeus, so Lucan tells us (*Phars.*, IV, 597), did not participate in the fight, and therefore he is unbound in Dante's Hell; in *Phars.*, IV, 593 ff., his misdeeds and his defeat by Hercules are related at length.   The "fable" of the battle of Phlegra doubtless represented to Dante merely the old pagan sages' idea of the revolt of the angels; the giants are stricken down by "il sommo Giove," the supreme Power.   The Biblical Nimrod, then, is not out of place among them.   The following particulars are culled from Gen. x, 8–10, and xi, 2–9, also vi, 4: "And Cush begat Nimrod: he began to be a mighty one in the earth.   He was a mighty hunter before the Lord. ... And the beginning of his kingdom was Babel, and Erech, and Accad, in the land of Shinar. ... And it came to pass ... that they found a plain in the land of Shinar; and they dwelt there. ... And they said, Go to, let us build us a city and a tower, whose top may reach unto heaven. ... So the Lord scattered them abroad from thence upon the face of all the earth: and they left off to build the city.   Therefore is the name of it called Babel."   Nimrod, then, was held responsible for the audacious enterprise, and as early as Orosius and St. Augustine he was regarded by Christians as a giant.   According to *De Vulgari Eloquentia*, I, vii, 4, it was "sub persuasione gigantis" that man presumed to surpass his maker.   In the confusion of tongues Dante's Nimrod has suffered more than his misguided fellows, for he speaks a language understood by no one else and can comprehend no other soul.   His mind, too, is as dazed as his words are senseless.   He can vent his feelings only by blowing the big horn with which, as a "mighty hunter," he is equipped.

The manifold crimes of the Lower Hell are due to pride and envy, and these sins are personified in Satan and the giants.   Embedded in the central point of his kingdom, the arch-sinner, surrounded by a ring of fellow rebels, holds his eternal court.   The spirits that thought to rise so high are sunken at the bottom of the universe; their monstrous forms are fixed and impotent forevermore. This, rather than the Circle of Violence, is artistically their fit place; and here, no doubt, Dante would have put them, even if Virgil had not pointed the way (*Aen.*, VI, 580–581):

> hic genus antiquum Terrae, Titania pubes
> fulmine deiecti fundo volvuntur in imo.

(Here the ancient sons of Earth, the Titan's brood, hurled down by the thunderbolt, writhe in the lowest abyss.)

4. Virgil's tongue has the same power as the magic spear of Achilles and his father Peleus, which could both wound and cure: *Met.*, XII, 112, XXIII, 171; *Tristia*, V, 2, 15-18; *Remedia Amoris*, 47. In Provençal and early Italian poetry there are many references to this spear; it was believed in the Middle Ages that a hurt inflicted by it could be healed only by another wound from the same weapon.

14. It attracted my eyes to one spot, and my sight went out toward that place, following (in the opposite direction) the course of the sound that came from it.

16. At Roncesvalles Charlemagne lost his rear guard, led by his peers (the 'blessed band') under the command of his nephew Roland. When all was lost, Roland blew his horn so loud that it was heard thirty leagues away: *Chanson de Roland*, ll. 1753-1757.

24. On several different occasions Virgil warns Dante against overhasty judgment and impatient curiosity. Cf. *Inf.* III, 76-81.

41. Montereggioni, a strong castle built by the Sienese, early in the 13th century, on a hill not far from the city, was surrounded by a circle of very high walls surmounted by twelve towers. The bases of the towers are still to be seen on the circular wall of the ruins. See illustration in Singleton (1970).

45. Because of their attack upon Heaven: cf. *Met.*, I, 151 ff.

49. I.e., ceased to produce such destructive creatures.

52. Nature continues to produce elephants and whales, but they have no intelligence and therefore are harmless. Her suppression of giants, then, shows fine discrimination.

59. A pine cone of gilt bronze, originally perhaps ten or eleven feet in height, which is said to have been one of the adornments of the Mausoleum of Hadrian, stood in Dante's day in the forecourt of St. Peter's, and is now to be seen, in a somewhat mutilated condition, in the court of the Vatican. See Singleton (1970).

61. The bank covered them — 'was an apron to them' — from the waist down. *Perizoma* is used in Gen. iii, 7: "fecerunt sibi perizomata" (made themselves aprons).

64. 'Three Frisians (standing on one another's shoulders) would have boasted in vain' that they could reach from the bank to the giant's hair. Frisians were noted for their tall stature.

67. These words have no meaning: cf. l. 81.

78. Cf. Gen. xi, 1: "And the whole earth was of one language, and of one speech."

89. I.e., the part visible above the edge of the cliff. The chain coils spirally around him.

95. Cf. XIV, 52-58. *Fer = fecero.*

98. *Thebaid*, II, 596: "immensus Briareus."

115. In the valley of Bagrăda, near Zama, Scipio conquered Hannibal.

118. *Phars.*, IV, 601-602:

> Haec illi spelunca domus; latuisse sub alta
> Rupe ferunt, epulas raptos habuisse leones.

(Yonder cave was his dwelling; men say that he hid beneath the towering cliff and feasted on the lions he had carried off.)

120. Cf. *Phars.*, IV, 596-597:

> Caeloque pepercit,
> Quod non Phlegraeis Antaeum sustulit arvis.

(And she dealt mercifully with the gods when she did not raise up Antaeus on the field of Phlegra.)

123. 'Where the cold locks Cocytus': at the bottom of the well, in the 9th circle, Cocytus is frozen into a plain of ice.

124. *Phars.*, IV, 595–596:

> Nec tam justa fuit terrarum gloria Typhon,
> Aut Tityos, Briareusque ferox.

(She had more cause to boast of him than of Typhon or Tityos and fierce Briareus.)

132. The story of the combat between Hercules and Antaeus is told in *Phars.*, IV, 609–653.

136. Bologna has two famous leaning towers. (See illustration p. 103.) The shorter but more inclined is called Garisenda or Carisenda; it was much taller in Dante's time. In 1286 the town demolished the buildings around it. Dante has left us a curious sonnet about these two towers; we find it copied by a Bolognese notary in 1287. Notaries of Bologna wrote in the empty spaces of their records scraps of Dante from 1287 to 1321: a part of the *canzone*, *Tre donne*, in 1310; bits of the *Inferno* in 1317. Pieces of the work of other poets are thus preserved for us.

137. To an observer standing beneath the overhang and looking upward, a cloud passing over the tower, in the direction opposite to its slope, makes the structure seem to be falling. Dante, in all probability, observed this phenomenon himself when he was in Bologna.

143. 'Set down,' on the 'bottom that swallows up Lucifer and Judas,' the 9th circle.

145. He rose like a mast that is being hoisted into its step on a ship. Possibly the meaning is 'rose high as a mast.'

Canto XXXII

Argument

The hardest, coldest heart is that of the traitor; from it all the warmth of human affection has been banished. The symbol of treachery is ice; and at the bottom of the well, buried in the circular plain formed by the freezing of Cocytus, are the sinners of the ninth and last circle. In the middle of the plain, at the center of the earth, is Lucifer or Satan, called Dis by the ancients. Ice is used as a means of punishment in other visions of Hell, and in the *Visio Alberici* we find a graded immersion in ice; but nowhere else has it the significance that our poem gives it. Dante's traitors have no desire to be remembered on earth: the best they can hope is to be forgotten. Their evil disposition is unchanged, and even in Hell they are eager to betray one another. The cold, cruel spirit that pervades their congregation communicates itself to the beholder; the mere thought of their odious crimes arouses an instinct of vindictiveness. Scorn and hatred possess Dante as he contemplates them, and he feels impelled to pay them in their own coin.

The traitors fall into four divisions, according to the relation between themselves and their victims. They are arranged in the round plain in four concentric circles; taking them in order, from circumference to middle, these rings are called *Caìna*, *Antenòra*, *Tolomèa* ('Ptolemea'), *Giudecca* ('Judecca'). They are distinguished only by the position of the sinners in the ice: in the first three the souls are embedded up to their heads; in the last, Giudecca, they are entirely

Torri degli Asinelli e Garisenda

The two towers, of which Garisenda is the shorter, still remain in Bologna. Below appears the artist's reconstruction of the *torri gentilizie* of medieval Bologna.

covered.   In Caina the heads are bowed down; in Antenora they are apparently erect; in Tolomea they are thrown back.   Caina contains traitors to kindred, Antenora traitors to country or party, Tolomea traitors to guests, Giudecca traitors to benefactors (or, according to Del Lungo, to constituted authorities). In all cases the treachery involves murder.   Caina and Giudecca are named respectively for Cain and Judas.   Antenora derives its title from the Trojan Antēnor, who bears an excellent character in the *Iliad*; in the later narratives, however, ascribed to Dares and Dictys and regarded in the Middle Ages as an authentic account, he figures as the archtraitor who hands over the Palladium to the Greeks (cf. Servius's commentary on *Aen.*, I, 242). Tolomea is so called after the Ptolemy of 1 Macc. xvi, 11–16, a captain of Jericho, who murdered his father-in-law and two brothers-in-law at a banquet to which he had invited them.

9. Nor one fit for a childish tongue.   An example of rhetorical understatement, or litotes.

10. The Muses, thanks to whom Amphion's lyre charmed the rocks to move and form the walls of Thebes.   Cf. Horace, *Ars Poetica*, 394 ff.; *Thebaid*, X, 873 ff.

19. The two brothers who thus address Dante from the ice are, as we learn presently, the counts of Mangona.

26. The Danube in Austria.

27. The Tanăis, or Don.

28. *Tambernicchi* (or *Tamberlic* or *Taberlic*) is an unidentified mountain.

29. *Pietrapana*, now called Pania della Croce, is a rocky mountain in the Tuscan Apennines.

30. *Cricchi* or *cric* is a word made to imitate the sound.

33. In the summer, the season when the country woman is apt to dream of gleaning.

34. As far as their faces: shame manifests itself by a blush.

36. Their teeth chatter like a stork's bill.   Cf. *Met.*, VI, 97: "Ipsa sibi plaudat crepitante ciconia rostro" (and claps her rattling bill, a stork).   Also Hugh of St. Victor, *De Bestiis*, I, 42: "Ciconiae sonum oris pro voce quatiente rostro faciunt."

38–39. The chattering teeth bear witness to the cold; the weeping eyes, to the sadness of the heart.

46. Their eyes until now 'were wet only within' because they were frozen over on the outside.   A new flood of tears bursts the icy coat for a moment.

56. The Bisenzo is a little stream that runs near Prato and empties into the Arno.

57. Alberto, count of Mangona.   Two of his sons, Napoleone and Alessandro, quarreled over their inheritance and killed each other.

61. Mordrec, or Mordred, the treacherous nephew of King Arthur, was pierced by such a blow from Arthur's spear that, when the weapon was pulled out, a ray of sunlight traversed his body.   The story is told in the Old French *Lancelot du lac*, the romance which Paolo and Francesca were reading in V, 127.

63. Focaccia de' Cancellieri, of the White party of Pistoia, lay in wait, with other ruffians, for one of his relatives, Detto de' Cancellieri, a Black, and killed him in a tailor's shop.

65. Sassol Mascheroni is known to us only through an early commentator, who says he murdered a nephew to secure his inheritance.

68. Of Camicion de' Pazzi nothing certain is known.   He is said to have treacherously slain a kinsman named Ubertino.

69. Carlino de' Pazzi is still alive and has not yet committed his great crime.   It was in June, 1302, that he was bribed to surrender to the Florentine Blacks the castle of Piantravigne,

containing a number of the foremost White and Ghibelline exiles, many of whom were slain. When he dies, he will come to the second division of the 9th circle, Antenora, reserved for betrayers of their country or party.

70. The sight is so horrible that Dante ever afterward will shudder at the sight of frozen pools.

72. The notion of "fording" thus introduced bears indirectly the subtle suggestion of a "crossing over," which, in fact, now takes place, as the two wayfarers cross into the second division from the first.

81. The mention of Montaperti arouses Dante's suspicions. This was the disastrous defeat of the Florentine Guelfs in 1260 by the Sienese Ghibellines and their German allies. The rout was attributed to the traitor Bocca degli Abati, who, in the thick of a charge, cut off the hand of the standard bearer to the Florentine cavalry. In 1266, when the Guelfs returned to power, he was banished.

113. Formula of adjuration: cf. X, 82.

116. Buoso da Duera of Cremona, notorious for his faithlessness, was distrusted by friends and enemies. In 1265, being bribed by the French, he allowed the army of Charles of Anjou, on its way to the conquest of Naples, to pass by the Ghibelline forces that had been detailed to oppose it. He was accused also of appropriating money sent by Manfred to pay his soldiers.

117. This is supposed to be the origin of the modern phrase, *star fresco*, 'to be in for it.'

119. Tesauro dei Beccheria of Pavia, abbot of Vallombrosa, was tortured and beheaded by the Guelfs of Florence for conducting secret negotiations with the Ghibelline exiles.

121. *Gianni de' Soldanier* was a Ghibelline, who, after the defeat of his party in 1266, headed a mob against his former associates.

122. Ganelon is the famous traitor to Charlemagne, in the *Chanson de Roland*; it was he who brought about the destruction of the rear guard at Roncesvalles and the death of Roland, his own stepson; cf. XXXI, 16–18. — The Ghibelline Tebaldello, a bastard of the Zambrasi family, surrendered to the Bolognese Guelfs his own city of Faenza in order to avenge himself on some Ghibellines from Bologna who had taken refuge there.

126. Two more political traitors are frozen in one hole in such a position that the head of one lies upon the head of the other like a hat.

130. Tydeus, one of the seven kings who attacked Thebes, was mortally wounded by Menalippus, whom he succeeded in killing. Before dying, he called for the head of his opponent and, when it was brought him by Capaneus, gnawed it fiercely. Cf. *Thebaid*, VIII, 736 ff.

Canto XXXIII

Argument

In this canto occurs an episode second only to that of Francesca da Rimini in its appeal to popular sympathy. It is in Antenora that Dante hears from Count Ugolino the frightful story of his death. Here, as in the case of the "injured souls" of Francesca and her lover, the poet is stirred to the depths by the wrong done on earth to the lost sinner. Francesca's fate moves him to an agony of pity not unmixed with indignation; that of Ugolino and his children kindles in him even more wrath than compassion. In the two narratives we find the same exclusion of all detail that might blur the one overwhelming impression to be produced upon the reader; in both, the same concentration on that part of the experience to which no human heart can be indifferent. As Francesca's guilty love follows her to Hell and binds her forever to the partner of her sin, so Ugolino is coupled to the object of his just hate, on whom he wreaks eternal vengeance.

Ugolino della Gherardesca, count of Donoratico, belonged to an old and power-ful family and held vast estates in western Tuscany. A careful scrutiny of the available documents and chronicles of the time suggests the following line of events, which led to the final downfall of the count. After her disastrous defeat by Genoa in the great naval Battle of Meloria (August 6, 1284), Pisa, traditional Ghibelline city *par excellence*, found herself threatened on all sides by powerful Guelf forces, Genoa immediately joining with Florence, Lucca, Siena, and Pistoia in league against her; and it was in such a time of crisis and grave emergency that Count Ugolino was elected *podestà* of the city for a period of ten years, being chosen for such high office not only for the competence which he had already shown in public affairs, but also as one who could, now being himself a Guelf (although of a family which was Ghibelline by tradition), best negotiate with the hostile Guelf powers which now threatened the city.

The so-called "tradimento delle castella" with which Ugolino was later charged took place in the spring and summer of 1285, the castles of Ripafratta and Viareggio being ceded to Lucca, and Pontedera, among others, to the Guelf party of Florence, and later, officially, to the city. But, given the time of crisis in which Pisa found herself, obliged as she was to propitiate the hostile Guelf powers surrounding her, the ceding by Count Ugolino of these castles was entirely in line with the new policy of conciliation and in no sense an act of treachery or betrayal. Such negotiations had, of course, to be shrouded in the greatest secrecy, for sundry and obvious reasons — a fact which could later be used in pointing to it as an act of treason on the part of the count.

Meanwhile Ugolino's grandson and namesake, Nino Visconti, who had now reached the age of 20, emerged upon the scene as a young man who clearly aspired to replace his late father Giovanni as leader of the Guelf party of Pisa, which he soon gave every promise of doing when, toward the end of that same year (1285), he was called to share with his grandfather the high offices of *podestà* and *capitano del popolo*. But personal ambitions on the part of both grandfather and grandson soon led to dissension and open armed strife between them and their respective factions, until they were finally persuaded, for the good of the city, to relinquish their office. They continued to clash, however, until in March, 1288, taking advantage of riots deliberately provoked by the count, they came to a temporary accord and, storming the *palazzo del governo* by armed force, seized control of the city.

Meanwhile the Ghibellines throughout Tuscany and the peninsula generally were enjoying better fortunes, owing to some important military victories, and their party was accordingly showing new strength in Pisa herself, and in June, 1288, after the victory of Ghibelline Arezzo over Guelf Siena in the Battle of the Pieve del Toppo, Count Ugolino, aware that the Ghibelline party of Pisa might gain control of the city once more, fell to conniving with their faction, headed by the Archbishop Ruggieri degli Ubaldini, in this way aspiring to better his own political fortunes and rid himself of further interference from his grandson and political rival, Nino.

It would appear that the count came to secret terms with Archbishop Ruggieri and other prominent leaders of traditionally Ghibelline families, such as are named in Dante's verses (Gualandi, Lanfranchi, Sismondi), agreeing among other things that Nino was to be driven from the city; whereupon the count deliberately withdrew to an estate of his in the country that this plan might be carried out in his absence. Nino, sensing the threat, turned to his grandfather for assistance but, when he got none, fled the city.

Being now acclaimed *podestà*, the archbishop took over and sent word to the count that he might return; on June 30, 1288, the count did return, trusting in the archbishop (*fidandomi di lui*, as Dante has him say); but he came to the city gates with some 1,000 armed men, such a large force that he was not allowed to enter until he agreed to come in with only a few of them. Outraged that the archbishop should have seized the office and power that he himself had aspired to gain by betraying his party and his grandson, the count managed, on the following day, to bring all his forces into the city, despite the archbishop; whereupon the latter and the Ghibellines in league with him stirred up the people against the count and his guard, causing them to shout throughout the city the charge of his "treachery of the castles." Afterward, having taken refuge in the *palazzo del popolo*, the count and his sons and grandsons were taken captive and imprisoned for more than a fortnight, when they were removed to the tower in which they were to die.

This was a complete triumph for the Ghibellines of Pisa. Within a few months the archbishop resigned the office of *podestà* in favor of another, who in turn yielded to Guido da Montefeltro (*Inf.*, XXVII), who, being called as *podestà*, entered the city in March, 1289, perhaps, as Villani suggests, in the very days in which the tower was nailed shut and the count and his children endured death by starvation.

Thus, the deed of treachery for which Count Ugolino is condemned to Dante's Antenora is, when seen in this light, at once his betrayal of his own Guelf party, the party which had first entrusted him with the rule of the city, and his own

Guelf grandson Nino Visconti; and it is not, therefore, for the "tradimento delle castella" with which he was later falsely charged by the archbishop and his faction, nor, as another view would have it, for any act of treason against his native city in the earlier disastrous defeat of Pisa at Meloria.

Treachery to a traitor was thought to be not only permissible but meritorious, and this belief is illustrated by Dante's treatment of one of the wretches in Tolomea. To be rude to him, he avers, was the part of true courtesy. In this division of the ninth circle are those who assassinated their own guests. Such betrayal as this severs all social bonds and puts the betrayer outside the pale of humanity. Dante expresses this idea allegorically by a startling device, which at the same time enables him to place in his lower world two or three heinous offenders still alive in 1300. As soon as this crime is committed — so we are informed — the sinner's soul descends to Hell, leaving the body, which, however, seems to remain alive, being occupied by a devil during the remainder of its natural term of existence. Thus it is written of Judas, at the Last Supper: "after the sop Satan entered into him"(John xiii, 27). In Ps. lv, 15, it is said of treacherous friends, "let them descend quick [i.e., alive] into hell."

4. Cf. *Aen.*, II, 3: "Infandum, regina, iubes renovare dolorem." (Beyond all words, O queen, is the grief thou bidst me revive.)

9. Cf. V, 126.

22. 'Mew': a loft where birds are kept while they moult. Ugolino gives this name to the tower known as dei Gualandi (having once belonged to the Gualandi family, though by this time it had been taken over by the city), where he was confined. After his death it was called "la torre della fame," which name is now given to the relatively modern tower which occupies its site.

24. It was not until 1318 that the municipal authorities decided to discontinue the use of this prison, which was described as foul-smelling, devoid of conveniences, and very small.

26. Several moons had appeared through the cleft of the little slit that served as a window: i.e., several months had passed — from July 20, or thereabout, to the beginning of February, 1289. Just before dawn of the day when the door is to be nailed up, Ugolino has an allegorical dream; from ll. 38–39 we learn that his companions have ominous dreams, but of a more literal character.

30. The mountain which prevents the Pisans from seeing Lucca is San Giuliano, a long, flat mountain conspicuous from the Leaning Tower.

31. The 'thin, eager, trained hounds' evidently represent the furious Pisan mob.

32. The leaders of the Pisan Ghibellines; in the dream they figure as huntsmen.

50. *Anselmuccio*: the younger of the two grandchildren.

75. Hunger did more than grief could do: it caused my death.

79. For the imprecation, cf. *Phars.*, VIII, 827–830.

80. Dante, like some others, classified the languages of Europe according to the word for "yes," Italian being the language of *sì*: cf. *Vulg. El.*, I, viii, 8. Provençal was called the *langue d'oc.*

81. Lucca and Florence, which waged bitter war against Pisa.

82. Two small islands in the sea not far from the mouth of the Arno, beside which Pisa lies. Dante calls upon these islets to move up and dam the stream at its outlet. Gorgona is visible from The Leaning Tower. Capraia, sometimes called *Caprara*, is farther out.

85. The archbishop represented to the Pisans that Ugolino, in 1285, had betrayed them in the matter of five strongholds which he had allowed Lucca and Florence to occupy. In reality the cession of these castles was a necessary piece of diplomacy.

87. *Dovei = dovevi.*

88. Gaddo and Uguccione were Ugolino's sons, Brigata and Anselmuccio his grandsons. Gaddo and Brigata were in reality of mature age.

89. Thebes being the wickedest city of the ancients, Dante calls Pisa the 'modern Thebes.'

93. Not turned face downward, like those in Caina, but all upturned.

105. In other words, how can there be wind (commonly called a "vapore") in this ice-locked place, to which the heat of the sun — which causes wind — never penetrates?

111. This spirit thinks that Dante and Virgil must be going to Giudecca.

117. This oath seems to be uttered with false intent, as Dante's way lies, in any case, through 'the bottom of the ice.'

118. Alberigo de' Manfredi of Faenza, a *frate gaudente*, had two of his family murdered at a dinner, in his presence, in 1285. He gave the signal to the assassins by calling: "Vengano le frutta!"

120. 'Am being repaid with interest,' a date being worth more than a fig.

126. 'Before Atròpos (the Fate who cuts the thread of life) gives it a start, i.e., sends it forth from life.

137. Branca d' Oria, of the famous Genoese family of Doria, was a rich and powerful noble of Genoa, who had great estates in Liguria, Corsica, and Sardinia. Apparently he lived until 1325. Aided by a relative not known to us by name, he treacherously murdered, probably in 1275, his father-in-law, Michel Zanche, the Sardinian barrator whom we met in "the sticky pitch" of the 8th ditch of Malebolge (XXII, 88), at a banquet to which he had invited him.

141. Cf. *Measure for Measure*, III, ii: "I drink, I eat, array myself, and live."

145. Branca's soul, leaving a devil in its stead, reached this 9th circle as soon as the murdered man's soul reached the 8th.

154. Alberigo de' Manfredi.

155. Branca d' Oria.

Canto XXXIV

Argument

The souls in the fourth division of the last circle are entirely covered by the frozen lake, through which they are seen like bits of straw blown into glass. They lie pell-mell in the ice, some curled up, some horizontal, some vertical — these last with head or feet upward, as they chanced to fall. Three sinners only — the worst of all humankind — have a different and more awful fate: they are crunched by the three mouths of Satan himself. Judas sold Christ, the founder of the Church; Brutus and Cassius betrayed Caesar, the founder of the Empire. Church and Empire being coordinate powers, divinely established for the spiritual and temporal government of men, their founders were both sacred. But inasmuch as the spiritual kingdom is holier than the temporal, and inasmuch as Jesus was not only man but God, treason to Christ is wickeder than treason to the merely human Caesar. Judas, then, is more tortured than his two companions; his back is rent by Satan's claws, and his head is inside the demon's mouth, while his legs, like those of the Simonists, dangle outside. He is chewed by the red face of Love of Evil, whereas Brutus and Cassius, head downward, hang respectively from the black face of Ignorance and the sallow face of Impotence.

In this Giudecca, the home of betrayers of their benefactors, the central figure is the archtraitor and archingrate, Lucifer. Here he fell when he was cast headlong from Heaven, and here he will remain, huge, hideous, and impassive, through all eternity. "How art thou fallen from heaven, O Lucifer, son of the morning! how art thou cut down to the ground, which didst weaken the nations! For thou hast said in thine heart, I will ascend to heaven, I will exalt my throne above the stars of God: I will sit also upon the mount of the congregation, in the sides of the north: I will ascend above the heights of the clouds; I will be like the Most High. Yet thou shalt be brought down to hell, to the sides of the pit" (Isaiah xiv, 12–15). Christian interpretation applied these verses not only to an earthly ruler but to a fallen angel as well. They naturally linked themselves to Luke x, 18: "And he said unto them, I beheld Satan as lightning fall from heaven"; and to Rev. xii, 7–9: "And there was war in heaven: Michael and his angels fought against the dragon; and the dragon fought and his angels, and prevailed not; neither was their place found any more in heaven. And the great dragon was cast out, that old serpent, called the Devil, and Satan, which deceiveth the whole world: he was cast out into the earth, and his angels were cast out with him."

Taken together, these passages corroborate the ancient tradition of the revolt and fall of the angels (cf. the note to III, 7), and at the same time furnish ground for an identification of Lucifer with Satan, the Devil, the Serpent, and the Dragon. As we shall see from l. 127, Dante regarded Beelzebub as still another name for the same demon.

In spite of the abundance of realistic detail that makes us share with Dante the experiences of this canto, we must consider his portrayal of Satan as essentially allegorical. His Devil is the image of sin, the principle of evil, the negative counterpart of God, who is the principle of good. As the Godhead comprises three persons — Father, Son, and Holy Ghost, representing the three attributes, Power, Wisdom, and Love — so Lucifer is pictured three-faced: his red visage betokens Love of Evil, or Hate; the black face is the emblem of Ignorance, the opposite of Wisdom and the source of pride; the pale yellow one signifies Impotence, the opposite of Power and the begetter of envy. Just as the Holy Ghost, or Love, continually proceeds from Father and Son, so, in Satan, Hate is the result of ignorant Pride and impotent Envy. Dante's Lucifer, though less grotesque and fantastic than the usual diabolical monster of vision literature, is ugly beyond description. Like the four beasts surrounding God's throne in Rev. iv, 8, and like the seraphim of Isaiah vi, 2, he has six wings; a pair of them sprouts beneath each face, and the three winds produced by their flapping freeze Cocytus. Immovable and helpless in the ice of his own making, he holds sway over his "doloroso regno" — so it would seem — by these winds alone. They are the Satanic instigations, the inspiration of sin. Presumably they correspond to the three great divisions of Hell, the "tre disposizion che 'l ciel non vuole" of XI, 81–83. From the wings of Love of Evil issues the blast of Fraud or Malice; from the wings of Ignorance, the blast of Violence or Bestiality; from the wings of Impotence, the wind of Incontinence or weakness to resist the passions. In Ephesians ii, 2, Satan is called "Prince of the power of the air."

Having explored all the manifestations of sin, and having finally scrutinized its very essence, Dante, with the help of Reason, turns his back upon it and laboriously wrests himself from its attraction. That is the allegory of the long and uneventful climb from the bottom of Hell, at the earth's center, out to the surface on the other side: it is the steady, monotonous effort by which the re-morseful wrongdoer is weaned from evil practices. In this journey Dante has no light to guide him — only the encouraging murmur of a streamlet of dis-carded sin (perhaps the tears of penitence), flowing constantly from Purgatory, where wickedness is washed away, down to its original Satanic source.*

When the practice of evil has been brought to a stop, there still remains the duty of penitentially restoring the soul to its first purity and cleansing it of all disposition to sin. This discipline is symbolized by the ascent through the torments of the mountain of Purgatory, a task which is performed in the light and under heavenly direction.

---

* Ed. note: Not all interpreters of Dante's allegory, indeed perhaps not many, would agree with Grandgent's view of it as expressed in this paragraph. For another view, involving broader conceptions, see Singleton (1954).

1. Virgil derisively adapts and applies to Satan the opening lines of a hymn written in honor of the Cross by Venantius Fortunatus in the 6th century:

Vexilla Regis prodeunt	Abroad the regal banners fly,
Fulget crucis mysterium.	Now shines the Cross's mystery.

It is sung at vespers on the Feast of the Exaltation of the Cross and also on Monday of Holy Week.

9. *Grotta* here, as usually in Dante, means 'bank.' In Tuscany the banks of a sunken road are still called *grotte.*

10. Cf. *Aen.*, II, 204: "Horresco referens." (I shudder as I tell the tale.)

27. 'Bereft of both,' i.e., neither alive nor dead.

30, 31. 'I compare better with a giant than giants do with his arms.' If we assume Dante's height to have been 5½ ft., and that of a giant (like one of those in the well) to have been 80 ft., and the length of an arm to be a third of the whole height, a rough computation makes Dis more than a third of a mile in stature. It is not likely, however, that Dante intended to convey anything more than a vague impression of almost inconceivable size.

34–36. If his beauty, as God created him, was equal to his present ugliness, his revolt against his Creator was an act of such monstrous ingratitude as to be a fitting source of all subsequent sin and sorrow.   It is characteristic of Dante that he was especially shocked by the thought of Satan's ingratitude.

42. The three faces blend together at the top of the head.

45. The faces that come from Egypt are black.

54. Cf. Virgil, *Georgics*, III, 203: "spumas aget ore cruentas" (fling from his mouth bloody foam); III, 516: "mixtum spumis vomit ore cruorem" (from his mouth he spurts blood, mingled with foam).

56. 'Heckle': a hemp brake, an instrument that crushes hemp stalks and separates the fiber.

67. We do not know why Cassius is described as 'sturdy of limb.'   It has been suggested that Dante confused him with the Lucius Cassius described by Cicero in the third Catilinian oration.

68. By the time of Jerusalem, it is the evening of Saturday, April 9.   The poets have spent 24 hours in their downward journey.   We are not told exactly how much more time is subsequently consumed in creeping down Satan's flank and up his thigh; from l. 96 it would seem to be about an hour and a half.

75. Between the ice and Satan's hip there is evidently a crack, through which Virgil, carrying Dante, descends like a man climbing down a ladder.

77. 'Haunches': the place, halfway down the body, where the thigh thickens into the haunch.

79. They have reached the center of the earth, and any further movement in the same direction is no longer downward, but upward.   Therefore Virgil, with Dante on his back, turns himself upside-down, so as to proceed head first, and not feet first, as hitherto.   In climbing a ladder, one goes down feet first, but up head first.   They are now ascending toward the opposite surface of the earth, where Purgatory is.

85. Through the chink between Satan's thigh and the rocky bottom of the ice, they emerge into a cavern which is situated on the other side of the earth's center.   Virgil puts Dante down on the brink of the crevice and then 'extends to him his prudent step,' i.e., steps cautiously from the 'tufts' to the rock.

90. Inasmuch as Satan traverses the center of the earth, having his head in the Jerusalem hemisphere and his legs in the Purgatory hemisphere, his feet, with reference to Purgatory, are pointed upward.

91. 'Let ignorant people conceive' how disturbed I must have been.

96. *Terza*, 'tierce,' embraces the three hours following sunrise.   'Midtierce' is, then, about half-past seven o'clock in the morning.   In Hell Dante computes time by the nocturnal bodies; now that Hell is left behind, he refers to the sun again.

102. Probably 'doubt'; cf. IV, 48 and X, 114.

105. In reality, as Dante presently learns, the change from evening to morning is due, not to any unusual movement of the sun, but to the altered position of the observers, who have passed from one hemisphere to the other.   Throughout Hell, they go by the time of Jerusalem, which is directly over the bottom.   As soon as they pass the center, they take their time from the Island of Purgatory, toward which they ascend.   Jerusalem and Purgatory being on opposite sides of the earth, or 180° apart, the difference in time between them is 12 hours. Dante therefore represents himself as gaining 12 hours when he crosses the center.   He has before him a new Saturday.

108. *Vermo* is any kind of a dragon or monster; cf VI, 22.   In the *Visio Alberici*, IX, beside the pit there is a "vermis ... infinitae magnitudinis, ligatus maxima catena" (monster of infinite size, bound by a huge chain).

112. *Emisperio* means here hemisphere of the sky, not of the earth.   It is the celestial hemisphere which covers the terrestrial Hemisphere of Water.   Opposite to it is the celestial hemisphere 'which covers the great continent (the terrestrial Hemisphere of Land) and beneath

whose zenith' lies Jerusalem, where Jesus was slain. Jerusalem is exactly in the middle of the Hemisphere of Land: "Thus said the Lord God; This is Jerusalem: I have set it in the midst of the nations and countries that are round about her" (Ezekiel v, 5).

113. "And God called the dry land Earth" (Gen. i, 10).

116. On the Hell side it is ice, the part called Giudecca; on the other side it is stone, forming the floor of the cavern into which Dante emerges. *Spera* in early Italian often meant a round mirror, glass on one side and lead on the other. It is still so used.

121. When heaven and earth were just created, "and the earth was without form, and void" (Gen. i, 2), sea and land were not separated. Then Satan fell, and all the land shrank away from the surface of the side where he descended, leaving a vast empty bed to be filled by the sea. Cf. Gen. i, 9–10.

125. As Satan pierced the earth in his headlong fall, the ground which he traversed "perhaps" fled away from him, and issued forth to form the Island of Purgatory, leaving a vacant cavern near the center. Cf. Isaiah xiv, 9: "Hell from beneath is moved for thee to meet thee at thy coming."

126. The land 'which appears on this side' is the lone Island of Purgatory, in the middle of the Hemisphere of Water.

127. The 'place down there' seems to be the farther end of the passage emptied by Satan's fall. It is just beneath the crust of the earth's surface that supports the Island of Purgatory, and therefore is separated from Beelzebub by the whole length of his "tomb" — the grave he dug for himself in falling. If this is the case, Dante omits all description of his climb from Satan to this point. See *Twenty-Ninth Annual Report of the Dante Society of Cambridge, Massachusetts*, 39. Satan is held fast in a strip of ice and rock between the cavity of Hell and a cavern on the other side, the upper part of his body projecting into Hell, the lower part into the cavern. Between ll. 126 and 127, Dante seems to skip the whole journey between the center of the earth and the outlet opposite the one where he entered. We are not told the nature of the passage beyond Satan's feet: whether it is a winding corridor, a vast conical cavity similar to an inverted Hell, or a big cylindrical hole. [For a somewhat different interpretation of these verses, see Singleton (1970).] — Dante identifies "Beelzebub the prince of the devils" (Mat. xii, 24) with Lucifer; they were sometimes regarded as different demons.

136. The descent through Hell occupied Friday night and Saturday; the climb from the center of the earth to the other side lasts through Saturday again and the following night. The poets emerge on the Island of Purgatory before daybreak on the morning of Easter Sunday. If we assume the existence of a great hollow, corresponding to Hell, between Lucifer and Purgatory, the *tomba* of l. 128 will probably refer to this cavity, which was dug by the demon as he fell. In that case the *luogo* of l. 127 and the *sasso* of l. 131 may both designate, perhaps, the crust of earth that covers the pit; and Dante will apparently skip some 3000 miles between ll. 126 and 127. But see Singleton (1970). The *intrammo* of l. 134 may mean simply 'started': cf. *Purg.* III, 101; XXIV, 110.

139. Each of the three great divisions of the poem ends with the sweet and hopeful word *stelle*.

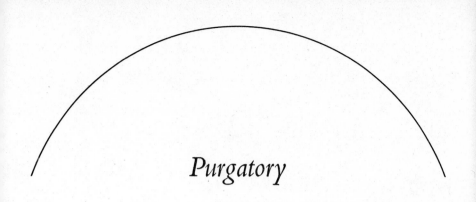

Purgatory

Preliminary Note

In the beginning all eternal things were directly created by God — namely, brute matter, the spheres, and the angels. The angels, operating by means of the heavenly bodies, constitute Nature, the power that first resolved matter into its four elements and combined them into a globe of earth and water surrounded by air and fire. God by his own act shaped Adam and Eve, whose flesh is therefore imperishable; and every human soul is made by God. The rest of the world is the work of Nature. Even when the Lord said (Gen. i, 9), "Let the waters under the heaven be gathered together unto one place, and let the dry land appear," it was the influence of the stars (directed by angels) that actually caused the land to rise, on a part of the earth's surface, above the normally higher element. According to Dante's cosmogony, the earth is a sphere, solid except for the cavity of Hell; its circumference is 20,400 miles. Most of this spherical surface is covered by water, but in the Hemisphere of Land — which lies, in the main, north of the equator — is a great continent composed of Europe, Asia, and Africa, stretching from east to west 180°, or 10,200 miles, between the Strait of Gibraltar and the mouth of the Ganges. Its two western parts are separated by the Mediterranean, which was thought to extend 5100 miles, or 90° — more than twice its real length. This sea, however, was well known and was charted with considerable accuracy at a time when general maps were still quite fantastic. The extreme north and the extreme south of the Hemisphere of Land were inhabited respectively by the Scythians and the Garamantes. The great ocean surrounding the land was an object of terror, full of mysterious dangers — monsters, rocks, whirlpools, chasms.   In the exact center of the land, midway between Gibraltar and Ganges, is Jerusalem.   "Thus saith the Lord God; This is Jerusalem: I have set it in the midst of the nations and countries that are round about her" (Ezekiel v, 5).   Halfway between Gibraltar and Jerusalem, in the middle of the western world, is Rome.   Somewhere on the globe is the Garden of Eden, where Enoch and Elijah still abide in the flesh, awaiting the Day of Judgment.   Although it was reached by sundry ancient travelers, opinions were diverse concerning its exact whereabouts.   Generally it was placed in Asia.   The English Bible says (Gen. ii, 8): "And the Lord planted a garden eastward in Eden."   But in the usual text of the Vulgate the "eastward" does not appear.   Some located it on the summit of a lofty mountain, some on an island, especially the island of Ceylon.   Bede and Peter Lombard record a belief that it projected upward to the sphere of the moon, and thus escaped the flood; but St. Thomas (*Summa Theologiae*, Prima, Qu. cii, Art. 1) does not accept this estimate of prodigious height as literal fact.   Whether there was land on the watery side of the earth was a question hotly debated; the doctrine of the antipodes — that is, of a race of men separated by an impassable ocean from Adam and from Christ — was denied by St. Augustine and condemned by the Church.   Dante chose for his Eden, the scene of man's fall, a point directly opposite Jerusalem, the scene of his redemption.   Dante's love of symmetry shows itself in the construction of his poem and of his universe: a high mountain balances a deep Hell; an Antipurgatorio balances an Antinferno; the Valley of the Princes, on the mountain, balances the Nobile Castello of the lower world.   His Earthly Paradise is situated on the top of a huge mountain which rises on a solitary island in the midst of the Hemisphere of Water.   There is no reason to believe that he regarded it as enormously higher than a real mountain might be.[1]

The upper part of the conical mountainside is occupied by the seven terraces of Purgatory, where repentant souls come after death to cleanse themselves for Heaven.   After leaving the body, they are brought to the island in a boat guided by an angel.   Dante apparently agrees with St. Ambrose in holding that all human spirits destined to be saved (except Christ and Mary) must pass through Purgatory; on this point St. Thomas seems to be of different mind.   Furthermore, according to Dante's belief, no souls ever went to Purgatory until the redemption was accomplished; before the Crucifixion, unrepentant souls went to Hell, as they still do, while penitent souls descended to the Limbus to await the Savior's coming.   The lower part of the mountain slope, on Dante's island, is a place of waiting for Christians who postponed repentance until the very end of life.

[1] See C. R. Beazley, *Prince Henry the Navigator*, 1895; H. F. Tozer, *A History of Ancient Geography*, 1897; Moore, III, 109.

There we find those who were overabsorbed by cares of state, those whose career was prematurely ended by a violent death, those whom indolence retarded.   On the shore, slowly circling around the mountain, are the excommunicated who died repentant though still under the anathema of the Church.   All of these are excluded for a time from the penance they are eager to begin.   Dante and Virgil emerge on the east side of the edge of the island, on the morning of Easter Sunday.   There they meet the guardian of the realm, Cato, the personification of Free Will.   They laboriously ascend the cliffs, still on the eastern side, toward the gate of Purgatory.   Over a considerable part of the way, however, Dante is mysteriously carried in his sleep by Lucia.   We therefore do not know how high up on the mountain the entrance to Purgatory really is; but we may naturally infer that it is more than halfway, since all of Purgatory proper is above the region of atmospheric change.   At the gate is an angelic keeper, the representative of Ecclesiastical Authority.   Steps cut into the steep rock lead from one terrace of Purgatory to another; on each terrace Dante and his guide turn to the right and proceed for some distance around the northern side of the cone, so that on leaving the last shelf they are on the west side, having made half the circuit.   They reach the Garden of Eden, which covers the circular mountaintop, on Wednesday morning.   Here the presiding genius, the embodiment of Innocence, is a lovely maiden, Matelda.   On Wednesday noon they rise to Heaven.   It will be seen that three nights are spent on the island; they are passed by Dante in rest and sleep, night being the time for meditation as day is the time for activity.   In the course of each night he has a symbolic dream.[2]

Led by one of his happiest inspirations, the poet has placed the action of this *cantica* in the open air, not in the gloomy cavern of tradition.   As the theme of the *Purgatorio* is betterment, release from sin and preparation for Heaven, its atmosphere is rightly one of hope and progress, and for that reason it appeals peculiarly to the modern mind.   There are two elements in sin: the turning away from God and the turning toward temporal good.   The first naturally ceases with repentance, and is forgiven.   The second is due to vices, or faults of character, which must be cured.   According to established Christian doctrine, of these fundamental defects there are seven, known as the "capital vices": pride, envy, anger, sloth, avarice, gluttony, lust.   Dante, in harmony with St. Gregory and St. Bonaventure, arranges them in this order.   There was, however, among Church writers, no absolute agreement as to their sequence, although pride was always regarded as the worst.   St. Thomas, in various passages, arranges them in four somewhat different ways and apparently regards the order as unimportant; once he has them as they appear in the *Commedia*.   At the

[2] See the diagrams on p. x.

beginning of the *Inferno* we see Dante, moved by grace, turning back to God. He is already repentant. On quitting Hell, he puts sin behind him, but there still remains the positive task of regeneration. The whole ascent of the mountain signifies this reformatory effort, an undoing of the work of sin — the passage through the seven circles of Purgatory representing specifically the accomplishment of penance under ecclesiastical direction. The torment on each terrace is a symbol of the particular form of discipline needed to remove from the spirit one of the seven capital vices. When the soul is entirely cleansed, it regains the perfect freedom of will that sin has restricted; it finds itself once more in the state of original innocence which man enjoyed before the fall. The recovery of innocence is symbolized by the entrance into the Garden of Eden. Then comes the sacrament of penance, ending with absolution, after which the soul is ready to see Heaven.[3]

Every sin consists in an act of the will, and is judged according to its motive, not according to its effect. The will is fundamentally a "craving for good," which produces evil incidentally in the attempt to acquire good that is not real but apparent. The guilty act is therefore a yielding to the desire for this apparent or unreal good. But although sin is not in the first place perpetrated for the sake of evil, indulgence in it creates a "habit" that begets "malice," the love of evil for itself. All sins fall, then, into two classes, those of passion and those of malice. The seven capital vices are all due to passion, and from them all sins of passion derive, whether they be sins of desire or sins of irascibility; a capital vice may, in fact, bring about a sin quite different from itself, but the act is classified in accordance with its source. Sins of malice, are due, not directly to passion, but to a habit caused, as we have seen, by repeated yielding to guilty impulse. All deliberate and "habitual" sins may be called "malicious." Inasmuch as the sinner's guilt is proportionate to his understanding, the blindly impetuous or ignorant sinner is less culpable than the malicious sinner, who consciously prefers temporal to spiritual good. The capital vices are responsible for sins of weakness; offenses against justice, on the other hand, are all due to malice. In Purgatory there can be no malicious souls, because a soul in a state of malice cannot repent, and only the repentant reach Purgatory; the moment a malicious sinner repents, his sin ceases to be one of malice, and must be attributed to the capital vice that first produced it. Furthermore, heresy (or *infidelitas*) is unknown in Purgatory; for, to admit of repentance, unbelief must give way to faith, and then there is left only the vice (presumably pride) that led to infidelity. It is

3 On this whole question of a "Return to Eden" and the impossibility of recovering, literally, the state of original innocence, see Singleton (1958), pp. 204–253. What is recovered is "personal justice," not the "natural justice" which Adam had.

evident, then, that in a portrayal of Purgatory malice and heresy, as such, may be left out of account, and only the seven capital vices need be directly considered.

As Hell is a place of punishment for the unrepentant and Purgatory a place of reformation for the penitent, it is comprehensible that Dante should look at sin in these two regions from different standpoints.   In Hell malice and heresy are at home.   Furthermore, the conception of Hell is universal, while the idea of Purgatory is peculiarly Christian.   In *Monarchia*, III, xvi, 7, Dante describes the two goals of human endeavor, temporal and eternal happiness; the first we reach through "philosophical," the second through "spiritual" teaching.   Following a similar distinction, Dante treats wickedness in the *Purgatorio* from the theological, in the *Inferno* from the philosophical or moral side.   Only in the offenses against faith do we find in Dante's lower world (where Christ is never named) a distinctively Christian element; and even in the circle of heresy Epicurus is chosen as the leading example, as is Capaneus, another heathen, in the realm of blasphemy. The whole system is Aristotelian, and its fitting expounder is the ancient Virgil. Of the seven capital vices of Christian theology, four, to be sure, are included in the plan of the *Inferno* — lust, gluttony, avarice, and anger; but these four were familiar to the moral philosophers of antiquity.   Sloth, on the other hand, was unknown to Aristotle, and envy was to him not a vice, but a culpable passion; it is natural, then, that these forms of evil should have no specific place in Dante's Hell.   As to pride, Aristotle (with whom Cicero in the main agrees) does discuss it, under the name of "vainglory," as an excess of "magnanimity"; an appropriate enough place for it, according to his description, would seem to be somewhere between Incontinence and Malice, and Dante does, in fact, there illustrate, in the person of Farinata, pride as a cause of heresy.   St. Thomas more than once regards *superbia* in this light.   It will be remembered that Dante's Hell falls into two great parts, an upper and a lower.   The sins in the upper section are directed against temperance, those in the lower against justice.   All the evil in the first may be attributed to infirmity; all in the second, to malice.   But malice itself, in the *Commedia*, is of two distinct kinds.   The sins in Dante's Hell are classified, not simply under two heads ("upper" and "lower"), but, in partial accordance with Aristotle's terminology, under the three heads of Incontinence, Bestiality, and Malice.   The last two, which belong to the Lower Hell, correspond more nearly, however, to St. Thomas's "bestial malice" and "human malice."   Cicero's "violence" and "fraud" are cited by the poet apparently as equivalents. Fraud is "de l' uom proprio male," that is, *malitia humana*.   But St. Thomas, like almost all other moralists, considers *vis* as worse than *fraus;* Aristotle, who also distinguishes violence and fraud, does not commit himself as to their relative iniquity. Dante, combining the Ciceronian and Aristotelian *vis* with St. Thomas's *bestialis malitia*, makes of Bestiality a third distinct state of the will, different both from Incontinence (or *infirmitas*) and from Malice (or *malitia humana*), more culpable than the first and less so than the second.   Their order follows, it would seem, the Gregorian maxim, "The greater the infamy, the less the guilt." In this arrangement Dante stands really alone.   On the other hand, while St. Thomas regards the bestial sins as offenses against temperance, Dante considers them as offenses against justice, and therefore worthy of the Lower Hell.   The only two phases of bestial wrongdoing that are discussed at any length by St. Thomas — ferocity and sodomy — are illustrated in the first and third *gironi* of Dante's seventh circle.

Canto I

Argument

As at the beginning of his tale of Hell (*Inf.* II, 79), so at the outset of his second narrative Dante invokes the aid of the Muses, the embodiment of poetic inspiration.   In the Letter to Can Grande we are informed that poets frequently prefix an invocation to their works (18, 47): "Et hoc est eis conveniens, quia multa invocatione opus est eis, cum aliquid contra comunem modum hominum a superioribus substantiis petendum est, quasi divinum quoddam munus." (And this is to their purpose, for they have need of ample invocation, since they have to implore something above the common scope of man from the higher beings, as in some sort a divine gift.)   Calliope, in particular, is here apostrophized, as in the *Aeneid*, IX, 525:

> Vos, o Calliope, precor adspirate canenti.

(Do thou, O Calliope, thou and thy sisters, I pray, inspire me while I sing.)

She was probably known to Dante as the patroness of style and rhetoric.   The mention of her name reminds the author of the story of the daughters of Pieros, whom she defeated in song.

The appeal to the Muses is followed by a beautiful description of dawn.   The journey up the mountain begins on the morning of Easter Sunday: both hour and day are full of the promise of hope, which is the dominant note of the *Purgatorio*. It will be remembered that the descent into Hell began on the evening of Good Friday.   The action of the second *cantica* opens, then, just before sunrise on Easter Sunday, April 10, 1300.

The Island of Purgatory being in the southern hemisphere, some of the celestial phenomena seem inverted.   As the traveler faces the east, for instance, he must turn to the right to look at the nearer, or south, pole.   Lucan, in his *Pharsalia*, repeatedly touches upon the aspect of the sky over Africa; and Dante himself, in *Convivio*, III, v, 9–21, gives a remarkably accurate description of the sun's course as seen from the two poles and the equator.   The stars of the extreme south, however, were of course unknown to our poet's generation, and there his imagination had free scope.   He invents a constellation of four bright lights, corresponding to the Great Bear of the north.   These luminaries symbolize the four cardinal virtues — Prudence, Temperance, Fortitude, Justice — which belong to the active life and have existed since humanity began; whereas the three theological virtues — Faith, Hope, Love — especially adapted to the life of contemplation, are distinctively Christian.   Adam and Eve before the fall ("the first people"), dwelling at the top of the mountain, beheld these stars; but fallen man, inhabiting the northern hemisphere, is bereft of their light.

These four shining virtues illumine with sunlike clearness the custodian of Purgatory, the example of that Free Will which the souls in his domain are striving, by purification, to regain; for although he appears only on the shore, the whole mountain, up to the Garden of Eden, is in his keeping.   This guardian is Cato the Younger, who on earth, after heroic resistance, killed himself in Utica rather than submit to Caesar.   His suicide was evidently regarded by Dante, not as a sinful revolt against God's law, but as a divinely bidden assertion of liberty.   Some suggestion of this interpretation is to be found in Lucan's *Pharsalia*, from which, in the main, Dante's conception of Cato was drawn.   In *Monarchia*, II, v, 15, Dante says: "Accedit et illud inenarrabile sacrificium severissimi vere libertatis auctoris Marci Catonis ... ut mundo libertatis amores accenderet, quanti libertas esset ostendit dum e vita liber decedere maluit quam sine libertate manere in illa."   (And that sacrifice, beyond narration, of the severest champion of true liberty, Marcus Cato. ... and the latter, to kindle the love of liberty in the world, gave proof of how dear he held her by preferring to depart from life a free man rather than remain alive bereft of liberty.)   He continues (17), quoting from Cicero's *De Officiis*: "'Non enim alia in causa Marcus Cato fuit, alia ceteri qui se in Affrica Cesari tradiderunt.   Atque ceteris forsan vitio datum esset si se interemissent, propterea quod levior eorum vita et mores fuerunt faciliores; Catoni vero cum incredibilem natura tribuisset gravitatem, eamque perpetua constantia roborasset, semperque in proposito susceptoque consilio permansisset, moriendum ei potius quam tyranni vultus adspiciendus fuit.'"   (The cause of Marcus Cato was no other than that of the rest, who surrendered to Caesar in Africa; but yet perchance it would have been counted a fault in the rest had they slain themselves, because their life was lighter and their ways were less austere: but since nature had given to Cato a weight of character past belief, which he had confirmed by unbroken constancy, ever remaining true to the purpose and resolve which he had taken, for him it was more fitting to die than to look upon the face of a tyrant.)

As a virtuous pagan, Cato went, on dying, to the Limbus, whence he was rescued with the patriarchs when Christ descended into Hell.   Then it was that souls first mounted to Purgatory; and from that time dates Cato's ministry, which is to continue until the Judgment Day.   How he became (or is to become) a Christian, we are not told — perhaps he received the faith on his release, having beheld Christ; but a Christian he must be on the day of resurrection, for Dante states that his body will then be glorified, like those of the other blest.   Del Lungo, in spite of this evidence, thinks that Cato was not saved.

The idea of giving him this sacred charge probably came to Dante from a passage in the *Aeneid* (VIII, 670), where, pictured on a shield, are scenes from the other world, the wicked in one spot, in another the good with Cato (presumably, in Virgil's intention, the Elder) for a lawgiver:

> Secretosque pios, his dantem iura Catonem.

(Far apart, the good, and Cato giving them laws.)

Cato was, however, Dante's favorite hero in antiquity, and he would, in any case, have found a dignified place for him.   Cato is, indeed, an example of the higher reason, or contemplation; Marcia represents the lower reason or temporal care.   Thus man and woman are defined by St. Augustine in *De Trinitate*, XII, vii–xiv.

For the shaggy, unkempt Cato of *Pharsalia*, II, 374–376, a man in the prime of life, Dante substitutes a figure all venerable and august, appropriate to his high office.   In the common legend of the Earthly Paradise two aged men appear in the Garden — Enoch and Elijah, who were transferred from earth to Eden, to await, in the body, the Day of Judgment.   Although Dante, in all likelihood, believed in this myth, he wished his Garden of Eden to be entirely suggestive of innocent youth, the springtime of humanity, and for that reason suppressed the inharmonious image of the two elders, which may, however, have lurked in his memory and contributed to his portrait of Cato.   In the *Voyage of St. Brendan*, a tale widely current in the Middle Ages, the monk Barinthus reaches an island where he finds, on the shore, "a man of great brightness," who gives him directions, and later, in the interior, St. Brendan meets a youth who calls him and his companions by name.   These two figures — originally, no doubt, identical, but differently described and occurring at the beginning and the end of the story — correspond, in a way, to Dante's Cato and Matelda.   After imparting the required information, the elder in the narrative of the Irish monk suddenly vanishes; and our Cato, contrary to the usual habit of Dante's spirits, does the same.

7. *La morta poesì* probably means the poetry that has sung the death of the soul.

11, 12. The wretched Magpies once heard such music from the lips of Calliope that they 'despaired of forgiveness' for their presumption. These Magpies were the nine daughters of King Pieros; they challenged the Muses to a contest and, being worsted by Calliope, became so insolent that they were turned into birds. Cf. *Met.*, V, 300–340, 662–678.

14, 15. The 'clear face' of the sky, which was pure from the center, or zenith, to the horizon.

21. Venus was dimming, by her brighter light, the Fishes, the constellation preceding Aries, in which was the sun. The time indicated is an hour or more before sunrise. According to the ecclesiastical calendar of 1300, Venus was in Pisces in March and April of that year. See Moore, III, 372.

29. *Altro*, i.e., north. The Wain, or Big Dipper, had sunk below the horizon; in Europe, as Dante repeatedly notes, this constellation never sets.

39. As if the sun were shining upon Cato's face.

42. The 'venerable plumage' is his gray beard.

48. 'Banks' (as almost always in Dante), i.e., the cliffs of the mountain.

71. See Romans viii, 21: "the glorious liberty of the children of God." Cf. *Purg.* XXVII, 140. See also John viii, 38.

75. The body, which, on the day of resurrection, shall be clothed with the glory of brightness. See *Summa Theologiae*, III, Suppl., Qu. lxxxv.

77. Dante is still alive, and Minos, the judge of Hell, does not bind Virgil, who dwells in the Limbus.

79. Marcia was mentioned among the dwellers in Limbus in *Inf.* IV, 128.

80. The appeal to Marcia is introduced here probably to reinforce the hard doctrine that the fate of the lost cannot affect the state of the elect. Cf. *Inf.* II, 82 ff. See E. G. Parodi in *Bull.*, XIX, 225: Peter Lombard, in *Sententiae*, IV, Dist. I, i, says that "justorum animae tanta rectitudine constringuntur ut nulla ad reprobos compassione moveantur." (The souls of the just are bound by such straitness that they simply are not moved at all by compassion for the damned.) Cf. C. H. Grandgent, *Quid Ploras?* in the 42^d, 43^d, and 44th Annual Report of the Dante Society of Cambridge, Mass. (1926), p. 8.

82. The seven circles of Purgatory.

89, 90. When Cato, with the patriarchs, was released from Limbus by Christ, he became subject to the law which forbids the blessed to be moved by the fate of the damned. Cf. *Inf.* II, 91–93; XX, 28–30. Before the descent of Christ the law did not exist, because there were no blessed: cf. *Inf.* IV, 52–63.

94, 96. Cf. *Aen.*, VI, 635–636. The rush, the symbol of humility, takes the place of the girdle of self-confidence which Dante cast off in *Inf.* XVI, 106 ff. The washing in pure dew removes *tristitia*, the gloom of past sin. Dante starts on his upward journey in a spirit of humility and cheerfulness.

99. The guardians of Purgatory are angels.

107. The sun, here as elsewhere, symbolizes intelligence, or righteous choice.

115–116. The early morning breeze dies away as the sun rises.

117. Cf. *Aen.*, VII, 9: "splendet tremulo sub lumine pontus." (The sea glitters beneath her dancing beams.) In Virgil, however, the light is that of the moon.

121–123. The dew resists the sun, because, being in a cool, moist breeze (*ad orezza*) it evaporates but little.

128–129. He uncovered my natural complexion, hidden under the fumes of Hell.

132. Witness the fate of Ulysses: *Inf.* XXVI, 130 ff.

133. 'As it pleased another,' i.e., Cato, but also God. Cf. *Inf.* XXVI, 141.

134–136. Cf. *Aen.*, VI, 143–144:

> Primo avolso non deficit alter
> Aureus; et simili frondescit virga metallo.

(When the first is torn away, a second fails not, golden too, and the spray bears leaf of the selfsame ore.)

Canto II

Argument

The souls destined to pass through Purgatory to Heaven are wafted across the great ocean in a swift bark directed by an angelic pilot, even as the boatman of Hell ferries the wicked over Acheron.   In the *Inferno*, III, 93, Charon referred to this "lighter craft" as the boat which is to carry Dante after death.   From the shore of the island, the two poets watch its approach, and at first neither can make out what is coming; all that is seen is a bright star on the horizon — the shining face of the angel.   Then the wings appear on either side and finally the white robe beneath.   Virgil is the first to recognize the stranger's heavenly office. The celestial visage is too dazzling for human sight, and Dante's eyes are blinded, as they are subsequently by the guardian angels of Purgatory.   The souls in the skiff, happy and eager to begin their purification, are all singing together Psalm cxiv (Vulg. cxiii), "When Israel went out of Egypt."   In *Convivio*, II, i, 6–7, Dante uses this psalm as an example of anagogical, or spiritual, symbolism: thus understood, it means — he says — that the soul going forth from sin becomes holy and free.   In the Letter to Can Grande, 7, the same passage serves to illustrate all four modes of interpretation, and the literal, allegorical, moral, and anagogical significances are all explained.   As sung by the released spirits, the verses evidently celebrate "the going forth of the blessed soul from the slavery of this corruption to the freedom of eternal glory."

Among the newly arrived, Dante recognizes his friend Casella, the musician, and vainly tries to embrace his ethereal form.   The apparent tangibility or intangibility of spirits in Dante's Hell and Purgatory was discussed in the Argument to Canto VI of the *Inferno*, and for the sake of convenience the commentary there given may be repeated here.   Throughout Hell the souls, though without weight, are not only visible and audible, but tangible.   On the lower slopes of the mountain of Purgatory, however, Dante cannot touch a shade (*Purg.* II, 79 ff.), although two spirits can still embrace (*Purg.* VI, 75); and near the summit one soul apparently cannot clasp another (*Purg.* XXI, 130 ff.).   In *Purg.* XXV, 79 ff., we are informed that after death the atmosphere collects around the departed spirit, forming an aerial body, which reflects all the emotions of the soul itself.   Although Dante nowhere says so explicitly, it would seem that he chose to regard this airy shape as more substantial in proportion to its proximity to the center of gravity of the universe (which is also the center of sin), and more ethereal as it rises above the earth's surface.   This conception of the shade appears to be to a great extent Dante's own, although St. Thomas mentions the power of angels and devils to assume aerial forms.

Our poet was addicted not only to mystery and enigma but also to puzzles of all kinds, especially astronomical riddles; and he credited his readers with the same proclivity. We find many of them in the *Purgatorio* and the *Paradiso*, oftenest in the opening lines of a canto. The one with which the present canto begins is not altogether easy. It must be understood that the *meridian* of any place on earth is a great circle in the sky, passing directly over that spot and crossing the two heavenly poles. The *horizon* of a given place is a great circle in the sky, running around the globe 90° from its meridian. The planes of the meridian and the horizon are therefore always at right angles to each other; the horizon of the north pole, for instance, is the celestial equator — which is also the horizon of the south pole, because the two poles are 180° apart. Inasmuch as Jerusalem and Purgatory are on opposite sides of the earth, 180° from each other, they have a common horizon: when Jerusalem sees the sun rise, Purgatory sees it set, and vice versa. The difference in time between the two places is just twelve hours, so that Jerusalem's noon is Purgatory's midnight, 6 A.M. in Jerusalem is 6 P.M. in Purgatory, etc. The first three lines of the canto mean, then, that the sun, in its daily revolution, has descended to the horizon of Jerusalem — "that horizon, the highest point of whose meridian is over Jerusalem." But this is also the horizon of Purgatory: the sun, which is setting for Jerusalem, is rising for Purgatory. Now Dante often speaks of *night* as if it were a point in the heavens directly opposed to the sun; so here he says that night, "circling opposite" the sun, was rising for Jerusalem. He represents it as coming forth from the Ganges; this river, which flowed on the eastern confines of the inhabited world, 90° from Jerusalem, stood for the *east* just as the Strait of Gibraltar (or Cadiz or Seville) stood for the *west*. The sun, then, for an observer in Jerusalem, was on the western horizon; night was on the eastern. In Purgatory, of course, these conditions were reversed. But Dante states, furthermore, that night was rising "with the Scales." The sun, from March 21 to April 21, is in the sign of Aries; and the sign of the Zodiac opposite Aries is Libra: night, therefore, conceived as a point 180° from the sun, may be described as being, on April 10, in Libra, the constellation of the Scales. Libra remains a night constellation until September 21, the autumnal equinox, when the sun passes into that sign; and as September 21 is the date after which the nights begin to grow longer than the days, Dante fancifully adds that the Scales in question are those which fall from the hands of Night at the time when she surpasses the Day. In this devious and ingenious way we are told that for the spectators on the Island of Purgatory the sun was rising.

6. 'She exceeds,' i.e., grows longer than the day.

9. *Rance*, 'orange.' The poet playfully transfers to the face of the goddess of dawn the changing colors of the morning sky.

16. 'As I hope to behold it again,' i.e., after death, when my soul shall in reality be wafted to Purgatory.

30. The guardians of Purgatory are 'such ministers' as this: namely, angels.

44, 46, 48. In Dante's day *tt* was very often written *ct* or *pt*; here the Latin *pt* is kept, to preserve, for the eye, the correspondence with *Aegypto*, which was (and in Italy is still) pronounced *Egitto*. *Parea beato per iscripto*, 'he seemed blest by inscription,' i.e., 'he seemed to have the word "blessed" inscribed upon him.'

57. At dawn the constellation of Capricorn was on the meridian; it is effaced by the rays of the rising sun.

70. Bearers of good tidings used to carry an olive branch.

74. The souls on this island all seem to Dante 'fortunate,' elect, and happy because they have come to 'make themselves beautiful' for Paradise.

80. So Aeneas, on meeting the shade of Anchises (*Aen.*, VI, 700–701):

> Ter conatus ibi collo dare bracchia circum,
> Ter frustra comprensa manus effugit imago.

(Thrice there he strove to throw his arms about his neck; thrice the form, vainly clasped, fled from his hands.)

91. Of Casella we know only that he was a musician of Florence; he is mentioned as a musician in a Vatican ms., Vat. 3214. From this passage we may infer that he was a close friend of the poet and, perhaps, that he set to music Dante's *canzone* (the second in the *Convivio*), *Amor che ne la mente mi ragiona*.

92. Dante's present experience is intended to fit him to return to Purgatory after death.

93. 'How hast thou been robbed of so much time?' Casella, evidently, had died some time before, and Dante is astonished to see him just arrived in the other world.

95. The angelic boatman.

97. His will depends on that of God. The greater or less delay imposed upon various souls appears to be a manifestation of God's mysterious judgment, the same predestination that assigns ranks in Heaven. This curious detail was probably suggested by the scene on the bank of the Styx in *Aen.*, VI, 313 ff.

98. The souls of the dead are allowed to participate in the plenary indulgence granted by Boniface VIII, from Christmas, 1299, to pilgrims to the great Jubilee of 1300.

101. The Tiber's mouth signifies allegorically the Church of Rome. There congregate the souls of those who die in the bosom of the Church. The souls of the unrepentant, on the other hand, descend to Acheron.

103. The angel has already started back toward the Tiber.

119. Cato reappears, rebuking the souls for their negligence. When we have assumed the task of cleansing our souls from guilt, no pleasure, however innocent, should divert us from our purpose.

122. 'Slough,' i.e., the old skin shed by a snake.

Canto III

Argument

Where the circular mountain descends to the shore, a high cliff forms its base all around, and outside this cliff creep the souls of those who died excommunicated but repentant. Like the other classes of the "negligent," whom we shall meet later, they are compelled to postpone their entrance into Purgatory until they have made amends for their neglect. The contumacious spirits of this canto are condemned to wait thirty times as long as their contumacy lasted.   Dante here insists upon the doctrine that the eternal fate of the soul depends upon its real state at the moment of death, and not upon the blessing or anathema of the Church.   "By their curse" — the curse of the clergy — "the eternal love is not irrevocably lost, so long as hope has a bit of green."   According to St. Thomas, *Summa Theologiae*, Tertia, Suppl., Qu. xxi, Art. 4, an unjust excommunication is ineffective.   Nevertheless, their rebellion against God's earthly vicar demands expiation, and their humble waiting at the very foot of the mountain is a fitting atonement.   This penalty Dante seems to have assigned on his own authority.

Among the excluded is Manfred, the natural son of the Emperor Frederick II, crowned King of Sicily in 1258.   Handsome, cultivated, winning, able in war and peace, he was the idolized chief of the Ghibellines and, like his father, the hated and excommunicated opponent of the Papacy.   In February, 1266, on a plain near Benevento, he was defeated and slain by St. Louis's brother, Charles of Anjou, to whom two Popes, Urban IV and Clement IV, had offered the throne of Sicily.   His body was interred on the battlefield, at the end of the Valentino bridge, on the right bank of the Calore; and a mound of stones was piled over the grave.   But this land was Church property.   When Clement heard of the burial, he sent the Archbishop of Cosenza to cast out the corpse, and Manfred's remains were deposited, with no funeral rites, outside the kingdom he had lost, on the bank of the Garigliano, or "Verde," which formed a part of its northern boundary.   Dante's is the earliest account we have of this episode.   The wretched disposal of Manfred's bones is in striking contrast to the magnificent translation of Virgil's body, to which reference is made in this canto.

When Manfred has appeared to Dante, and the latter has "modestly disclaimed" previous acquaintance with him, he reveals himself as the grandson of the Empress Constance, who, in the *Paradiso* III, 118, is called "la gran Costanza." Daughter and heiress of Roger II of Sicily, the last of the Norman kings, she married the Emperor Henry VI, the second of the Swabians, and gave birth to Frederick II.   Manfred named his daughter after her.   This second Constance, wedded in 1262 to Peter III of Aragon (cf. VII, 112 ff.), was the mother of Frederick and James, who became kings respectively of Sicily and Aragon.   Their loving grandfather here calls them "the glory" of these kingdoms; Dante himself, as we learn from various passages in his works, had a different opinion of them. Manfred hopes that his daughter, when she knows his state, will shorten by prayer his term of exclusion.   The belief that the journey of repentant souls to Heaven is hastened by the prayers of the living is an accepted doctrine of the Church, and Dante repeatedly dwells upon it.   Manfred's repentance and consequent salvation are probably not of Dante's invention.   In the *Imago Mundi* of Jacopo da

Acqui, written only some ten or twenty years after Dante's time, it is recorded that Manfred saved himself by exclaiming just before death: "Deus propitius esto mihi peccatori!" The incident as it appears in the *Purgatorio* is, therefore, presumably based on a tradition already current. If the passage was written as late as 1317, it has a particular significance, for in that year another great Ghibelline leader, Dante's patron, Can Grande della Scala, was excommunicated by John XXII. He remained under the ban until his death.

For the doctrine of prayers for the dead: 2 Macc. xii, 46; St. Thomas, *Summa Theologiae*, Tertia, Suppl., Qu. lxxi, Art. 2 and 6.

15. 'Unlakes itself,' i.e., rises from the great lake of the ocean.

16. The poets begin their journey on the east side of the island. When Dante turns and faces the mountain, the rising sun is behind him.

17, 18. The shadow has the same outline as the body which, by obstructing the sunlight, casts the shade.

21. Until now Dante has not had occasion to observe that spirits cast no shadow, and he is startled on seeing his own shadow without Virgil's. In several passages of the *Purgatorio* the poet makes effective use of the opaqueness of the human body.

25–27. *Vespero* is the last three hours of the day. Italy, according to Dante's geography, is midway between Jerusalem and Gibraltar, that is 45°, or three hours, west of Jerusalem; its time is therefore three hours earlier than that of Jerusalem. It is some time after sunrise in Purgatory, as long after sunset in Jerusalem, and the same amount after mid-afternoon in Italy. — Virgil died in Brundusium, but was buried by Augustus in Naples.

30. The nine concentric heavens being transparent, no one of them screens the sun's light from another.

31. Cf. *Inf.* III, 87.

37. In scholastic logic a demonstration *a priori*, from cause to effect, was called *propter quid*, and a demonstration *a posteriori*, from effect to cause, was called *quia*. The meaning of this line, therefore, is as follows: be satisfied with knowing the effects, and, through them, as far as may be, the maker; do not try to put yourselves in his place and guess his motives.

38, 39. If man had been all-knowing, there would have been no sin, and consequently no atonement: 'Mary would not have had to bear child.'

40, 41. If human knowledge had sufficed, the vain longing of the ancient sages (which torments them through eternity) would have been satisfied. Cf. *Georgics*, II, 490:

Felix, qui potuit rerum cognoscere causas.

(Blessed is he who has been able to win knowledge of the causes of things.)

45. Once more we have a pathetic reminder that Virgil is one of those whose desire will never be stilled.

49. *Turbia* is near Monaco; *Lerice*, now Lerici, is on the Gulf of Spezia, near Sarzana, where Dante was in 1306. Between these places the mountains descend steeply to the sea.

56. Virgil questions 'his mind about the road.' Reason is accustomed to look within itself for knowledge; the human Dante, however, looks without, and in this particular instance it is apparent that his method is the more successful.

65. In Hell the regular course is to the left; in Purgatory the course is always to the right. Virgil and Dante, however, now turn to the left (i.e., the south) to mingle with the slowly approaching crowd; hence the astonishment of the shades, ll. 70–72.

73. The fate of the souls on this island seems to Virgil the more happy by comparison with his own.

89. As Dante is now facing south, the morning sun is at his left, and his shadow falls on the cliff at his right.

107. Cf. 1 Samuel xvi, 12: (David) "Now he was ruddy, and withal of a beautiful countenance and goodly to look at."

122. Cf. Ps. li (Vulg. l); also John vi, 37, "him that cometh to me I will in no wise cast out."

126. If the Archbishop of Cosenza, sent by Clement IV to hunt me down, 'had read aright this page in God's book' — i.e., one of the passages referred to in the preceding note.

132. Without candles, as was customary in the burial of the excommunicated.

135. Green is the color of hope.

138. Cf. *Aen.*, VI, 327–330.

139. Why thirty? See E. G. Gardner in the *Modern Language Review*, IX, 63. In Deut. xxxiv, 8, we read: "the children of Israel wept for Moses in the plains of Moab thirty days." Hence the early Christian practice of saying prayers for the dead for thirty days after decease. Out of this grew the "Trental of St. Gregory," or thirty masses on thirty feast days through the year.

144. The 'prohibition' of entering Purgatory.

Canto IV

Argument

The top of the cliff can be reached only by crawling up through a crack in the rock, so narrow that it crowds the climbers on either side. Above is an open slope, difficult of ascent. On this declivity, lazily reclining in the shade of a boulder, are the shades of the "negligent" of the second class — those who postponed repentance through indolence. They must wait outside of Purgatory for a period equal to their life on earth. Among them is the mocking, humorous Florentine called Belacqua, evidently a friend of our poet and, according to the early commentators, a maker of musical instruments. His real name was probably Duccio di Bonavia. He first betrays his presence by his amusement at Dante's naïve surprise on seeing the sun at the left, or north, as he faces east. As the sun's course is confined within the tropics, it is always south of the north temperate, and north of the south temperate zone. The European observer, in the middle of the morning, sees the sun in the southeast; Dante now beholds it in the northeast. Something similar was noted by Lucan in his *Pharsalia*, III, 247–248 and IX, 538–539:

> Ignotum vobis, Arabes, venistis in orbem,
> Umbras mirati nemorum non ire sinistras.

(the Arabs entered a world unknown to them, and marveled that the shadows of the trees did not fall to the left.)

At tibi, quaecumque es Libyco gens igne dirempta,
In Noton umbra cadit, quae nobis exit in Arcton.

(But the shadow of people, if such there be, who are separated from us by the heats of Libya falls to the South, whereas ours falls northwards.)

4. 'It (the soul) seems to care for no other power': the intellective power is inoperative.

5, 6. Dante adds parenthetically that this absorption of the soul in one faculty is a proof that the Platonists and the Manichaeans, who maintain that man has several souls — 'one kindled upon another' — are wrong: if we had two souls, we could attend to two things at once. Cf. St. Thomas, *Summa Theologiae*, Prima, Qu. lxxvi, Art. 3.

10. Dante is using *potenza* here in the more restricted meaning of a single sense or faculty (namely, the hearing, *quella che l'ascolta*) of one of the major *potenze* of the soul. Thus: "It is one faculty which heeds it," i.e., the passing of time. The use of *ascolta* in this case has caused some perplexity among the commentators, and E. G. Parodi (1957, pp. 368–369) has judged it a lax use, in part dictated by the rhyme. We should remember, however, that time was commonly told, in Dante's day, by the ringing of bells, which makes appropriate the verb "to hear." It is essential, in any case, to understand that *l'* (*lo*) here refers to the passing of time (*vassene 'l tempo*, l. 9) and that the faculty in question is that faculty which perceives the passing of time, by observing the position of the sun, by hearing bells, or howsoever.

11. 'And another (power) is that which holds the whole soul (concentrated on it),' as in ll. 3–4. The reference, in this particular case, is to Dante's complete absorption in Manfred.

12. The power which holds the whole soul is absorbed (*legata*) in listening and looking (as is the case here) and accordingly pays no attention to the power that observes the passing of time, which would be the *estimativa*, a function of the *intellettiva*. — *E quella è sciolta*: And the faculty (the *estimativa*) which notes the passing of time is inoperative, unengaged.

15. Inasmuch as fifteen degrees correspond to an hour of time, three hours and twenty minutes have passed since sunrise.

25. San Leo, or Leone, is on Monte Feltrato, a huge rock of sheer precipices. Noli, a little town on the shore, not far from Genoa, is at the foot of steep cliffs.

26. Bismantova was a former hamlet in Emilia on a steep mountain by the same name about twenty miles south of Reggio and not far from Canossa. Nothing now remains except the huge sheer semicircular rock, known as the Pietra di Bismantova.

42. The hillside was far steeper than a line (*lista*) drawn from the center of a circle to the middle of one of its quadrants. Such a line makes an angle of 45°.

54. 'For it always cheers a man to look back' on the difficulties he has overcome.

60. 'Aquilo,' the north wind, often used, as here, for 'the north.'

61. Castor and Pollux compose the sign of Gemini, which accompanies the sun from May 21 to June 21. The clause means, then, 'if it were June (instead of April).'

62. The sun is often called a 'mirror,' because it reflects the divine light.

63. The sun 'leads with its light' on both sides of the equator, being half the year 'above' it, half the year 'below.'

64. The zodiac comprises the belt of constellations through which the sun passes as it takes its annual slanting course around the earth. The 'ruddy zodiac' consists of the part in which the sun is — or, in other words, the sun itself.

65. The sun, in that case, would be 'circling' farther north — 'closer' to the Big and Little 'Bears,' or Dippers — because June 21 is the day on which it reaches the point of its course farthest north of the equator.

66. Its 'old road' is the ecliptic, the annual path of the sun, which crosses the equator diagonally on March 21 and September 21 (the equinoxes). On June 21 it is farthest north, on December 21 farthest south.

70. See the third paragraph of the Argument to Canto II.   It must be remembered that Mt. Zion, or Jerusalem, and the mountain of Purgatory are on opposite sides of the earth, separated by 180°, so that they have a common horizon midway between them.

72. 'The road which, unhappily for him, he knew not how to drive' is the ecliptic.   The story of Phaëthon's disastrous attempt to drive the chariot of the sun is told in *Met.*, II.

73, 74. The ecliptic 'must pass on one side' of Purgatory when it passes 'on the other side' of Zion.   Jerusalem and Purgatory being in different hemispheres, on different sides of the equator and the tropics, it follows that when the sun is approaching one of these places, it is receding from the other; the more it is south of Jerusalem, the less it is north of Purgatory, and the less it is south of Jerusalem, the more it is north of Purgatory.

79. The 'mid-circle' of the 'upper motion' — the revolution of the spheres — is the celestial equator.

80. 'A certain science': astronomy.

81. When it is winter in any place, the sun is on the other side of the equator from that place.

82. The equator is as far north from Purgatory, one side of the globe, as it is south from Jerusalem, on the other.

123. Dante sees that Belacqua is, after all, among the elect.

129. The guardian angel at the gate of Purgatory.

137. It is noon in Purgatory, midnight in Jerusalem; the whole Hemisphere of Water is light, the Hemisphere of Land is dark.   The sun has reached the meridian of Purgatory; night, striding across the other hemisphere from the bank (of the Ganges), has already set foot on Morocco (the Strait of Gibraltar) — that is, it extends from the eastern to the western extremity of the habitable world.

Canto V

Argument

The third class of the "negligent" comprises those who, cut short by a violent death, repented at their last gasp.   They come wandering horizontally across the mountainside.   Their principal spokesman is Count Buonconte da Montefeltro, a Ghibelline leader, captain of the Aretines in the disastrous battle of Campaldino in 1289.   There he met his death, but, as we are told by Dante (who almost certainly took part in this fight), his body was not found on the field.   This curious circumstance allows the poet to introduce a romantic account of Buonconte's end — his appeal to Mary with his dying breath, his salvation "by one little tear" of genuine contrition, and the contest between angel and demon for the possession of his soul.   Such a conflict we find portrayed in ancient Etruscan art and, in Christian times, described as early as Gregory I and Bede.   In the *Commedia* it occurs — with a different outcome — in only one other instance, that of Buonconte's father, Guido (*Inf.* XXVII, 112–129), whose fate is thus contrasted with his son's.   By means of these two extreme examples Dante illustrates the dependence of everlasting welfare or perdition upon the real fitness of the soul at the instant of departure.

The foiled devil wreaks his vengeance on the corpse. He conjures up a storm, and Buonconte's body is swept into the Arno. In Ephesians ii, 2, the fiend is called "prince of the power of the air." According to St. Thomas, the elements are subject to spiritual beings; and demons, who dwell partly in Hell and partly in the dark air, are able to produce wind and rain.

For Guido da Montefeltro, see Argument to *Inf.* XXVII.

5. As Dante is climbing straight up the east side of the mountain, facing west — the sun being now in the north — his shadow falls on the left (or south) side.

17. The man in whose mind one thought immediately begets a different one 'puts the target further from him,' i.e., makes his goal more difficult of attainment. Dante is particularly fond of metaphors taken from archery.

21. Shame is becoming in women and youths, not in mature men: cf. *Conv.*, IV, ix, 8–9.

24. Ps. li (Vulg. l): 'Have mercy upon me, O God.' — *A verso a verso* probably indicates a division of the singers into two choirs, which sing the verses alternately.

36. 'It may profit them,' because they are in need of the prayers of the living, which Dante may procure for them.

37. *Vapori accesi* comprise both meteors and lightning. Meteors, cleaving the clear sky in the early night, and lightning, cleaving the August clouds at sunset, move less swiftly than the messengers.

69. The March of Ancona is the country between the Romagna and the land of Charles — i.e., the kingdom of Naples, which belonged to Charles II of Anjou. The speaker is Jacopo del Cassero, a leading citizen of Fano, who in 1296 was mayor of Bologna. He fell out with Azzo VIII of Este, and in 1298, while on his way to take the place of mayor of Milan, he was murdered by the marquis's hirelings.

74. Cf. Levit. xvii, 14: "anima enim omnis carnis in sanguine est"; the English version is not so close — "for the life of all flesh is the blood thereof."

75. The territory of the Paduans. According to an ancient tradition, Padua was founded by Antenor (cf. *Aen.*, I, 247–249), who, as we have seen, was regarded as an archtraitor: see the second paragraph of the Argument to *Inf.* XXXII.

79. Mira is a village between Padua and Oriaco, now Oriago. The speaker cannot forgive himself for having, in his terror, turned in the wrong direction, when he was 'overtaken' by the assassins: had he fled toward the village, instead of running into the swamp, he might still be in the land of the living, in which case he would have repented in due season and so spared himself, after death, this long waiting outside of Purgatory.

89. Giovanna was his wife.

94. The Casentino is a mountainous district in Tuscany, on the upper Arno.

95. The Archiano is a mountain torrent that runs into the Arno not very far from Bibbiena.

96. The 'Hermitage' is the monastery of Camaldoli, founded, in the moutains, by St. Romualdo in the 11th century.

97. The 'name' of the Archiano 'becomes useless' when it joins the Arno.

116. Pratomagno, a ridge on the southwest of the Casentino, the 'great chain' being the main range on the northeast.

122. The 'royal stream' is the Arno.

132. The unexpected intervention of this 'third spirit' is as startling as her reticence is pathetic.

133. Pia de' Tolomei of Siena, it was said, was wedded to Nello della Pietra de' Pannocchieschi, who, wishing to marry another woman, murdered her, or had her murdered, in his castle in the Tuscan Maremma.

Canto VI

Argument

The leading personage of this canto is that "Lombard soul" who so fired the imagination of two great poets. Browning saw in Sordello the representative of a changing age, an infinitely varied and interesting civilization; in Dante's eyes he was the critic of corrupt and incompetent government. The real Sordello was one of those roving Italians who, in the 13th century, helped to maintain the waning glory of Provençal verse and profited by its immense vogue in foreign countries. Born in the Mantuan town of Goito, he lived the restless and sometimes scandalous life of a handsome adventurer and clever poet at various courts in Lombardy and Piedmont, then in France and Spain, and found at last a mighty protector in the Count of Provence. Passing into the service of the count's son-in-law, Charles of Anjou, he probably saw the Sicilian campaign and the battle of Benevento. By this time he was certainly a man of considerable importance. Charles, after a reproof from Pope Clement IV for his neglect of the poet, bestowed upon him some castles in the Abruzzi. Sordello had evidently risen to knighthood, and we may assume that the notoriety of his youthful career was overshadowed by the fame of his later years. Dante, in De Vulgari Eloquentia, I, xv, 2, describes him as a man of great eloquence who had renounced his native dialect not only in poetry but in speech. His lyric work, as we possess it, does not rise above mediocrity; but his Ensenhamen d'Onor, a long didactic poem, though not brilliant in style, contains much that surely appealed to Dante — a high standard of chivalrous conduct and a vigorous invective against the mean-spirited rich. Dante's conception of him, however, was obviously based, in the main, upon a single short piece of verse, a lament over the death of Blacatz, a Provençal patron of letters; Sordello compares the virtues of the departed with the vices and weaknesses of those that are left, and turns his elegy into scathing satire, fearless and merciless condemnation of the potentates of his time, from the Emperor down. Dante regards him, then, as the type of the unflinching patriot and reformer, the scourge of kings. He invests his figure with more than regal dignity. It is likely that he knew but little of the real Sordello. He puts into the figure much of himself, as he did with Statius. Though a member of the fourth class of the "negligent" (those whose minds were over-engrossed by public cares), Sordello sits "all alone," apart from the monarchs whom he judged. The instant kindling of the flame of love by the mere mention of his native Mantua — contrasted as it is with the majestic indifference of his first attitude, and rendered the more effective by the amazing swiftness of the action — leads up naturally to the apostrophe to Italy which concludes the canto, a denunciation that vents all the pent-up bitterness of the exile's heart.   Its savage irony recalls the poem and the letter addressed by Guittone d'Arezzo to the Florentines on the morrow of their great defeat at Montaperti.   For many centuries it bore a stern message to Italians.

1. 'Hazard,' a game played with three dice, was very much in vogue, in spite of prohibitions.

13. The 'Aretine' is Benincasa of Laterina in the county of Arezzo, a jurist, who visited Florence in 1282; he was murdered in Rome, while sitting in court, by the famous robber Ghino di Tacco (Boccaccio, *Decamerone*, X, 2), whose brother he had condemned to death.

15. 'The other' Aretine is said to be Guccio Tarlati of Pietramala, who was drowned in the Arno while 'hunting' the enemy, or, possibly 'hunted by.'

17. 'Frederick, junior,' the son of Count Guido Novello and a daughter of Frederick II, was killed in war in the Casentino in 1291. — *Quel da Pisa* is apparently Giovanni or Gano, called Farinata, the son of the Marzucco of l. 18.

18. Marzucco was a Pisan, prominent in public affairs, who in 1287 left the world and became a Franciscan friar.   According to the most plausible of the conflicting early explanations, his fortitude was shown by pardoning the murderer of his son.   A certain Marzuchus Scornigianus was "syndicus" of Pisa in 1275; he is recorded also in Arezzo, Florence, Venice (1275).   Dante may have known Marzucco between 1291 and 1295, when the latter was very old, at the monastery of Santa Croce in Florence.

19. Count Orso of Mangona was murdered, it is said, by his cousin Albert.   The fathers of Orso and Albert killed each other: cf. *Inf.* XXXII, 55-58.

22. Pierre de la Brosse of Turenne — 'the soul parted from its body by hate and envy' — was chamberlain of Louis IX and Philip III of France.   Through the wiles of Philip's second wife, Mary of Brabant, whom Pierre had accused of the murder of the heir to the throne, he was hanged in 1278. — 'Let her look to it,' while she is alive, that she be not consigned, after death, to the 'worse flock' of the damned.   Mary lived until 1321.

29. When the shade of the unburied Palinurus begs Aeneas to take him over the Styx, the Sibyl replies (*Aen.*, VI, 373-376):

> Unde haec, o Palinure, tibi tam dira cupido?
> Tu Stygias inhumatus aquas amnemque severum
> Eumenidum aspicies ripamve iniussus adibis?
> Desine fata Deum flecti sperare precando.

(Whence, O Palinurus, this wild longing of thine?   Shalt thou, unburied, view the Stygian waters and the Furies' stern river, and unbidden draw near the bank?   Cease to dream that heaven's decrees may be turned aside by prayer.)

33. Dante questions his own understanding, not Virgil's statement.

37. 'The summit of justice (*apex juris*) is not overturned.'   Cf. Shakespeare, *Measure for Measure*, II, ii, 75-77:

> "How would you be
> If He who is the *top of judgment* should
> But judge you as you are?"

39. Satisfaction, an atonement for the injury done, can be made by other loving hearts as well as by the guilty one.   See the last paragraph of the Argument to Canto III.

42. Palinurus was a pagan, not 'living in grace' (IV, 134), and his prayer was not addressed to God or received by him.

43. A question involving the doctrine of grace transcends the power of reason, and is not to be 'settled' without revelation.

46. This mention of the name — the first since the beginning of the journey — makes Dante more eager to climb.

51. Cf. *Eclogue* I, 83: "Maioresque cadunt altis de montibus umbrae." (And longer shadows fall from the mountain heights.)

57. In the middle of the afternoon the whole eastern side of the mountain is in the shade, and Dante no longer casts a shadow.

66. Cf. Gen. xlix, 9: "he couched as a lion."

75. See the second paragraph of the Argument to Canto II.

78. Several old writers call Italy "domina provinciarum"; cf. Lamentations of Jeremiah i, 1, "princess among the provinces (*princeps provinciarum*)." Cf. Isaiah i, 21: "How is the faithful city become a harlot!"

88. In ll. 88–102 Italy is pictured as a horse. Justinian (*Par.* VI) "adjusted its bridle" by codifying the laws, but there is no Emperor to fill the saddle.

93. Mat. xxii, 21: "Render therefore unto Caesar the things which are Caesar's."

96. Ever since the clergy usurped temporal authority.

97. Albert of Hapsburg was elected King of the Romans in 1298, but never went to Italy to be crowned.

100. In 1307 Albert's oldest son died after a short sickness; the next year Albert himself was murdered by his nephew, John the Parricide. If Dante was apostrophizing Albert as still alive at the time of writing, this canto must have been composed between these two events. If, on the other hand, the poet was putting himself back into the year 1300, the 'judgment' would naturally be the assassination of Albert, and the 'successor' would be the next Emperor, Henry VII, who descended into Italy. According to Parodi, the passage was probably written shortly after the events of 1307 and 1308, presumably late in 1309 or early in 1310.

103. Rudolph, who was as remiss as his son.

104. 'Held by greed of things up yonder': the desire to increase their German states.

106, 107. Dante cites a few of the great houses that were ravaged by strife: the Montecchi of Verona, Ghibellines; the Cappelletti of Cremona, of the Church party; the Monaldi and Filippeschi, rival familes (Guelf and Ghibelline) of Perugia and Orvieto. There is no evidence that the 'Capulets' were ever neighbors of the 'Montagues' in Verona. The story of Romeo and Juliet comes from Bandello, who took it from Luigi da Porto, who got it from Masuccio da Salerno (1476). It has been suggested that the legend of the rival families in Verona is due originally to a misinterpretation of Dante's words.

109. Cf. Luke xxi, 25, "pressura gentium," (distress of nations).

111. The Counts of Santafiora, a great Ghibelline family, lost, at the close of the 13th century, a great part of their territory to Siena. Santafiora is in the Maremma.

125. C. Claudius Marcellus, "Marcellus ... loquax" (Marcellus, that man of words), as Julius Caesar calls him in Lucan's *Pharsalia*, I, 313, was a strenuous opponent of Caesar and a partisan of Pompey.

129. Ll. 127–144 are bitterly ironical.

135. 'I bend my back' for the 'common burden' of public service.

141. Athens and Lacedaemon 'offered but a slight suggestion of right living,' compared to Florence.

142. Dante plays upon the double sense of *sottile*, which means 'shrewd' and 'flimsy.' The fabric of laws which Florence spins in October does not last until mid-November. The two months were perhaps suggested by the vicissitudes of 1301, in which year the White priors who took office on Oct. 18 were deposed by the Blacks on Nov. 8.

151. Cf. St. Augustine, *Confessiones*, VI, xvi, 3: "Versa et reversa in tergum et in latera et in ventrem, et dura sunt omnia." (Turned it has, and turned again, back, sides, and belly, yet found all places to be hard.)

Canto VII

Argument

"Walk while ye have the light, lest darkness come upon you: for he that walketh in darkness knoweth not whither he goeth" (John xii, 35). In ll. 107–108 of the first canto the wayfarers were told that the sun — the emblem of spiritual enlightenment, or righteous choice — was to be their guide in their upward journey; now (and again in XVII, 62–63 and XXVII, 74–75) they learn that without that guidance they cannot ascend at all. The life of the penitent is divided between the day of active advancement on the path of reformation, where every step must be wisely directed, and the night of prayerful meditation. Day is ushered in by the constellation of cardinal, or practical, virtues, Prudence, Temperance, Fortitude, Justice (I, 22–27); night, by the three bright stars of Christian contemplation, the theological virtues of Faith, Hope, and Love (VIII, 85–93).

Each of the three nights passed by Dante on the island is spent in repose. His first resting place is the beautiful Valley of the Princes, a hollow in the mountainside, where are gathered great rulers whose worldly cares made them postpone until the last moment their reconciliation with God. Those who were enemies on earth sit side by side in fraternal harmony, Rudolph of Hapsburg with Ottocar of Bohemia, Charles of Anjou with Peter of Aragon. Here, as in the first life, Sordello is the judge of kings: he points out and describes to the travelers the dwellers in the dale. The conception of this charming, peaceful spot was probably suggested to Dante — as was that of the Noble Castle of *Inf.* IV, 106 — by Virgil's picture of the Elysian Fields in *Aen.*, VI, 637 ff. As Sordello shows the dell to Virgil and Dante from a bank, so Anchises leads the Sibyl and Aeneas to a height (754–755):

> Et tumulum capit, unde omnis longo ordine posset
> adversos legere et venientum discere voltus.

(Then chose a mound whence, face to face, he might scan all the long array, and note their countenances as they came.)

In both poems the spirits are seen reclining on the greensward, singing together (656–657):

> Conspicit ecce alios dextra laevaque per herbam
> Vescentis laetumque choro paeana canentis.

(Lo! others he sees, to right and left, feasting on the sward, and chanting in chorus a joyous paean.)

Like Sordello, Anchises surveys and recognizes souls destined to rise (679–681):

> At pater Anchises penitus convalle virenti
> Inclusas animas superumque ad lumen ituras,
> Lustrabat studio recolens.

(But, deep in a green vale, father Anchises was surveying with earnest thought the imprisoned souls that were to pass to the light above.)

One may compare also Lucian's Isle of the Blest in the *True History*, II.

3. Not until he has lovingly greeted his countryman several times does Sordello ask his name.   Dante remains comparatively unnoticed until Canto VIII, l. 62.

4. Before the descent of Christ into Hell no souls went to Purgatory or Heaven: cf. *Inf.* IV, 63.   Ever since the redemption the souls of the elect have reached Heaven through Purgatory. Virgil died in 19 B.C.

6. Cf. III, 27.

15. 'The inferior lays hold' — i.e., clasps his superior — either under the arms or at the feet (XXI, 130).

18. Mantua issued coins bearing Virgil's image, and in the 14th century erected a statue to him.

30. Cf. *Inf.* IV, 26.

33. Before baptism: cf. *Inf.* IV, 35–36.

36. Though the virtuous souls in Limbus were ignorant of the three theological virtues, 'they knew the others' — the four cardinal virtues — 'and followed them all.'   See the third paragraph of the Argument to Canto I.

72. The sloping valley opens out as it descends, and its banks diminish until they blend into the mountainside.

73. 'Cochineal and white lead,' from which red and white colors were extracted.   The pigments named here were really used by artists.

74. As pointed out by M. Cook (1903, p. 356), several interpretations of this verse have been proposed: one is that *indaco*, taken by itself, means indigo; another is that the words *indaco legno* taken together mean 'amber,' the tree gum that sometimes comes from India. The most persuasive interpretation advanced so far is that *legno* taken by itself, intended to be in apposition to *indaco*, means, 'lychnis' (or 'lignis'), mentioned as a bright purple gem by Pliny, Solinus, and Isidore of Seville.

76, 77. 'Each (of the things just enumerated) would be surpassed in color by the grass and flowers set within that dale.'

82. *Salve Regina* is an antiphon recited after sunset in the service of certain seasons.   It is an appeal to Mary from the "exiled sons of Eve ... in this valley of tears."

94, 95. Rudolph of Hapsburg, crowned Emperor at Aix-la-Chapelle in 1273, was the first of the Austrian Emperors. Cf. VI, 103.

98. Bohemia.

100. Ottocar II, King of Bohemia and Duke of Austria, was killed, in 1278, in war with Rudolph, whom he would not recognize as King of Rome. — *Fasce*, 'swaddling clothes': he was worth more in his infancy than his son Wenceslaus in mature age.

101. Wenceslaus IV, son and heir of Ottocar, son-in-law of Rudolph.   He lived until 1305.

103. 'Small Nose' is Philip III, the Bold, of France, son and successor of Louis IX, and nephew of Charles of Anjou.   To help his uncle against Peter of Aragon (l. 112), whom the Sicilian revolutionists had elected king, he invaded Catalonia by land and by sea; but his fleet was defeated, and his army, which had contracted the plague, was obliged to flee.   The king himself died at Perpignan in 1285.

104. Henry the Fat of Navarre, brother and successor of the Thibault of *Inf.* XXII, 52, died in 1274.

109. Philip the Bold was father, Henry the Fat was father-in-law, of the 'Curse of France,' Philip IV, the Fair.   In the many passages in which Dante assails this sovereign (who did so much harm to Italy and the Church), he avoids mentioning his name.   He died in 1314.

112. The 'large-limbed' sovereign is Peter III of Aragon, the husband of Manfred's daughter Constance (cf. III, 115), elected king of Sicily when the French were expelled in 1282.   He died in 1285.

113. 'The one with the masculine nose' is Charles of Anjou, brother of Louis IX of France, and conqueror of Naples and Sicily.

114. Cf. Isaiah xi, 5: "And righteousness shall be the girdle of his loins, and faithfulness the girdle of his reins."

116. The reference is probably to Pedro, the last-born son of Pedro III of Aragon.   Some commentators have understood the reference to be to Alfonso III of Aragon, the eldest son of Pedro III.   But Alfonso actually did become king after his father, reigning from 1285 to 1291.

117. 'Goodness would indeed have been emptied from vessel to vessel.'   Cf. Jeremiah xlviii, 11.

119. James and Frederick, 'the other heirs,' i.e., the second and third sons of Peter, were kings of Aragon and Sicily when Dante wrote.   Cf. III, 115.

120. The 'better heritage' is the father's goodness.

123. "Crist," who bestows it, "wol we clayme of him our gentilesse" (Chaucer, *Wyf of Bath's Tale*, 1117).   Cf. Epistle of James i, 17.

126. Apulia and Provence 'mourn' under the rule of Charles's degenerate son, Charles II, who died in 1309.

127, 128, 129. Charles II is as much inferior to Charles I as Charles I is to Peter III.   Beatrice of Provence and Margaret of Burgundy were the successive wives of Charles I; Constance (daughter of Manfred) was the wife of Peter; and Charles I was not a devoted husband.   'The plant (the son) is inferior to the seed (the father) to the same extent that Constance boasts of her husband (Peter) more than Beatrice and Margaret boast of theirs (Charles).'

130, 131 132. Henry III of England was reputed to have little wit; his son, Edward I, was highly esteemed.

134. William VII, or 'Longsword,' sits in a lower place on the ground because he is of lower rank than the others.   He was, however, Marquis of Montferrat and Canavese, Imperial vicar, a great feudal lord and Ghibelline leader.

135, 136. In 1292 he was treacherously captured at Alessandria in Piedmont, and was kept in an iron cage until his death.   His son, to avenge him, attacked Alessandria, but was defeated, unhappily for his domains.

Canto VIII

Argument

The penitent who, completely renouncing his past life, has once begun his expiation under the protection of grace and the guidance of the Church is exempt from temptation or fear of sin; so the souls within Dante's Purgatory have no apprehension.   Those outside the gate, however — the remorseful evildoers who are still waiting and striving — are exposed to the wiles of the serpent and feel the "chaste dread" (*timor castus*) of wickedness itself, different from the "servile terror" (*timor servilis*) of the consequences of wrongdoing (cf. *Inf.* I, 44).   But inasmuch as they are on their way to God, he constantly watches over them; in time of need he sends the green Angels of Hope, armed with the blunted sword of defense, to protect them from the adversary.   Such is the lesson which Dante expressly bids us discover behind the "thin veil" of allegory.   Once before, in *Inf.* IX, 61–63, he warned us to look "under the veil of the strange verses."

It is in the evening that temptation creeps upon the repentant sinner — evening, which softens the hearts of sailors just parted from home, and "pricks with love" the unhardened traveler as he hears the bell of compline, or *compieta*, tolling the knell of "dying day." That is the hour at which the Church sings the hymn (attributed to St. Ambrose) *Te lucis ante* and recites a prayer calling for the guardianship of holy angels and protection against the snares of the enemy. This hymn is now sung by the souls in the valley. The first two of the three stanzas are as follows:

Te lucis ante terminum,   Ut tua pro clementia
Rerum Creator, poscimus,   Sis praesul et custodia.
Procul recedant somnia   Hostemque nostrum comprime,
Et noctium phantasmata;   Ne polluantur corpora.

They are translated by M. Britt as follows:

Before the ending of the day,   From all ill dreams defend our eyes,
Creator of the world, we pray   From nightly fears and fantasies;
That, with Thy wonted favor, Thou   Tread under foot our ghostly foe,
Wouldst be our guard and keeper now.   That no pollution we may know.

Among the singers, two are singled out for special notice: one, Nino Visconti, was known to Dante in the first life; the other, Conrad Malaspina, belonged to a family whose hospitality the poet once enjoyed. Nino, a grandson of the Ugolino of *Inf.* XXXIII, was judge, or governor, of Gallura, one of the four provinces into which the Pisans divided their Sardinian domain; Fra Gomita (*Inf.* XXII, 81) was his dishonest vicar there. Moreover, he ruled Pisa with his grandfather, and on the death of the latter waged war for five years — 1288–1293 — against that city and the Ghibelline forces of Guido da Montefeltro (*Inf.* XXVII). He was an ally of Florence — to which he made several visits in 1289 — and other Guelf towns of Tuscany and became captain general of the Guelf league. We learn from *Inf.* XXI, 94–96, that Dante had a hand in one of his campaigns, being present at the siege of Caprona in 1289. Although Nino's life was devoted mainly to politics and strife, he seems to have been fond of poetry. He lived until 1296. Conrad Malaspina, who died two years earlier, was the lord of Villafranca on the Magra (which flows into the sea near the Gulf of Spezia) and other holdings in the northwest. For a century his house had been famous for its gallantry and its liberality to troubadours; and "the glory of the purse and the sword" had not declined. In October, 1306, Dante acted as attorney for the family in concluding a treaty of peace. One of the letters ascribed to him (Epistola III) is addressed to Moroello Malaspina, his former host, to whom obscure reference is made in *Inf.* XXIV, 145–150. The poet's splendid tribute of just praise is a grateful return for kindness to the exile.

7. Cf. IV, 1–12: Dante becomes so absorbed in gazing that he can hear nothing.

9. Cf. Acts xiii, 16: "Then Paul stood up, and beckoning with his hand said ..." etc.   Also *Met.*, I, 205–206; *Aen.*, XII, 692.

18. The 'upper wheels' are the revolving heavens.

46. The bank is not high (VII, 72), and Dante has been observing the spirits at close range (VII, 88–89).

51. It was not too late for the darkening air to 'disclose what it had locked up (concealed) before': now that they are so near, Dante and Nino can discern each other's features.

62. Sordello, up to this time, has not noticed that Dante is alive.

65. This Conrad reappears in l. 109.

71. Joan was Nino's only child.   In 1308 she was married to Rizzardo di Camino.

73. Nino's wife was Beatrice, daughter of Obizzo II d'Este (cf. *Inf.* XII, 111).   In June, 1300, she married Galeazzo di Matteo Visconti.   As it is now April, 1300, we may suppose, either that Dante did not know the exact date of the marriage or that Nino is here speaking of it only as something contemplated.

74. Married women wore as veils certain bands called *bende;* the widow's veil was white.

75. In 1302 the Visconti were driven from Milan, and Galeazzo and his wife were compelled to take refuge with her family in Ferrara.

77. Cf. *Aen.*, IV, 569–570: "varium et mutabile semper femina.'   (A fickle and changeful thing is woman ever.)

80. The cognizance of the Visconti, the lords of Milan, was a blue viper swallowing a red Saracen.   These arms will not adorn her tomb so well as would Nino's, the cock, the emblem of Gallura.   In the 13th century the Milanese, when at war, never pitched their camp until they had hoisted the Visconti standard.

87. Near the pole, the end of the axis of the heavens, the stars revolve slowest.

89. The 'three torches' represent the three theological virtues: see the first paragraph of the Argument to Canto VII.

91. Cf. I, 22–27.

97. Apparently from the lower end, where the valley opens.

99. Gen. iii, 4–6.

112. The meaning is: 'As thou hopest that illuminating grace (the lantern which leads thee up) may find in thy free will the responsive spirit (the wax, food for the flame) that is needed to take thee to the Earthly Paradise.'

114. *Smalto*, 'enamel,' is used figuratively by Italian poets in two senses, 'stone,' and 'greensward' or 'garden': here it has the second meaning.

116. The valley of the Magra (*Inf.* XXIV, 145) is a part of the district of Lunigiana.

119. The older and more famous Conrad Malaspina, who lived in the first half of the 13th century, was the grandfather of the present speaker.

122. In 1300 Dante had not been there.

133, 134, 135. The sun will not return seven times to the sign of Aries, the Ram: seven years will not pass.   The sun is in Aries from March 21 to April 21.   The prophecy is made in April, 1300.   Dante's 'courteous opinion' of the Malaspina is, then, to be confirmed ('nailed in his head') by experience before March 21, 1307.   We know that he was with them on Oct. 6, 1306.

Canto IX

Argument

During each of the three nights that Dante spends on the island he has an allegorical vision, related to his present state or his immediate future. In the first dream he fancies himself carried up through the sky by a golden eagle; and this flight is but the image of a real spiritual ascent. Souls earnestly striving to reach God are always mysteriously assisted by grace, which comes to meet them and so speeds them on their way that their swift progress passes their understanding. "They that wait upon the Lord," says Isaiah xl, 31, "shall renew their strength; they shall mount up with wings as eagles."

Lucia, then, the symbol of Illuminating Grace, who came to Dante's assistance at the beginning of his struggle (*Inf.* II, 97–108) and who reappears to him at his long journey's end (*Par.* XXXII, 137), now lifts him up while he is asleep and bears him, just at daybreak, over the long, steep incline up to the very gate of Purgatory.

There he beholds, seated on the steps, an angelic guardian, who represents Ecclesiastical Authority. In the hand of this celestial "porter," reflecting the sun's rays, gleams a bare sword, "the sword of the Spirit, which is the word of God" (Ephesians vi, 17).

From beneath his garment he draws the keys entrusted by Christ to Peter and his successors — "I will give unto thee the keys of the kingdom of heaven" (Mat. xvi, 19). They are two, the golden key of power and the silver key of discernment; or, as Peter Lombard describes them in his *Sententiae*, IV, xviii, 502, "scientia discernendi peccata et potestas judicandi de peccatis" (the science of discerning sins and the power of judging sins). The priest needs not only the requisite authority to loose and bind, delegated to him by God, but also must have judgment to direct him in the use of it. The golden key, which was purchased with Christ's blood, is "the more precious"; but the other, the silver key of discrimination, "requires vast skill and wit" to "disentangle the knot."

The stone threshold of Purgatory, which is the angel's seat, appears to Dante to be made of adamant; it evidently typifies the firm foundation upon which ecclesiastical power rests — "thou art Peter, and upon this rock I will build my church" (Mat. xvi, 18).

Leading up to it are three steps: the first is of white, smooth marble; the second, of rough, dark stone, scorched and cracked; the third, "piled upon" the second, is blood-red. Apparently they stand for the three stages in the career of man which led up to the founding of the Church: original innocence, sin, and atonement. It is obvious that the same three stages are bound to recur in the life of every transgressor who finds salvation. The feet of the gatekeeper rest upon the red step of atonement; there it is that Dante humbly prostrates himself and beats his breast.

Most commentators see in the three stairs the three parts of the sacrament of penance — contrition, confession, satisfaction. But according to the literal sense of the poem the souls who have reached the gate should have accomplished these duties (for the most part at least) before death; otherwise they would not have attained the mountain at all. And in Dante's symbolical journey through Purgatory (indicating the purification of his soul as a result of discipline on earth) he is not yet ready to receive this sacrament, which forms the culmination of his expiatory task. Contrition, confession, and satisfaction await him upon his arrival at the top of the mountain, where they are administered by Beatrice herself: *Purg.* XXX, 97–99; XXXI, 1–36, 88–90.

1. In two places in the *Aeneid* — IV, 584–585 and IX, 459–460 — we find the lines:

> Et iam prima novo spargebat lumine terras
> Tithoni croceum linquens Aurora cubile.

(And now early Dawn, leaving the saffron bed of Tithonus, was sprinkling her fresh rays upon the earth.)
In the *Georgics*, I, 447, the second line occurs once more. Tithonus was therefore well known to Dante as the husband of Aurora, the dawn. Having to describe moonrise, the lunar dawn, — two or three hours after sunset on the island — the poet fancifully calls the lunar aurora 'the concubine of old Tithonus,' as contrasted with sunrise, his lawful spouse.

2. The lunar aurora 'was already whitening in the balcony of the east': the white light of the moon was appearing on the eastern horizon.

4, 5, 6. In the eastern sky, where the moon was to appear, was the constellation of Scorpio. This is astronomically correct: see Moore, III, 74–85. For the description of the 'cold creature,' cf. Rev. ix, 5: "and their torment was as the torment of a scorpion, when he striketh a man" — "cum percutit hominem" (i.e., "percuote la gente"). See also *Met.*, XV, 371:

> Scorpius exibit, caudaque minabitur unca.

(A scorpion will come forth threatening with his hooked tail.)

7. The 'steps' with which night ascends are the hours between sunset and midnight. Nearly three hours have passed since nightfall.

9. The third step 'was bending its wings downward': the third hour had nearly finished its flight. Such incongruous mixed metaphors are not uncommon in Dante.

10. The 'stuff of Adam' is the body.

12. Sordello, Virgil, Dante, Nino, Conrad.

15. An allusion to the familiar and tragic story of Philomela and Progne, told by Ovid in *Met.*, VI, 423–674. According to the version followed by Dante, it was the outraged princess Philomela who was turned into a swallow: cf. XVII, 19, 21.

18. Cicero, *De Senectute*, XXII, 81: "Atqui dormientium animi maxime declarant divinitatem suam." (And yet it is when the body sleeps that the soul most clearly manifests its divine nature.) Dreams that occurred shortly before dawn were thought to be prophetic: cf. *Inf.* XXVI, 7.

22. On Mt. Ida, in Phrygia, whence the youthful hunter Ganymede was caught up by an eagle, from the midst of his guardians and dogs, to be cupbearer to the gods: *Aen.*, V, 252–257; cf. *Met.*, X, 155–161.

27. 'He disdains to carry off on high in his feet' (*pedibus ... uncis: Aen.*, V, 255). Help comes from above only to those who have climbed as high as their own power will take them.

30. The sphere of fire is between the earth's atmosphere and the heaven of the moon.

34. To prevent her son Achilles from going to the Trojan war, Thetis took him in his sleep from his teacher, the centaur Chiron (*Inf.* XII, 71), to the court of the peaceful Lycomedes on the island of Scyros. When Achilles awoke, he did not know where he was. See Statius, *Achilleid*, I, 104–250.

39. Ulysses and Diomed discovered Achilles disguised in women's garments and took him away.

44. It is the morning of Easter Monday. The poets are still on the eastern side of the mountain.

50. A ledge — *balzo* (cf. IV, 47) — runs around the mountain outside of Purgatory.

59. There was no ascent until the sunlight appeared: cf. VII, 44.

97. 'Perse' is a very dark purple color: cf. *Inf.* V, 89.

111. In remorse for sins of thought, word, and deed.

112. *P* stands for *peccatum*, 'sin': the seven letters are the emblem of the seven capital vices, of which Dante's soul is to be cleansed by penance. Cf. Rev. xiii, 16; xx, 4.

116. The gray color of the angel's garment betokens the humility of the priest, who is God's servant.

132. The sinner must enter upon the course of penance with no mental reservation; if he looks back upon his former life, at the moment of leaving it, he is unworthy to proceed. Cf. Luke ix, 62: "No man, having put his hand to the plough, and looking back, is fit for the kingdom of God." Also Gen. xix, 17: "Escape for thy life; look not behind thee, neither stay thou in all the plain; escape to the mountain, lest thou be consumed." See, furthermore, Boethius, *Cons.*, III, Met. xii (the story of Orpheus and Eurydice) near the end:

> Ne dum Tartara liquerit   That when from hell he takes his flight,
> Fas sit lumina flectere.   He shall from looking back refrain.
>
> . . . .
>
> Vos haec fabula respicit,   But you this feigned tale fulfill,
> Quicumque in superum diem   Who think unto the day above
> Mentem ducere quaeritis.   To bring with speed your darksome mind.

This warning applies only to the entrance: once within the gate, souls are safe from temptation.

136. When Caesar entered Rome, after crossing the Rubicon, he wished to take possession of the public treasure, kept in the temple of Saturn at the foot of the Tarpeian rock. The tribune Metellus, after a futile resistance, departed, leaving the temple unprotected. Then the gates were opened and the rock resounded (Lucan, *Phars.*, III, 153–155):

> Protinus abducto patuerunt templa Metello.
> Tunc rupes Tarpeia sonat magnoque reclusas
> Testatur stridore fores.

(Metellus was drawn aside and the temple at once thrown open. Then the Tarpeian rock re-echoed, and loud grating bore witness to the opening of the doors.)

The gate of Purgatory roars because, owing to the perversity of man, it is so seldom opened: cf. X, 2.

138. After the spoliation of the temple the Tarpeian rock 'was left lean.' Cf. *Phars.*, III, 167–168:

> Tristi spoliantur templa rapina,
> Pauperiorque fuit tunc primum Caesare Roma.

(Dismal was the deed of plunder that robbed the temple; and then for the first time Rome was poorer than a Caesar.)

139. *Tuono* here, apparently, means not 'thunder' but 'tone,' and refers not to what precedes but to the following line: I seemed to hear *Te Deum* from within the gate, and 'turned attentive at the first note.'

140. This hymn of praise to God, who opens Heaven to the faithful, is appropriate to the place.

144. On reading these lines, one is reminded of the old and immensely heavy bronze doors in the ancient baptistery of S. Giovanni in Laterano, in Rome; when they are slowly pushed open, these doors emit a succession of loud musical notes that sound like organ peals. One thinks also of Keats's *Lamia*:

> Sounds Aeolian
> Breathed from the hinges, as the ample span
> Of the wide doors disclosed a place unknown.

Canto X

Argument

Purgatory proper consists of seven flat, narrow terraces running around the mountain and separated from one another by steep cliffs. On each shelf are souls doing penance for one of the capital vices — pride, envy, anger, sloth, avarice and prodigality, gluttony, lust. These wicked dispositions are the source of all sin. Inasmuch as pride is an ingredient in every transgression (which is an assumption of superiority to law), all souls have to suffer in the first circle; in the ensuing circles they are punished according to the nature of their wrongdoing. The terraces are connected by stairways cut into the precipice. When a spirit has cleansed itself of the evil that is expiated on one shelf, it passes on upward to the next terrace that claims it — or, if it has no other stain, to the top of the mountain. At the beginning of each ascent a friendly angel is seen, who removes the last impress of the discarded vice; and a beatitude (Mat. v, 3–8) is heard, appropriate to the circle that is left below. To sustain them, the souls are furnished, on every terrace, with examples of the particular sin that belongs to that spot, and of the opposite virtue. The latter examples — the "goad" — generally appear to Dante as he enters each circle, the former — the "check" — as he is about to depart from it. They take different shapes on the various shelves; on the first, they present themselves to the eye as beautiful carvings on the upright wall of the mountain and on the floor. These illustrations of good and evil are drawn from both Christian and pagan lore, but the first example of each of the seven virtues is taken from the life of the Virgin. In the *Speculum Beatae Mariae Virginis* by Friar Conrad of Saxony, a Franciscan contemporary of St. Bonaventure, the Virtues of the Virgin are opposed to the seven vices: Gardner, 254–255.

Allegorically the torments cheerfully endured on the several terraces represent the forms of discipline to which the sinner must subject himself, under priestly direction, in order to restore his lost innocence and thus fit himself for Heaven.   In the first circle, for instance, the spirits crouching under heavy burdens are the image of self-imposed humiliation, the painful subjugation of pride.   Dante's journey up through Purgatory signifies the moral training by means of which, obedient to ecclesiastical authority, he removes from his soul every disposition to evil and regains the purity of heart that enables him to see God.   While in the literal sense of the poem he is only an observer of the spirits and their punishments, symbolically he is himself the punished spirit; in the circles of pride, envy, anger, and lust — if we look for the inner beneath the external meaning — we can see the poet in the throes of penance.

2. Love, wrongly directed, so perverts human souls that few of them attain Purgatory: the gate falls into disuse.

5. Cf. IX, 131–132.

8. The narrow crack by which the poets ascend runs zigzag up through the cliff.

12. The climbers have to cling now to one side, now to the other, according to the changing direction of the crack.

14. The waning moon, which, of course, sets later than the full moon; it is several hours after sunrise.

16. 'Needle's eye,' i.e., the narrow passage: cf. Mat. xix, 24.

18. 'Gathers itself': withdraws, leaving a flat terrace.

24. The width of the shelf, from its outer edge to the foot of the upright cliff, is three times the length of a human body.

32. The Greek sculptor Polycletus was known by name to medieval writers.

34. 'The angel' is Gabriel.   The first example of humility represents the Virgin at the Annunciation.   Cf. Luke i, 26 ff.

40. *Ave*, 'hail,' the greeting of Gabriel to Mary: Luke i, 28.

44. 'Behold the handmaid of the Lord,' Mary's reply to Gabriel: Luke i, 38.

47, 48. Virgil had Dante on his left.   On Virgil's right was another carving.

56. The second example of humility pictures King David dancing 'with all his might' before the ark of the covenant, as it is drawn into the city on a 'new cart': 2 Samuel vi, 12–16.

57. We have here a brief, parenthetical reference to an incident not represented in the carving — the story of Uzzah, which makes us chary of assuming offices not entrusted to us. Uzzah, one of the drivers of the cart, seeing the ark shaken and fearing it would fall, "put forth his hand ... and took hold of it"; whereupon "God smote him" for his presumption, and "there he died": 2 Samuel vi, 3–7.

59. The 'seven choirs' appear in the Vulgate, but not in the English Bible: 2 Samuel vi, 12.

65. "And David was *girded* with a linen ephod" (2 Samuel vi, 14).   When he returned home, his wife, Michal, Saul's daughter, reproached him for uncovering himself "in the eyes of the handmaids of his servants, as one of the vain fellows shamelessly uncovereth himself": 2 Samuel vi, 20.

66. David replied to Michal: "I will yet be more vile than thus, and will be base in mine own sight: and of the maidservants which thou hast spoken of, of them shall I be had in honour" (2 Samuel vi, 22).

67. "Michal, Saul's daughter, looked through a window, and saw King David leaping and dancing before the Lord; and she despised him in her heart": 2 Samuel vi, 16.

74. The third example of humility is furnished by Trajan, the 'Roman prince' who acknowledged the justice of the poor widow's claim.   This story had wide currency in the Middle Ages.

75. According to a legend universally believed in Dante's time, St. Gregory was so moved by the thought of Trajan's justice that he interceded with God for him; whereupon Trajan's soul was allowed to return from Limbus to earth and inhabit its body long enough to embrace Christianity, thus winning salvation: cf. *Par.* XX, 43–48, 106–117. This was the 'great victory.'

80. The Roman eagles on a golden background, in banners.

106. Dante fears that the horror of the penance may divert the reader from his "good resolution" to make amends.

111. In any case the suffering will stop at the Day of Judgment.

124. Cf. Job xxv, 6: "man, that is a worm."

125. Cf. Mat. xxii, 30: "For in the resurrection they ... are as the angels of God in heaven."

133. The 'unreal' suffering of the caryatid arouses a 'real pang' of pity in the beholder. In the Florentine Baptistery, caryatids support a round Paradise in mosaic.

138, 139. Even the most patient among them seemed to be at the limit of his endurance.

Canto XI

Argument

Among the victims of pride are representatives of three types — the arrogance of noble birth, the vanity of artistic excellence, and the haughtiness of power. Humbert, son of William, of the ancient and mighty Ghibelline family of the Aldobrandeschi, was count of Santafiora in the Maremma (cf. VI, 111). Like his father he was hostile to Siena, and in 1259 he was killed by Sienese troops at his stronghold of Campagnatico, in the valley of the Ombrone, after a fierce and bloody fight. Oderisi of Gubbio, in the Duchy of Urbino, was a famous illuminator of manuscripts in the second half of the 13th century. He spent some years in Bologna and Rome and died, it would seem, in the latter city in 1299. Provenzano Salvani, a sagacious and valiant Ghibelline chief, was all-powerful in Siena at the time of her defeat of Florence at Montaperti in 1260. Nine years later, at the battle of Colle di Valdelsa, Florence was victorious, and Provenzano, the leader of the Sienese army, was defeated and beheaded. It is related of him that when he was at the height of his power, to save the life of a friend held for ransom by Charles of Anjou, he meekly begged of the passers-by until he had collected the 10,000 florins which were demanded.

The practice of soliciting alms to pay fines was common enough in the Middle Ages, but usually the mendicants went from house to house; Provenzano — who might have procured the money by force, and who, moreover, was acting in behalf of another — took his stand in the Campo, or great public square, of Siena, where he was exposed to the sight of all. This act of generous humility, according to Oderisi, so atoned for his many acts of presumption that, although he had postponed repentance until the end of his life, he was admitted to Purgatory immediately after his death.

1. The canto opens (ll. 1–24) with an expanded paraphrase of the Lord's prayer (Mat. vi, 9–13), recited by the spirits of the first circle.   Such paraphrases were not uncommon in the Middle Ages.

2. God dwells in Heaven, not because he is 'circumscribed,' restricted to one place, but because he is fondest of his 'first works' — the angels and the heavens.

6. 'Emanation': the goodness that flows from God.

11. 'Hosanna': Mat. xxi, 9, 15.   Cf. *V. N.*, XXIII, 25, l. 61.

13. The 'daily manna' (Exod. xvi, 14, 31) is spiritual food.   The souls in Purgatory, toiling to reach Paradise, are like the Israelites in the desert on their way to the Promised Land.

19. The figure is that of a rider (the devil) taming a horse (our virtue).

23. Once inside the gate, souls are free from temptation.

27. The incubus, or nightmare.

28. Some had heavier weights than others.

32, 33. What can be done for them here on earth by those whose will is rooted in the divine will?

48. It was not clear from whom the words came, because the faces were all hidden.

60. It is evident that the speaker has already learned modesty.

63. The 'common mother' is the earth: cf. Ecclus. xl, 1.

73. This humble attitude (cf. l. 78), which is natural enough in the literal sense, seems to indicate allegorically Dante's participation in the penance.   See XIII, 136–138.

81. The art of 'illuminating' (French *enluminer*, Ital. *miniare*), or illustrating and decorating manuscripts, was held in great esteem before the invention of printing.   In a medieval book factory were to be found the *scriba* (or 'writer'), the *corrector*, the *rubricator* (who inserted the capital letters), the *illuminator* (who decorated the margins), the *miniaturista*.

83. Franco of Bologna was known to Vasari, who possessed some of his drawings.   We have no other information about him.

92. How quickly fame withers!

93. 'If it is not followed by barbarous times,' in which no successor comes to obscure the fame of the departed.

94. The Florentine Giovanni Cimabue, who lived in the second half of the 13th century, put new life into the Byzantine style and was regarded as the restorer of painting in Florence.

95. Giotto, Cimabue's pupil, was the greatest painter of Dante's time, and also a famous architect and sculptor.   Dante probably knew him.   He was two years younger than Dante.

97. Guido Cavalcanti, Dante's 'first friend,' still alive in April, 1300, surpassed Guido Guinizzelli of Bologna (XXVI, 92), the father of the "sweet new style."

99. This conjecture of Oderisi is simply a general deduction from antecedent probability. Dante, however, in writing it, must have known that the reader would immediately apply it to him.   Obviously whatever pride is betrayed by the remark belongs to Dante the author, rather than to Dante the protagonist of the poem.

100. Cf. Boethius, *Cons.*, II, Pr. vii: "populares auras inanesque rumores" (popular blasts and vain rumors).

103. 'What more repute shalt thou have,' a thousand years hence (l. 106), 'if thou strippest off thy flesh when it is old' than if thou hadst died young?

105. Baby talk, childish prattle.   *Pappo* and *dindi* are childish pronunciations of *pane* and *denaro*.

108. 'The circle which is slowest turned' — the eighth or starry sphere — moves only one degree in a hundred years.

115. Cf. Isaiah xl, 7: "The grass withereth, the flower fadeth: because the spirit of the Lord bloweth upon it: surely the people is grass."

138. 'He brought himself to quiver in every vein': a forceful picture of the mortification of a haughty spirit.   Dante, in the time of his exile, knew this feeling all too well.

142. 'This deed relieved him of those restrictions,' enabled him to enter Purgatory without waiting outside among the 'negligent.'

Canto XII

Argument

The conception of the lifelike carvings on the floor, which, in this canto, furnish the warning illustrations of pride, was manifestly a delight to the artistic soul of the poet.   In the very phrasing of his descriptions Dante affects a kind of architectural symmetry: first we have four tiercets beginning each with *Vedea* (ll. 25, 28, 31, 34), then four with *O* (ll. 37, 40, 43, 46), next four with *Mostrava* (ll. 49, 52, 55, 58), and finally one tiercet (ll. 61–63), in which the three lines begin with these same three words.   The list of examples presents an alternation of biblical and mythological instances.

1. Once more we have an indication that Dante, in an allegorical sense, shares in the penance.

7. Dante's penance is ended.

8. An abiding meekness has resulted from the penance.

17. Tombs in the floor of a church or cloister, the covering stone being part of the pavement and bearing the graven image of the dead one there buried.

24. 'All that juts out of the mountain to form a road,' i.e., the whole floor of the terrace.

27. Luke x, 18: "I beheld Satan as lightning fall from heaven."

28. Briareus was one of the giants who fought against the gods: cf. *Inf.* XXXI, 98.

31. Thymbraeus is one of the appellations of Apollo, who had a temple at Thymbra in the Troad: Cf. *Aen.*, III, 85. — The carving represents the bodies of the defeated giants, upon which Apollo, Pallas, Mars, and Jove are gazing.   Cf. *Met.*, X, 150–151:

Cecini plectro graviore Gigantas
Sparsaque Phlegraeis victricia fulmina campis.

(I have sung the giants in a heavier strain, and the victorious bolts hurled on the Phlegraean plains.)

34. For Nimrod, the builder of the tower of Babel in the land of Shinar, see Gen. x, 8–10, and xi, 2–9. Cf. *Inf.* XXXI, 77.

37. Niobe, wife of King Amphion of Thebes, proud of her seven sons and seven daughters, presumptuously disparaged Latona, who had only two children, Apollo and Diana.   These gods avenged their mother by shooting with arrows all of Niobe's offspring; Niobe then turned to stone. See *Met.*, VI, 165–312.

40. Defeated by the Philistines on Mount Gilboa, King Saul threw himself upon a sword and killed himself: 1 Samuel xxxi, 1–6.

42. In his lamentation over Saul and Jonathan, David said (2 Samuel i, 21): "Ye mountains of Gilboa, let there be no dew, neither let there be rain, upon you."

43. Arachne, who had challenged Pallas to a trial of skill in weaving, was turned by her into a spider: *Met.*, VI, 5–145.

46. After having threatened to add to the burdens of the people of Israel, "king Rehoboam sent Adoram, who was over the tribute; and all Israel stoned him with stones, that he died. Therefore king Rehoboam made speed to get him up to his chariot, to flee to Jerusalem" (1 Kings xii, 18).

49. Amphiaraus, the soothsayer (*Inf.* XX, 34), to avoid going to the Theban war where he knew he would be killed, hid himself, but was betrayed by his wife Eriphȳle and met his death at Thebes.   As Eriphyle had been bribed by an ill-fated golden necklace, Dante chooses to regard her as an example of vanity or pride.   Dante was perhaps thinking of vainglory,

which the earlier theologians regarded as the lowest of the seven vices, pride being somewhat different, outside the seven and the root of them all.   She was killed by her son Alcmaeon in vengeance for the loss of his father: cf. *Par.* IV, 103–105.   See Statius, *Thebaid*, II, 265 ff.; IV, 187 ff.

52. Sennacherib, the haughty king of the Assyrians, despised the Israelites and their God. "And it came to pass, as he was worshiping in the house of Nisroch his god, that ... his sons smote him with the sword: and they escaped into the land of Armenia" (2 Kings xix, 37).

55. Thamẏris (or Tomyris), queen of the Scythians, to avenge the death of her son and the defeat of her army, lured Cyrus, king of Persia, and his 200,000 men into an ambush and destroyed them.   She then had Cyrus's head put into a skin full of human blood, and addressed it in terms similar to those cited by Dante: Paulus Orosius, *Historia adversus paganos*, II, vii.

58. Judith delivered the Israelites by cutting off the head of the Assyrian king, Holofernes. When his troops heard of his death, "fear and trembling fell upon them" and "they fled into every way of the plain, and of the hill country" (Judith xv, 1, 2).

60. By 'the remnants of the killing' is probably meant the headless body of the king. "Behold Holofernes lieth upon the ground without a head" (Judith xiv, 16).

61. Cf. *Aen.*, III, 2–3:

Ceceditque superbum
Ilium et omnis humo fumat Neptunia Troia.

(Proud Ilium fell, and all Neptune's Troy smokes from the ground.)

77 Cf. Luke xxi, 28: "look up, and lift up your heads, for your redemption draweth nigh."

81. The sixth hour of daylight is drawing to a close; it is nearly noon.

94. Cf. Mat. vii, 14: "Because strait is the gate, and narrow is the way, which leadeth unto life, and few there be that find it."

101–102. 'The church that dominates the well-governed city across the Rubaconte bridge' is San Miniato. *Ben guidata* is of course ironical.   The bridge, now called Ponte alle Grazie, was first named after honest Messer Rubaconte da Mandello, who was mayor when it was begun in 1237.

105. By way of contrasting the 'age' of Rubaconte with later, degenerate times, Dante here refers to two notorious local scandals of his own day.   In 1299 a certain Niccolò Acciaiuoli, to conceal a false entry made in his favor with the connivance of the mayor, tore a leaf out of the municipal record (*quaderno*).   A salt commissioner, Durante de' Chiaramontesi, enriched himself by receiving the salt from the commune with an honest measure, and dealing it out with a measure diminished by one stave (*doga*): cf. *Par.* XVI, 105.

108. The flight of steps is so narrow that the wall 'grazes' on either side.

110. Mat. v, 3: "Blessed are the poor in spirit."   This beatitude suits those who are leaving pride behind.

116. It is now easier for Dante to climb than it has been for him to walk on the level terrace. By the removal of pride, the foundation of all evil, Dante is relieved of the greater part of his other sins.   The angel has obliterated the *P* of *Pride*, and the other six letters have thereby become dim (l. 122).   See Ecclus. x, 15: "the beginning of all sin is pride."   Cf. St. Thomas, *Summa Theologiae*, Prima Secundae, Qu. lxxxiv, Art. 2.

133. Cf. the surprise of Cipus when he saw in a spring the reflection of horns on his head (*Met.*, XV, 566–568):

Vidit enim, falsamque in imagine credens
Esse fidem, digitis ad frontem saepe relatis,
Quae vidit, tetigit.

(For he saw them and, thinking that he was deceived by the reflection, lifting his hands again and again to his forehead, he touched what he saw.)

Canto XIII

Argument

To purge ourselves of envy, we must cultivate a spirit of humility and resolutely shut our eyes — agonizing as the effort may be — to all that has beguiled them. The spirits in the second circle, then, sit in a row, meanly clad, like beggars, their eyes sewed up with an iron wire. Falcons that were tamed full-grown used to have their eyes closed in this cruel way. In the *Magnae Derivationes* of Uguccione da Pisa the poet had read: "*Invideo tibi*, idest non video tibi, idest non fero videre te bene agentem"; (I envy you, that is, I do not see you; that is, I cannot bear to see you faring well); and this definition of envy may have suggested to him the particular form of punishment. Line 57 is probably intended to indicate that, in the mystic (but not the literal) sense, Dante himself is subjected to this discipline; but we learn from lines 133–135 that he merits but a slight penance here, having sinned far less from envy than from pride.

Turning to the right — as they do on every terrace of Purgatory — the travelers proceed toward the north, facing the noonday sun, the symbol of enlightenment. Here they find no carvings on wall or pavement: such lessons would have been wasted on the sightless penitents. Instead, the examples of love — the opposite of envy — are called aloud by mysterious voices. The first illustration is drawn, as in the other circles, from the life of the Virgin.

Among the willing sufferers is a certain woman of Siena, who (as she declares), in spite of her name, Sapía, was not wise. In 1269, having passed the age of thirty-five (she was, in fact, about sixty), she was still so full of envy of her fellow-townsmen that when, under the leadership of Provenzano Salvani (XI, 121), they met the Florentines in battle at Colle di Valdelsa, she prayed God that they might be worsted. This, as it proved, was what the Lord had already decreed, for the Sienese were overwhelmingly defeated by a smaller force of Florentines. Thereupon Sapia's exultation was so mad that she did not care what fate God might send her. Only the intercession of one of her countrymen, Pier Pettinagno (or Pettinaio) — a poor comb dealer, so honest, pious, and kindly that he was regarded as a saint — secured for her prompt admission to Purgatory.

Siena and Florence, like other rival cities, had many standing jokes at each other's expense. Dante puts into the mouth of Sapia, who in life had hated her own people, two of Florence's stock gibes at Siena. This ambitious town aspired to become a maritime power, like Venice and Genoa; in 1303 she succeeded in acquiring a little seaport on the shore of the Tuscan Maremma, called Talamone, and in improving it she spent large sums of money. At one time the Florentines asked for a concession there. Furthermore, Siena, perched on the top of a hill, had difficulty in getting water; it was said that her inhabitants were continually digging to find an underground river, the Diana, which was supposed to flow under the city.

7. Cf. XII, 65.

9. A 'livid color' is the proper hue of envy: cf. XIV, 84.

12. 'Choice': whether to turn to the right or to the left, as they face the cliff.

15. He turns to the right, wheeling on his right foot.

29. At the marriage feast in Cana, "when they wanted wine, the mother of Jesus saith unto him, They have no wine" (John ii, 3); and Jesus turned the water into wine. This speech is cited here as an example of loving solicitude; in XXII, 142–144, it appears again as an example of temperance.

32. When the tyrant Aegisthus had condemned Orestes, whom he did not know by sight, Orestes and his friend Pylades both claimed that name, each wishing to save the other. Cf. Cicero, *De Amicitia*, VII, xxiv. In *De Finibus Bonorum et Malorum* (a work which Dante repeatedly cites), V, xxii, Cicero tells how excited the audience at the theater becomes on hearing the words "I am Orestes" in Pacuvius's tragedy.

36. A condensation of Mat. v, 44: "Love your enemies, bless them that curse you, do good to them that hate you, and pray for them which despitefully use you and persecute you."

40. By 'the check' is meant the examples of the sin of 'this belt' — envy.

42. 'The pass of forgiveness' is the beginning of the ascent to the next circle.

48. Cf. l. 9.

51. 'I heard Michael, etc., called upon, invoked.' The souls seem to be repeating the Litany of Saints.

57. 'I was milked of hard pain through my eyes,' i.e., painful tears of sympathy were drawn from my eyes. For the curious figure, cf. *Inf.* XII, 135–136.

62. On the 'pardon' days of various churches, pilgrims come in crowds for indulgences, and beggars collect at the doors.

73. This delicate scruple reveals a fineness of feeling, an instinctive gentleness, that contrasts strangely with Dante's sterner moods.

81. The outer 'side of the shelf' is 'wreathed with no rim,' i.e., has no parapet.

82. Virgil is on Dante's right; on his left, against the wall, are the 'devout shades.'

85. Notice that in this instance Dante begins his speech with words of good cheer.

90. So that the conscience shall retain no recollection of sin.

94. Ephesians ii, 19: "Now therefore ye are no more strangers and foreigners, but fellow-citizens with the saints, and of the household of God."

102. If anyone should ask me how it showed its expectancy, I should reply that 'it was lifting up its chin like a blind man.'

123. This characteristic of the blackbird was probably known from general observation.

133. Dante's 'eyes shall be taken' from him, in the literal sense of the poem, when he shall return to this circle after death.

138. 'The load' of the circle of pride 'already weighs' upon Dante.

151–154. The meaning seems to be: 'But those who shall spend, or waste, most upon Talamone shall be those who expect to be admirals,' to command the nonexistent Sienese fleet.

Canto XIV

Argument

There is an uncanny realism in the discussion of Dante by two blind spirits from Romagna; the poet is standing close beside them, but in their sightlessness they converse about him as if he were miles away.   One of the speakers is Guido del Duca, a gentleman of Bertinoro, probably a Guelf, who lived in the first half of the 13th century.   The other is the Guelf Rinieri (or Ranieri) of the powerful family of the lords of Cálboli, a stronghold near Rocca San Casciano in the valley of the Montone; prominent in peace and war, he was *podestà* of various cities, was defeated by Guido da Montefeltro (*Inf.* XXVII) in 1276, and was killed at Forlì in 1296.

Questioned by the penitents, Dante modestly withholds — as in the *Vita Nuova* — not only his own name but that of his city and that of the river Arno. This reticence leads to a description of the stream and a satirical picture of the dwellers on its banks.   The passage falls into three parts of twelve lines each. First comes a general introductory portrayal of the river and of the Tuscans, who "avoid virtue as if it were a snake" and resemble those unhappy men whom the enchantress Circe had turned into beasts.   Next we have four tiercets devoted to the inhabitants of the Casentino, Arezzo, Florence, and Pisa, who are likened respectively to swine, curs, wolves, and foxes.   The mountainous Casentino, on the upper Arno, was, in fact, a pig-raising country, and the stream near its source flows by a hill called Porciano; in at least one of his lyrics (*Rime*, CXVI, 67-70) Dante complains of the rudeness of its people.   The Aretines — those "curs who snarl more than their strength warrants" — were described in nearly the same terms by Sacchetti in a letter to R. Gianfigliazzi, captain of Arezzo (Tor., 437).   The greed of the Florentines and the cunning of the Pisans made the wolf and the fox their proper symbols.   The general suggestion of the beast names came, no doubt, from Boethius (*Cons.*, IV, Pr. iii).   Following this characterization, the closing twelve lines of the passage contain a prophecy of the slaughter of the Florentine wolves by a bloodthirsty nephew of Rinieri da Calboli.

10. 'The one' is Guido del Duca.

17. *Falterona*: one of the highest mountains in the Tuscan Apennines.

25. 'The other' is Rinieri da Calboli.

30. The valley is the Valdarno. — Cf. Job xviii, 17: "His remembrance shall perish from the earth."

31. Its 'source' is in the Falterona, which was regarded also as the source of the Tiber.

32. 'The Alpine range from which Pelorus is severed' means the Apennine chain, of which Pelorus, at the eastern end of Sicily, is the continuation.   Cf. *Phars.*, II, 438: "Extremi colles Siculo cessere Peloro."   (That end of the Apennines was surrendered to Pelorus in Sicily.)

33. Only a few of the Apennine peaks are wetter than Falterona.

34. Down to its mouth, 'where it (the Arno) gives itself up to replace' the water that evaporates from the sea.

36. 'What goes with them' is their supply of water.

37. All along the Arno, from source to mouth, 'virtue is shunned.'

45. Down to Romena the Arno is nothing but a brook.

48. The Arno, which descends south through the Casentino and then flows eastward toward Arezzo, suddenly turns off to the west when it has come within three miles of that city.

58. The reference is to the nephew of Rinieri, Fulcieri da Calboli, who while *podestà* of Florence in 1303, had many White Guelf and Ghibelline citizens tortured and put to death on accusations of treason. He was *podestà* again in 1312.

78. Dante has avoided giving his name: ll. 20, 21.

85. Cf. Galatians vi, 7: "whatsoever a man soweth, that shall he also reap."

87. Upon earthly possessions, in which there can be no sharing, because no two men can own the same thing. In the next Canto, ll. 44-45, Dante asks for an explanation of this difficult phrase. Cf. *Cons.*, II, Pr. v: "vestrae vero divitiae nisi comminutae in plures transire non possunt." (But your riches cannot pass to many, except they be diminished.)

91. His is not the only family in Romagna that has become 'bare' (cf. *Inf.* XVI, 30; XXXIV, 60), i.e., destitute of goodness.

92. Romagna is bounded on the north by the Po, on the south by the Apennines, on the east by the Adriatic, on the west by the river Reno.

97-107. In these lines are enumerated sundry noble and famous citizens and houses of Romagna in the 12th and 13th centuries. For Dante, Romagna included Bologna.

102. Unlike the others mentioned, he was of lowly birth, and rose to importance by his merit alone. In 1249 he was mayor of Siena and Pisa.

112. *Bretinoro* (now Bertinoro), a little town between Forlì and Cesena, was the birthplace of Guido del Duca. The family of the counts of Bertinoro died out in 1177. They and others who have departed are represented as having left the world to avoid the contamination of modern life.

115. Bagnacavallo is a little place near Ravenna. Its counts left no male heirs after Dante's generation. Among the heiresses was the wife of Guido da Polenta, Dante's host in Ravenna.

117. The counts of Castrocaro (near Forlì) and Conio, now Cunio (near Imola), were very numerous in 1300. — The good pass away, and the wicked multiply.

118. 'The Pagani,' a noble family of Faenza, 'will do well' to get no more sons, 'when their demon,' Maghinardo di Susinana (*Inf.* XXVII, 49-51), shall have died. Maghinardo, the head of the family, died in 1302, leaving two daughters and a grandson.

119, 120. But they will not do so well as ever to leave 'clean witness of themselves,' i.e., an undefiled reputation. To do that, they should have died out before Maghinardo came.

121. Ugolino was a worthy gentleman of Faenza, who died about 1278. His two sons died not many years later, and then his daughters came into possession of the inheritance.

129. We knew that if the 'dear souls' had heard us taking the wrong way, they would have warned us.

133. The first of the examples of envy, proclaimed by spirit voices, is that of Cain: "every one that findeth me shall slay me" (Gen. iv, 14).

139. The princess Aglauros, of Athens, envious of her sister Herse, who was loved by Mercury, tried to prevent the god from reaching her, and was turned into a statue. Cf. *Met.*, II, 708 ff.

143. Ps. xxxii (Vulg. xxxi), 9: "whose mouth must be held in with bit (*camo*) and bridle (*freno*)."

145. Cf. Eccles. ix, 12: "sicut pisces capiuntur hamo" ('hook'); in the English version, "as the fishes that are taken in an evil net."

151. 'He who sees all' is God: cf. 2 Macc. ix, 5.

Canto XV

Argument

The most important feature of this canto is a discussion — adroitly introduced in explanation of an obscure phrase — of the difference between spiritual and temporal possessions. In earthly property there can be no companionship, because what one man has another must lack. Not so with heavenly goods, knowledge and love, which all can possess together. God's love is poured out in proportion to the readiness of each soul to accept it, and upon every one of the blessed is lavished all the love that it is capable of receiving. The divine love runs to meet the aspiring human affection and, uniting with it, doubles its ardor and its joy. The more happy spirits there are in Paradise, the greater is the sum total of divine love bestowed; and — inasmuch as every soul receives love, not only from God directly, but from all its fellows as well — the greater is the share of each participant.

This doctrine is expounded by Virgil while the two poets are climbing up the stairway from the second terrace to the third. In the circle of wrath the punishment consists of a blinding, suffocating cloud of smoke, which rolls along the path, enveloping the penitents — a symbol of the energetic stifling of angry passion. In this discipline Dante evidently shares.

At the foot of the steps, before their ascent, the travelers are met by an angel so shining that Dante's mortal eyes are blinded. At first he imagines that he is dazzled by the sun, which is directly in front, halfway between the meridian and the horizon; but when he shades his brow with his hands, the blaze is in no wise diminished. Then it seems to him that the brightness, from which his arched hands cannot shield him, must be a reflection of the sunbeam from some pool before him. A ray descending at a slant of 45 degrees to a mirror on the ground would be reflected up into his eyes at the same angle. Not until Virgil tells him the truth is he aware of the presence of the heavenly guardian; and he does not note the removal of one *P* from his forehead. He has been saved from envy not so much by conscious renunciation of worldly things as by unconscious contemplation of the divine.

1, 2. As much of the ecliptic as is visible between the end of the third hour (9 A.M.) and the beginning of day (6 A.M.). Between dawn and mid-morning there is a difference of three hours, or 45°.

2, 3. 'The circle that is always playing like a child' is probably the ecliptic (the sun's annual revolution through the sky), which dodges now to one side, now to the other, of the equator: cf. IV, 63.

4, 5. So much (45°) of the sun's course seemed to be left on the evening side : the sun still had 45° to descend. It was three hours before sunset, or mid-afternoon; the sun was therefore in the northwest.

6. 'Vespers,' as Dante uses it, means the last of the four canonical divisions of the day, i.e., from 3 to 6 P.M.: cf. III, 25; *Conv.*, IV, xxiii, 16. 'It was the beginning of vespers there, in Purgatory; here, in Italy (where I am writing), it was midnight.' The time of Italy is three hours earlier than that of Jerusalem. It was 3 P.M. in Purgatory, 3 A.M. in Jerusalem, midnight in Italy.

9. The poets, who climbed up the east side of the mountain as far as the first shelf, and walked to the right (or north) on each terrace, are now on the northeast side, facing the declining sun in the northwest.

10. An excessively bright light produces on the beholder an impression of heaviness over the eyes.

15. A shade, or visor, 'files down the excess of visibility,' i.e., reduces the excess of visible light.

17. A ray of light, falling on a horizontal surface of glass or water, is reflected upward at the angle at which it descends, but 'in the opposite direction.'

20. The angle of reflection is equal to the angle of incidence.

21. Experiment and science.

36. Note that Dante, in this particular instance, omits any mention of the obliteration of one of the letters from his forehead.

38. Mat. v, 7: "Blessed are the merciful." Mercy (*caritatis effectus*) is here regarded as the opposite of envy: cf. St. Thomas, *Summa Theologiae*, Secunda Secundae, Qu. xxxvi, Art. 3.

39. Cf. Mat. v, 12: "Rejoice, and be exceeding glad: for great is your reward in heaven." Also Rev. ii, 7: "To him that overcometh will I give to eat of the tree of life."

42. Profit from Virgil's teaching.

45. The words of Guido del Duca in XIV, 87.

48. 'He rebukes (men) for it': in order that men may have less cause to mourn for it.

52. 'The highest sphere' is the Empyrean, the abode of God, the angels, and the blest.

54. The 'fear' of sharing.

55. 'For there (in the Empyrean), the more there are to say "our,"' i.e., the more sharers there are. Cf. St. Gregory, *Moralia*, IV, xxxi.

69. Naturally bright objects were thought to attract the sun's rays.

72. In other words, God's blessing corresponds to the measure of affection of the loving soul, and is really added to it.

81. 'Which are healed by being painful.'

85. The examples of gentleness — the opposite of wrath — appear as 'ecstatic visions.'

86. The first vision represents the child Jesus, who, after three days' absence, is found in the temple disputing with the doctors. See Luke ii, 42–50.

88. Mary. Cf. Luke ii, 48: "and his mother said unto him, Son, why hast thou thus dealt with us? behold, thy father and I have sought thee sorrowing."

94. This is the wife of Pisistratus, ruler of Athens, enraged because a young man has dared to embrace their daughter, with whom he is in love. Cf. Valerius Maximus, *Facta et Dicta Memorabilia*, V, i, Ext. 2.

97. Athens.

98. The contest between Neptune and Minerva (as to which should name the city) and the victory of Minerva are told in *Met.*, VI, 70–82.

107. For the stoning of St. Stephen, the first Christian martyr, see Acts vii, 54–60. From early times Stephen was always pictured as a youth.

131. The visions were intended to teach Dante to cool the heat of anger with the waters of peace.

133. 'I did not ask "What ails thee?" for the same reason that he does' who looks with undiscerning eye.

144. The smoke covered the whole width of the terrace, so that 'there was no room to turn out from it.'

Canto XVI

Argument

The human soul, created just before the birth of each infant, is guileless and naturally inclined to good and to gladness; the child of a happy maker, its first tendency is to seek happiness.   All that seems excellent, all that appears to promise joy attracts it.   But in its inexperience it may mistake false delight for true.   It needs guidance; and for this end society, with its laws and rulers, was constituted.   The laws still exist, but there is no one left to execute them, since the Papacy has usurped the Imperial power and joined the sword of worldly supremacy to the crosier of ecclesiastical authority.   In the old days, when mankind fared well, Rome was the seat of two brother monarchs, neither of whom encroached upon the other — the Pope and the Emperor.   Now the temporal chief is gone, and the spiritual leader does not suffice; for he whose province is religious thought cannot possess the gift of practical discrimination. This difference of office is indicated allegorically in the Bible in the Mosaic law which restricts the meat of the Israelites to "whatsoever parteth the hoof, and is clovenfooted, and cheweth the cud" (Levit. xi, 3; Deut. xiv, 6).   According to St. Thomas, *Summa Theologiae*, Prima Secundae, Qu. cii, Art. 6, chewing the cud signifies meditation of the scriptures, and the cloven foot means, among other things, the distinction of good and evil.   The Pope may ruminate, but his own acts show that he does not "part the hoof."   Lack of temporal direction, then, rather than universal corruption of the human heart, is the cause of modern depravity.   The stars are not to blame.   The heavenly bodies, indeed, governed by angels, determine, to a certain extent, our characters, so that our first inclinations are generally under their control; but we have the innate knowledge of right and wrong, as well as free will to combat wicked desires, if only our first steps are guided aright.

Thus speaks Mark the Lombard, a penitent in the circle of wrath.   Nothing is known of his family or history, but Villani and the *Novelle Antiche* corroborate his excellent reputation.   With his companions he marches in the smoke, chanting the "Lamb of God": "Agnus Dei, qui tollis peccata mundi, miserere nobis; Agnus Dei, qui tollis peccata mundi, miserere nobis; Agnus Dei, qui tollis peccata mundi, dona nobis pacem."   Joining Dante, he deplores with him the decline of courtesy and virtue.   In all Lombardy, he declares — the province which, less than a century before, was the favorite resort of courtiers and poets — there are but three worthy men left, noble survivors of an elder generation. We are reminded of the "giusti son due" of *Inf.* VI, 73, and the "tre men rei di nostra terra" of *Rime*, XCI, 97.   The first of the three Lombards is Conrad

(Corrado or Currado) da Palazzo, of Brescia, vicar general of Charles of Anjou in Florence in 1276, *podestà* of Piacenza in 1288.   The second is Gherardo da Camino, captain general of Treviso from 1283 to 1306, upon whom Dante incidentally bestows high praise in the *Convivio* (IV, xiv, 12).   The third, Guido da Castello, of Reggio, is also favorably mentioned in the *Convivio* (IV, xvi, 6); Mark says of him that he is most fitly called, "in the French fashion, the 'simple Lombard,'" but we do not know why.   To emphasize the fame of the second of the three — to whom, one would think, he must have been bound by ties of personal gratitude — the poet resorts to an ingenious device.   Mark refers to him merely as "the good Gherardo," and Dante, asking who is meant, calls forth the statement that no Tuscan can be unfamiliar with that name.   If any other epithet than "good" is needed to identify him, the only suitable one is that suggested by the name of his daughter, Gaia.   Some early commentators take the name Gaia to mean that the lady in question was virtuous and beautiful; others understand the opposite, that she was gay and frivolous.   It is not possible to determine the true meaning here, but it seems probable that Dante meant to imply that Gaia's reputation was *not* good and that he mentions her in ironical contrast to her *good* father.

For the influence of the stars and its limitations, see St. Thomas, *Summa Theologiae*, Prima, Qu. cxv, Arts. 4 and 6.

15. *Mozzo*, 'severed.'   Cf. *Inf*. XXVIII, 103.
19. The first words of each verse of the prayer are "Agnus Dei."
20. The souls sing in unison, after the fashion of a Gregorian chant.
27. In Dante's time the Florentines still gave the names of 'calends' to the first days of each month.
54. Dante represents himself as enveloped in a 'doubt,' which binds him so tight that he will 'burst' if he does not 'extricate' himself from it.   He wonders what is the cause of the degeneracy of modern times.
55. When the doubt was first suggested to him by the words of Guido del Duca in XIV, 37–41, it was 'single'; now it is 'doubled' by Marco's 'speech' in l. 48, which assures him of that with which he 'couples it' (namely, Guido's utterance).
57. Here in the circle of wrath and down in the circle of envy.
63. Note that *il cielo*, here and in ll. 68, 73, 77, means 'the planets and the stars.'   Some attribute modern wickedness to planetary influence, some to innate human depravity.
74. The stars initiate only bodily impulses; they have no control over the will, which belongs, not to the senses, but to the intellect.
79. The 'greater power and better nature' than the stars is God, who sets the will of man in motion and gives it a general inclination toward the good, leaving to man himself, however, a free choice between the real and the apparent good.
80. Without God, man can will nothing at all, but the particular object of his will rests with himself.
81. The planets and the starry heaven.
85. 'He who loves it before it exists' is God.
95, 96. The 'king' should be one who had at least some inkling of justice — 'who could discern at least the tower (the most conspicuous part) of the city of truth.'

101. The flock sees its 'shepherd, who walks ahead,' 'snatch only at the kind of good for which it is greedy' — i.e., temporal possessions.

109. In 1300 Italy had known no Imperial guidance since the death of Frederick II, fifty years before.

114. Cf. Mat. vii, 16: "Ye shall know them by their fruits." Also Luke vi, 43–44.

115. Lombardy in the Middle Ages included most of northern Italy.

117. Frederick II was at odds with the Church during the latter part of his life.

132. The 'children of Levi,' or Levites, are the priests. — Cf. Numbers xviii, 20: "And the Lord spake unto Aaron, Thou shalt have no inheritance in their land, neither shalt thou have any part among them: I am thy part and thine inheritance among the children of Israel." Also Deut. x, 8–9.

142. 'The brightness that beams through the smoke' is the gleam of the white angel.

Canto XVII

Argument

A thick mist in the mountains, gradually clearing until "the sun's disk" can be faintly discerned — such is the picture which, with a few strokes, Dante sets vividly before us, to convey an idea of the passing of the cloud of smoke on the third terrace. An apostrophe to Imagination, that mysterious power which receives images within the mind, introduces the examples of wrath, presented in ecstatic visions. At the top of the stairway leading to the next shelf, night overtakes the travelers and compels them to stop. Just as in Hell (*Inf.* XI) the Latin poet utilizes a necessary halt, halfway down the abyss, to set forth the general arrangement of the lower world, so here, halfway up the slope of Purgatory, he explains to Dante the categories of sin and atonement.

To begin with, the "seed" of every act in the universe, good or evil, is love. God himself is impelled by love, and none of his creatures is devoid of it. But love is of two kinds, instinctive and elective. Instinctive love — the only kind felt by inanimate things, plants, and beasts — is directly inspired by God and consequently unerring. Aristotle, in his *Ethics*, III, xi, 3 and 4, taught a similar doctrine. This primal impulse to return to the maker and conform to his law is innate in man also; but man, endowed with free will, has power to divert his love to other objects, good or bad. The elective love, then, is subject to error. As long as it is bent upon heavenly things, it cannot go astray; nor is it harmful when turned to the good things of earth in due measure. But when man is lukewarm in his affection for the divine, or immoderate in his craving for worldly good, and when he loves evil, he misuses his liberty and opposes the will of his creator.

The choice of a bad object, insufficient devotion to a heavenly object, excessive attachment to a temporal object not evil in itself — these are the three wrong courses open to man's love.   The first error results in the sins of the spirit, the three vices punished in the three lower circles; the second produces the negative vice of sloth, expiated in the fourth, or middle, circle; the third is responsible for the sins of the flesh, the three vices of the three upper circles.   The last two categories are not further discussed by Virgil, but the first — the love of evil — is treated in detail.   At the outset this question arises: what kind of evil can man love, or, in other words, to whom may he wish harm?   Having proved that it is impossible to hate oneself, or to hate God, Virgil shows that man is capable of hating his fellow creatures alone — he may wish harm to his neighbor, but to no one else.   Hatred of our neighbor springs up in three ways and manifests itself accordingly in the three vices of pride, envy, and anger, which are defined in three consecutive tiercets.

For St. Thomas's definitions of pride (*amor propriae excellentiae*, 'the desire of one's own excellence'), envy (*tristitia de alienis bonis*, 'sorrow for another's good'), and anger, see *Summa Theologiae*, Secunda Secundae, Qu. clxii, Art. 3; Qu. xxxvi, Arts. 2 and 3; Qu. clvi, Art. 4.   See also St. Thomas, Prima Secundae, Qu. clxii, Art. 3; Qu. xxxvi, Arts. 2, 3; Qu. clvi, Art. 4.

3. According to Aristotle and medieval authorities, the eye of the mole is covered by a membrane which prevents it from seeing.

7. *Imagine* means a mental picture, generally derived from visual impression.   *Imaginativa* (l. 13) and *fantasia* (l. 25) signify the faculty of receiving such pictures.

12. The 'shores' of the Island of Purgatory.

16. What is it that arouses the faculty of mental vision when no impression of sight comes from without?   Is it some physical stellar influence, or the divine will operating through the stars?   Cf. St. Thomas, *Summa Theologiae*, Prima, Qu. lxxxiv, Art. 6.

19. The first example is that of Progne (or Procne), who, to avenge the cruel and infamous wrong done by her husband, Tereus, King of Thrace, to her sister Philomela, made him eat of the flesh of his own child, Itys.   Tereus and the two sisters were then turned into birds. According to Aristotle (*Rhetoric*, III, 3) and most of the Greeks, Progne became a nightingale and Philomela a swallow; the Latins, followed by modern poets, usually made Philomela the nightingale.   But Ovid (*Met.*, VI, 424 ff.), the Latin poet from whom Dante got the story, does not tell, and Virgil (*Eclogue* VI, 79) seems to follow the Greek version, which Dante also adopted.   Cf. IX, 13–15.

26. The 'one crucified' is Haman, minister of King Ahasuerus, who "reigned from India even unto Ethiopia" (Esther i, 1).   Enraged at the independence of the Jew, Mordecai, 'so upright in word and deed' (l. 30), who "bowed not, nor did him reverence" (Esther iii, 5), "Haman sought to destroy all the Jews that were throughout the whole kingdom" (v, 6); but through the influence of Esther, Mordecai's cousin and adopted daughter, who had become the wife of Ahasuerus, he was himself "hanged on the gallows that he had prepared for Mordecai" (vii, 10).   In the Vulgate, the "gallows fifty cubits high" (vii, 9) is a "cross." The scene of the execution is not described in the Bible.

32. 'Bubble': the air that is enclosed in a spherical film of water.

35. The 'queen' is Amata, wife of King Latinus, who hanged herself in a fit of rage on hearing a premature report of the death of Turnus, the intended husband of her daughter Lavinia (cf. *Inf.* IV, 126).   She feared that her daughter would be taken from her by the victorious Aeneas.   See *Aen.*, VII, 341 ff.; XII, 604 ff.   Cf. Dante, Epistola VII, vii, 24.

39. Lavinia has to 'mourn' the death of her mother before that of Turnus.

67. Cf. XII, 98. It appears that the third *P* is now removed from Dante's brow.

68, 69. Mat. v, 9: "Blessed are the peacemakers."

85, 86. 'The love of the good diminished of its due (i.e., less than it should be), is here restored.' The sin punished is *acedia*, or sloth.

98. 'And while it is moderate in its attachment to secondary goods,' i.e., worldly blessings.

100, 101. When it runs to wordly good with more ardor, or to heavenly good with less ardor, than it should.

106, 107. 'Now, since love can never avert its gaze from the welfare of its own subject,' i.e., can never be hostile to the interest of the person in whose heart it dwells.

108. 'Things are safe (i.e., exempt) from self-hate': we cannot hate ourselves. Cf. Ephesians v, 29: "For no man ever yet hated his own flesh."

109, 110. 'And since no being can be conceived of as severed from the primal being and existing independently.' Cf. Acts xvii, 28: "For in him [the Lord] we live, and move, and have our being."

111. 'Every product (i.e., every creature) is debarred from hating him.' It is impossible to hate God, in whom we exist. Cf. *Conv.*, IV, xii, 14–15.

115, 116. 'There is the man who hopes to excel through his neighbor being crushed down,' i.e., 'by the abasement of his neighbor.'

126. 'In perverted measure': too sluggishly toward heavenly good, too eagerly toward worldly good.

128. Cf. St. Augustine, *Confessions*, I, i: "Fecisti nos ad te et inquietum est cor nostrum, donec requiescat in te." (Thou hast created us for thyself, and our heart cannot be quieted till it may find repose in thee.)

135. Cf. St. Thomas, *Summa Theologiae*, Prima, Qu. vi, Art. 3: "solus Deus est bonus per suam essentiam." (God alone is good essentially.)

Canto XVIII

Argument

Acedia is defined by St. Thomas (*Summa Theologiae*, Prima, Qu. lxiii, Art. 2) as "a certain sadness by which man is made slow to spiritual acts on account of physical difficulty." Elsewhere (Secunda Secundae, Qu. xxxv, Art. 1) he calls it "weariness of doing," and "sorrow over apparent ill which is real good." It is the "noonday devil," particularly rife in monastic life. Throughout the Middle Ages it was regarded as a capital vice. In our day we should be likely to attribute its most characteristic manifestations to a disease, melancholia or neurasthenia. To Dante, as we have seen, it meant a spiritual sluggishness due to insufficiency of love. Our poet, therefore, somewhat extends the theological definition of sloth. The cure must obviously be enforced spiritual activity, and consequently the souls in the fourth circle are represented as rushing at the top of their speed around their ledge, filled with righteous zeal. Dante takes no part in the penance. The examples on this terrace are recited by the penitents themselves, two at the head of the band proclaiming instances of celerity, two at the rear calling tales of sloth.   Startling is the swiftness with which the whole throng comes and goes.

When the spirits appear, the moon is newly risen.   Not far from the horizon, but already "making the stars seem fewer," its half disk looks like a red-hot kettle.   The moon, in its monthly circuit around the earth, moves from west to east, and therefore passes through the constellations, night after night, in a direction opposite to the general course of the heavens.   The annual march of the sun, too, is backward — not directly, however, but diagonally, as Dante points out in *Conv.*, III, v, 13.   When he speaks of the moon as "running contrary to the sky" (l. 79), he refers to this continuous backing, not to any motion visible to an observer in a single night.   The moon's revolution is accomplished in a little less than twenty-eight days.   On its fourteenth day, or thereabouts, it is full, and rises at sunset; on or near its twenty-first day it enters into its last quarter, when it rises at midnight.   Inasmuch as the moon was full on the night when Dante was lost in the wood (*Inf.* XX, 127–129), it has now reached its eighteenth or nineteenth day, and is 'delayed' in its rising 'almost until midnight' (l. 76).   Furthermore, it is moving 'over that road which the sun kindles at the time of year when the Roman sees it (the sun) set between Sardinia and Corsica' (ll. 79–81).   That is to say, the moon is now in that part of the sky where the sun is to be found at the season when a line drawn from Rome toward sunset would pass between Sardinia and Corsica.   Of course the Roman cannot really see the two islands; he merely perceives the sun disappearing in that direction.   Now, such a line points nearly west-southwest, the quarter where the sun, as seen from Rome, descends toward the end of November; and at that time the sun is in Sagittarius.   Against this constellation, then, the moon shows itself to Dante as it rises.

The time before the arrival of the spirits is employed by Virgil to expound to his pupil the doctrine of love (which, as he has already stated, is the motive power of the whole universe) and of free will.   But inasmuch as the full comprehension of free will transcends mere Reason, the teacher must leave the completion of his exposition to Beatrice, who, in fact, discusses the subject in *Par.* V, 19 ff.   In every soul, from its creation, love is latent, ready to be aroused to activity by a pleasing object.   This theory we find already formulated by Dante — as far as the love of gentleman and lady is concerned — in the tenth sonnet of the *Vita Nuova*, XX, 3–5, *Amor e 'l cor gentil sono una cosa*.   The senses convey to the mind the impression of some attractive object in the material world; the understanding then develops this impression in such a way that it is brought to the notice of the will, which may or may not lean toward the object in question.   Or, in Dante's words, 'the human perception derives from a real being (*esser verace*, l. 22) a conception (*intenzione*, l. 23), and unfolds it within the mind, so that it makes the desire turn towards it; and if, having thus turned, the desire inclines to it, that inclination is love.' This definition follows that of St. Thomas in the *Summa Theologiae*, Prima Secundae, Qu. xxvi. The process is illustrated in dramatic form by Dante in *Rime*, CXVI, ll. 16–36, where it is especially interesting to compare the 'colà dov' ella è vera' of l. 35 with the 'esser verace' of the present passage. The poet adds that this inclination is the natural human instinct (*natura*, l. 26), which, through a pleasing impression (*piacer*, l. 27), is once more bound in the soul. Before it is awakened to action, it is 'bound,' because it exists only in a potential state; after it is quickened and fixed, it is 'bound' again, in the sense that it is restricted to one object. Passion, according to St. Thomas (*Summa Theologiae*, Prima Secundae, Qu. lxxvii, Art. 2), is a sort of bodily modification which 'binds' the reason. The captive will, then, is moved to desire, and has no rest until it attains its object. This motion of the will is as natural, in the spiritual world, as, in the physical universe, the upward tendency of the flame, which is constantly striving to regain the sphere of fire, where its element is eternal. It is the 'form,' or character, of fire to rise, as it is the 'form' of the soul to love.

From the principle that love, in the abstract, is a general craving for good the Epicureans have deduced the conclusion that all love is, in itself, praiseworthy; but they overlook the fact that the especial object of desire may be evil, possessing only a false semblance of goodness. Even as a poor seal may stamp on excellent wax a bad imprint, so an unworthy object may kindle the good instinct of love to a wrongful passion. The first impulse to a particular affection comes from without, and is therefore not under our control; nevertheless, we are responsible, because we have the inborn knowledge of good and evil, and the free will to take or reject. 'Every substantial form,' says Dante in ll. 49–51, 'which is distinct from matter and yet combined with it, has, appropriated to itself, a specific faculty.' A 'substance,' in scholastic language, is something that has an independent being (*Summa Theologiae*, Prima, Qu. iii, Art. 5); the 'form' is the fundamental character of a thing; 'substantial form' (cf. *Conv.*, III, ii, 4) means the particular basic principle, that which gives an object its separate existence (*Summa Theologiae*, Prima, Qu. lxxvi, Art. 4), and the substantial form of mankind is the intellective soul, which is utterly different from matter, and yet is united with it in the human body. A 'specific faculty' is one that is common and peculiar to a whole species. The specific faculty possessed by the intellective soul of man is an instinct which comprises innate knowledge and the inborn disposition to love. This instinct is apparent only through its works, just as in a plant life manifests itself by green leaves. Hence we are not aware of the source of our axiomatic notions or of our natural inclination toward all that seems good: these things are a part of us, as the honey-making proclivity is a part of the bee. Since they are not of our own begetting, they call for neither praise nor blame. This God-given instinct is necessarily innocent; we must see to it that the inclinations which we do control are equally harmless. To this end we have judgment — "the faculty that counsels" (l. 62) — which "defends the threshold of consent." Judgment tells us which desires are right and which are wrong: and although our first impulses may always take us unawares, our decisions are subject to our own free will.

For the position of the moon, see Moore, III, 71–73. — With regard to the inborn, we must distinguish "innate ideas," which the Church does not admit, and "innate principles." Certain fundamental principles, according to St. Thomas, are inborn. See *Summa Theologiae*, Secunda Secundae, xlvii, 6 and 15: "praeexistunt quaedam ut principia naturaliter nota" (certain things preexist, as naturally known principles) ... "prima principia universalia sunt naturaliter nota" (the primary universal principles are known naturally).

18. Mat. xv, 14: "they be blind leaders of the blind."

23. Intention, 'image,' abstract conception. It is interesting to note that 'intention' has been so used in English.

28. *Met.*, XV, 243: "Alta petunt aer atque aere purior ignis." (Air and fire, purer still than air, fly to the upper realms.) Cf. Aristotle, *Ethics*, II, i, 2.

50. St. Thomas, *Summa Theologiae*, Prima, Qu. lxxvi Art. 4. "Anima intellectiva unitur corpori ut forma substantialis." (The intellectual soul is united to the body as its substantial form.)

56. 'Primal ideas': the things that appear as axiomatic truths.

57. 'Nor the liking for the primal objects of desire,' i.e., goodness and happiness.

60. Cf. St. Thomas, *Summa Theologiae*, Prima, Qu. lx, Art. 2.

61. 'Now, in order that every other (wish) may conform to this (primal wish),' which is instinctively good.

67. 'Those' are the philosophers.

76. It is the 18th or 19th day of the moon, which on its 21st will rise at midnight.

79–81. West-southwest. Sagittarius. End of November.

82. Virgil was born at Andes, now commonly identified with Piètola, or Piètole, near Mantua.

84. 'Had put off the burden of my loading (i.e., with which I had loaded him),' had discharged the duty I had set him.

91. Ismēnus and Asōpus are rivers in Boeotia, near Thebes, the birthplace of Bacchus.

92. The Bacchic orgies. Cf. Statius, *Thebaid*, IX, 434 ff.

100. Luke i, 39: "And Mary arose in those days, and went into the hill country with haste," to see Elizabeth.

101. *Ilerda*, Lerida, a city in Spain, held by the adherents of Pompey. Cf. *Phars.*, III, 453–455; also, for the general swiftness of Caesar's movements, I, 151–157.

102. Caesar began the siege of Marseilles, and then, leaving it to a lieutenant, hastened on to Spain. Cf. Paulus Orosius, *Historia adversus Paganos*, VI, xv.

118. We know nothing of this abbot of the monastery of St. Zeno.

120. The Emperor Barbarossa destroyed Milan in 1162.

121. Alberto della Scala, lord of Verona, who died in 1301. Alberto was the father of Can Grande.

124. Giuseppe della Scala, the illegitimate son of Alberto, was abbot of St. Zeno from 1292 to 1313. — In Levit. xxi, 16–23, "whatsoever man he be that hath a blemish" is excluded from divine office.

133, 134, 135. The Hebrews who had crossed the Red Sea were sluggish and rebellious, and all perished, except Caleb and Joshua, before the Promised Land was reached. Cf. Numbers xiv, 16–33; Joshua v, 6.

136. Some of Aeneas's companions, weary of hardship, stayed behind in Sicily with Acestes. See *Aen.*, V, 700–778; especially l. 751: "*animos nil magnae laudis egentes*" (souls with no craving for high renown).

Canto XIX

Argument

Dante's sojourn beside and in the realm of sloth occurs at night, the time when activity is suspended, and he tarries there much longer than in the other circles. In these coincidences we are to see, no doubt, an artistic rather than a symbolic relevancy; the delay of the traveler makes more effective, by contrast, the haste of the penitent. Here, in the prophetic hour that precedes dawn, he has the second of his three allegorical dreams. This one reveals to him the true nature of the sins of the flesh, whose penitent victims he is to visit during the ensuing day; at the same time it illustrates, in concrete, dramatic form, the doctrine of temptation, discretion, and resistance expounded in the foregoing canto (XVIII, 49–66). A hideous, impotent female — stammering, cross-eyed, handless, club-footed, pale — is gradually transformed, as Dante looks on her, into a siren of perilous beauty; thus evil desire, hateful and powerless at first, becomes alluring if we let our minds dwell upon it. While the poet is listening to the sweet voice of the temptress, a "lady quick and holy" springs up to confound her. This heaven-sent counselor (the "*virtù che consiglia*" of XVIII, 62) arouses Reason; and he, gazing steadfastly on this pure image of Conscience, never allowing his eyes to stray to the dangerous charms of the deceiver, discloses to the shocked dreamer the real foulness of her who has so attracted him. Even so, in one of the tales of Caesarius of Heisterbach (*Dialogus Miraculorum*, XII, chap. iv), a sweet-voiced cleric, who has bewitched all by his song, collapses, when exorcised, into a putrid corpse.

The myth of the sirens had survived in medieval folklore and literature. Hugh of St. Victor, for instance, in *De Bestiis et Aliis Rebus*, II, chap. xxxii, likens dissolute men, in the devil's clutches, to sailors lulled and killed by sirens. Dante's siren boasts that she once "turned Ulysses from his wandering way." While this is allegorically true — since Ulysses was led into forbidden seas by his eagerness to have experience of "human vices and virtue" (*Inf.* XXVI, 97–99) — it is not literally in accordance with Homer's narrative. Dante had never read the *Odyssey*, and probably got his knowledge of the episode from a passage in Cicero (*De Finibus*, V, xviii, 49), which, taken by itself, might easily give the impression that Ulysses succumbed

The worst of the sins of the flesh is avarice, which, in Purgatory as in Hell (*Inf.* VII), is coupled with the contrary vice of prodigality. Both hoarding and squandering consist, when reduced to their underlying principle, in immoderateness with regard to property; the virtue opposed to both is moderation, the golden mean between the two extremes. But while Dante, for theoretical reasons, insists on this combination, he evidently centers his attention on avarice in his description of penance and penitents. Those whose eyes were fixed on vile earthly goods must lie with their faces in the dust; those who eschewed useful activity are now tight bound and motionless. Allegorically the discipline signifies the averting of the mind from worldly things and the humble renunciation of glory and power. As love of money has much in common with envy, so there is a resemblance between the punishments in the 2nd circle (XIII) and the 5th, which Dante now enters.

1, 2, 3. The coldest hour is just before dawn. The earth itself was regarded as naturally cold, and a chill was supposed to descend from the moon, as well as from Saturn when it is above the horizon.

4. 'Geomancers' foretold the future by means of figures constructed on points that were distributed by chance. Their specialty was the selection of favorable spots for burial. They were the first in Europe to use the compass. One of their figures, called *fortuna major*, or "greater fortune," resembled a combination of the last stars of Aquarius and the first of Pisces. As these constellations immediately precede Aries, in which the sun is from March 21 to April 21, the figure in question can be seen in the east shortly before sunrise at that season.

6. The 'road' by which *fortuna major* rises is 'kept dark for it only a little while,' because the sun, following close after, makes the stars fade.

32. Cf. Ezekiel xvi, 37: "I will ... discover thy nakedness (*ignominiam*) unto them, that they may see all thy nakedness (*turpitudinem*)." Cf. also Isaiah iii, 16–17: "Because the daughters of Zion are haughty, and walk with stretched forth necks and wanton eyes, ... the Lord will discover their secret parts."

39. The poets are now on the north side of the mountain, walking toward the west.

42. Boccaccio describes Dante as stooping thoughtfully.

48. The 'two walls of hard rock' enclose the stairway cut into the cliff.

49. Thus it is apparent that one more P is effaced from Dante's brow.

51. 'Who shall have their souls mistresses (i.e., possessed) of comfort' — a periphrasis of Mat. v, 4: "Blessed are they that mourn, for they shall be comforted." This beatitude is here interpreted as a praise of those who, unlike the slothful, have the courage to face pain.

59. In the three upper circles.

63. The 'lure' of 'the great wheels' is the uplifting influence of the revolving heavens. Cf. XIV, 148–150.

69. Dante climbs to the fifth terrace, the circle of avarice and prodigality.

73. Ps. cxix (Vulg. cxviii), 25: "My soul cleaveth unto the dust."

81. In order to keep their right hands on the outer side of the cornice, it is evident that the poets must walk, according to their usual custom, to the right.

84. The speaker's face, turned to the ground, cannot be seen.

92. 'That without which one cannot return to God' is the fruit of repentance.

97. They are lying on their bellies.

99. 'Know that I was a successor of Peter.' The language of the Church is appropriate in the mouth of a Pope, and the majestic Latin emphasizes, by contrast, his present humiliation. The speaker is Adrian V, of the Fieschi family of Genoa, who held the Papal office for 38 days in 1276.

101. The Lavagna 'descends' into the Gulf of Genoa between the towns of Sestri and Chiavari. The Fieschi were counts of Lavagna; the name of the river was the 'pinnacle' of their title.

109. Even in the Papal chair itself, beyond which no man can climb on earth.

117. I.e., more humiliating: cf. *Inf.* VI, 48, The wickedness of avarice is shown by the severity of the penance of the 'converted souls.'

122. 'So that our activity was lost,' i.e., our good works ceased.

134. Cf. Rev. xix, 10: "And I fell at his (the angel's) feet to worship him. And he said unto me, See thou do it not: I am thy fellow servant, and of thy brethren that have the testimony of Jesus."

137. Mat. xxii, 30: "For in the resurrection *they neither marry*, nor are given in marriage, but are as the angels of God in heaven."

141. Cf. l. 92.

142. Alagia de' Fieschi, the daughter of Adrian's brother Niccolò, was the wife of Marquis Moroello Malaspina and was therefore probably Dante's hostess in 1306.

144. One of the Fieschi, Bonifazio, appears in the circle of gluttony (XXIV, 29); a second, Innocent IV, is mentioned slightingly in Epistola XI, vii, 16; at least one other probably incurred Dante's displeasure.

Canto XX

Argument

As the rueful souls lie flat on the outer edge of the terrace, their faces turned to the ground, they meditate, at the close of all their prayers, comforting examples of virtue and of punished vice, which they now murmur softly to themselves, now cry aloud, according to their mood. By day they recite instances of indifference to wealth and of the proper use of it; by night, anecdotes of the fatal results of cupidity. Of these last stories, seven are quoted, corresponding to the seven sins which St. Thomas (*Summa Theologiae*, Secunda Secundae, Qu. cxviii, Art. 8) derives from avarice. With a curse upon the "old wolf" of immoderateness, Dante invokes that savior whom the heavens shall send to banish this devourer and restore justice to the world. Once before, in *Inf.* I, 94–111, the havoc done by the "wolf" was described, and the rescuing "hound" was foretold. Once again, in *Purg.* XXXIII, 34–51, after a picture of corruption by greed, we find the promise of a divinely ordained reformer; this latter prophecy is linked to our present passage by the repetition of a rhyme in -*eda* (XX, 11–13–15; XXXIII, 35–37–39).

In the prostrate throng is Hugh Capet, king of France from 987 to 996, founder of the Capetian line, whose descendants, in 1300, ruled over France, Spain, and

Naples.   Before that year four Philips and four Lewises (as well as a Robert and a Henry), sprung from him, had mounted the throne of France.   In Dante's day he was often confounded with his father, Hugh the Great, Duke of France, who really governed the country in the time of the last Carolingians; in our poem these two persons are fused into one.   According to a generally accepted but incorrect tradition, Hugh the Great came of a family of rich Parisian cattle dealers or butchers.   When "the old kings" — the offspring of Charlemagne — "died out" with Louis V, there remained of the elder dynasty only Charles, duke of Lorraine, son of Louis IV; the feudal lords refused to accept him as sovereign, and crowned Hugh Capet in his stead.   For Dante's assertion that the last of the Carolingians became a monk, "a devotee in gray clothes" (l. 54), there is no historical warrant.   Here again he seems to have followed a confused literary tradition.

Hugh Capet, in Dante's account, gained such firm control of the state that his son was promoted to the "widowed crown," and from him descended the "consecrated bones" of all the subsequent royal anointed.   In reality, Robert I was almost immediately associated with his father in the government and was crowned in 988.   While the means and the domain of his family were comparatively small — Hugh declares — it remained insignificant but harmless; but when, by trickery, Charles of Anjou, brother of Louis IX, contrived to marry Beatrice, heiress of Provence, and so secured "the great Provençal dowry," his descendants lost all sense of shame.   Since then their history has been a chronicle of crimes, in which Philip IV, the Fair (VII, 109), has played the leading part.   England was robbed, "by violence and by falsehood," of Ponthieu, Normandy, and Gascony.   Charles of Anjou (VII, 113, 124) came to Italy in 1265 to wrest the kingdom of Sicily from Manfred, who was defeated and slain the next year (III, 112); in 1268, in Naples, after the battle of Tagliacozzo (*Inf.* XXVIII, 17), he put to death Conradin, a lad of sixteen, grandson of Frederick II; he was accused also of having instigated, for political reasons, the poisoning of St. Thomas Aquinas, who died, probably in 1274, on his journey from Naples to the Council of Lyons.   Another Charles, continues Hugh Capet — Charles of Valois, called Lackland or *Senza terra*, brother of Philip IV — will come out of France in 1301, armed only with treachery ("the lance with which Judas tilted"), to betray Florence into the hands of the Blacks and to contend vainly with Frederick of Aragon (VII, 119) in Sicily.   A third Charles — the Cripple of Jerusalem, Charles II, king of Apulia, son of Charles of Anjou (VII, 127; *Par.* XIX, 127) — after having been taken prisoner in 1284 in a sea fight in the Bay of Naples by Ruggero di Lauria, the admiral of Peter of Aragon (VII, 112), will sell his young daughter Beatrice in marriage to the old Marquis of Ferrara, Azzo VIII d'Este.   But the crowning infamy of the race, that which shall throw into the shade all past and future outrage, shall be the seizure of Pope Boniface VIII at Anagni in the Roman Campagna, in 1303, by Guillaume de Nogaret and Sciarra Colonna.   Seated on his throne and clad in the Papal raiment, Boniface was roughly taken prisoner; he was then conveyed to Rome, where he was wounded in the head, and, after a little while, died of rage and shame.   In spite of Dante's hostility to Boniface, whom he regarded as an unworthy prelate (*Inf.* XIX, 52–57), the enemy of Florence and the author of his own misfortunes (*Par.* XVII, 49–51), this humiliation of the head of the Church shocked him beyond measure.   The fate of Christ — so it seemed to the poet — was renewed in that of his vicar, crucified, not between two thieves condemned to die with him, but between two mocking villains — Guillaume and Sciarra — who were allowed to live. These men were bearers of the *fleur-de-lis*, creatures of Philip the Fair.   That "modern Pilate," not satisfied even with this crime, directed his "greedy sails," like a pirate ship, toward the Order of the Templars; having brought against that body a false accusation of heresy, and having arrested all the Templars in 1307, without waiting for Papal authorization, he turned them over to the Inquisition, possessed himself of their treasure, and finally caused the abolition of their order in 1312.   The head of the Order, Jacques de Molay, was burned to death in 1313.   Such is the "evil plant" of which Hugh Capet was the root.   By means of its control of the Papacy, it "overshadows all Christendom," and "seldom is good fruit plucked therefrom."   If the cities of Douai, Lille, Ghent, and Bruges had the strength, they would soon wreak vengeance on Philip the Fair, who conquered Flanders in 1297.   That vengeance came, in fact, in 1302, when Philip's troops were crushingly defeated in Bruges and Courtrai, and the French were driven from the country.

It is noteworthy that Dante never mentions the saintly Louis IX, who was canonized in 1297 by Boniface VIII for political reasons.   Dante regarded the House of France as the worst menace to Christendom, as it was acquiring both the ecclesiastical and the temporal power.

One may ask: For what sin is Hugh Capet here?   According to Pio Rajna, *Hugues Capet dans la "Divine Comédie,"* 1924, Hugh is probably doing penance for prodigality rather than avarice.

1. The 'better will' is that of Adrian V: cf. XIX, 139.
6. The poets step carefully along on the inner side of the cornice, close to the upright cliff, just as soldiers march on the top of a narrow rampart, close to the battlements.   Such battlemented walls still surround Carcassonne and Aigues-Mortes, and may be seen also at Avignon and Florence.
25. Caius Fabricius Luscinus, the Roman consul famous for his incorruptibility, who refused the bribes of the Samnites: *Conv.*, IV, v, 13; *Mon.*, II, v, 11.   Cf. *Aen.*, VI, 843–844.
32. St. Nicholas, bishop of Mira in the fourth century.   According to the legend, he secretly

threw, on three successive nights, into the window of his neighbor's house enough money to provide dowries for the three daughters who would otherwise have been forced by poverty to a life of dishonor.

90. Cf. Mat. xxvii, 38: "Then there were two thieves crucified with him, one on the right hand, and another on the left."

91. Philip the Fair, who had played the part of Pilate toward Christ's vicar.

92. Papal decree.

94. Cf. Ps. lviii, 10 (Vulg. lvii, 11): "The righteous shall rejoice when he seeth the vengeance."

97. Having replied to Dante's first question (l. 35), Hugh proceeds to answer his second (l. 36). — Cf. Mat. i, 20: "that which is conceived in her (Mary) is of the Holy Ghost."

103. Pygmalion, king of Tyre, brother of Dido, killed Dido's husband Sichaeus (*Inf.* V, 62) for the sake of his wealth: *Aen.*, I, 343–359.

106. Midas, king of Phrygia, asked of Bacchus that all he touched might be turned to gold, but was compelled to pray for a revocation of the gift, and was finally presented with ass's ears: *Met.*, xi, 85–193.

109. Achan, having stolen and hidden some of the forbidden spoils of Jericho, was stoned to death at Joshua's command: Joshua vi, 17–19; vii.

112. Ananias and his wife Sapphira, having sold a piece of land and deceitfully withheld from the apostles a part of the price for their own use, were rebuked by Peter and fell down dead: Acts v, 1–10.

113. Heliodorus, minister of King Seleucus, having entered the temple of Jerusalem to take possession of the treasure, was kicked half to death by a mysterious horse: 2 Macc. iii, 7, 25–27.

115. Polymnestor (or Polymestor), king of Thrace, murdered and robbed his young brother-in-law, Polydorus, who had been entrusted to him by Priam; Hecuba, maddened by the death of her son, tore out the traitor's eyes and killed him (*Inf.* XXX, 16–21): *Met.*, XIII, 429 ff.; cf. *Aen.*, III, 41–57.

117. Marcus Licinius Crassus, triumvir with Caesar and Pompey, was famous in antiquity and in the Middle Ages for his wealth and his greed. It is related that when he was defeated and slain by the Parthians, their king had molten gold poured down his throat, saying: "Thou hast thirsted for gold, now drink it!" Cf. Paulus Orosius, *Historia adversus Paganos*, VI, xiii.

130. Delos, before Latona took refuge there to bring forth Apollo and Diana (sun and moon, "the two eyes of heaven"), was a wandering island: *Met.*, VI, 189–192; *Aen.*, III, 73–77.

136. Luke ii, 14: "Glory to God in the highest."

140. Luke ii, 9.

145. Cf. Wisdom of Solomon xiv, 22: "they lived in the great war of ignorance."

Canto XXI

Argument

Left, like Dante himself, in agonizing suspense at the end of the preceding canto, we now learn why the mountain trembled and why all the souls up and down its slope cried out together. This rejoicing occurs whenever any spirit has completed its penance and feels itself free to rise to heaven. St. Thomas, and others after him, distinguished the "absolute" from the "conditioned" will. The absolute will is a constant inclination toward the good; the conditioned will is a modification of this inclination by circumstances. When we sin, we follow, not our absolute, but our conditioned will, which has been perverted by false appearances. So when we make atonement, it is not the absolute will that seeks punishment, but the conditioned will, shaped by the knowledge that good can come through penance alone. A soul in Purgatory is held there only by its own conditioned will. As soon as this conditioned will, or desire, coincides with the absolute and eternal inclination to seek blessedness, the penitent knows that his expiation is over and he is at liberty to rise. "The only proof of purity is the will itself, which suddenly finds the soul quite free to change its company, and by its volition enables it to do so": ll. 61–63. "Before that moment (*prima*), to be sure (*ben*), the soul wills absolutely to rise (*vuol*), but it is prevented by its desire or conditioned will (*ma non lascia il talento*), which divine justice inclines to suffering (*che pone al tormento*), its operation being now contrary to the tendency of the absolute will (*contra voglia*), just as was the case when it sinned (*come fu al peccar*)": ll. 64–66.

Purgatory itself, like the Garden of Eden, is exempt from physical change, and only spiritual causes operate there. "The law of the mountain never experiences anything that is unregulated or abnormal": ll. 40–42. A spiritual phenomenon — the release of a soul — may move both spirits and earth to a display of gladness, but even this manifestation is in accordance with the everlasting nature of the sacred mount. Although the peak does not rise above the earth's mantle of air, its upper part, like the Isle de Voirre, described in the Old French *Erec* (ll. 1947–1951), is beyond the reach of atmospheric change. As Lucan says, in *Pharsalia*, II, 271–273:

> nubes excedit Olympus.
> Lege deum minimas rerum discordia turbat,
> Pacem magna tenent.

(Olympus rises above the clouds. It is heaven's law, that small things are troubled and distracted, while great things enjoy peace.)

Wet vapors are unknown; "no rain, hail, snow, dew, nor frost falls any higher up than the short stairway of three steps," where is the entrance to Purgatory: ll. 46–48. Dry vapors, which cause lightning, meteors, comets, wind, and earthquake, are absent also. "Lower down on the slope, the earth may quake, much or little; but up here its shaking was never due" — as it is elsewhere — "to the mysterious confinement of wind in the belly of the globe": ll. 55–57. "It trembles when any soul feels itself clean enough to arise and start on its ascent, and such a shout" as its companions have just raised "accompanies" the upward faring spirit: 58–60.

The penitent whose liberation from the fifth circle has produced such a commotion is Statius, a famous Latin poet of the first century of our era.   His two great epics, the *Thebaid* and the *Achilleid* (the second unfinished), highly artificial and ornate in style, were assiduously studied throughout the Middle Ages, and were looked upon as models of rhetorical elegance.   Dante, who knew them thoroughly, must have found in them a vast storehouse of classical mythology; with characteristic gratitude he honored Statius for the good he had derived from him.   A third work, a miscellany known as the *Silvae*, in which the author names Naples as his birthplace, had not been recovered in the 14th century, and Dante and his contemporaries seem to have confounded the epic poet with another Statius, a certain rhetorician from Toulouse.   The admiration of Statius for Virgil is attested by a passage at the close of the *Thebaid* (XII, 816 ff.), in which he bids his narrative "follow, at a distance, the divine *Aeneid*, and ever adore its steps."   The meeting between these ancient poets is described by Dante in a vein of demure humor quickened by love.   At the end of the canto is a scene that reminds one of the encounter of Virgil and Sordello (VI, 75); but whereas Sordello embraces his brother Mantuan, it is apparently impossible for Statius to clasp the feet of Virgil.

The real Statius was a pagan, and the story of his conversion, related in the next canto, is, as far as we know, of Dante's invention, although he may have found it suggested in some lost source or deduced it from Statius's own work. The author of the *Thebaid* represents, in the *Commedia*, Reason illumined by Faith, and seemingly has the mission of elucidating certain questions that transcend unassisted Reason; he is doubtless to be regarded, then, as an auxiliary to Virgil and a secondary guide to Beatrice, or, in other words, as an intermediary between human Reason and Revelation.   At the same time he serves as an example of a soul in transit from earth to Heaven.   He may illustrate also the influence of inspired paganism on Christianity.   With Dante's extraordinary love of symmetry, it is rather surprising that he should have furnished only two great conductors for the three journeys.   One is almost tempted to surmise that in his original conception Statius played a more important part.

For St. Thomas on the absolute and the conditioned will of souls on Purgatory, see *Summa Theologiae*, Tertia, Suppl., App., Qu. ii, Art. 2.
                                        St. Thomas, in his commentary on Aristotle's *Ethics*, II, Lectio xi, declares that Aristotle uses the simile of straightening warped pieces of wood by bending them the other way, thus bringing them back to the mean; similar is Dante's conception of the straightening of the will by purgation.— For the absence of atmospheric change, cf. *Thebaid*, II, 32–40.

2. Cf. John iv, 7–26, especially 13–15: "Jesus ... said unto her, Whosoever ... drinketh of the water that I shall give him shall never thirst ... The woman saith unto him, Sir, give me this water, that I thirst not."

7. Luke xxiv, 13–15: "And, behold, two of them went that same day to a village called Emmaus ... and they talked together of all these things which had happened.   And it came to pass, that, while they communed together and reasoned, Jesus himself drew near, and went with them."   One of the two was Cleopas; the other is unnamed.

13. Cf. Luke xxiv, 36: "And as they thus spake, Jesus himself stood in the midst of them, and saith unto them, Peace be unto you."

22. The letters on Dante's brow.

24. "Then shall the King say unto them on his right hand, Come, ye blessed of my Father, inherit the kingdom prepared for you from the foundation of the world" (Mat. xxv, 34).

25. Lachesis, the second of the three Fates, spins the thread of life, which Clotho prepares and Atropos cuts off.

36. 'Its moist feet': referring, of course, to the base of the mountain.

50. Thaumas's daughter is Iris, the rainbow, Juno's messenger.

51. The rainbow, in the land of the living, appears sometimes in the east, sometimes in the west.

53. Cf. IX, 100–104.

68. Statius, who died near the close of the first century of our era, has passed a little more than 1200 years on the Island of Purgatory; of these, upward of 400 were spent in the circle of sloth (XXII, 92), and over 500 in the circle of avarice and prodigality.

82. The capture of Jerusalem by the Emperor Titus, which took place in the year 70, was regarded as a vengeance for the crucifixion of Christ by the Jews.

89. *Tolosano*, 'though I was from Toulouse.' — Cf. Juvenal, *Satires*, VII, 82 ff., for the popularity of Statius in Rome.

92. Statius did not live to finish the *Achilleid*.

101. Virgil died in 19 B.C.; Statius, more than a century later.

105. 'The faculty that wills,' the willpower.

Canto XXII

Argument

In his fourth Eclogue, Virgil rejoices in the conclusion of peace during the consulate of his protector, Caius Asinius Pollio, under the second triumvirate; and, in strangely obscure language, celebrates the birth of a son to Pollio himself.   The last of the periods predicted by the Cumaean Sibyl has come, he declares — the return to the golden age, which was to be restored after the ages of silver, bronze, and iron.   A vast cycle of years is starting afresh.   The virgin Astraea, goddess of Justice, the last of the gods to forsake mankind, is now returning, with the good old times when Saturn, father of Jupiter, ruled the world.   A new offspring is sent down from high Heaven.   Verses 4–7, the last three of which are translated by Dante in ll. 70–72 of this canto, run as follows:

> Ultima Cumaei venit iam carminis aetas;
> magnus ab integro saeclorum nascitur ordo.
> iam redit et Virgo, redeunt Saturnia regna;
> iam nova progenies caelo demittitur alto.

(Now is come the last age of the song of Cumae; the great line of the centuries begins anew. Now the Virgin returns, the reign of Saturn returns; now a new progeny descends from heaven on high.)

Early Christian writers often discussed the question whether the Sibyls were truly inspired, and the belief was tolerably common that, although these prophetesses were possessed by demons, God occasionally allowed them, in consideration of their virginity, to foretell the truth. From the fourth and well into the sixteenth century, the verses just cited were generally regarded as a genuine announcement of the coming of Christ, unwittingly formulated by Virgil some forty years before the event. It may be assumed, perhaps, that Virgil was illumined by *gratia gratis data*, in order that he might serve others. According to a pious legend recorded by Comparetti, *Virgilio nel medio evo*, I, vii, 137 (ed. 1896), three persecutors of Christians, suddenly illumined by these verses, were turned from paganism to the true religion. Dante represents Statius as having been converted in the same way, but as having concealed his new faith and succored his fellowbelievers by stealth. Thus another legend, cited by Torraca, 518, pictures a sister of the Emperor Domitian as secretly visiting and comforting imprisoned Christians and listening to the sermons of St. Paul. We may compare also the story of Joseph of Arimathea, who, according to John xix, 38, was "a disciple of Jesus, but secretly for fear of the Jews."

While the effectiveness of this hidden conversion, as a tribute to Virgil, and its allegorical appropriateness, in a figure symbolic of Reason enlightened by Faith, are obvious enough, we have small clue to the causes that led our author to select Statius for this experience. Dante presumably interpreted the name Statius as "the dallier." He believed Statius was really converted when he reached the middle of the *Thebaid*. The introduction to this poem is distinctly pagan, in that the divinity of the Roman Emperor is explicitly proclaimed (I, 22–31). In the opening lines of the *Achilleid*, on the other hand (I, 14–19), Domitian is not called a god, and the whole passage is susceptible of a Christian interpretation, the *progeniem* suggesting l. 7 of Virgil's famous fourth Eclogue. Statius's Achilles may, indeed, be taken as a symbol of Christ, in which case Hippomedon, who led the Greeks to cross the river in *Thebaid* VII, might represent John the Baptist.

Nor do we know why Dante chose to make Statius a spendthrift — for as such he reveals himself in the present canto — unless he got the idea from Juvenal's words about the poet, in *Satire* VII, 87: cf. l. 14 of this canto. But whatever may have occasioned the attribution of prodigality to the author of the *Thebaid*, it seems likely that Dante blamed himself for this vice and ascribed to Statius some of his own feelings and ideas. Was it not our poet himself who really discovered a mysterious warning in the whimsical distortion of Virgil's apostrophe to the "auri sacra fames" (ll. 37–42)? We know that Dante, before his exile, between 1297 and 1301, incurred heavy debts, and we know that he was a close friend of the happy-go-lucky Forese Donati, who appears in the next canto. When he leaves the circle of spendthrifts, he is "lighter than at the other outlets" (XXII, 7). The insistence, both in Hell and in Purgatory, upon the doctrine that prodigality is just as much a sin as avarice — although people do not think so (ll. 46–48) — may be accounted for in part by a desire to illustrate the Aristotelian arrangement of vices in pairs of extremes; but it appears to have behind it also some more cogent and personal reason. It is Statius, the prodigal, who asserts (ll. 49–51) that each sin is coupled with its opposite, although this scheme is carried out nowhere else in Purgatory or Hell. Many little indications, in fact, combine to suggest that Dante was eager to protect his readers from the consequences of an insidious vice from which he had miraculously escaped.

The next vice on the stairway of purification is gluttony, and the proper discipline is rigid abstinence, which, embittered by continual exposure to temptation, wastes the penitent to skin and bone. As, in the *Visio Sancti Pauli*, the souls of those who neglected fasts are tantalized by fruits, so Dante's gluttons have to pass, in their circuit, two fruit trees moistened by waterfalls. These trees, with the large branches at the top and the small ones at the bottom, are so shaped that no one can climb up — a symbol of prohibition. From their foliage issue voices proclaiming examples of temperance and intemperance.

4. Mat. v, 6: "Blessed are they which do hunger and thirst after righteousness" — in the Vulgate, "Beati qui esuriunt et sitiunt *justitiam*." Dante here takes "justice" in the special sense of moderation, the golden mean between avarice and prodigality, the virtue opposed to both these sins.

6. The verse as recited by the angel is: "Beati qui sitiunt justitiam," the *esuriunt* ('hunger') being left out. In the circle of gluttony the same verse is given, in a different sense, the *esuriunt* being retained and the *sitiunt* ('thirst') omitted. To get the requisite number of appropriate beatitudes, Dante used this one twice, and in both cases somewhat distorted its form and meaning.

10, 11. Virgil here says of spiritual love what Francesca said of carnal passion in *Inf.* V, 103.

14. The Latin poet Juvenal was a contemporary of Statius, whom he praised in his *Satires*, VII, 81–87.

36. 'Thousands of months': over 500 years (XXI, 68), or more than 6000 months.

40, 41. *Aen.*, III, 56–57:

> Quid non mortalia pectora cogis,
> Auri sacra fames?

(To what dost thou not drive mortal hearts, accursed hunger for gold?)

Statius took from these words the warning that the opposite vice, prodigality, was also to be avoided. For a more detailed discussion of this much-debated point, see Singleton (1970).

42. 'Rolling (a heavy weight), I should (now) be engaged in the dismal tilts' of the misers and the prodigals in Hell: cf. *Inf.* VII, 25–30.

46. The 'cropped hair' is a symbol of prodigality: *Inf.* VII, 56–57.

47. Many are lost because they do not understand that prodigality is a sin, as well as avarice. Their ignorance, which 'robs them of repentance,' is not a sufficient excuse, because it is not insuperable or 'invincible' ignorance: they had a chance to learn better. Cf. St. Thomas, *Summa Theologiae*, Prima Secundae, Qu. lxxvi, Art. 2.

56. By the 'twofold affliction of Jocasta' is meant her two sons, Eteõcles and Polynīces, whose strife and death are related in the 11th book of the *Thebaid*. Cf. *Inf.* XXVI, 52–54.

57. This mention of the *Bucolics*, or *Eclogues*, of Virgil prepares the reader for the quotation from the 4th Eclogue in ll. 70–72.

58. 'Judging from that (i.e., the music) which Clio plays with thee there': judging from the narrative which the pagan muse inspired. Clio, the muse of history, is invoked twice in the *Thebaid* and once (as 'goddess') in the *Achilleid*.

61. What heavenly or earthly light 'scattered thy darkness'?

63. The 'fisherman' is St. Peter. In the *Thebaid*, XII, 209, Statius speaks of his work as a voyage.

65. Parnassus is the mountain sacred to Apollo and the muses.

68. Cf. St. Augustine, *Confessions*, IV, xvi.

83. Domitian was Emperor toward the close of the first century of our era.

87. See, in the *Thebaid*, XII, 481 ff., the description of the altar to Clemency, refuge of the afflicted, open to all, without ceremony or sacrifice. It is to be noted that after the Greeks reach the Asopus, Apollo and Diana are impotent to save their favorites (*Thebaid*, IX, 653 ff.).

88. The arrival of the Greeks at the rivers of Thebes marks the middle of the *Thebaid*. Cf. VII, 424–425:

Iam ripas, Asope, tuas Beotaque ventum
Flumina.

(Already they were come to thy banks, Asopus, and the Boeotian streams.) Statius, then, in Dante's belief, was baptized before the poem was half done.

93. Statius circled around the fourth circle (of sloth) 'over four centuries' before his penance of 500 years and more in the circle of prodigality. Cf. XXI, 67–68.

98. *Varro*, popular form of the name Vario. This is Lucius Varius Rufus, Roman poet of the Augustan age and intimate friend of both Virgil and Horace. He wrote a tragedy and epics, a few fragments of which have been preserved.

100. Persius, the Latin satirist.

101. Homer: cf. *Inf.* IV, 88.

103. The 'first belt' is the Limbus.

105. 'Our nurses' are the muses: cf. l. 102.

106, 107. The Greek lyric poet Simonides is mentioned with the Greek tragic poets Euripides, Antiphon, and Agathon.

109. By 'thy people' Virgil means the characters in Statius's poems. The first six enumerated are found in the *Thebaid*, the last two are found in the *Achilleid*.

110, 111. Antigone and Ismēne were daughters of Oedipus and Jocasta (l. 56); after fearful misfortunes, both were condemned to death by Creon. Deiphīle and Argīa were daughters of Adrastus, king of Argos; the first was the wife of Tydeus (*Inf.* XXXII, 130), the second of Polynices (see note to l. 56); Argia once possessed the "ill-fated ornament" of XII, 51.

112. It was Hypsipȳle who pointed out the fountain of Langīa to Adrastus and the other Greek kings, when their troops were dying of thirst (*Thebaid*, IV, 716 ff.): cf. *Inf.* XVIII, 92; *Purg.* XXVI, 95.

113. Tiresias's daughter was Manto, whom Dante consigned (*Inf.* XX, 55), with the other soothsayers, to the 4th *bolgia* of the 8th circle of Hell; for a discussion of this curious inconsistency, see the Argument to Canto XX of the *Inferno*. — Thetis, the sea-goddess, was the wife of Peleus and the mother of Achilles: cf. IX, 37.

114. Deïdamīa and 'her sisters' were daughters of Lycomedes, king of Scyros, with whom Thetis hid Achilles: IX, 34–39. Deidamia was loved by Achilles: *Inf.* XXVI, 62.

118. The 'handmaids of the day' are the hours of daylight: cf. XII, 81.
119. The hours are here represented as drawing in turn the car of day.
120. The 'blazing horn' is the bright tip of the pole, which now points 'only upward,' as it is approaching the meridian.
126. The 'worthy soul' who gives his silent assent is Statius.
136. On the inner side, where the path was enclosed by the cliff.
143. The story of Mary at the wedding feast in Cana (John ii, 1–3), which she tried to make 'honorable and perfect,' was used in XIII, 29, as an example of loving solicitude; here it appears among the noteworthy examples of temperance.
144. 'Than of her own mouth (i.e., of gratifying her own appetite), which now answers (pleads) for you.'
145. St. Thomas says that, according to Valerius Maximus, the women, at the time of the early Romans, drank no wine: *Summa Theologiae*, Secunda Secundae, Qu. cxlix, Art. 4.
147. Daniel i, 8–17: "But Daniel purposed in his heart that he would not defile himself with the portion of the king's (Nebuchadnezzar's) meat, nor with the wine which he drank ... and Daniel had understanding in all visions and dreams."
148. The golden age is described in *Met.*, I, 89–112.
151. Mat. iii, 4: "his (John the Baptist's) meat was locusts and wild honey."
154. Mat. xi, 11: "Among them that are born of women there hath not risen a greater than John the Baptist." Cf. Luke i, 15.

Canto XXIII

Argument

Just as, in Hell, Dante's old master, Brunetto Latini, scorched almost beyond recognition, suddenly greets his former disciple with the exclamation "Qual maraviglia!" (*Inf.* XV, 24), so among the disfigured gluttons in Purgatory one of the souls, after peering at the poet "from the depths of his skull," reveals himself by the cry "Qual grazia m'è questa!" The same gentle, caressing rhythm in which the traveler accosted Francesca, Ciacco, and Belacqua (*Inf.* V, 116; VI, 58; *Purg.* IV, 123) recurs here in the line "Ed io a lui: 'Forese, da quel dì' ..." For this is the shade of Bicci Novello, called also Forese, of the Donati family, brother of that famous Corso Donati who led the Blacks, and a kinsman of the Gemma Donati who became Dante's wife. He died in 1296. From the present passage we learn that he and our poet, at one time (we cannot tell exactly when), were close friends and that they pursued together a course which it is now painful to recall, a life symbolized by the dark wood from which Virgil, or Reason, rescued the sinner at the beginning of the *Inferno*. The nature and the degree of their worldliness we have no means of knowing; but we have evidence of their intimacy, and of a common coarseness of taste, in a series of six sonnets exchanged, either in anger or in blackguard jest, by the two companions. In these, Dante reproaches Forese with desertion of his wife, gluttony, thievishness, and illegitimate birth; Forese retaliates with accusations of beggary and cowardice, and a couple of incomprehensible references to some scandal connected with Dante's father.   The genuineness of these sonnets has been questioned, but it is still almost universally accepted.   Although Bicci Novello was a rimester, he was probably no scholar; at any rate, in the present canto the poet does not think it worth while to tell him Statius's name, and when Virgil is introduced to him he seems to show no interest.   But, for the really bad name he gave Forese in the vituperative sonnets, Dante now makes all possible amends. He puts into his mouth a sweet phrase of loving penitence and a stern reprobation of Florentine immodesty.   Still more notable is the rehabilitation of Forese's wife, Nella, whom Dante had cruelly ridiculed in the first sonnet, jeering at her perpetual colds and her husband's neglect.   Forese now describes her as his "dear widow," whom he "loved so much," and to whose tears and prayers he owes his speedy admission to the heavenward path.

3. Bird hunting was the favorite aristocratic sport in the Middle Ages, and is still (in different forms) ardently pursued in Italy.   Dante draws many similes from it.

11. Ps. li, 15 (Vulg. l, 17): "*O Lord, open thou my lips; and my mouth shall shew forth thy praise.*"   The mouth, which was put to a bad use on earth, now makes amends: cf. XXII, 144.   This verse is from the beautiful psalm of repentance and faith called the "*Miserere,*" which was sung by the waiting spirits in V, 24.

26. Erysichthon was punished for sacrilege, by Ceres, with consuming hunger, so that, having devoured all he possessed, he finally began to eat himself: *Met.,* VIII, 738–878.

27. 'Fear': when he found himself obliged to feed on his own body: *Met.,* VIII, 877–878.

30. The Jews besieged in Jerusalem were horribly reduced by famine, until they were at last compelled to open the gates to the Emperor Titus.   A lady named Mary killed, cooked, and 'stuck her beak into' her own child: Flavius Josephus, *De Bello Judaico,* VI, iii, 8.

32. Capital M, in the handwriting of Dante's time, resembled two O's side by side, the second a little open at the bottom.   Inasmuch as this figure is not unlike a nose between two eye sockets, it was sometimes said that man (*homo*) had his name (*omo*, i.e., *uomo*) written in his face, the two sockets furnishing the initial and the final *O*, and the whole contour of the sockets and nose furnishing the medial *M*.   In a skull the likeness is much more striking.

39. Scaliness and discoloration of the skin were regarded as signs of extreme starvation.

74. Mat. xxvii, 46: "And about the ninth hour Jesus cried with a loud voice, saying, Eli, Eli, lama sabachthani, that is to say, My God, my God, why hast thou forsaken me?" — That same love of sacrifice which led Christ gladly to the crucifixion leads us to our penance.

78. 'Five' is here a round number.   In fact, as Forese died on July 28, 1296, the time is less than four years. — Dante wonders why Forese is not waiting outside of Purgatory, since he postponed repentance until the end of life.   Cf. IV, 130–135.

94. *Barbagia* is the name of a wild and mountainous region in Sardinia, whose inhabitants, converted late to Christianity, were said to be only half-civilized in Dante's time.

96. Dante calls Florence a second Barbagia, on account of its godlessness.

100. We have no other knowledge of such a prohibition from "the pulpit," nor have we other evidence that the Florentine women deserved such a reprimand.

111. The prophecy seems to relate to an event about 15 years off.   On Aug. 29, 1315, occurred the defeat of Montecatini, disastrous for the leading families of Florence.

119. 'The other day,' actually five days before.   Cf. *Inf.* XX, 127.

Canto XXIV

Argument

When Dante wrote the first *canzone* of the *Vita Nuova*, "Ye ladies who understand what love is," he felt that he was inaugurating a new era in poetry. The prose introduction to the verses testifies to the solemnity of the event. Following in part the indications of his master, Guido Guinizzelli of Bologna (XXVI, 91–102), and strongly influenced in style by Virgil (*Inf.* I, 85–87), the youthful poet was creating — or renewing — a type of composition based directly upon truth, inspired by, and faithfully recording, the author's own emotions and the fruits of his eager study (*V. N.*, XLII, 1–2). In Dante's opinion, his Italian forerunners and probably (in spite of frequent protestations of sincerity) their Provençal forbears had regarded poetry as a rhetorical, metrical, and musical exercise, a working out of old themes in new keys, with fresh variations of technique; while the "sweet new style" of the young Florentine made rhetoric, meter, and music subservient to the expression of real thought and feeling. For him, *amore* meant not only love, but also the enthusiastic pursuit of knowledge (*Conv.*, II, xv, 10). The phrase *dolce stil nuovo* is nowadays employed rather loosely to designate all the work of a little group comprising Guido Cavalcanti, Lapo Gianni, Dante Alighieri, and Cino da Pistoia, who are mentioned together in *De Vulgari Eloquentia*, I, xiii, 3, as experts in the vulgar tongue; but as our author uses it in Canto XXIV, it evidently refers only to the maturer lyric product of Dante himself and those who followed him — perhaps excluding Cavalcanti, who did not share in the cult of Virgil (*Inf.* X, 62–63). Italy had already seen in the 13th century more than one glorious artificer of modern speech: Giacomo da Lentini — or, as he signed himself, "the Notary" — a secretary at the court of Frederick II, a prolific and versatile composer, perhaps the inventor of the sonnet, leader of the Sicilian school (*Vulg. El.*, I, xii, 2–4), to which Pier delle Vigne (*Inf.* XIII) belonged; Guittone d'Arezzo (*Vulg. El.*; I, xiii, 1; *Purg.* xxvi, 124), an ingenious but uninspired and laborious love poet and a rugged satirist, the chief of the early Tuscan versifiers; and his follower, Bonagiunta Orbicciani of Lucca (*Vulg. El.*, I, xiii, 1), a not altogether servile imitator of Provençal and Italian models. But they and their fellows substituted convention for introspection, and this fundamental error, from which all their faults of conception and diction derived, was the "knot" that bound them, keeping them always "on the hither side" of the heights scaled by unfettered genius.

The last of the above-mentioned predecessors of the new style, Bonagiunta Orbicciani, is presented to Dante by Forese. In this region, where aspects are so altered by fasting, there is no discourtesy in pointing at people and calling them by their names. In fact, all the shades designated by Forese are glad to serve as warning examples to the newcomer, and not one of them scowls, or shows "a dark mien," at having his former weakness disclosed. This, indeed, may be regarded as a part of their penalty. Among them, "plying their teeth on empty air," are seen: Martin IV of Tours, Pope from 1281 to 1285, the supporter of Charles of Anjou (VII, 113) in Sicily and the stubborn opponent of Guido da Montefeltro at Forlì (*Inf.* XXVII, 43–44) — a liberal dispenser of excommunications after the Sicilian Vespers, who, for all his honesty and valor, was overfond of white wine and of the fat eels of Lake Bolsena, in the province of Rome (there is an old picture of him with a goose on his mitre and an eel beside him); Ubaldino dalla Pila, brother of Cardinal Ottaviano (*Inf.* X, 120) and father of Archbishop Ruggieri (*Inf.* XXXIII, 14), a Ghibelline prominent among those who triumphed at Montaperti in 1260, a jovial personage in one of Sacchetti's stories (*Novelle*, CCV); Bonifazio de' Fieschi, the "shepherd of many people," archbishop of Ravenna from 1274 to 1294, a rich man, holder of a grand court, with famous feasting, who, in his will, devoted his fortune to the recovery of the Holy Land; Messer Marchese (or Marchesino) degli Orgogliosi of Forlì, mayor of Faenza in 1296.

There was a rimester called Bonagiunta in Florence, where the name was very common; but the one our poet meets among the gluttons is from Lucca (where he had several homonyms), a judge and notary for some fifty years, whom we find recorded in documents from 1250 to 1296. Although his city has been condemned as a nest of bribery (*Inf.* XXI, 37–42), he foresees that a lady, a certain Gentucca, who does not yet, in 1300, wear the married woman's veil (cf. VIII, 74), shall one day make Lucca a pleasant sojourn for Dante. In this dim prophecy we doubtless have one more of those discreetly gracious compliments offered in grateful return for hospitality to the exile in his wanderings. Who his kind hostess was, we do not know. The name Gentucca occurs several times in Lucchese records.

A very different prophecy — though similarly cloaked in vagueness — is made by Forese concerning his brother, Corso Donati, the Cataline of Florence. This great leader of the Blacks, noble, handsome, proud, ambitious, daring, crafty, and cruel, at last fell out with the other chiefs of his party, who accused him of treason and had him condemned and arrested. As he was being led into the city on a horse or a mule, on October 6, 1308, he threw himself upon the ground, where a Catalan guardsman dispatched him with a lance thrust in the throat. According to one story, his foot caught in the stirrup, and he was dragged some distance before the Catalan overtook him. In Dante's version, which is not found elsewhere, Corso is kicked to death by the animal that is hauling him. "Him who is most to blame for Florence's downfall," says Forese, "I see dragged, at the tail of a beast, toward that valley where there is no remission of sin" — in other words, dragged to death, which, for Corso, means Hell; "the creature runs faster at each step, ever increasing, until it strikes him and leaves his body ignominiously destroyed." This end is the more disgraceful in that dragging at a horse's tail was a punishment inflicted upon particularly vile criminals.

The conversation in this canto is a continuation of a discussion held in real life between Bonagiunta and Guido Guinizzelli. We have a sonnet by the former, criticizing the latter for his "new style," and we have Guido's reply.

8. The shade of Statius, mentioned in XXIII, 131.

9. In order to be longer with Virgil.

10. Piccarda Donati, Forese's sister, appears in *Par.* III.

24. *Vernaccia*, a Genoese and Ligurian white wine.

54. It is said that Dante has been offered by Carlo Martello the post of "dictator pulcherrimus."

64. Cf. *Phars.*, V, 711–716.

82–87. The story of Corso's death is simplified to a picure of a death ride on a Hell horse.

84. 'The valley' of Hell, 'where sin is never cast off.'

96. Single combat with one of the enemy.

101, 102. My eyes could no more follow his form than my mind could follow his words.

105. 'Because I had just then turned that way': Dante had been watching Forese in the distance.

115. Cf. Gen. ii, 17: "But of the tree of the knowledge of good and evil, thou shalt not eat of it."

116. The 'tree higher up' (in the Garden of Eden), 'which was bitten by Eve' (Gen. iii, 6), and of which the present fruit tree is a slip, is the tree of knowledge, the symbol of law: XXXII, 37–42.

119. 'Drawing close together,' to pass, on the left, between the tree and the cliff.

121. The 'accursed' centaurs were the offspring of Ixion and a cloud.

123. The centaurs, who were invited by the Lapithae to the wedding of their king, Pirithous, attempted, when 'drunken,' to carry off the bride and other women; as a consequence a fierce battle ensued, in which the centaurs were defeated, with great slaughter, by Theseus (Pirithous's friend) and his followers.

125. Of the 10,000 Hebrews ready to fight against Midian, the Lord bade Gideon choose only the 300 who, when led to water, drank without kneeling, merely lifting the water to their lips; the others were sent home: Judges vii, 4–7.

130. 'Spreading out again,' after having passed through the narrow passage on the inner side of the ledge.

138. Cf. Rev. i, 15: "And his (Christ's) feet like unto fine brass, as if they burned in a furnace." Red is the color of love.

154. Mat. v, 6: "Blessed are they which do hunger and thirst after righteousness." — "Beati qui *esuriunt* et sitiunt justitiam." In the circle of avarice and prodigality (XXII, 4–6) this beatitude was used, with the omission of the *esuriunt*, in a changed sense. Here it is the *sitiunt* that disappears, and the *justitiam* is ingeniously rendered by *quanto è giusto*, which means both 'after all that is righteous' and 'as much as is right.'

Canto XXV

Argument

In response to Dante's question how, when there is nothing in common between souls and matter, a bodiless spirit can grow thin from hunger, Virgil cites, as examples of things equally wonderful, a familiar incident from Ovid and a common physical phenomenon. The life of Meleager (*Met.* VIII, 273 ff.) was made by the fates to depend on that of a firebrand, which his mother plucked from the flames; there was no visible connection between the youth and the brand, and yet when the stick, restored after many years to the fire, burned itself out, Meleager simultaneously wasted away. Furthermore, we can see no bond between a mirrored image and the body before the glass; nevertheless the reflection — a thing as unsubstantial as a shade — follows every movement of the solid form. Having thus prepared his disciple's mind, Virgil leaves the real explanation to Statius; and he accepts the task, but not without an apology so phrased as to suggest that the matter is not absolutely beyond the reach of pure Reason. In Lucian's *Dialogues of the Dead*, in a conversation between Menippus and Tantalus, the question is raised as to how a ghost can suffer thirst; the answer is that the punishment consists in desiring to drink when there is no possible need.

The main problem to be solved is the relation of soul to body, and to grasp it one must understand the physical and spiritual processes which lead up to the birth of both flesh and ghost. The limbs and organs of man are fed by his blood, which contains within it, potentially, all the parts of his frame. Not all of the blood, however, is used in this way: some of it remains, intact and unsullied, in the heart, retaining its complete formative power. This "perfect blood," once more "digested," or transformed, becomes the parent seed. In the act of generation it unites with the blood of the female. The active male blood then operates upon the passive female blood, which it first condenses into an embryo and then quickens into life. This life, or *anima*, is at first merely that of a plant — the "vegetative soul." Next — by means of the formative power transmitted, through the seed, from the begetter's heart — the senses are developed, the embryo changes little by little from a plantlike creature to an animal, and its life is that of the "sensitive soul." Both of these "souls" are perishable. The real incorruptible spirit, the "intellective soul," is breathed into each child by God at the moment it is ready for birth, and immediately takes unto itself the vegetative and sensitive functions, absorbing the powers of life and sense which had been previously developed by physical activity.

Every man has, then, but one soul, specially created for him and endowed with life, sense, and intellect. "And the Lord God formed man of the dust of the ground, and breathed into his nostrils the breath of life; and man became a living soul" (Gen. ii. 7). This is the orthodox view, supported by Lactantius, St. Augustine, and their followers, among whom are St. Thomas, Hugh of St. Victor, and Peter Lombard. At the outset it had to contend with other doctrines. Origen had adopted the Platonic theory that all souls were created together at the beginning of the world; this opinion the Church condemned as heretical. Tertullian had maintained that one soul is begotten by another at the moment when the body is generated — nearly the view supported by present day post-Thomistic philosophy, which places the creation of the soul at the moment of conception. St. Jerome says that in his day Tertullian's doctrine is the common belief of the western church. Dante follows, in the main, St. Thomas (apparently preferring Aristotle, however, when it comes to the origin of the "sensitive soul"), but he doubtless gathered from other Christian sources as well — for instance, from Hugh of St. Victor, *De Anima*, II, xii (Migne XL, p. 788). In the *Convivio*, IV, xxi, 4–5, he treats, very summarily, the same subject. It was Aristotle, in *De Anima*, III, who distinguished the "potential" or passive, *internal*, perishable intelligence, which receives impressions or images, from the active, *external*, imperishable intellect ($\nu o\hat{v}\varsigma\ \pi o\iota\eta\tau\iota\kappa\acute{o}\varsigma$). a sort of oversoul which interprets images and forms ideas. His teaching was carried further by his great commentator, the Spanish Moor, Averroës (cf. *Inf.* IV, 144). This philosopher, who had an immense vogue in the 13th and 14th centuries, combined the two intellectual principles, active and passive, into one universal mind, situated outside the individual soul and only temporarily connected with it; to the latter he allowed only the functions of sense and instinct, thus denying the immortality of the individual intelligence. As far as we can judge, Dante accepts the combination of the passive and active principles, but rejects for man the theory of the external, impersonal mind. He has nothing to say of the "active intellect," and his *possibile intelletto* appears to comprise both the capacity to receive impressions and, stimulated by grace, the ability to understand and reason. Now, in our canto, ll. 61–66, he says that the problem of the transformation of the "vegetative," "sensitive" embryo into a child is "a point which once led astray a wiser man than thou, so that in his philosophy he parted the potential intellect from the soul, because he saw no organ appropriate to that intellect." It seems likely, on the whole, that the "wiser man" is Aristotle, interpreted more or less through the medium of Averroës. For the actual separation of the "potential intellect" from the soul, the Moor is responsible; on the other hand, it is Aristotle who states (*De Anima*, III, iv, 4) that the passive intelligence has no organ of its own.

To complete the answer to Dante's question, which has led to wide and important digressions, Statius describes the acquisition, by the soul, of an aerial body (cf. the Argument to Canto II).   In this invention Dante seems to run counter to St. Thomas, who denies (*Summa contra Gentiles*, II, xc; *Summa Theologiae*, Prima, Qu. lxxvi, Art. 5) that the human soul can unite formally with the elements, although he affirms (*Summa Theologiae*, Prima, Qu. li, Art. 2) that angels and devils can shape for themselves bodies of condensed air.

1. It is early afternoon.

3. The sun, in the sign of Aries, has passed the meridian, or 'noonday circle,' leaving it to Taurus, the constellation that follows Aries; and the night, conceived as a point opposite the sun, has left the meridian circle to Scorpio, the constellation opposite Taurus.

31. 'If I unbind to him the eternal view,' i.e., 'if I set forth to him the full truth of the matter, which goes beyond the operation of nature alone and involves God's direct intervention finally,' hence the 'eternal.'

45. *Altrui*: of the female.

49. The male blood united with the female blood.

50. Cf. Wisdom of Solomon, vii, 2: "Decem mensium tempore *coagulatus* sum in sanguine, ex semine hominis." (In the time of ten months being compacted in blood of the seed of man.)

52. 'The active principle (first derived from the heart of the begetter) having become a soul.'

54. The soul of the fetus is on its way to further development, while that of the plant is at the end of its course.

56. The sea fungus is a sponge, which is intermediate between vegetable and animal. Cf. Aristotle, *De Animalibus Historiae*, VIII, i. See also Pliny, *Historia Naturalis*, IX, 45.

57. 'To organize the faculties of which it is the germ': namely, the senses.

73, 74. 'Which absorbs into its own substance all that it finds active here (in the embryo), — i.e., the vegetative and sensitive powers — 'and a single soul is created.'

77, 78. The 'new spirit,' when it has absorbed the already existing powers of the embryo, becomes a complete soul (vegetative, sensitive, and intellective), just as the sun's heat, uniting with the 'juice that flows from the vine,' is transformed into wine.

79. Láchesis is the fate who spins the thread of life from Clotho's 'flax': cf. XXI, 25.

80. The soul carries with it the divine part of man's powers and, potentially, the human part.

82. 'The other faculties being all of them dumb,' i.e., the faculties of sense being useless and therefore inactive.

83. Cf. St. Augustine, *De Trinitate*, X, xi, 17 and 18.

84. 'Much keener in their activity than before': these purely spiritual faculties gain by release from matter.

86. The soul 'falls' to the bank either of Acheron or of Tiber, according as it merits Hell or Purgatory.

91. The radiation of the soul's formative power upon the surrounding air, producing the appearance of a body, is compared to the action of the sun's rays on wet atmosphere, forming a rainbow.

100. Since the soul thus takes on a visible aerial "body," that body is called a 'shade' (as something that has form and yet is not substantial, as real flesh).

103. Cf. *Aen*, VI, 733: "Hinc metuunt cupiuntque, dolent gaudentque" (hence their fears and desires, their griefs and joys).

114. The upright bank on the left shoots forth, all the way around, a continuous horizontal flame, which extends across the terrace; but a wind blows up vertically along the mountainside, and, deflecting upward the outer edge of the ring of flame, 'secures a path from it' on the outside rim of the shelf.   Fire is the symbol of purification from lust.

121. *Summae Deus clementiae*, 'God of clemency supreme,' is the beginning, in old breviaries, of the hymn sung on Saturday at matins, praying for purification by fire and cleanness of heart and body.   It is attributed to St. Ambrose.

128. "I know not a man," is the reply of Mary to the angel at the Annunciation: Luke i, 34.   After each singing of the hymn the souls call aloud an example of chastity.   The examples of lust are proclaimed (as we shall see in the next canto) by two troops of shades as they pass.

131. The chaste goddess Diana banished her nymph Helĭce, who had been seduced by Jupiter: *Met.*, II, 453–465.   Helice (or Callisto) and her child form the constellations of the Great and Little Bear.

Canto XXVI

Argument

Around the ledge of carnal vice there go circling through the fire, in opposite directions, two ghostly companies, composed of the abnormally and the normally lecherous.   As they meet, they exchange a kiss of pure brotherly affection, such as the early Christians gave one another in their services.   Then, on parting, they all rebuke themselves, the members of the second troop shouting "Sodom and Gomorrah!" (Gen. xix, 1–28), those of the first recalling the bestial sin of Pasiphaë.   This woman, the wife of King Minos of Crete (*Inf.* V, 4), being cursed by Venus with a passion for a bull, satisfied her lust by concealing herself in a wooden cow: *Aen.*, VI, 24–26; *Met.*, 132–137.   The fruit of their union was the Minotaur (*Inf.* XII, 11–13).   In the Middle Ages her story was interpreted allegorically.

Among those whose offence was not contrary to nature is Guido Guinizzelli of Bologna, the most important Italian writer before Dante.   He was mayor of Castelfranco in 1270 and died in 1276.   Like Arnaut Daniel, he is doubtless consigned to this circle on the general ground that he was a sincere poet of love. At first he looked upon Guittone d' Arezzo (XXIV, 56) as his literary master, and followed the current artificial fashion; but later he took a new direction, expressing real feeling and earnest thought in verse whose ease, clearness, and harmony made him an excellent model for the next generation.   In his famous poem, *Al cor gentil rempaira sempre amore* (*Vulg. El.*, II, v, 4; I, ix, 3), is rhymed for the first time the new symbolic conception of love, which was adopted by Dante and his group.   Guido was thus doubly a predecessor of the *dolce stil nuovo* (XXIV, 57); and Dante's affectionate cry of admiration and gratitude, in lines 94–98, testifies to the magnitude of his debt.   In the tenth sonnet of the *Vita Nuova*, XX, 3, l. 2, Dante refers to him as "il Saggio"; in the *Convivio*, IV, xx, 7, he is "quel nobile Guido Guinizzelli"; and in *De Vulgari Eloquentia* he is cited four times, once (I, xv, 6) as "maximus."

It must have been this same sentiment of gratitude, always dominant in

Dante's heart, that led him to award the palm in modern Gallic literature to the twelfth-century troubadour Arnaut Daniel, who to our taste seems, to be sure, the most minutely ingenious and metrically resourceful, but at the same time one of the most laborious and tiresome of the Provençal versifiers. His works are a mosaic of odd conceits and rare and difficult forms. The *sestina*, imitated by Alighieri and Petrarch, is one of his inventions. Three of his compositions are cited in *De Vulgari Eloquentia*, where he is mentioned four times. Dante — as he tells us in the *Vita Nuova*, III, 9 — learned by himself "the art of uttering words in rhyme," and he can have done so only by studying attentively the works of his predecessors, preeminent among whom was surely Arnaut Daniel. To Arnaut, then, more than to anyone else, he owed (or thought he owed) his command of metrical form; as far as the *sestina* is concerned, he expressly acknowledges his indebtedness in *De Vulgari Eloquentia*, II, x, 2. That is why, in our canto, Guido rates the clever troubadour above himself, calling him "a better smith of the mother tongue." "Verse of love and prose of romance ..." continues Guido, "he surpassed them all." Provençal was the first language of amatory poetry (*Vulg. El.*, I, x, 3), French the recognized idiom of narrative and didactic literature and of any kind of prose (*Vulg. El.*, I, x, 2); "romance" signified originally a literary composition in the vulgar tongue. Arnaut, as far as we are aware, never wrote in French nor in prose; Guido means simply that he was superior to all other authors of Gaul, whether they used verse or prose, Provençal or French.

"Let fools talk on" — adds Guido — "who think that the Limousin poet excels." Many songsters (among them Arnaut himself) were of Limousin origin, but the particular one here indicated is evidently Giraut de Bornelh, a younger contemporary of Arnaut; according to his Provençal biographer, he was called "the master of the troubadours," and others bear witness to his high repute. His poetry, much of which has survived, justifies in some measure his great fame. He was the principal champion of the clear style, as Arnaut was perhaps the best representative of the purposely obscure. Dante cites him once in the *Convivio* and four times in *De Vulgari Eloquentia*. In the latter work, II, ii, 9–10, he speaks of Bertran de Born as a poet of arms, Arnaut and Cino da Pistoia as poets of love, and Giraut and himself as poets of righteousness. When he wrote the *Purgatorio*, he evidently regarded Giraut as artistically inferior to Arnaut — perhaps too popular and commonplace to merit the highest rank, which "fools" had accorded him.

The same undeserved glory had been enjoyed by Guittone d' Arezzo (XXIV, 56), on whom alone "many people of old" bestowed praise — following fashion "from cry to cry" — until at last "the truth has got the better of him, as concerns more men than one" — that is, the superiority of several other writers (Guinizzelli, Cavalcanti, Dante, Cino?) is now acknowledged. This Guittone, though a prolific imitator of the Provençal school in his amatory verse, had a good deal of vigor and eccentric ingenuity and originality but was poor in sentiment and unhappily destitute of the sense of beauty. He is better in his religious, moral, and especially his political poetry, where his fierce irony is very effective. He was also one of the first to attempt artistic Italian prose. He joined the order of the Frati Gaudenti (*Inf.* XXIII, 103), founded a monastery in Florence, and died in 1294. In *De Vulgari Eloquentia*, I, xiii, 1, Dante blames him for using his local dialect.

4. The travelers are now on the west-northwest side of the mountain, which receives the direct rays of the sun in the latter part of the afternoon. Dante, facing south-southwest, has the sun on his right.

7. As Dante passes along close to the mass of flame, in which the spirits are walking, his shadow, cast on the fire at his left, restores to it its natural 'ruddy' hue, which the sunlight has paled.

21. Cf. Pr. xxv, 25: "As cold waters to a thirsty soul, so is good news from a far country."

35. In *Aen.*, IV, 402–407, and *Met.*, VII, 624–626, there are descriptions of ants at work, but the trait here cited seems to have been first noted by Dante.

43. The 'Riphaean mountains' were placed by early geographers in the extreme north.

44. The two flocks of cranes, one flying north and the other south at the same time, are hypothetical, as is shown by the imperfect subjunctive *volasser*. — 'The sands' are the deserts of Libya.

45. Cf. *Phars.*, VII, 832–834:

> Vos, quae Nilo mutare soletis
> Threicias hiemes, ad mollem serius Austrum
> Istis, aves.

(The cranes that each year leave the Thracian winter for the Nile were late in migrating to the warm south.)

59. *Donna*: possibly the Virgin Mary or, more immediately now, Beatrice herself.

62. The Empyrean.

77. Uguccione da Pisa in his *Magnae Derivationes* (cited in *Conv.*, IV, vi, 5), combining two anecdotes from Suetonius, relates that Caesar, returning to Rome in triumph, was hailed by some one as 'queen': Toynbee, 118.

82. Hermaphroditus was the son of Hermes and Aphrodite, and resembled both his parents, whence his name: *Met.*, IV, 290–291. He fused with the nymph Salmacis into one body that was of both sexes: *Met.*, IV, 285–388.

94. Hypsipyle (*Inf.* XVIII, 92), to show the thirsty Greeks the fountain of Langia (*Purg.* XXII, 112), left Archemorus (*Conv.*, III, xi, 16), the child of King Lycurgus of Nemea, who had been entrusted to her. A serpent killed the child, and the father, blinded by 'grief' and rage, was about to have her put to death, when her two sons suddenly rushed in and saved her. Cf. Statius, *Thebaid*, V, especially 718 ff.

96. Dante is as full of delight and love as Hypsipyle's sons 'on seeing their mother again,' and would like to plunge into the fire and clasp Guido to his heart, as they embraced their mother, but he does not 'rise to such a pitch,' being afraid of the flame.

108. Lethe is the traditional river of oblivion.

113. The 'modern use' of the vulgar tongue in poetry was still comparatively new in 1300: cf. *V. N.*, XXV, 3–5.

129. Cf. St. Bonaventure, *Soliloquium*, IV, § 3: "omnium sanctorum collegium." (the company of all the saints).

140–147. These Provençal verses are presumably of Dante's own composition.

Canto XXVII

Argument

The time described is the approach of sunset. The sun was in the position it occupies when it "shoots its first rays" upon Jerusalem. Dawn in Jerusalem is simultaneous with sunset in Purgatory.

In medieval legend the Earthly Paradise is generally situated in an inaccessible spot, often surrounded by a barrier of flame. In both Germanic and Celtic myth a wall of fire occurs. The Bible also offers a hint of it, in Gen. iii, 24: "And he placed at the east of the garden of Eden Cherubim, and a flaming sword which turned every way." Tertullian, Lactantius, St. John Chrysostom, Isidore, and, after him, many others speak of the fiery wall. Dante makes his encircling fire serve a double purpose: it obstructs, according to tradition, the road to the home of terrestrial bliss, and at the same time it constitutes the punishment of the last cornice. "Mortify therefore your members which are upon the earth" — says St. Paul in Colossians iii, 5 — "fornication, uncleanness, inordinate affection." In the *Moralia*, XXI, xii, 688, St. Gregory declares: "Si per cordis munditiam libidinis flamma non extinguitur, incassum quaelibet virtutes oriuntur." (If the flame of lust is not extinguished through cleanness of heart, in vain do any virtues arise.) The burning path signifies the quenching of carnal desire by purification of the heart. This penance is imposed upon Dante, who now, for the first time in Purgatory, recoils from his duty. A high pitch of excitement is reached in the brief scene of Virgil's impassioned exhortation and his pupil's stubborn refusal. Not until the master invokes the name of Beatrice, whose image once before turned the youthful poet from unworthy love (*V. N.*,

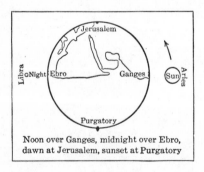

Noon over Ganges, midnight over Ebro, dawn at Jerusalem, sunset at Purgatory

XXXIX, 1–3), can Dante be induced to obey. Then, preceded by Virgil and followed by Statius (who apparently do not feel the heat), he traverses the flames.

After this trial, there comes to Dante, in the hour before dawn, the third of his prophetic dreams. He is in reality about to visit the Garden of Eden, the abode of innocence and harmless activity, from which he is to rise to Heaven, the goal of contemplation. Consequently the active life and the contemplative life are revealed to him in the form of Laban's daughters, Leah and Rachel, the fertile and the barren wife of Jacob (Gen. xxix, 10–35). From early Christian times their story has been interpreted as an allegory of work and meditation: cf. St. Thomas, *Summa Theologiae*, Secunda Secundae, Qu. clxxix, Art. 2. In *Monarchia*, III, xvi, 7, Dante distinguishes two kinds of divinely ordained human blessedness: "beatitudinem scilicet huius vite, que in operatione proprie virtutis consistit et per terrestrem paradisum figuratur; et beatitudinem vite eterne, que consistit in fruitione divini aspectus ad quam propria virtus ascendere non potest, nisi lumine divino adiuta, que per paradisum celestem intelligi datur." (The blessedness, to wit, of this life, which consists in the exercise of his proper power and is figured by the terrestrial paradise, and the blessedness of eternal life, which consists in the fruition of the divine aspect, to which his proper power may not ascend unless assisted by the divine light. And this blessedness is given to be understood by the celestial paradise.) Leah's innocent activity is symbolized by picking flowers to adorn herself; Rachel's contemplation, by gazing into a mirror, where she is "eager to see her own beauteous eyes." In the *Convivio*, III, xv, 2, the eyes of Wisdom are defined as "its *demonstrations*, with which the Truth is unerringly beheld" (cf. Canzone II, 55–58).

3. It is midnight at the Strait of Gibraltar: the river Ebro is coming under the constellation of Libra, which is opposite Aries.

4. The sun, in Aries, is over eastern Asia, so that the waters of the river Ganges are 'scorched by noon.'

8. Mat. v, 8: "Blessed are the pure in heart."

18. Burning to death was not an uncommon punishment. Dante was himself condemned to death by fire, if taken in Florentine territory.

23. *Gerïon*: cf. *Inf.* XVII, 91–136.

27. Luke xxi, 18: "But there shall not an hair of your head perish." Cf. Daniel iii, 25, 27.

37. The tragic story of the young lovers Pyramus and Thisbe is told in *Met.*, IV, 55–166. See especially 145–146:

> Ad nomen Thisbes oculos a morte gravatos
> Pyramus erexit visaque recondidit illa.

(At the name of Thisbe, Pyramus lifted his eyes, now heavy with death, and having looked upon her face, closed them again.)

39. The mulberry turned red on being spattered with the blood of Pyramus, who stabbed himself when he thought Thisbe slain by a lion: *Met.*, IV, 125–127.

48. Cf. XXII, 127–128.

58. Mat. xxv, 34: "Then shall the King say unto them on his right hand, *Come, ye blessed of my Father*, inherit the kingdom prepared for you from the foundation of the world."

59. The 'light' of course refers to an angel, perhaps the guardian of Eden. We have no information as to how the last letter is removed from Dante's brow.

65. The stairway, on the west side of the mountain, goes straight up, from west to east, so that the climbers turn their backs to the setting sun and Dante's shadow falls on the steps in front of him.

87. 'Swathed,' i.e., hemmed in by the 'high wall' on either side of the narrow stairs, which are cut into the rock.

90. Seen through the narrow crack, the stars look big and bright.

95. Cytherēa is Venus, so called from the island of Cythera, where she rose from the sea. Venus shines on Purgatory shortly before sunrise: cf. I, 19–21.

102. Garlands of flowers were often worn by ladies in Dante's time.

109. Cf. Wisdom of Solomon, xi, 23: "Tamquam gutta roris antelucani" (As a drop of dew preceding dawn).

111. 'As, on their way back, their lodging is less distant,' i.e., as they approach home on their return journey.

115. The 'sweet fruit' seems to signify earthly happiness. Cf. *Inf.* XVI, 61.

127. The 'temporal fire' is that of Purgatory, the 'eternal' that of Hell.

131. Now that Dante's soul has been cleansed and his will set free from the bondage of vice, all his impulses are necessarily good.

137. Cf. *Inf.* II, 116.

140. The freedom after which all the souls in Purgatory are striving (I, 71) has been attained. The will turns naturally toward God. Evil inclinations have been purged away, although remorse still remains, to be removed in the Garden of Eden. In order to see God, Dante must earn and obtain remission of sin.

142. Virgil's final words, 'crowning' and 'mitering' Dante over himself, complete his declaration to him that he has brought him to justice, inner justice. On which conception and its full allegorical implications, see Singleton (1958) pp. 64–69.

Canto XXVIII

Argument

"And the Lord God planted a garden eastward in Eden ... And the Lord God took the man, and put him into the garden of Eden to dress it and to keep it" (Gen. ii, 8, 15). This terrestrial paradise naturally offered itself to Dante as a symbol of the youth or golden age of mankind, the life of innocent activity which, but for Adam's sin, humanity would have enjoyed, without death, until the Judgment Day. But the garden was to him not a symbol alone: it was a real spot, still in existence in a remote quarter of the globe. Medieval literature is rich in tales of journeys to it. Ephraim the Syrian, deacon of Edessa in the fourth century, tells us that it is circular, situated on a high mountain surrounded by the sea, and divided into an outer and an inner, more sacred, part. Barinthus, in the *Voyage of St. Brendan* (p. 4), finds on his island paradise a river which cannot be crossed; and St. Brendan himself, in his "terra repromissionis sanctorum" (p. 35), sees fruit trees and a river running through the middle. In the Old Venetian version of the story (chap. xxxi, xxxvii), the beautiful trees and birds are enlarged upon, and the river occurs again (chap. xlii). This stream goes back to the Bible, Gen. ii, 10: "And a river went out of Eden to water the garden; and from thence it was parted, and became into four heads," namely Pison (or Ganges), Gihon (the Nile), Hiddekel (Tigris), and Euphrates. Those who located the garden on an island were hard pressed to account for the transfer of these "four heads" to the mainland; it was sometimes maintained — by St. Augustine, for example (*De Genesi ad Litteram*, VIII, vii) — that they burrowed under ground. Dante perhaps had some such idea, but he wisely refrained from expressing it. His river is divided, from its very source in the middle of the earthly paradise, into two branches, Lethe and Eunoe, which flow out on opposite sides. So Brendan and his companions (p. 7) "viderunt ripam altissimam sicut murum et diversos rivulos discendentes de summitate insule, fluentes in mare" (saw a very high bank like a wall and several streams flowing down from the top of the island and pouring into the sea). It may be their spray which falls upon the two trees in the circle of gluttony. It is perhaps Lethe, with its burden of sinful recollection, that bores its crooked way from the shore of the island to the feet of Satan; in that case Eunoe would presumably have to be, at some spot, the source of the four great streams of the inhabited world. On these points Dante is silent. What concerns him is the allegorical significance of the waters. Of Lethe, the ancient river of oblivion, and Eunoe, a stream of his own devising, he makes the symbol of absolution, the remission of sin, the complete restoration of purity. Lethe means forgetfulness of past wrongdoing; Eunoe, memory of past good work. This last name our poet seems to have constructed for himself out of the Greek εὔνοια, or directly from εὖ, "well," and νοῦς or νόος, "mind."

In Pliny's *Natural History*, XXXI, 11, we read: "In Boeotia ad Trophonium deum iuxta flumen Hercynnum e duobus fontibus alter memoriam alter oblivionem adfert, inde nominibus inventis." (In Boeotia by the temple of Trophonius near the river Hercynnus are two springs; one brings remembrance, the other forgetfulness; hence the names that have been given them.) Cf. Isidore, *Etymologiae*, XIII, xviii, 4. In the Orphic mysteries the novitiate found in Hades two springs, Lethe on the left, Mnemosyne on the right. Avoiding Lethe, he drank of Mnemosyne, to dwell with the heroes.

It is on the morning of Wednesday, April 13, the sixth day of his journey, and the fourth of his sojourn on the island, that Dante enters the abode of earthly happiness. His daintily phrased account of it combines into an artistic whole the various conventional elements of the medieval Eden. One factor, however, is lacking — the traditional inhabitants, Enoch and Elijah. In the *Apocalypse of St. Paul* (p. 18), after the apostle has seen the four great rivers in the terrestrial paradise, he is greeted by Enoch, Elijah, and seven other patriarchs. The first two became almost constant features of the garden. Fra Benedetto d' Arezzo, in his journey to the terrestrial paradise, also meets at the foot of a mountain a beautiful youth, who shows him the way up. In the Latin *Navigatio Sancti Brendani*, the youthful figure is already present beside the river (p. 35): "Ecce juvenis occurrit illis obviam osculans eos cum magna leticia et singulos nominatim appellabat." (Behold, a young man ran to meet them, and, kissing them with great rejoicing, called each of them by name.)   Earlier in the tale (p. 4), near the stream, a "vir quidam magni splendoris" (a certain man, all resplendent) appears to the travelers and forthwith calls them by name; he will not reveal his own identity, but tells them that the island has been unchanged from the beginning of the world.   It has already been intimated, in the Argument to Canto I, that Dante — who, unwilling to mar a scene of youthfulness by the introduction of elderly dwellers, kept Enoch and Elijah out of sight and apparently out of mind — may have utilized the suggestion of the *Navigatio* in the creation of his Cato, at the foot of the mountain, corresponding to his Matelda, at the top.   Another contrasted pair that may possibly have impressed his imagination is furnished by St. Augustine's *De Mirabilibus Sacrae Scripturae*, ch. iii, *De Abel et Enoch primatum tenentibus in hominum justitia*: "Abel totius humanae justitiae princeps et secundus post eum Enoch, ... quibus summa justitiae in initio ipso mundi et fine committitur." (Abel, the summit of all human justice, and, second after him, Enoch, ... to whom all justice from the beginning to the end of this world is committed.)   Matelda, like Abel, represents original goodness; Cato, like Enoch, goodness after evil.   But such parallels could be multiplied almost to infinity.   Whatever may have been his starting point, Dante evolved, as guardian of his Eden and personification of its spirit, a lovely girlish form, one of his prettiest conceptions.   Such a figure had always haunted his fancy: it lurks in nearly all his lyric verse, whether dedicated to Beatrice, to the Donna Pietosa, to Philosophy, or to the unknown lady of the Casentino.   In her solitude, her joyousness, her amorous song, her association with birds and flowers, Matelda belongs to the pastoral type.   All her attributes and surroundings indicate that she symbolizes the early, immaculate stage of humanity, the life of harmless activity, the purity and gladness that can and should be regained. It is she, the embodiment of Innocence, who, by the remission of sin through Lethe and Eunoe, restores innocence to Dante.   Even so, Cato, the personification of Free Will, showed Dante how his free will was to be restored.   Perhaps she is more accurately described as the Perfect Earthly Life (M. Porena), combining activity (plucking flowers) with contemplation (hymn *delectasti*).

12. The direction in which the mountain casts its shadow in the morning is, of course, the west.

20. The pine grove of Classe, or Chiassi — the old port of Ravenna, from which the Adriatic has now receded — was exposed to the *Scirocco*, or southeast wind. — Cf. *Met.*, XV, 603–604.

21. *Aeolus*, king of the winds: *Aen.*, I, 52–57.

26. Dante, who reached the Garden of Eden on its west side, is walking east. As the stream which 'prevents him from going further' flows towards his left, it must, at this point, be running north.

36. In some parts of Italy a branch, called *maio* or *maggio*, is used in the celebration of May Day, serving the purpose of either Maypole or of May basket.

50. When Proserpine, the daughter of Ceres, was suddenly carried off to the lower world by Pluto, she had been picking flowers in the 'perpetual springtime' of the valley of Henna: *Met.*, V, 385–408, especially 391.

66. It was contrary to the custom of Cupid to wound unintentionally, as he did when, coming to kiss his mother, he pricked her with an arrow projecting from his quiver, and caused her to love Adonis: *Met.*, X, 525–532.

68. No doubt, she is plaiting a garland now of the flowers she has plucked — and in this recalls the figure of Leah, XXVII, 101–102.

70. The 'three steps' may signify simply a very short distance which separates Dante from that which he is eager to reach: cf. VIII, 46. If the words have an allegorical meaning, they probably refer to the three stages of the sacrament of penance through which Dante must pass to attain perfect happiness on earth: cf. XXXI, 1–90.

71. Xerxes, king of Persia, crossed the Hellespont with a vast army to conquer Greece, but was defeated and forced to flee ignominiously. Cf. *Phars.*, II, 672–675:

> Tales fama canit tumidum super aequora Persen
> Construxisse vias, multum cum pontibus ausus,
> Europamque Asiae Sestonque admovit Abydo
> Incessitque fretum rapidi super Hellesponti.

(Such, by the report of fame, was the road built over the sea by the proud Persian, when, greatly daring, he brought Europe near to Asia and Sestos to Abydos by his bridges, and passed on foot over the straits of fast-flowing Hellespont.)

74. The Hellespont 'swelled' between Leander in Abydos and his beloved Hero in Sestos: Ovid, Epistulae XVII and XVIII.

80. Ps. xcii (Vulg. xci), 4: "For thou, Lord, *hast made me glad* through thy work."

82. Dante, who was third in the circles of gluttony and lust (XXII, 127–128; XXXVI, 16–17), and second in traversing the fire (XXVII, 46–47), is now first.

87. The statement of Statius in XXI, 43–54, seems to be contradicted by the presence of water and wind at the top of the mountain.

91. As God alone is perfect, he can be altogether satisfied only with himself.

104. The air that envelops the earth is surrounded by a layer of fire, which in turn is enclosed in the heaven of the moon. As there are no intervals of empty space between these spheres, the two mobile elements — air and fire — are swept around the earth by the heavens in their 'primal revolution,' or daily circuit. Dante can hardly have estimated the velocity of such a motion of the atmosphere; or, if he did, he must have assumed a considerable drag or retardation.

105. On the rugged surface of the earth the daily revolution of the air encounters so many obstacles that it is not felt; but this mountaintop, rising so high that it is 'quite free in the quick air,' receives the atmospheric current unobstructed.

111. The air, in its revolution around the earth, scatters far and wide the vital power of the plant.

120. The Garden of Eden contains all the flora of the rest of the world, and some besides.

121. The water of this stream comes from a miraculous fount, not from any natural spring fed by condensed aqueous vapor.

131. To be operative, the water must be tasted in both streams.

140. The golden age was 'poetized' by Ovid, *Met.*, I, 89–112. The ancient poets were gifted with sight beyond that of their contemporaries (cf. the "nobile castello" in *Inf.* IV), and had some inkling of the truth. When they sang of Parnassus and the golden age, they may have been dimly conscious of the real origin of man.

Canto XXIX

Argument

At the solemn moment when Dante is to pass through the stages of contrition, confession, and satisfaction to absolution, the Church, with Beatrice, or Revelation, as its guiding power, appears to him in all its majesty. He is following the stream of Lethe up toward its source, when a splendid pageant approaches on the other bank. At a signal from Heaven, it comes to a halt opposite him. Then, after the sacrament of penance and the remission of sin, Dante joins the radiant host. Thus does the Church come to meet the penitent sinner; thus does it reveal itself to him and finally receive him into its bosom. In all this episode the poet makes use of a symbolism more formal and more minute than is his wont. The kind of ceremonial that he describes is remote from modern experience, though not unfamiliar to Dante's contemporaries. In his day elaborate allegorical processions, both religious and secular, were common enough. We find something similar in the *Arbor Vitae Crucifixae Jesu*, written in 1305 by Ubertino da Casale, the leader of the Franciscan sect known as the *Spirituales* (*Par.* XII, 124). At a later date the type was developed by Petrarch in his *Trionfi*. Dante's procession may, indeed, be called "the Triumph of Revelation."

Not long after Dante, we find the Corpus Christi procession, with the Host under a canopy whose bearers are crowned with flowers, while boys scatter rose petals. The principal theological interest from the 9th to the 13th century was concentrated in the doctrine of the Eucharist, which was formulated by the Lateran Council in 1215. The festival was authorized apparently in 1311, but must have existed before. Through Communion, we unite with Christ and may see God, although our vision may be veiled in a symbol. It has therefore been suggested that Beatrice, on this occasion, represents especially the Eucharist.

Dante's inspiration came, in large measure, from the Apocalypse and from Ezekiel. His procession is in the shape of a cross, in the middle of which is the Chariot of the Church, drawn by Christ, its founder, in the form of a griffin. Christ, to Dante's mind, was always a divine figure, a part of the triune God, who could be conceived by the human intellect only through the medium of symbols. He seldom thought of him as an historical person or as a model for human life. What particularly impressed him was the mystery of his dual nature, a union of man and God; and this duality he expresses by means of the griffin, a creature half eagle, half lion, belonging both to heaven and to earth. He may have got the idea of this beast from St. Isidore's *Etymologiae*, XII, ii, 17, where it is described; in the same chapter, but not in connection with the griffin, Christ is compared both to a lion and to an eagle (43, 44). The griffin is often pictured in ancient art, notably in the frieze of the temple of Faustina in Rome. In Christian art, too, it is not uncommon; it is the emblem of the city of Perugia, and is displayed everywhere in that old town; it is seen also on the eleventh-century façade of the cathedral of Assisi. In Dante's portrayal there are several traits taken from the Song of Solomon, which from very early times was interpreted as an allegory of Christ and the Church. Beside the two wheels of the chariot are two groups of figures symbolizing the Theological and the Cardinal Virtues.

At the head of the procession, at first unrecognizable, then gradually revealing themselves as they approach, are seven golden candlesticks. Seven lamps or candlesticks are repeatedly mentioned in the Bible. Exod. xxv, 37: "And thou shalt make the seven lamps thereof." Rev. i, 12: "I saw seven golden candlesticks." Rev. i, 13: "And in the midst of the seven candlesticks one like unto the Son of man" (cf. ii, 1: "who walketh in the midst of the seven golden candlesticks"). Rev. i, 20: "the seven candlesticks which thou sawest are the seven churches" (cf. 11). Rev. iv, 5: "and there were seven lamps of fire burning before the throne, which are the seven Spirits of God." This last interpretation is apparently the one that Dante chose: his candlesticks represent the sevenfold Spirit of God. The flame of each candle leaves, as it passes, a trail of colored light, which stretches as far as the eye can reach. These seven streaks of brightness, all of different hues, form a canopy over the marching band. They probably symbolize the gifts of the Spirit of the Lord, mentioned in Isaiah xi, 2, 3: "And the spirit of the Lord shall rest upon him" (the "rod out of the stem of Jesse"), "the spirit of *wisdom* and *understanding*, the spirit of *counsel* and *might*, the spirit of *knowledge* and of the *fear of the Lord*. And shall make him of quick understanding in the *fear of the Lord*." The Vulgate, instead of repeating "fear of the Lord," has in the first verse *pietatis*, in the second *timoris*, making seven gifts in all.

After the candlesticks, come twenty-four old men. Rev. iv, 4: "And round about the throne were four and twenty seats: and upon the seats I saw four and twenty elders sitting, clothed in white raiment; and they had on their heads crowns of gold" (cf. also 10 and 11). St. Jerome, in the *Prologus Galeatus* to the Vulgate, refers to an interpretation of these elders as the books of the Old Testament, namely: the five books of Law, written by Moses (Genesis, Exodus, Leviticus, Numbers, Deuteronomy); eight books of Prophets, i.e., seven major prophets and one book made up of the twelve minor prophets; nine books of sacred writings, historical and didactic; Ruth and Lamentations, which Jerome himself was inclined to regard as not canonical. Dante's elders are clad in white and crowned with lilies, white being the color of faith: the Old Testament is the expression of faith in the coming Savior.

Next, surrounding the chariot and the griffin, are four animals representing the Gospels; they are crowned with green, the color of hope.   Each has six wings, to carry it abroad through the world; and the wings seem full of eyes, for nothing can escape its flight.   Ezekiel i, 4, 5, 6, 11, 12: "And I looked, and, behold, a whirlwind came out of the north, a great cloud, and a fire infolding itself, and a brightness was about it, and out of the midst thereof as the color of amber, out of the midst of the fire.   Also out of the midst thereof came the likeness of four living creatures.   And this was their appearance; they had the likeness of a man.   And every one had four faces, and every one had four wings ... And their wings were stretched upward. ... And they went every one straight forward; whither the spirit was to go, they went."   Rev. iv. 6, 7, 8: "and round about the throne, were four beasts full of eyes before and behind.   And the first beast was like a lion, and the second beast like a calf, and the third beast had a face as a man, and the fourth beast was like a flying eagle.   And the four beasts had each of them six wings about him; and they were full of eyes within: and they rest not day and night, saying, Holy, holy, holy, Lord God Almighty, which was, and is, and is to come."   These four beasts were early adopted by Christian art as emblems of the four Evangelists.   Ezekiel x, with its account of Cherubim and wheels, may be compared also.   At the end of the troop, dressed in white and garlanded with red, are seven personages, who stand for the remaining books of the New Testament.

For an interpretation of the meaning of this whole procession as the triumph of Beatrice, in analogy to Christ, see Singleton (1958), pp. 72–85. — For the "living creatures," cf. Virgil's description of Fame in *Aen.*, IV, 180–183:

> monstrum horrendum, ingens, cui, quot sunt corpore plumae,
> tot vigiles oculi subter (mirabile dictu),
> tot linguae, totidem ora sonant, tot subrigit auris.

(A monster awful and huge, who for the many feathers in her body has as many watchful eyes below — wondrous to tell — as many tongues, as many sounding mouths, as many pricked-up ears.)

2. Matelda continued her song 'at the end' of her speech.

3. Ps. xxxii (Vulg. xxxi), 1: "*Blessed is he* whose transgression is forgiven, *whose sin is covered.*"

8. Matelda on one side of the river and the three travelers on the other turn to Dante's right and proceed upstream, i.e., to the south.

12. At this point the river turns a right angle, and Dante and his companions, still walking upstream, face the east, as they did before they came to the water.

27. 'She could not endure remaining under any veil' of ignorance.   Cf. Gen. iii, 4–6.

30. If Eve had not yielded to temptation, all mankind would have been born in the Garden of Eden and would have continued to live there until the final Day of Judgment.

37. Dante appeals once more to the Muses, as in I, 8.

40. Cf. *Aen.*, VII, 641:" Pandite nunc Helicona, Deae, cantusque movete." (Now fling wide Helicon, ye goddesses, and wake your song.)   Helicon was a mountain near Parnassus, sacred to the Muses.

41. Urania, muse of astronomy, genius of the 8th or starry heaven, is regarded as the leader of the 'choir.'

44. 'The long stretch' of intervening space 'produced a false impression' of seven golden trees.

47. By the *obietto comun* Dante seems to mean the *sensibile comune*, the sum of attributes perceptible to more than one sense, the 'variously recognizable character' of a thing. Such attributes are shape, size, number, and motion or stillness; whereas color and light are perceived by the eye alone: *Conv.*, III, ix, 6. In *Conv.*, IV, viii, 6, we learn that we are often deceived by our senses, especially with regard to 'variously recognizable characters,' or *sensibili comuni.*

49. 'The faculty that supplies procedure for the reason': the power of estimation, or discernment.

60. 'They would have been outstripped' by a bride in a wedding procession.

66. Cf. Mark ix, 3: "And his raiment became shining, exceeding white as snow; so as no fuller on earth can white them."

67. Dante, walking upstream on the left bank, has the water on his left. The procession is coming downstream on the opposite side.

68. Though released from sin, Dante is not yet free from remorse; in the light of the 'seven Spirits of God' he sees his own worst part, his 'left side.'

75. 'And they looked like moving paintbrushes,' i.e., 'brushes drawn' across a wall or ceiling, leaving lines of color behind.

78. *Delia = Diana*, born in Delos, goddess of the moon.

81. 'The (two) outer ones,' representing *wisdom* and *fear of the Lord.* All seven gifts are contained within the ten commandments, by which God transmitted them to man.

85. The books of the Old Testament anticipate the greeting to Mary uttered by Gabriel and by Elizabeth (Luke i, 28, 42) at the time of the Annunciation.

95. The hundred-eyed Argus was the guardian of Io: cf. *Met.*, I, 625–629.

100. Ezekiel i, 4–6, 11, 12.

105. In the Revelation of St. John the Divine iv, 6–8, the animals have six wings, while in Ezekiel they have only four.

108. Song of Solomon i, 3: 'Draw me, we will run after thee.' Cf. *Mon.*, III, iii, 12: "dicit Ecclesia, loquens ad Sponsum: Trahe me post te." (The Church says, speaking to the Bridegroom, "Draw me after thee.") Here the passage in the song is distinctly applied to the Church and Christ.

109. The wings extending up out of sight indicate the divine origin of Christ, his miraculous descent from Heaven without really leaving it.

110. The wings extend upward on either side of the middle strip of the colored canopy, the strip representing *might.* On the right of the right wing are *wisdom, understanding*, and *counsel*; on the left of the left wing, *knowledge, piety*, and *fear of the Lord.*

111. The supernatural advent and return of Christ were entirely in accord with the prophecy of the gifts of the Holy Spirit.

113. The eaglelike, or divine, part is of gold, the symbol of purity. Cf. Song of Solomon v, 11: "His head is as the most fine gold."

114. The lionlike, or earthly, part is white and red, like human flesh. These are the colors of faith and love. Cf. Song of Solomon v, 10: "My beloved is white and ruddy."

115, 116. 'Not only did Rome never gladden Africanus (Publius Cornelius Scipio, the conqueror of Hannibal) or Augustus with a chariot so beautiful (on their returning in triumph).'

118. At the prayer of the scorched earth, Phaethon, the unsuccessful driver of the chariot of the sun, was stricken down by Jove, who thus punished the crime which, for unknown reasons, he had allowed: *Met.*, II, 227–332. Cf. *Inf.* XVII, 107.

122. Red is the color of Love, or Charity, the greatest of the three Christian virtues. Cf. VIII, 88–93.

124. 'The next' is Hope, whose color is green.

127. Hope must arise either from Faith or from Love: cf. St. Thomas, *Summa Theologiae*, Secunda Secundae, Qu. xvii, Art. 7 and 8. Love, the foundation of all goodness (1 Cor. xiii, 2), sets the pace by her song for the other two virtues.

130. The four beside the left wheel are the cardinal virtues, Prudence, Temperance, Justice, and Fortitude. Cf. I, 22–27.

131. They are clad in 'purple' (in the Middle Ages nearly identical with red) to indicate that they depend for their existence on Love, and are therefore the *infused* cardinal virtues. See Singleton (1958), pp. 159–167.

132. Their leader is Prudence, who sees past, present, and future.

138. Nature created Hippocrates, the famous Greek doctor and father of medical science, for the benefit of mankind. His follower represents the book of the Acts of the Apostles, written by "Luke, the beloved physician" (Colossians iv, 14).

139. 'The other,' who was more disposed to cut than to cure, represents the Epistles of Paul. St. Paul is often pictured with a sword, perhaps "the sword of the Spirit, which is the word of God" of Ephesians vi, 17; cf. Hebrews iv, 12.

142. The 'four of humble mien' are the minor Epistles, those of Peter, James, John, and Jude.

144. The 'old man' stands for the Revelation of St. John the Divine, the last book of the New Testament. In art John is often depicted asleep. It was commonly believed that he was sleeping in Ephesus, not to wake until the Judgment Day.

145. They were dressed 'like the first band,' the 24 elders.

147. Instead of white wreaths, they had red, symbolic of love.

154. 'The first ensigns' are the candlesticks with their streamers.

Canto XXX

Argument

At the culmination of a climax subtly contrived at every step to whet increasingly the reader's curiosity and to intensify his impression of majesty and loveliness, Beatrice emerges into view from the midst of a rain of flowers. And before he sees her features, Dante recognizes her by the love that fills him. Inasmuch as the Christian Church is founded on Revelation, from which it derives its authority, Beatrice now appears as its dominating spirit and mouthpiece and takes back to herself its power and its functions. By an interesting coincidence, in the *Anticlaudianus* of Alanus de Insulis, Prudence journeys to Heaven under the guidance of Reason, who is there replaced by Theology. Beatrice it is who leads the penitent through contrition, confession, and satisfaction to the final remission of sin, administered under her direction. Contrition, the first stage of the sacrament of penance, must spring from a full recognition of guilt. Just as Lady Philosophy greets with stern rebuke the captive Boethius, in the *Consolatio Philosophiae*, I, Pr. ii, so the divine Beatrice bitterly chides Dante for his recreancy after the death of her mortal part. Without entering upon specific charges, she accuses him of having forsaken the true way and "given himself to others," following "false images of good." Worldliness, ambition, unworthy companionship or unworthy love — among these is perhaps to be found the fault so discreetly recalled. Canto XXXI will perhaps afford a clue. The first word the accuser speaks (l. 55) is Dante's name, which occurs nowhere else in the poem. "Di necessità qui si registra," the author explains (l. 63): without this humiliating record of his identity, his confession would have been incomplete.

1. The Septentrion is the constellation of Ursa Minor, the Little Dipper, which contains the North Star, the sailors' guide. The seven candlesticks, representing the sevenfold Spirit of the Lord, are called the Septentrion, or sevenfold guiding light, of the 'first heaven,' or Empyrean.

3. Nothing but man's sinfulness has ever hidden from him the light of the Spirit of the Lord.

7. The 'truthful people' are the elders representing the prophetic Old Testament.

10. The one who stands for the Song of Solomon.

11. Song of Solomon iv, 8: "Come with me from Lebanon, my spouse." The "spouse" is the Church. In the Vulgate the word *veni*, 'come,' occurs three times.

15. Rev. xix, 1: "And after those things I heard a great voice of much people in Heaven, saying, Alleluia."

17. A hundred angels suddenly arose 'at the voice of so great an elder.' The Latin, appropriate enough to the ecclesiastical tone of the whole passage, is evidently needed here to prepare for the coming rhymes.

19. Mat. xxi, 9: "And the multitudes that went before, and that followed" (Christ as he entered Jerusalem), "cried, saying, Hosanna to the son of David: *Blessed is he that cometh* in the name of the Lord." The last clause is taken from Ps. cxviii (Vulg. cxvii), 26. Dante changes *venit*, 'cometh,' to *venis*, 'comest.' These are the last words sung by the assistants before the canon of the Mass; they express the expectation of the bodily coming of Christ. — The elder has sung the invitation of Christ to the Church; the angels in the chariot of the Church now respond with the greeting to Christ.

21. *Aen.*, vi, 883: "Oh, give lilies with full hands!" On the point of dismissing Virgil from his narrative, Dante pays him the supreme honor of putting a phrase from his *Aeneid* into the mouth of angels, together with words from the Bible. The exclamation "Oh" is inserted by Dante.

31. Olive is the emblem of peace and is also the crown of Minerva, goddess of wisdom. Cf. l. 68. It suggests also the aureole of the doctor. In these three lines are the colors of the three Christian virtues; but green, the symbol of hope, really occurs twice. In XXXI, 116, Beatrice's eyes, too, are green.

35, 36. Cf. *V. N.*, II, 4; XI, 3; XIV, 4; XXIV, 1. As Beatrice had died in 1290 (*V. N.*, XXIX, 1–4), Dante had not seen her, except in dreams, for ten years: cf. *Purg.* XXXII, 2.

42. When Dante first saw Beatrice, he was not yet nine years old: *V. N.*, II, 1–2.

48. Cf. *Aen.*, IV, 23: "Agnosco veteris vestigia flammae." (I recognize the traces of the olden flame.)

57. Hebrews iv, 12: "For the word of God is quick, and powerful, and sharper than any two-edged sword, piercing even to the dividing asunder of soul and spirit, and of the joints and marrow, and is a discerner of the thoughts and intents of the heart."

70. Her anger shows itself in the impetuousness of the following speech.

74. From the imperiousness of the first line, she passes abruptly to the irony of the second, and thence, with equal suddenness, to the direct rebuke of the third.

77. Contrition is caused by seeing our real selves.

83. Ps. xxxi (Vulg. xxx): "In thee, O Lord, do I put my trust." It expresses trust and gratitude, and prays for continued defense and deliverance.

84. Verse 8 (Vulg. 9) ends with: "thou hast set *my feet* in a large room" (Vulg.: "statuisti in loco spatioso *pedes meos*"). After this verse the tone of the psalm is rather mournful than jubilant.

85. The 'living rafters' are trees.

86. The 'back of Italy' is the Apennine range.

89. 'The land that loses shadow' is the African desert, where the sun is sometimes directly overhead.

93. In harmony with the music of the spheres. Cf. *Par.* I, 78, 82.

98. It is the pity of the angels that finally awakens complete contrition of the heart, the first stage of the sacrament of penance.

101. The 'kindly substances' are the angels.

104. 'Steals not from you' a single step of the world's course.

109. The 'great wheels' are the revolving heavens, which determine, by the arrangement of the stars at his birth, the disposition of every human being.

112. God bestows upon every individual a special degree of grace, upon which his keenness of spiritual vision depends. The reasons that govern God's uneven distribution of grace neither men nor angels can fathom. His graces rain down from so high — 'have such high vapors for their rain' (l. 113) — that no eye can approach their source. See St. Thomas, *Summa Theologiae*, Prima, Qu. lvii, Art. 5.

125. The 'second age,' *gioventù*, begins at 25: see *Conv.*, IV, xxiv, 1, 2. — Dante was born (probably) in May, 1265. Beatrice, who was nearly a year younger (*V. N.*, II, 2), was doubtless born in the first third of 1266. She died in June, 1290: *V. N.*, XXIX, 1–3.

132. Cf. *Cons.*, III, Pr. viii: "haec quae nec praestare quae pollicentur bona possunt" (these goods, which can neither perform that which they promise).

144. It would be contrary to God's justice to allow forgetfulness of sin without previous contrition.

Canto XXXI

Argument

Contritio cordis (contrition of the heart) is followed by *confessio oris* (confession by the mouth) and *satisfactio operis* (satisfaction of works), after which comes remission of sin. This whole solemn and elaborate episode — far more elaborate than the allegory itself would seem to require — strikes one as having been devised by the author partly for the purpose of making real amends for past wrong and setting himself right before the world. What may have been the nature of the guilt thus expiated, as it were, by avowal? Was it a mundane love or an undue literary or scientific ambition? Our evidence is slight.

On the completion of Dante's confession Beatrice rebukes him once more, "that he may be stronger another time when he hears the sirens" (ll. 44–45). It will be remembered that in Dante's second dream a siren (XIX, 19) represented the sins of the flesh. On the other hand, in *Consolatio Philosophiae*, I, Pr. i, in a situation somewhat analogous to the one under discussion, Philosophy, finding the exiled and imprisoned author in the company of the muses of poetry, drives them away, saying: "Sed abite potius, Sirenes usque in exitium dulces, meisque eum Musis curandum sanandumque relinquite." (Rather get you gone, you Sirens pleasant even to destruction, and leave him to my Muses to be cured and healed.) The sirens of poetry must yield the place to the muses of philosophy. Beatrice's "sirens," then, can be used on either side of the argument.

A few lines further on (58–60), after recalling the keen sorrow and disappointment that came to him from her own departure from this world, Beatrice declares that he should not have allowed any "little maid, or other so shortlived novelty," to attach him to earth, to be wounded again.   Here the question arises anew: Is the *pargoletta* to be taken literally, or does she symbolize some intellectual pursuit (for instance, poetry, as the author's son Pietro thought)? Dante's sixth ballad (*Rime*, LXXXVII) begins 'I' mi son *pargoletta* bella e nova.' Now this lyric, from its tone and style, seems distinctly to belong to the same group as ballad CVI and the first two *canzoni* of the *Convivio* (also, probably, Canzone XC and a few miscellaneous shorter poems), all concerned with a maiden who, Dante tells us (*Conv.*, II, ii), is identical with the compassionate lady of the latter part of the *Vita Nuova* (chap. xxxv–xxxix, Son. XIX–XXII).   This young person attracted his notice and then his affection by her apparent pity for him after the death of Beatrice.   Of his passion for her — a harmless enough infatuation, as far as one can judge — he was profoundly ashamed (*V. N.*, XXXVII–XXXIX); his acquaintances, no doubt, and his literary circle were likewise dissatisfied and expressed their disapproval of his celebration of this *pargoletta*. When, therefore, he undertook the *Convivio*, he did so partly to defend himself from such criticism (*Conv.*, I, ii, 15–17) by showing that the poems in question are allegorical, the lady being none other than Philosophy (*Conv.*, II, xii).   For the unprejudiced reader of the *Vita Nuova* it is difficult, if not impossible, to believe that the sympathetic young lady there described is a purely allegorical figure. The incident is peculiarly lifelike; and such an allegory is quite foreign to the spirit of that early work.   It is certainly true that Dante found comfort in the study of philosophy at about the same time that he was consoled by the sight of this *donna gentile*.   It would have been, then, quite in accordance with his practice (with the example of Boethius before him) to make her the symbol of the consolation of Philosophy, and of Philosophy herself; and it would have been equally natural for him, when his moody yearning for her had died away, to try to forget that she had ever been anything more to him than the embodiment of the subject of his absorbing study.   To make others accept her as a pure symbol was one of the objects of the *Convivio*.   It is noteworthy that this treatise was never finished.   Dante's conscience, apparently, was ill at ease; and here, in the *Commedia*, he at last tells the whole truth, admitting that his love for the *pargoletta* was not merely an innocent devotion to that "figlia di Dio, regina di tutto, nobilissima e bellissima Filosofia" (*Conv.*, II, xii, 9), but also, and originally, a sentiment deserving reprobation.   Now, as far as we can see, Dante's devotion to Philosophy never ceased, his admiration never waned; throughout the *Commedia*, as in the *Convivio*, she is the handmaid of religion and, though not omniscient, the guide to revelation.   That she ever was a dangerous companion for him, or that he ever thought of his pursuit of her as excessive, there is no clear indication. He could scarcely have referred to her, at any time, as a "short-lived novelty." If, then, we are to see in the *pargoletta* of the *Commedia* anything more than a woman, it is more likely that she represented, to Dante's repentant mind, a whole mode of life and thought, a practical, imaginative, and artistic materialism inconsistent with the spiritual ideal he always cherished.

2. Her speech is compared to a sword: cf. XXX, 57.

3. I.e., addressed to me indirectly, being ostensibly directed to the angels: cf. XXX, 103–108.

21. Cf. *Aen.*, XI, 150–151:

haeret lacrimansque gemensque,
et via vix tandem voci laxata dolore est.

(He clings to him weeping and moaning, and scarce from sorrow at the last does his speech find open way).

25. Obstacles, such as were used to prevent the passage of a hostile army or fleet.

40. The use of *gota*, 'cheek,' instead of 'lips,' was perhaps suggested, not only by the rhyme, but also by the idea of the blush of shame that accompanies the words.

42. 'The grindstone turns back against the edge': the sword of justice is blunted, i.e., tempered with mercy.

46. The odd phrase 'the seed of weeping' is evidently due to a reminiscence of Ps. cxxvi (Vulg. cxxv), 5: "They that sow in tears shall reap in joy."

51. Cf. Gen. iii, 19: "unto dust shalt thou return."

68. In the Middle Ages, *barba*, in many regions, meant both 'beard' and 'chin.' Dante apparently plays on the double sense of the word.

72. Iarbas was king of Libya: *Aen.*, IV, 196.

75. The 'venom of her speech' consists in the implication that the beard, the plumage of the full-fledged (cf. I, 42), is inconsistent with Dante's youthful vagaries.

80. 'Turned toward the animal,' evidently referring to the griffin.

84. *Vincer*, 'surpass,' is insistently repeated. — *Che l'altre*, 'than she surpassed all other women.'

88. *Riconoscenza*, 'remorse.' — This swoon evidently represents *satisfaction*, the last stage of the sacrament of penance.

92. *Donna*: Matelda, as she is finally named, XXXIII, 119.

98. Ps. li, 7 (Vulg. l, 9): "*Purge me* with hyssop, and I shall be clean: wash me, and I shall be whiter than snow" — a verse that accompanies blessing of the holy water.

106. The cardinal virtues, here the *infused* cardinal virtues, specifically Christian. See Singleton (1958), pp. 158–183, also for the three theological virtues of l. 111.

111. The theological virtues, who are beside the right wheel.

116. The eyes of Beatrice are called emeralds: green is considered to be the color of hope. The emerald, too, was thought to preserve and strengthen the sight.

120. The eyes of Revelation are fixed upon Christ alone.

123. Now with its human, now with its divine 'bearing.' Revealed theology analyzes the nature of Christ into its two component parts, although in reality they are eternally joined into one.

138. The first beauty is the eyes; the second, the mouth.

144. The 'harmonizing heaven' is the canopy of the seven streamers of light which, like a rainbow, hang over the procession and over Beatrice now unveiled. Cf. XXIX, 76–81, and 82, where it is called a *bel cielo*. It is, in symbolic meaning, the sevenfold Spirit of the Lord. Cf. Singleton (1965), p. 47.

Canto XXXII

Argument

When the sinner has chosen the road to reformation, the Church comes to meet him, takes him to itself, directs him in the way he should go, and leads him Heavenward. Such is the spiritual meaning of the procession which comes out of the east, stops opposite Dante, receives him as a companion, and then, turning to the right, wheels about and marches eastward, with the sun and the seven candlesticks in front — with God-given intelligence and the sevenfold Spirit of the Lord as its guides. These movements, however, probably contain also an historical allegory: the Church originated in the Orient, made its way westward to the Atlantic, and then took up its abode in Rome, midway between its eastern and its western frontier. This last event is symbolized by the halt of the band after it has gone back a distance of some three arrow shots — that is, perhaps, has crossed Spain, France, and Italy. Then Beatrice descends from her chariot beneath the tree of Law: the Church puts itself under the authority of the State. Christ himself is careful not to trespass on the field of temporal power, as is shown by the griffin's forbearing to harm the tree. "Let every soul be subject unto the higher powers," says St. Paul in Romans xiii, 1. "For there is no power but of God: the powers that be are ordained of God."

Law naturally takes the form, "thou shalt not"; and the tree of knowledge of good and evil, the subject of God's first prohibition to man (Gen. ii, 17), is a fit symbol of divine Law. This tree, of vast height, is shaped like those in the circle of gluttony (XXII, 132-135), its offshoots: it tapers downward, the branches being long above and short below, so that no one can climb it — a token of prohibition. According to a legend widespread in the Middle Ages, Seth, returning to the Garden of Eden, found there a bare tree of lofty stature, the tree of knowledge, thus denuded since his parents' disobedience (Gen. iii, 6, 17); taking a branch — or, as another version says, three seeds of the apple eaten by Adam — he planted another tree, from which, later, the Cross was made. Thus sin and atonement sprang from the same wood. Dante's tree is likewise bare until the griffin, Christ, draws up the chariot of the Church and, fastening the pole — which is the Cross — to the mother trunk, "leaves bound to it that which came from it" (l. 51). Then the tree clothes itself in purple foliage — divine Law is revived in the form of Empire. Church and State being thus allied, humanity enjoys (or would have enjoyed, had this ideal condition lasted) a perfect tranquillity, which is symbolized by the deep sleep into which Dante now falls, as he listens to a mysterious hymn of peace.

When the sleeper comes to himself, he finds that the scene has been transformed.   Christ and the Scriptures have left the earth and returned to Heaven, whence they came.   They have left below as their representative the Church, with Revelation for its guide, and the sevenfold Spirit of God in the keeping of the seven Virtues.   A change as wonderful as this was experienced once before, when the three disciples who had witnessed the Transfiguration recovered from their fright.   Mat. xvii, 1–8: "And after six days Jesus taketh Peter, James, and John his brother, and bringeth them up into an high mountain apart.   And was transfigured before them: and his face did shine as the sun, and his raiment was white as the light.   And, behold, there appeared unto them Moses and Elias talking with him.   Then answered Peter, and said unto Jesus, Lord, it is good for us to be here ... While he yet spake, behold, a bright cloud overshadowed them: and behold a voice out of the cloud ... And when the disciples heard it, they fell on their face, for they were sore afraid.   And Jesus came and touched them, and said, Arise, and be not afraid.   And when they had lifted up their eyes, they saw no man, save Jesus only."   Dante discusses the moral sense of this episode in the *Convivio*, II, i, 5, and refers to its allegorical significance in *Monarchia*, III, ix, 11.

There is now revealed to Dante, for the benefit of mankind, a picture of the vicissitudes of the Church.   The persecution of the Christians by the early Roman Emperors, harmful to the State even more than to the victim, is represented by the descent of an eagle, which breaks flowers, leaves, and bark from the tree, and shakes the chariot.   A fox, rebuked and put to flight by Beatrice (Truth revealed), stands for a more insidious foe, heresy, which attacks the Church within.   The Song of Solomon ii, 15, speaks of "little foxes, that spoil the vines."   According to Origen (and others after him), these foxes, in the "third," or "spiritual," sense, signify false doctrines distracting the Church.   If Dante had in mind any particular heresy, it must have been an early one, Gnosticism or Arianism.   After the fox, the eagle returns, this time with no hostile intent but with more damaging effect, and leaves its feathers in the chariot.   The Emperor thus designated is Constantine, whose donation of his western possessions to the Church was accepted by Dante and his contemporaries as an historical fact: cf. *Inf.* XIX, 115–117; XXVII, 94–95; *Par.* XX, 55–60; *Mon.*, III, x.   Next is recorded a great schism, either the secession of the Greek Church or the Mohammedan movement, which was regarded as a departure from Christianity: cf. *Inf.* XXVIII, 31.   This disaster, brought about by Satan, is pictured as the removal of a part of the bottom of the chariot by the sting of a dragon that has emerged from the ground beneath it.   The figure is suggested by Rev. xii, 3, 4, 9: "And ... behold a great red dragon ... And his tail drew the third part of the stars of heaven, and did cast them to the earth ... And the great dragon was cast out, that old serpent, called the Devil, and Satan, which deceiveth the whole world" (cf. xx, 2).   Meanwhile the gift of temporal possessions has borne its inevitable fruit of corruption.   The love of wealth possesses the clergy and disfigures the Church.   Feathers suddenly cover the whole chariot; and seven heads, representing the seven capital vices, spring forth on its pole and its corners.   The three on the pole are two-horned, and stand for pride, envy, and anger, which are harmful to both the sinner and his neighbor (cf. XVII, 112–123); the other four, single-horned, symbolize sloth, avarice, gluttony, lust, which do not necessarily affect anyone but the vicious man himself.   Here again Dante drew his inspiration from the Apocalypse: "and I saw a beast rise up out of the sea, having seven heads and ten horns" (Rev. xiii, 1).   Riding fearlessly, "with swift roving eyes," upon the monstrous chariot — like the woman "upon a scarlet coloured beast, full of names of blasphemy, having seven heads and ten horns" in Rev. xvii, 3 — is an "unbridled harlot," who evidently personifies the corrupt Papacy. The House of France, her master, stands beside her in the form of a giant.   In Epistola VII, viii, 29, Philip the Fair, the worst offender among the French kings, is called Goliath.   Inasmuch as Philip and Boniface VIII were sometimes in accord for evil ends, the giant and the harlot are described as "kissing from time to time."   But when she turns "her greedy, restless eye" on Dante, her "fierce lover" beats her "from head to foot."   This scourging apparently signifies the outrage perpetrated by Philip on Boniface at Anagni (cf. XX, 85–90).   The eager glance at Dante is harder to interpret but seems to indicate the covetous designs of Boniface on Tuscany.   In that case Anagni would appear to be a retribution for the betrayal of Florence.   After the punishment, the giant drags off the chariot through the forest — an allegory of the removal of the Papal See to Avignon in 1305 by the French Pope, Clement V, who was thought to be under the control of Philip.   The chariot is drawn so far, Dante says, that the wood alone screens it from his eyes.   As the forest is used in l. 100 distinctly as a symbol of this world, contrasted with Heaven, the closing lines may mean that the worldliness of the Papal court, more than its physical distance from Rome, destroys its moral influence in Italy.

2. Ten years: from June, 1290, to April, 1300.

8. The 'Divinities' to which this reference is made are the three theological virtues, Faith, Hope, and Charity.

9. By 'Too fixedly!' the Virtues remind Dante that Revelation cannot be directly comprehended, in its entirety, by the ordinary human mind, but can be best understood through its manifestation in the Church.   A similar warning is uttered by Beatrice herself in *Par.* XVIII, 21.

13. The whole procession visible in its various parts, called *little* as compared to the vision of Beatrice as presented in the closing verses of the preceding canto.   This is high praise indeed!

19. The figure is that of a troop of soldiers retreating, with their shields locked over their heads.

24. The candlesticks and the 24 elders all 'passed us,' 'before the chariot bent its first wood,' i.e., its pole, which is the Cross.

25. The seven Virtues returned to their two wheels (XXIX, 121, 130), which they had left (XXXI, 109, 131.)

27. Christ set the Church in motion, by means of the Cross, without disturbing in any way his divine part.

28. Matelda: XXXI, 91–104.

30. The wheel 'that made its turn with the smaller curve' is the right wheel, inasmuch as the chariot is turning to the right. Dante and Statius, with Matelda, join the Theological Virtues.

37. Cf. 4 Esdras vii, 48: "O thou Adam, what hast thou done? For though it was thou that sinned, thou are not fallen alone, but we all that come of thee."

41. India was famous for high trees: cf. Virgil, *Georgics*, II, 122–124.

43. Cf. *Mon.*, III, x, 5: "Sed contra officium deputatum Imperatori est *scindere* Imperium." (But it is counter to the office deputed to the emperor to rend the empire.) — See *Mon.*, II, xi, xii; Mat. xxii, 21.

48. Mat. iii, 15: "For thus it becometh us to fulfil all righteousness." Cf. Rom. v, 19: "For as by one man's disobedience many were made sinners, so by the obedience of one shall many be made righteous." — Justice is identical with the divine will: *Mon.*, II, ii, 4–6.

53. When the sun's light descends 'mingled with that' of Aries — the constellation which follows Pisces, the 'heavenly carp' — it is spring.

57. The 'next constellation' to which the sun 'hitches his steeds' is Taurus, which follows Aries.

58. The color between red and violet is the Imperial purple.

65. The hundred eyes of Argus, the guardian of Io (cf. XXIX, 95), were put to sleep by Mercury's song of the nymph Syrinx, loved by Pan; Mercury then slew the overvigilant guardian: *Met.*, I, 568–747.

69. 'But let him who will make a good counterfeit presentment of the act of falling asleep!'

73. Cf. Song of Solomon ii, 3: "As the apple tree among the trees of the wood, so is my beloved among the sons."

74. The full glory of Christ.

75. Rev. xix, 9: "Blessed are they which are called unto the marriage supper of the Lamb."

76. Mat. xvii, 1. Peter, John, and James, representatives of the three Christian virtues, conduct Dante's examination in these virtues in Heaven: *Par.* XXIV–XXVI.

77. Mat. xvii, 5–7.

78. The sleep of death. Cf. Luke vii, 14–15; John xi, 43–44.

79. 'And saw their company diminished': Mat. xvii, 8.

80. 'Both by Moses and by Elias': Mat. xvii, 3.

81. 'And their Master's raiment changed,' no longer 'white as the light,' as it had been at the moment of the Transfiguration: Mat. xvii, 2.

87. Beatrice sits upon the root of the tree: Revelation (Religion) and Law (Empire) come from the same source.

88. The seven Virtues, Beatrice's handmaids.

99. 'Which are safe from Aquilo and Auster,' the north and the south wind: which no physical blast can extinguish.

100. Thou shalt dwell a little while on earth.

101. Then thou shalt dwell forever in Heaven. Cf. Ephesians ii, 19: "fellow-citizens with the saints, and of the household of God."

112. The emblem of the Roman Empire is the eagle, 'Jove's bird': *Aen.*, I, 394. — Cf. Ezekiel xvii, 3–4.

125. The 'ark,' like the 'cradle' above, means the body of the chariot.

153. Cf. Rev. xviii, 2, 3: "Babylon the great is fallen, ... and the kings of the earth have committed fornication with her."

158. The 'monster' is the chariot.

Canto XXXIII

Argument

The 13th and 14th centuries witnessed a considerable vogue of prophetic literature and mystic interpretation. Aside from the Kabbalistic method — which assigned numerical values to the letters, and explained one word by another whose letters added up to the same sum — the transposition of letters was used, and the attribution of special significances to letters and numbers. Lucian, in *Alexander or the False Prophet*, gives the name of the pretender as 'one, thirty, five, and twenty more' — which, substituting Greek letters for their numerical equivalents, reads 'Ἀλεξ. Speculation as to the secret meaning of numbers, which is so curiously illustrated in the *Vita Nuova*, chap. xxix, was common enough among scholars and theologians. A standing problem was the "number of the beast," in Rev. xiii, 18: "Here is wisdom. Let him that hath understanding count the number of the beast; for it is the number of a man; and his number is Six hundred threescore and six." Joachim and St. Thomas discuss the possible values of the letters and the numbers that make up DCLXVI, and point out (as Victorinus had done in the fourth century) that with a shift of its last two members the combination reads DIC LVX, the not very relevant Latin phrase *dic, lux.*

This idea of transposition seems to have been adopted by Dante when, in the present canto, he follows up the prophecies of a temporal redeemer uttered in *Inf.* I, 100–111, and *Purg.* XX, 13–15, with the solemn and mysterious announcement of an approaching heir to the vacant Imperial throne, a *cinquecento diece e cinque*, sent by God, who shall slay the harlot and the giant. The number DXV, with a shift similar to that noted above, gives DVX, the Latin word *dux*, or 'leader.' An Imperial leader of mankind, ordained by God, is soon to correct the greedy and unscrupulous Papacy and overthrow the power of the House of France. In choosing 515 as a symbol, Dante undoubtedly had in mind also the mystic attributes (whatever he may have thought them to be) of the numbers that compose it. His imagination may have been touched, furthermore, by the familiar abbreviation of the name of Christ, a Greek *X* (= *CH*) and *P* (= *R*), so combined as to look like a *P* superposed on an *X*, or a *D* connected by a downward prolongation of its upright line with a *V* which forms the upper half of an *X*. This sign was sometimes interpreted as D*eus* CH*ristus* V*enturus*, 'Lord Christ to come,' just as *I. H. S.*, the first three letters of *Jesus* in Greek spelling, is explained as *Jesus Hominum Salvator*. The word *Christ*, as Dante knew, means 'king'; and the temporal Christ, who is to appear near the end of the world, corresponds to the spiritual Messiah, who inaugurated our era.

To emphasize the mysteriousness of his prediction, Dante compares it to the utterances of the goddess Themis, whose obscure oracle is recorded in *Met.*, I, 377–394, and to the riddle of the bloodthirsty Theban Sphinx, finally guessed by Oedipus (*Met.*, VII, 759–761; *Thebaid*, I, 66–67). Dark though his words may be, he adds, the events shall ere long solve the problem — even as Oedipus, the son of Laius, unraveled the Sphinx's puzzle. Ovid, in *Met.*, VII, 759–760, relates that this son of Laius had cleared up the riddles which had never been understood before:

> Carmina Laïades non intellecta priorum
> Solverat ingeniis.

(Oedipus, the son of Laïus, had solved the riddle which had been inscrutable to the understanding of all before.)

Dante, however, evidently read the passage in a faulty text, which substituted *Naiades* for *Laiades* and *solvunt* for *solverat*, and was thus led to believe that Naiads, or water nymphs, were the successful guessers. Therefore, instead of saying "the events shall be the Oedipus (or Laiades) that shall explain the mystery," he puts it: "The facts shall soon be the Naiads that shall solve this hard enigma."

1. Ps. lxxix (Vulg. lxxviii), 1: "*O God, the heathen are come* into thine inheritance; thy holy temple have they defiled." This psalm, depicting the destruction of Jerusalem by the Chaldaeans, and closing with a prayer for restoration, is now applied to the profanation of the Church described at the end of Canto XXXII. The Theological and the Cardinal Virtues sing the verses alternately.

6. Mary at the foot of the cross — the *Mater dolorosa* of art and song — was scarcely more altered by grief than Beatrice.

10. In answer to the complaint and prayer of the Virtues, Beatrice repeats the prophecy of Christ to his disciples in John xvi, 16: "A little while, and ye shall not see me: and again, a little while, and ye shall see me." Truth, as revealed through the Church, shall be hidden for a time, but shall shine forth again.

14. She had no need to speak.

15. Matelda. — Statius.

17. The 9 to 10 steps probably represent a period of over 9 years, between 1305, when Clement V was induced by Philip the Fair to make Avignon the seat of the Papacy, and 1314, when both Clement and Philip died. After their death the world was in a better condition to expect a redeemer.

34. The 'vessel' is the chariot, and the 'serpent' is the dragon of XXXII, 131.

35. Rev. xvii, 8: "The beast that thou sawest was, and is not." The material Church has ceased to exist. — Clement and Philip shall both be stricken down.

36. 'God's vengeance fears no bullying,' like that of the harlot by the giant.

37. In *Conv.*, IV, iii, 6, Dante calls Frederick II, who died in 1250, the last Roman Emperor.

44. The 'thief' is the harlot who has usurped the place of the rightful authority.

51. Themis, to avenge the death of the Sphinx, sent the Thebans a beast to lay waste their flocks and fields: *Met.*, VII, 763 ff. But the followers of the new Oedipus, the Redeemer to come, will have nothing to fear from Themis, the goddess of Justice.

57. The tree of Law has been despoiled by Adam and by the giant.

62, 63. Adam longed for redemption by Christ, who took upon himself the punishment for Adam's sin, during more than 5000 years, i.e., 930 on earth (Gen. v, 5) and 4302 in Limbus (*Par.*

XXVI, 118–120).   According to the chronology of Eusebius, Christ was born in the year 5200 after the creation.

67.   The water of the Tuscan river Elsa coats with carbonate of lime anything that falls into it.   The 'vain thoughts' have petrified Dante's mind.

69.   His 'delight in them' has discolored his mind, as the blood of Pyramus stained the mulberry: cf. XXVII, 39.

77.   Pilgrims bring back their 'staff wreathed with palm' from the Holy Land, to show where they have been and what they have seen.

90.   The Primum Mobile, the swiftest and most distant of the heavens. — Cf. Isaiah lv, 9: "For as the heavens are higher than the earth, so are my ways higher than your ways, and my thoughts than your thoughts."

99.   Inasmuch as Lethe removes only the memory of *sin*, the fact that he has now forgotten his recreancy to Beatrice — which he remembered just before drinking of the stream (XXXI, 34–36) — proves that this estrangement was sinful.

103.   It is noon.   When the sun is overhead, it seems to move slower than when it is near the horizon.

105.   The 'noonday circle,' or meridian, 'shifts to one side and the other according to the point of view': it is not a fixed line, like the equator.

109.   The 'pallid shade' resembles a dark pool under the trees.

112.   Boethius, *Cons.*, V, Metr. i, 3–4:

Tigris et Euphrates uno se fonte resolvunt
Et mox abiunctis dissociantur aquis.

(The Tigris and Euphrates flow from a single source, but they quickly flow apart in separate streams.)

Cf. Lucan, *Phars.*, III, 256–259.   So Brunetto Latini in the *Trésor* and St. Isidore in the *Origines* (both citing Sallust as an authority) describe these two rivers as coming from the same source.

115.   John viii, 12: "I am the light of the world."

119.   This is the only mention of the lady's name.

125.   Remorse for his sin had made Dante forget the promise of good (XXVIII, 127–133); now the recollection of sin has been removed by Lethe, and the memory of the good that is his due must be revived by Eunoe.

128.   Apparently Matelda performs this office for all souls that reach this stage.   The complete restoration of Innocence implies that all evil is banished from the mind, and the memory of all good is revived.

135.   Statius now disappears from the narrative.

144.   Cf. Ephesians iv, 23: "And be renewed in the spirit of your mind."

145.   Like the first and third, this second *cantica* ends with the word *stelle* pointing to the goal of Dante's journey.

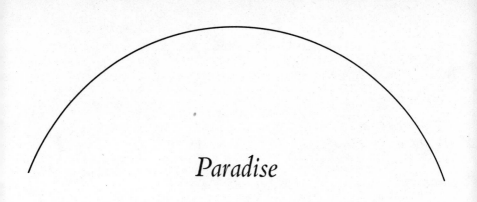

Paradise

Preliminary Note

Of the three parts of the *Commedia*, the *Purgatorio* seems to a 20th-century reader most modern, the *Paradiso* most medieval. The idea of everlasting progress, apparently so indispensable to latterday thought, is here quite absent. We of the present generation are so devoted to perpetual betterment that a state of perfection is almost abhorrent to us. It is the approach that concerns us, not the attainment. An eternity of absolute but unchanging and unproductive happiness does not attract mankind now as it did of old. Furthermore, the scholastic philosophy that pervades the third book of the poem has today lost much of its vital interest. The physical universe, too, is of course constructed by our author on the Ptolemaic model, a system rational in its assumptions and logically worked out, but long since abandoned in favor of the Copernican. The permanent charm of Dante's *Paradise* abides solely in its power to satisfy our craving for pure beauty and for purely religious emotion.

In this *cantica* the Almighty is disclosed to us, first through his works, then through Christian dogma, and lastly in his own essence. The real theme of the whole *Paradiso* is, in fact, an allegory of contemplation, of the human soul rising by stages from consideration of God's universe to the understanding of its Maker. Lacking the dramatic element of his *Hell*, and the human appeal of his *Purgatory*, Dante's *Paradise* reveals — especially in its unrivaled climax — a reach of imagination not to be found in either of the preceding parts. Out of such unsubstantial materials as light, motion, and sound the poet constructs those wondrous scenes which make visible to us the unseen and intangible realm of the spirit.

The reader of the *Paradiso* must be prepared for much instruction. Certain fundamental principles are established in the first five cantos, and the discussion of many difficult philosophical and theological questions runs through the following ones, although the very last are reserved for the divine vision. The didactic matter which here abounds must not be regarded as intrusive: it is an integral part, if not indeed the nucleus, of the whole conception. We must remember, too, that for a keenly inquisitive mind like Dante's a large share of the happiness which Heaven has in store must consist in the true solution of the great problems that have so vexed us during life. The blessed see all things in God; and the fullness of their knowledge is a source of intellectual satisfaction, as the vast love which they give and receive satisfies the affection.

The blessedness of Heaven is not the same for all. In proportion to the grace bestowed on them by divine predestination, human souls (as well as angels) have diverse powers of sight, and consequently see their Maker in diverse ways; and upon their vision of God their ardor and happiness depend. This variety in happiness is asserted by many theologians, Popes, and councils. "In my Father's house are many mansions"; and the "mansions," according to St. Augustine and St. Thomas, in their exposition of John xiv, 2, are different degrees of knowledge of God. The Divine Care, in itself, is equal for all, but is unequal in its gifts to one and to another (*Summa Theologiae*, Prima Secundae, Qu. cxii, Art. 4). Every soul, however, is perfectly content, being aware that it receives knowledge, joy, and love to the full extent of its capacity, and that its capacity has been fore-ordained by God's just but mysterious will. The mystery of predestination is the keynote of the 3rd *cantica*. The degree of celestial beatitude is not primarily determined, then, by one's earthly conduct, although admission to Heaven is, of course, contingent on the right use of free election in the first life.

Even more than his picture of Hell, and far more than his Purgatory, Dante's portrayal of Heaven is to be looked upon as visualized allegory rather than as an interpretation of concrete reality. The general structure of the physical world is, to be sure, conceived according to the astronomical science of the author's day; but, aside from this framework, nearly all the supermundane description is of purely symbolic import. For instance, the appearance of the various orders of the blessed in the several spheres, as Dante traverses them, does not indicate that these regions are really inhabited by souls, but is merely a visible token of the different grades of beatitude. The device has the further advantage of peopling with hosts of spirits the immense lonely spaces through which the journey lies.

Some figures in the *Convivio* give us an idea of the extent of these uninhabited expanses and of the size of the heavenly bodies. When Venus is nearest to us, she is 542,750 miles away (II, vi, 10); the diameter of the sun is 35,750 miles

(IV, viii, 7), that of the earth 6500 (IV, viii, 7), that of Mercury, the smallest planet, 232 (II, xiii, 11).   The earth, being so much smaller than the sun which illumines it, casts into space a tapering shadow, whose apex extends to the sphere of Venus. The three nearest heavens — those of the moon, Mercury, and Venus —'within reach of the earth's shadow, form the lowest group of spheres.   Then come the heavens of the sun, Mars, and Jupiter.   The highest group is composed of the heaven of Saturn, that of the fixed stars, and the Crystalline Heaven or Primum Mobile.   It will be remembered that each heaven is a transparent hollow sphere, or shell, of rare matter, invisible save for the heavenly body (or bodies) which it contains.   The spheres fit into one another, with no empty space between.   At the center of the universe is the solid, round, motionless earth, about which the heavens revolve, carrying with them their luminous orbs.   Dante's transfer from sphere to sphere is instantaneous, and he is conscious of no motion; as he reaches each sphere, he enters into its star — or, in the 8th heaven, into one of its constellations — and revolves with it as long as he remains there.   In the 9th sphere there is no heavenly body and therefore nothing visible and no special station for the traveler.

In the heavens upon which the earth's shadow falls appear the souls whose goodness was foreordained to have some earthly strain: in the moon, the religious but inconstant; in Mercury, the beneficent but ambitious; in Venus, the affectionate but sensual.   These enjoy the lower degrees of beatitude.   The sun, Mars, and Jupiter display spirits of masterful, righteous activity, the souls respectively of great teachers (mainly theologians), of warriors of the Faith, and of just rulers.   In Saturn are seen the contemplative spirits.   The seeming dwellers in these last four heavens may be said to exemplify the four cardinal virtues: prudence, fortitude, justice, temperance.   In the heaven of the fixed stars, Dante beholds the Apostles, Christ, and Mary; in the Crystalline Heaven he has a vision of God and the angels.   It must be understood that the real home of all of these is the true Paradise or Empyrean, the world of spirit, which lies outside the spherical universe of matter.

The operation of the heavens and the influence of their various stars constitute the power called Nature, which is governed by God, not directly, but through his ministers, the heavenly Intelligences or angels.   One order of angels presides over each sphere.   There are, then, nine orders, which fall into three groups, or hierarchies, of three orders each.   Every order has its own character and functions; the Cherubim, for example, embody divine wisdom, the Seraphim divine love.   The nine orders, with their spheres, and the classes of souls associated with them, may be tabulated as follows:

Angels	MOON	*Inconstant Nuns*
Archangels	MERCURY	*Ambitious Statesmen*
Principalities	VENUS	*Sensual Lovers*
Powers	SUN	*Teachers of Wisdom*
Virtues	MARS	*Soldiers of the Faith*
Dominations	JUPITER	*Just Rulers*
Thrones	SATURN	*Contemplatives*
Cherubim	FIXED STARS	*(Apostles)*
Seraphim	PRIMUM MOBILE	

According to *Conv.*, III, vii, and IV, ix, there is an infinite gradation from the lowest man to the highest angel.   In the mosaics in the Florentine Baptistery the angelic orders are depicted, though not in the sequence expounded in *Par.* XXVII.

Canto I

Argument

The keynote of the 3rd *cantica* is struck in its majestic opening verse, "La gloria di colui che tutto move."   Dante's *Inferno* deals with man's failure to appreciate God's goodness and his own opportunity; the *Purgatorio* illustrates God's mercy to his erring but repentant creatures; the *Paradiso* proclaims the splendor of the divine idea and its realization in the heavens.   It is God's love that moves the universe: so Dante has told us in the *Convivio* (III, xv, 15); and our poem closes with the words, "L'Amor che move il sole e l' altre stelle."   His glory penetrates everything; but, even as those objects that are inherently bright receive most of the sunshine, so the noblest parts of the world respond best to the spiritual radiance from on high (*Conv.*, III, vii, 2-5); so Dionysius, *De Divinis Nominibus*, IV, i and iv: Gardner, 934.   The realm in which the divine light shines brightest is the Empyrean, the abode of pure spirit, the real home of the angels and the blessed.

The universe is regulated by an order which reveals the Maker's plan and keeps the material world in harmony with its Creator.   To this order all things are subject, each in its own way.   Matter and spirit and their compounds, animate and inanimate, have an infallible instinct that tells them what to do.   This instinct impels fire to strive upward toward its sphere, which lies just below the heaven of the moon; it compresses the earth into a globe; it makes the Primum Mobile revolve, whirling the other spheres in their course.   This same instinct constantly inclines the human soul to mount up to its Creator; but, inasmuch as man's will is free, his primal instinct may be thwarted by a perverse use of this freedom, and his soul may sink instead of rising, just as, under certain conditions, fire may move downward, in the form of lightning. If, however, the original impulse is undisturbed by sin, spirit moves upward as naturally and inevitably as unhampered flame. Thus it is that Dante, cleansed of all impurity, shoots heavenward with Beatrice, passing through the light matter which constitutes the spheres.

His rise to God begins appropriately at noon, in the full glory of the day; with like fitness, the ascent of Purgatory began in the hopeful hour of morning, and the descent into Hell in the sad eventide. Furthermore, the season of his journey is the best season of the year. At the creation, the world was shaped in its vernal state, the sun in the sign of Aries; and the Conception and the Redemption found the sun in this same constellation. Coupled with the Ram, the sun molds the earthly wax better than it can fashion it from any other part of the zodiac. At noontide of a spring day Dante leaves the earth.

On quitting our globe, the poet apostrophizes Apollo and the Muses. Upon the latter powers he has already called, at the beginning of each of the first two *cantiche* (*Inf.* II, 7; *Purg.* I, 7–12). In the *Vita Nuova* (XXV, 9) Dante defines the Muses as the writer's "own science," the poetic art; this has sufficed for the portrayal of Hell and Purgatory. For the description of Heaven, divine inspiration is needed as well, and he invokes it under the name of Apollo, as did Statius in the *Achilleid* (I, 9–11). Parnassus, as Lucan tells us (*Phars.*, III, 173), has two peaks, one of which Dante assigns to Apollo, the other to the Muses. The invocation fills verses 13–36 of the canto, the preceding twelve lines being devoted to a proem; the proem and the invocation together, according to the Letter to Can Grande (Epistola XIII, xviii), form the prologue to the *Paradiso*.

For a discussion of St. Paul's rapture and the meaning of his "third heaven" (2 Cor. xii, 2), see St. Thomas, *Summa Theologiae*, Secunda Secundae, Qu. clxxv, Art. 3. According to the second sense of the vision, he declares it appropriate "ut primum caelum dicatur cognitio caelestium corporum; secundum, cognitio caelestium spirituum; tertium, cognitio ipsius Dei." (That the first heaven be called the knowledge of heavenly bodies, the second the knowledge of heavenly spirits, the third the knowledge of God himself.) Parnassus has two tops also in Lucian's *Charon* or *The Spectators*.

6. Cf. the Letter to Can Grande (Ep. XIII, xxviii); also Richard of St. Victor, *De Contemplatione*, IV, xxiii.

15. Daphne, loved and pursued by Apollo, was changed to a laurel. Cf. *Met.*, I, 452–567; especially 557–565.

18. 'Arena': the remaining *cantica* of the poem.

20. The satyr Marsyas, having challenged Apollo to a musical contest, was defeated and then flayed by him: *Met.*, VI, 382–400.

25. The 'beloved tree' is the laurel: cf. l. 15.

32. The 'joyous Delphic deity' is Apollo, whose most famous temple was at Delphi, below Mt. Parnassus.

33. The 'Peneian leaf' is the laurel: Daphne was the daughter of the river god Penēus.

36. 'Prayer will be made that Cyrrha may respond': i.e., poets will pray for Apollo's aid. Cyrrha was the seaport of Delphi.

37–44. In these lines Dante describes the season.   On every day of the year the sun rises from a particular point in the horizon, and this point differs from day to day.   The points are called *foci*, 'outlets.'   The best 'outlet' is the one from which the sun emerges on March 21, the vernal equinox.   This is the *foce* that 'brings together four circles with three crosses': it is the point where three great heavenly circles intersect the horizon, each of them forming a cross with it.   The circles are the equator, the ecliptic, and the colure of the equinoxes; this last is a great circle that traverses the two heavenly poles and crosses the ecliptic at Aries and Libra.   When the sun rises from this point, it is 'coupled with its best orbit, and with its best constellation,' namely Aries.   In that sign, the sun has the most benign influence on the earth. Now on the day when Dante rose to heaven, the sun had passed 'almost' through that *foce*: it was considerably later than March 21 (it was, in fact, Wednesday, April 13, 1300), but the sun was still in Aries; 'almost this outlet,' then, 'had made morning yonder (in Eden) and evening here (in the Hemisphere of Land).'

44–45. Here Dante tells the hour.   It was noon in Eden, midnight in Jerusalem: the Hemisphere of Water was all light, the Hemisphere of Land all dark.

62. Without knowing it, Dante has left the earth and is speeding heavenward.

64. The 'eternal wheels' are the revolving heavens.

66. It is by gazing on Beatrice, or Revelation, that Dante is 'transhumanized.'

68. The fisherman Glaucus, tasting of a certain herb that had revived his fishes, became a sea god: *Met.*, XIII, 898–968.

70. 'Transhumanizing,' rising above the human state, as Glaucus did.

71. 'The example' is that of Glaucus.

72. The experience of sanctification.

74. Dante is not sure whether he took his body with him to Heaven, or left it behind.   St. Paul expresses the same doubt with regard to his own experience, 2 Cor. xii, 2–4: " ... And I knew such a man (whether in the body, or out of the body, I cannot tell; God knoweth;) How that he was caught up into paradise, and heard unspeakable words, which it is not lawful for a man to utter."   St. Augustine (*De Genesi ad Litteram*, XII, iii–vi) and St. Thomas discuss the question, but leave it undecided.   The poet considers his rapture as similar in kind to St. Paul's, and therefore repeats St. Paul's words.   In the following narrative Dante seems to think of himself as still in the flesh, although he ultimately sees God.   Whether St. Paul actually beheld God or not is a matter on which theologians have disagreed, St. Augustine and St. Thomas holding the affirmative opinion.   Cf. Exod. xxxiii, 20: "Thou canst not see my face: for no man shall see me, and live."

77. The swift motion of the Primum Mobile, the outermost sphere of the material universe, is due to the eagerness of every one of its parts to come into contact with every part of God's own Heaven, the Empyrean; and the Primum Mobile imparts its revolution to all the heavens within it.

78. 'The harmony which thou dost attune and modulate' is the harmony of the spheres, imagined by Pythagoras, derided by Aristotle, and described by Cicero in the *Somnium Scipionis* (*De Re Publica*, VI, xvii).

79–81. As Dante approaches the sun, its fiery disk grows bigger and bigger. Cf. l. 61.

92–93. When lightning descends, it leaves its proper abode, the sphere of fire.   Dante's real home is the Empyrean, toward which he is returning more swiftly than lightning ever fell from the sky.

106. The 'exalted creatures' are angels and men, who have intelligence.

111. Their source, to which some are ordained to be nearer than others, is God.

118. The bow of instinct impels not only things which are devoid of intelligence but also angels and men, who possess love and understanding.

122. The Empyrean, within which the swift Primum Mobile revolves.

124. Thither the power of the bowstring of instinct is carrying us on.

127-129. Often the character (*forma*) of the product does not equal the intention of the artisan, because matter — the material with which the artisan (God) must work — is unresponsive.

132. Only a creature that possesses free will has 'power to incline in another direction.'

134-135. 'So the primal impulse (instinct), diverted by deceptive pleasure, brings it (the creature) down to earth.'

Canto II

Argument

In the *Paradiso* our author is now to expound to us not only the structure of the universe but also the fundamental truths of Christianity, a theme never before attempted in a poem. Setting sail on this untried sea — with wisdom (Minerva) for his favoring wind, Inspiration (Apollo) for his helmsman, and the nine muses for pilots — he warns his followers to turn back, save only those who have from early years accustomed themselves to feed upon sacred knowledge, "the bread of the angels." "Man," says Ps. lxxviii (Vulg. lxxvii), 25, "did eat angels' food (*panem angelorum*)." Even here on earth, then, one may eat of it, but one is never satisfied: cf. *Purg.* XXXI, 129; also Ecclus. xxiv, 29.

As he pictures himself rising with Beatrice to the sphere of the moon, the poet takes advantage of the occasion to explain — through the lips of his guide — the function of Nature, the power to which all the activities of the material universe are due. By Nature Dante means the operation of the heavenly bodies, directed by celestial Intelligences, or angels, which are the ministers of God. The world of matter, therefore, exactly corresponds to the world of spirit, and is its visible image. From the Maker, in his Empyrean abode, descends a vital principle, which is received by the 9th sphere, or Primum Mobile, the outermost of the revolving heavens. This sphere, which contains no stars, is alike in all its parts; and for that reason it does not analyze the force bestowed upon it, but imparts it, translated into material energy, to the heavens within its circuit. The 8th sphere — that of the fixed stars — by means of these bodies differentiates, in accordance with the needs of the world, the single but potentially multiform power that comes from the Primum Mobile: cf. *Quaestio de Aqua et Terra*, XXI, 70-71. This diversified power then sifts downward to the earth, passing through the other spheres, each of which combines with those energies which are akin to its own essence, and transmits them still further modified. The brightness of the heavenly bodies is due ultimately to this same power, derived from God, whose gladness is the source of all light.   The various stars, according to their nature, combine to a greater or less degree with this energizing and light-giving principle; and that is why one star differs from another in glory.   So it is with the moon.   Some parts of this orb are less sensitive than others to the illumining energy and hence, when seen from below, appear as spots on the lunar surface. Looked at from above, the moon has no such marks: *Par.* XXII, 139–141 (*Bull.*, VII, 385).   To the dwellers on earth the spots are the "man in the moon," whom ignorant people called Cain.   He was represented as carrying a bundle of thorns for his offering: cf. *Inf.* XX, 126.

Averroës and Albertus Magnus believed the moon spots to be the results of the presence, in some regions of the moon, of rarer matter, which was unfit to reflect the sun's light; and they attributed this opinion to Aristotle (Toynbee, 78–79).   The same view is expressed by Dante in *Conv.*, II, xiii, 9.   By the time he wrote the *Paradiso*, however, he had evidently become dissatisfied with such a material explanation and had worked out a more spiritual one, which applies to the stars as well as to the moon.   The refutation of his former theory is conducted, in scholastic style, by Beatrice, some of whose arguments may be found in Albertus Magnus, *De Caelo et Mundo*, Lib. II, Tr. ii and iii (Toynbee, 82).

In the first place, we must assume that the obscurity of some parts of the moon is due to the same cause as the comparative dimness of some of the stars.   The question then is, whether this difference in brightness is caused by a difference in density, or quantity of matter, or by a difference in quality.   Now we know that each of the several heavenly bodies and groups of stars has a special influence on the earth.   If the stars differed only in the density of their matter, the quality being the same, the effect of all would be the same in kind, and would differ only in degree.   Different influences must be the result of different fundamental principles; and these principles, if Dante's earlier view were correct, would be reduced to one.   Therefore the celestial bodies — and, by inference, the various parts of the moon — must differ in kind.

As far as the moon is concerned, there is another argument, a purely physical one.   Supposing the moon contained streaks of rarer matter, these layers would either extend through the moon, from side to side, or not.   If they did, we should see the sun shining through them at the time of a solar eclipse, when the moon is between the sun and the earth.   If they did not, there must be dense matter behind the rare; and in that case this dense matter would reflect the light, just as if it were on the surface.   But — it may be objected — the light reflected from farther back would be fainter than that reflected from the outside, and the fainter reflections would appear as spots.   To be convinced that this is not true, says Beatrice, try an experiment.   Aristotle has declared that experiment is the source of science (*Metaphysics*, I, i).   Place three mirrors upright at a distance from you, one a little farther back than the other two.   Somewhere behind you put a light in such a position that it will shine into the glasses and be reflected by them.   You will see that the reflection in the three mirrors is equally bright, although its image in the more remote one is of somewhat smaller dimensions.   If, as seems likely, Dante had actually performed this experiment, he must have done so under such conditions that, to the eye, his conclusion was shown to be correct.

9. The constellations of the Great and Little Bear, by which sailors are guided.

16. The bold Argonauts, who crossed to Colchis in quest of the golden fleece, were amazed to see Jason, their leader, compel two monstrous, fire-breathing bulls to draw a plow: *Met.*, VII, 104–122.

21. Our 'inborn and eternal thirst' for Heaven, 'was sweeping us on almost as swift as you see the sky' — a curious comparison, since we are ordinarily not conscious of the sky's motion. If, however, we follow the position of a heavenly body from hour to hour, we discover that in a very brief period it traverses an immense distance.   The sky, without seeming to move at all, is really traveling with inconceivable velocity; and so we were doing.   See also *Met.*, II, 70.

23–24. 'And perhaps in as much time as that in which a bolt (from a crossbow) stops and flies and quits the notch': the three incidents in the flight of the arrow are arranged in inverse order, to indicate that, to the eye, they are simultaneous.   The same device is used in XXII, 109.

35. A ray of light can penetrate water without displacing its particles.   Cf. IX, 114.

38. 'How one bulk brooked another': how one solid body could, without displacement, be penetrated by another.   It is possible for this, according to St. Thomas (*Summa Theologiae*, Tertia, Suppl., Qu. lxxxiii, Art. 3), to be brought about by a miracle.   See also St. Thomas, *De Veritate Catholicae Fidei contra Gentiles*, IV, lxxxvii.

41. In the 'essence' of Christ the human and the divine nature are miraculously united. The thought of my body and the matter of the moon occupying simultaneously the same space should make us eager to rise to Heaven and behold, in the person of Christ, the greatest miracle of the kind — a miracle which we accept on faith, without being able to understand it. In Heaven it will be as clear and natural as a 'primal truth,' or axiom.

51. 'People' (*altrui*) 'down on earth' called the dark spots Cain.

56. It is no wonder that men go astray in the interpretation of spiritual things, when they cannot even explain physical phenomena.

64. The 'eighth sphere' is that of the fixed stars.

67. 'If rarity and density alone produced this': i.e., this difference in apparent kind and size.

72. These principles, 'according to thine argument, would be obliterated.'   There would be one and the same nature in all the stars, and they would all have the same influence.

77. The body of an animal 'divides fat and lean' in layers which do not extend all the way through.

78. The moon 'would change pages in its volume.'   When a book is opened in the middle, and lies flat, the pages on each side extend only halfway through the volume.   Each set of pages comes to an end in the middle of the book.

89. 'Just as color comes back through glass' that is backed with lead, i.e., is reflected from a mirror, the glass corresponding to the rare matter, the leaden back to the dense.

112–114. The 'body' which revolves inside the Empyrean (the 'Heaven of divine peace,' which lies without the confines of the material universe) is the Primum Mobile, 'in whose power is the existence of all that it contains.'   All the rest of the material world derives its special mode of being from the outermost revolving sphere.

115. 'The next heaven' is the starry sphere.

129. The 'blessed motors' are the angels.

130. The sphere of the fixed stars.

131. The 'deep mind' is that of the heavenly Intelligences which preside over this 8th sphere: namely, the Cherubim, who are the repositories of divine wisdom.

138. The heavenly Intelligence is one and indivisible, self-contained, unerring and constant in its operation. Circular revolution would symbolize perfect and unending intellectual activity. Cf. *Purg.* XXV, 75. See also *Par.* XIII, 55–60.

139–140. Each 'different power' from on high 'makes a different alloy' with the 'precious' or incorruptible heavenly 'body which it quickens.'

145. The *virtù mista*, or fusion of the heavenly bodies, to different degrees and in different modes, with the power from above.

Canto III

Argument

"In my Father's house are many mansions" (John xiv, 2). By "mansions" are meant degrees of happiness: so says St. Thomas in the *Summa Theologiae*, Tertia, Suppl., Qu. xciii, Art. 2, 3; see also his Commentary on John xiv, and St. Augustine's Treatise on John, lxvii. Every soul in Heaven receives all the gladness of which it is capable, but the capacity differs. God, on creating each soul, endows it — according to his mysterious grace — with a certain degree of keenness of spiritual sight, upon which (if the soul attains Heaven) depends its vision of God, and upon the clearness of this vision depends the soul's love and joy. This is the doctrine of St. Thomas, which Dante upholds. According to a rival school, the fundamental gift of grace is love, on which vision depends. Every soul is contented with its kind of beatitude, because it knows that its condition was predestined by its Maker, and because it feels that its own state of happiness is the only one for which it is fit.

The real abode of the blessed is the Empyrean, the realm of pure spirit, outside the confines of the world of matter; there they dwell with God and the angels. But in order to make evident to Dante the difference in their degrees, and to illustrate the correspondence of the material universe to the world of spirit, the souls first reveal themselves to him in the spheres that symbolize their state. In his Commentary on Aristotle's *De Caelo et Mundo*, II, x–xviii, St. Thomas informs us that while the Primum Mobile has only one motion, eternal and immutable, the other spheres have two or more and therefore generate change; but they approach uniformity as they approach the Primum Mobile in position, the moon, which is the most distant from it, being the most variable. So it is fitting that the angels should be seen in the Primum Mobile, the Apostles in the next (or 8th) heaven, and the inconstant in the sphere of the moon.

In the heaven of Venus, and in all above it, the spirits appear merely as bright lights: the happiness that envelops them conceals their individual forms. In the sphere of Mercury, just below Venus, the poet has a glimpse of the soul within the light.   In the lowest heaven, that of the Moon, the spirits are discerned as faint translucent images of human shapes, like the reflections we sometimes catch in windowpanes or in shallow water, when there is no dark background to make the figure clear.   They are as difficult to see as a pearl against a white forehead.   These are the ghosts of nuns who were compelled to break their vows.   Among them he finds one for whom he had previously inquired (*Purg.* XXIV, 10), Piccarda Donati, a kinswoman of his wife and the sister of his old friend Forese (*Purg.* XXIII).   We may suppose that all weak and inconstant persons who win salvation at all are to be connected with this sphere, the nuns being chosen as extreme examples.

Piccarda was betrothed to a certain Rossellino della Tosa.   To avoid marriage, she entered, under the name of Costanza, the convent of the Suore Clarisse di Monticelli.   This sanctuary was invaded by her brother Corso and his followers, who dragged her forth and compelled her to wed.   According to one legend, she was blessed with a sickness which preserved her virginity until her death.

Dante leaves us in doubt whether, in the literal sense of his narrative, the souls actually leave their seats in the Empyrean and come to meet him, or merely project their images into the several spheres.   In the 8th heaven all the elect are seen by him, even those who have previously appeared below.   The idea that the blessed can change their places, without losing sight of God and thus interrupting their beatitude, is in no wise contrary to Christian doctrine.   St. Thomas tells us as much in his *Summa Theologiae*, Tertia, Suppl., Qu. lxix, Art. 3, and Qu. lxxxiv, Art. 1 and 2; also in *De Veritate Catholicae Fidei contra Gentiles*, IV, lxxxvi, where he discusses the active life of the spirits in Heaven.   For their existence does not wholly consist of passive receptivity; they have the power of locomotion, they take interest in one another and (without diminution of their everlasting joy) in the world beneath.   Their active and their quiet being may be symbolized by the physical heavens and the Empyrean.   The "essential reward" of the just is the vision of God, which never changes; their "accidental reward" is the enjoyment of good done by themselves or others, and this may vary. "Accidentally," then, their gladness is increased by the salvation of a fellow creature, and their love goes forth to him, as does that of the angels.   "There is joy in the presence of the angels of God over one sinner that repenteth."   In the *Convivio*, IV, xxviii, 5, Dante pictures the blessed coming to meet a new companion; and the same figure recurs in *Paradiso* XXI, 64–66.

In this sphere, as in most of the others, our author places sovereign and subject side by side.   With the simple nun Piccarda is the great Empress Constance. A similar contrast is to be found in the heavens of Mercury, Venus, the sun, Mars, and Jupiter.   In Saturn, where only monks appear, both hermit and cenobite are seen. And in the sun a grammarian, Donatus, accompanies the great theologians. It is curious, too, that only the planets with feminine names — Luna and Venus — show the spirits of women.

In *Summa Theologiae*, Prima, Qu. lxii, Art. 2, St. Thomas explains that the kind of beatitude of each soul depends on the nature of its vision of God, which is an effect of predestination. In *Summa Theologiae*, Prima, Qu. lxxxix, Art. 8, and Qu. cxvii, Art. 4, also Tertia, Suppl., Qu. lxix, Art. 1, he tells how souls may miraculously assume a body and appear to the living; cf. *Purg.* II, Argument. The question whether souls have a body before the Resurrection is discussed by St. Augustine in *De Genesi ad Litteram*, XII, xxxii–xxxiii.

1. The 'sun' is Beatrice, the symbol of Revelation.
18. Narcissus, who took his reflection in the fountain for a real form, whereas I took these real beings for reflections. Cf. *Met.*, III, 407–510.
32. The 'true light' is the visible God.
51. The sphere of the moon, being nearest to the center, turns slowest in the diurnal revolution of the heavens. This comparative sluggishness of motion symbolizes a relatively low degree of love and of beatitude.
53. The Holy Ghost is divine love.
66. 'In order to see more and make yourselves more intimate' with God. The souls that are spiritually nearest to God are endowed with the keenest intellectual vision; they therefore see God clearest and love him most.
82–87. Cf. Francis Thompson, *Epilogue to the Hound of Heaven*:

> Heaven, which man's generations draws,
> Nor deviates into replicas,
> Must of as deep diversity
> In judgment as creation be.

87. All that God's will creates by its own act, and all that is produced by Nature.
96. 'In which she did not draw the shuttle to the end': which she left uncompleted.
97–98. The lady is St. Clare, the friend of St. Francis; in 1212 she founded the order that bears her name.
106. The 'men more used to evil than to good' were her brother Corso Donati and his followers, who compelled her to marry.
117. 'She never was stripped of the veil of the heart': she remained at heart a nun.
118. Constance, the daughter and heiress of Roger II, in 1186 married Henry, son of Frederick I of Swabia, and brought him as a dowry the kingdom of Sicily. According to an unfounded tradition, she was taken from a nunnery and married against her will.
119. The Swabian Emperors are called 'blasts' because of the violence and the brief duration of their activity. Frederick I (Barbarossa) was the first; the 'second wind' was Constance's husband, Henry VI; the third and last was her son, Frederick II.

Canto IV

Argument

Plato sets forth in his *Timaeus* the idea that human souls were all created at once at the beginning of the world, each one being lodged in an appropriate star to await the birth of the body which it shall inhabit; and that after death the souls of those who have made a good use of earthly life shall go back to their stars again. Cicero's adaptation, the *Timaeus* (chap. xii), may have been Dante's source of information about the doctrine in question. Plato's theory appealed strongly to some of the early Christian theologians, but had to be abandoned after 540, when the Council of Constantinople decided that every soul is created by God at the birth of its body.

The real home of the elect, then, is not in the stars, nor anywhere in the material heavens, but in the Empyrean. Only to afford a visible image to Dante's understanding do they project their forms into the several spheres, illustrating at the same time the influence of Nature on human beings. In the lowest heaven, that of the inconstant moon, appear to him the souls least endowed with intellectual vision and therefore least capable of love and happiness in the realm of light. These, as we have seen, are the spirits of nuns who, under constraint, broke their vows and married. The compulsion does not justify their act, because no outside power can force the will. If these women returned to secular life and remained in it, they did so because they regarded such a course as better than death, ill treatment, or whatever the alternative might have been. Their "absolute will" still chose the veil: that is, the convent, in itself, was always more attractive to them than any other place. Their "conditioned will," on the other hand — namely, their preference as shaped by given circumstances — inclined them to the easier way.

For St. Thomas's views on violence, see *Summa Theologiae*, Prima Secundae, Qu. vi, Art. 4 and 5. For his references to absolute and conditioned will, see the note at the end of the Argument to *Purg.* XXI.

3. The familiar paradox later known as the Ass of Buridan, or the donkey and the two bales of hay, is here applied to Dante, who is eager to ask two questions and cannot decide which to put first. See Aristotle, *De Caelo*, II, xiii; St. Thomas, *Summa Theologiae*, Prima Secundae, Qu. xiii, Art. 6. Cf. *Met.*, V, 164–166.

13. Beatrice divined Dante's thought, just as Daniel, inspired by God, revealed the forgotten dream of Nebuchadnezzar (Daniel ii), saving the impotent astrologers from the senseless anger of the king (ii, 13).

24. This doctrine, expounded by Plato in the *Timaeus*, is contrary to Christian faith. Cf. *Summa Theologiae*, Tertia, Suppl., Qu. xcvii, Art. 5.

34. The '1st circle' is the Empyrean, which envelops the spherical universe of matter.

36. 'Because they are more or less susceptible to the eternal breath' of love.

48. Raphael, who cured the blindness of Tobit (Vulg. *Tobias*): Tobit xi.

51. 'Because he (Plato's Timaeus) seems to understand it as he expresses it': i.e., literally not allegorically.

58–60. 'If he means that the credit or the blame for influence (on human souls) reverts to these (heavenly) revolutions, perhaps the bow (of his speech) hits some truth.' Dante is evidently reluctant to impute fundamental error to such a philosopher as Plato.

61. 'This principle' of stellar influence.

63. 'It (the world) went astray' in attributing the stellar power to heathen gods and in naming the planets after them. Cf. VIII, 1–3, 10–11.

67–69. If man had not faith in the perfection of divine justice, he would not be troubled by apparent deviation from it.

73–75. Beatrice begins by establishing a definition of violence. If this definition is correct (as it surely is), the souls in question cannot invoke violence as a sufficient excuse.

83. St. Lawrence was a Christian martyr of the 3rd century.

84. Mucius Scaevola burned off his own right hand, with which he had failed to kill Porsena, the enemy of Rome.

91. The 'pass' that meets Dante's eyes is another problem through which he must make his way.

96. God, the source of truth.

103–105. Alcmaeon, to avenge his father, Amphiaräus (*Inf.* XX, 31–36), killed his mother, Eriphȳle (*Purg.* XII, 49–51), who had betrayed her husband's hiding place: *Met.*, IX, 407–408. Thus, 'not to be lacking in duty, he became undutiful.' Cf. "impietate pia" (pious in impiety) in *Met.*, VIII, 477.

109–111. Cf. Aristotle, *Ethics*, III, i; St. Thomas, *Summa Theologiae*, Prima Secundae, Qu. vi, Art. 6, and Tertia, Suppl., Qu. xlvii, Art. 1–3.

122. 'Grace (= thanks) for grace (= favor).' Cf. *Aen.*, I, 600–601.

126. The mind is satisfied only with that truth which contains within itself every other truth.

129. Cf. *Summa Theologiae*, Prima, Qu. xii, Art. 1: "Si igitur intellectus rationalis creaturae pertingere non possit ad primam causam rerum, remanebit inane desiderium naturae." (But if the intellect of the rational creature could not reach so far as the first cause of things, the natural desire would remain void.)

136–137. The question of 'making amends for unfulfilled vows with other goods' is discussed by St. Thomas in the *Summa Theologiae*, Secunda Secundae, Qu. lxxxviii, Art. 10–12. — *Vi* (*sodisfarvi*), 'you,' Heavenly powers.

Canto V

Argument

Once more we are reminded that happiness depends on love, which in turn depends on perfection of spiritual sight. Inasmuch as happiness manifests itself by light, the brightness of a soul grows with any increase of joy. Justinian, when he has an opportunity to add to Dante's knowledge, appears more shining; and Beatrice becomes more splendid when she perceives that Dante is already illumined by divine truth. 'Justinian's narrative falls in the next canto, but Beatrice's answer to a question put by her pupil is the main theme of Canto V.

Can one offer, for broken vows, reparation sufficient to win salvation? This is the problem suggested to Dante by the sight of the souls in the moon.   It was discussed by St. Thomas in the *Summa Theologiae*, Secunda Secundae, lxxxviii, Art. 10–12.   In the first place, it must be understood that a vow is a covenant between God and man, and must be accepted by both parties.   A bad promise is not received by God.   Men must be cautious in their pledges, for they may sin in keeping a foolish or wicked pact that has not been sanctioned by the Lord. Thus Agamemnon erred when he sacrificed his daughter to obtain from the gods a favorable wind to carry him and his army to Troy.   Equally mistaken was Jephthah (Judges xi, 30–40), who, having sworn, in return for victory, to offer up whatever first came to meet him on his return, made a victim of his only child.

There are two elements in a good vow: the promise itself and the thing promised.   The first can never be set aside, even by the highest earthly authority; it is an offering of the free will, accepted by God.   If we have once entered into such an agreement, we are bound to fulfill our obligation.   But may we not alter the terms of it, substituting another sacrifice for the one specified?   In other words, is not the second element — the thing promised — subject to change?   In Leviticus xxvii sundry privileges of this kind are accorded the Hebrews.   In the Christian Church, we are told, the thing originally pledged may sometimes be replaced, but only by something manifestly more valuable, and only with the approval of a properly authorized member of the clergy.

If, however, the thing promised is more precious than any other possession of the promiser, no exchange is possible. It follows that when we have vowed abdication of the will, there can be no release.   For the free will is the best of God's gifts to man, the one most in conformity with divine goodness.   Dante says, in *Mon.*, I, xii, 6: "hec libertas sive principium hoc totius libertatis nostre, est maximum donum humane nature a Deo collatum: quia per ipsum hic felicitamur ut homines, per ipsum alibi felicitamur ut dii."   (This freedom, [or this principle of all our freedom], is the greatest gift conferred by God on human nature; for through it we have our felicity here as men, through it we have our felicity elsewhere as deities.)

5. For the perfection of the beatific vision, see *Summa Theologiae*, Tertia, Suppl., Qu. xcv, Art. 5.

11. Unworthy things mislead the love of you mortals (*vostro amor*), not because they are evil, but because they have in them some 'trace' of the 'eternal light.'   *Mon.*, I, viii, 2: "cum totum universum nichil aliud sit quam vestigium quoddam divine bonitatis."   (The whole universe is nought else than a certain footprint of the divine excellence.)   Cf. *Summa Theologiae*, Prima, Qu. xciii, Art. 1–4.

29–30. 'This treasure' — free will — 'precious as I describe it, becomes the offering, and it does so by its own act,' i.e., by an act of the will itself.

32–33. If thou thinkest to make amends by putting to a good use that which thou hast promised and then withdrawn, thou art like a thief who is trying to do good deeds with ill-gotten gain.   Cf. *Inf.* XI, 36.

44–45. 'The thing of which the sacrifice is made' is the thing promised; 'the other' element in a vow 'is the act of agreement.'

50. The *offerere* (= *offrire*; cf. XIII, 140) is the act of offering, the *offerta* is the thing offered.

52. The other element, which has been described to thee as the subject matter of the vow: l. 44.

55. The 'burden' is the substance of the vow.

57. Cf. *Purg.* IX, 117–126. The 'turn' of the 'white key' of discrimination and the 'yellow key' of authority signifies ecclesiastical permission.

59–60. 'If the thing put aside is not contained, as easily as four in six, in the thing assumed.' Probably no exact proportion is intended, merely a manifest superiority of the new obligation to the old. It follows (ll. 61–63) that if the old is the most precious of our possessions, nothing can be substituted for it. That is the case when, on entering a religious order, we promise entire abdication of the free will.

66. 'First gift': because Jephthah vowed (according to the Vulgate) to offer up to the Lord the *first* person that should come to meet him after his victory: Judges xi, 31.

67–68. Cf. *Summa Theologiae*, Secunda Secundae, Qu. lxxxviii, Art. 2, where St. Thomas quotes St. Jerome as saying of Jephthah: "In vovendo fuit stultus, et in reddendo impius." (In vowing he was foolish, and in keeping his vow he was wicked.)

70. To Agamemnon's sacrifice of his daughter Iphigenia reference is made by Virgil in *Aen.*, II, 116; by Ovid in *Met.*, XII, 24–38. Her bewailing her fair face (which made her an acceptable offering) is a trait transferred probably by Dante from the story of Jephthah's daughter, who, before her death, "bewailed her virginity upon the mountains": Judges xi, 38.

72. *Cólto* = *culto*, 'act of worship.'

77. The Pope alone has power to absolve from the greater vows.

80. Cf. Ephesians iv, 12: "That we henceforth be no more children, tossed to and fro, and carried about with every wind of doctrine."

81. Cf. Epistola VIII, iii, 33–36: "Impietatis fautores, Judaei, Saraceni, et gentes sabbata nostra rident, et, ut fertur, conclamant: 'Ubi est Deus eorum?'" (The champions of impiety, Jews, Saracens, and Gentiles, scoff at our sabbaths; and, as it is written, cry out "where is their God?")

87. The Empyrean.

93. The heaven of Mercury, which symbolizes the degree of beatitude enjoyed by the souls of the ambitious.

107. Here, for the last time in the material universe, Dante sees the souls themselves; after this they are concealed by the light that emanates from them.

109. 'That which begins here' is the description of this heaven.

Canto VI

Argument

The "little star" of Mercury is "adorned with good spirits" whose activity was due rather to a craving for earthly honor and fame than to direct love of God. When human desires rise toward celestial things by such a devious course — that is, by fondness for worldly glory — it follows that "the rays of true affection mount heavenward less quick," for the degree of spiritual vision and zeal possessed by such souls is not of the highest. Their reward in happiness is proportionate to their innate merit; but they yearn for nothing greater, the exact correspondence between desert and wage being an endless source of joy to them.   The vast harmony of Heaven must be composed of various kinds of beatitude.

Among these spirits is a certain Romeo of Villeneuve, minister of Count Raymond Berenguier of Provence in the first half of the 13th century.   Romeo served his master ably, and helped to bring about the marriage of the count's youngest daughter, Beatrice, to Charles of Anjou.   The three elder daughters were also united to royal personages: Margaret to Louis IX of France; Eleanor to Henry III of England; Sancha to Henry's brother Richard, Earl of Cornwall, elected King of the Romans.   These alliances likewise were later ascribed to Romeo's diplomacy.   According to a legend followed by Dante, but not recorded before him, Romeo came to Raymond's court as a poor pilgrim, won his confidence, and increased his wealth and influence; then, being unjustly accused by jealous Provençal nobles, asked for his mule, his staff, and his scrip, and departed, never to be seen again.   The character of pilgrim attributed to him may have been suggested by his name: see *Vita Nuova*, XL, 6-7.   G. Villani, in his *Croniche*, VI, xc, tells the story in a fashion similar to our poet's.   The final touch — the mortification of the outcast "begging his livelihood crust by crust" — is evidently drawn from Dante's own bitter experience, pictured in the *Convivio*, I, iii, 4-5.   This part of Romeo's life, the most worthy, was hidden from the world, which knew and applauded his successful ambition.

This same celestial "pearl," Mercury, contains the soul of Justinian, Emperor of the East in the 6th century, under whose direction was achieved the great compilation of Roman law known as the Justinian Code.   In his day Byzantium was torn with religious strife; and, according to some, the Emperor himself, until converted to the true faith by Pope Agapētus I, shared in the Eutychian heresy to which his wife, Theodora, adhered.   Brunetto Latini tells this story in the *Trésor*, where the Pope is called "Agapit."   Euty̆ches, who lived in the century before, had taught that after the incarnation there was only one nature in Christ — the divine.

Justinian, who speaks throughout this canto, proceeds to unfold the marvelous course of Roman history in the form of a narrative of the vicissitudes of the Roman Eagle.   This emblematic bird, having followed Aeneas from East to West — from Troy to Italy — and having dwelt in Latium until the 4th century, was carried by Constantine, contrary to the revolution of the heavens, from West to East — from Rome to Byzantium — when the Eastern Empire was founded.   There it remained, on the edge of Europe, near the mountains of its native Troad, until it came into the keeping of Justinian, some 200 years after its transfer to the Orient.   Dante probably followed the chronology of Brunetto Latini, who put the conversion of Constantine in 333 and the accession of Justinian in 539 (Tor., 685), the correct date being 527.   The exploits of the Eagle, symbol of Roman sovereignty, from the time of Aeneas down, make it a sacred object, worthy of reverence by friend and foe — by the Ghibelline who wrongfully attempts to make it an emblem of his party alone, by the Guelf who would substitute for this "public ensign" the golden lilies of the House of France. The poet derives his incidents mainly from Virgil, Livy, Paulus Orosius, and Lucan. We find a similar outline of Roman history in the *Convivio*, IV, iv and v (cf. *Mon.*, II, iii–v). The culminating event in the chronicle of the Eagle is the crucifixion of Christ under Tiberius, the third Emperor — a "vengeance" for Adam's sin. This vengeance was in turn avenged by Titus, when he took Jerusalem. How a just punishment can itself be justly punished is a question that will demand an answer in the next canto.

3. 'The man of old who wedded Lavinia' is Aeneas, who brought the Eagle from Troy.

4. More than two hundred years, according to Dante's chronology, which is not quite exact.

7. Ps. xvii (Vulg. xvi), 8: "Hide me under the shadow of thy wings."

8. The Eagle, descending from Emperor to Emperor, 'there (in Byzantium) governed the world,' which was under the shadow of its wings.

10. Earthly titles have no place in Heaven.

13. The reformation and codification of law.

19–21. What he (and afterward I) accepted on faith, without being able to comprehend it, I can now see as a fact, as clearly as thou seest an axiomatic truth — for instance, that if a proposition is false, its opposite must be true (cf. *Mon.*, II, xi, 4). — Of the dual nature of Christ, Dante beheld a symbolic presentment in the Griffin: *Purg.* XXXI, 121–126.

25. I gave up warfare, entrusting my armies to my great general, Belisarius.

29. The reply has necessitated mention of the Roman Eagle.

35–36. It — the valor (*virtù*) of heroes — 'began from that hour when Pallas' — son of the Latin king Evander — 'died to give it (the *segno*) a kingdom.' Pallas, leading Latin troops to help Aeneas, was killed by Turnus (*Aen.*, X, 479–489); to avenge his death, Aeneas slew Turnus (*Aen.*, XII, 945–952), and gained possession of Latium.

37. Alba Longa was founded by Ascanius, son of Aeneas.

39. When the three Curiatii, who were the champions of Alba Longa, fought, for the Eagle's sake, against the three Horatii, the champions of Rome. After this contest, the Eagle dwelt in Rome.

40. 'From the time of the wrong': the rape of the Sabine women.

44. Brennus, leader of the Gauls; Pyrrhus, king of Epirus.

46. Titus Manlius Torquatus condemned his own son to death. — Quinctius, called Cincinnatus from his unkempt shock of hair (*cincinnus*, which is a synonym of *cirrus*), was called to the dictatorship from the plow.

47. The Decii and Fabii fought valiantly for Rome.

49. The 'Arabs' are the Carthaginians.

52. Scipio and Pompey won their first victories when they were mere boys.

54. The Eagle (*segno*) 'seemed bitter' to the hill of Fiesole, because the Romans destroyed that town and founded Florence below.

55. 'When the whole heaven strove' to bring the world to its own peaceful mood: all the heavens, in harmony, did their best to make the world equally harmonious.

59–60. 'The rivers Isère, Loire, and Seine beheld,' and all the tributaries of the Rhone.

62. After the Eagle, with Caesar, crossed the Rubicon, events came thick and fast.

65. *Durazzo*, 'Dyrrachium' in Illyria.

66. The consequences of Caesar's victory over Pompey at Pharsalia were felt in Egypt, where Pompey was murdered.

67. It was from the town of Antandros, near the river Simŏis, that the Eagle first set forth with Aeneas: *Aen.*, III, 5–6. When Caesar was pursuing Pompey, he stopped to visit the Troad: *Phars.*, IX, 961 ff.

69. 'And then shook itself, ill for Ptolemy,' who was deprived by Caesar of the kingdom of Egypt, and soon perished.

70. Juba, king of the Numidians, was an ally of Pompey.

71. Spain, where the followers of Pompey were defeated in the battle of Munda.

73. Augustus was the 'next keeper' of the Eagle.

74. Brutus and Cassius, defeated by the Eagle, 'bark' of its victory in Hell (*Inf.* XXXIV, 64–67).

75. Cf. *Phars.*, I, 41.   Mark Antony was beaten at Modena, his brother Lucius at Perugia.

77. After the final defeat of Mark Antony at Actium, Cleopatra, fleeing before the Eagle, killed herself with an asp (*colubro*).

79. The shore of the Red Sea.

81. The temple (*delubro*) of Janus, which was closed only in time of peace, was locked three times under Augustus, whereas it had been shut only twice during the whole period of the Republic.

86. 'If it (the *segno*) be contemplated in the hand of the third Caesar,' i.e., Tiberius, under whom Christ was crucified.

94–96. In 773 Pope Adrian I invoked the aid of Charlemagne against Desiderius, king of the Longobards or Lombards.   Charlemagne — who now, in Dante's mind, represented the Empire, although he was not crowned until 800 — came to the aid of the Church under the pinions of the Eagle.

98. Cf. ll. 31–33.

106. 'This younger Charles' is Charles II of Apulia, son of Charles of Anjou.

109–110. Charles is warned that the consequences of his folly may fall on his children.

111. God's ensign is the Eagle.

112. Justinian proceeds now to answer Dante's second question: V, 127–129.

142. The meaning is: 'Although it praise him much, it would praise him more.'

Canto VII

Argument

In his overflowing love, which is incompatible with envy, God created the universe, that there might be others to share his happiness. Some things he shaped by his own act, others by means of his agent, Nature, which consists of the celestial bodies, with their angelic directors. The heavens and the angels are his own handiwork, and so is every human soul. So, too, is brute matter, out of which the stars fashioned the elements and their compounds. All products of Nature are perishable, but whatever comes directly from the hand of God can never die. Inasmuch as he formed human flesh by his creation of Adam, it follows that the bodies of men, as well as their souls, are indestructible. If mankind, in the exercise of its free will, had remained faithful, soul and body would never have been parted; we should all have dwelt in the Garden of Eden until taken up to Paradise, in the flesh, on the Last Day. Death is the fruit of original sin; but that sin, thanks to Christ's vicarious atonement, is not an eternal heritage of man, and therefore the separation of body and soul is not everlasting. On the Judgment Day our flesh is to be resurrected.

Men and angels, the immediate products of God's creative act, possess three advantages over the works of Nature: in addition to immortality, they have free will and likeness to their Maker. By transgression our race forfeited the last two privileges, but not the first. The lost gifts might conceivably have been restored to sinful man either by outright forgiveness or in return for due amends. "All the paths of the Lord are *mercy* and *truth*," says Psalm xxv (Vulg. xxiv), 10 — "Universae viae Domini, *misericordia* et *veritas*"; and "truth" is interpreted as *justice*. Now any action is more perfect and more beautiful the more fully it represents all the good powers of the doer. Therefore God, who is perfect, chose to proceed by all his paths — in other words, to exercise both mercy and justice, pardoning humanity while exacting satisfaction. But man's presumption in defying the Lord's command was infinite, whereas his capacity for penance is but finite; hence he is incapable of any act of humility sufficient to atone for his first arrogance. And that is why God himself assumed human flesh, with all its burden of sin, and by his infinite self-abasement on the cross saved mankind from the consequences of its own proud disobedience.

1–3. 'Hail, holy God of hosts, doubly illumining with thy brightness the happy fires of these kingdoms.' The blessed souls — 'happy fires' of the heavens — are illumined first by their own intelligence and secondly by God's grace. — Of the three Hebrew words mixed with the Latin, *osanna* and *sabaòth* are used in the Bible, and *malacòth* (a mistake for *mamlacoth*) occurs in St. Jerome's preface to the Vulgate called *Prologus Galeatus*, where it is said to be equivalent to *regnorum*, 'of kingdoms.'

5. 'This substance' is Justinian. Angels and souls are often called substances because they exist independently of matter.

6. The 'double light' of natural intelligence and of illuminating grace 'is twofold' upon this spirit.

8. Cf. Wisdom iii, 7. — The souls, like swift sparks flying upward, return to the Empyrean.

14. *Be* is the name of the letter *b*, *ice* is the rest of the name *Bice*, the shortened form of *Beatrice*. Dante is filled with reverence at the thought of the mere earthly Beatrice, and the name by which she was called: how much more reverent must he be in the presence of the heavenly Beatrice, whose full name occurs two lines below! The usual Tuscan name of *b* is *bi*; *be*, however, is Aretine.

20. See VI, 88–92.

30. Christ. Cf. John i, 1.

36. Human nature was created pure and good, but by its own act became evil and forfeited Paradise.

39. Cf. John xiv, 6: "I am the way, the truth, and the life."

41. 'If it be measured by the nature assumed,' i.e., by the sinful nature of man, which Christ took.

48. Cf. Mat. xxvii, 51. — Earth quaked with horror and Heaven opened with joy.

60. 'Full-grown' in the flame of love. Only an infinitely loving mind can comprehend the boundless love which impelled God to sacrifice himself for man.

64–66. Divine Goodness, in its exuberant love, brings forth men and angels, just as a blazing fire sends out sparks.   Thus it 'reveals its eternal beauties,' by giving them a visible, objective form in the created world. — Cf. *Cons.*, III, Metr. ix, ll. 4–6 (Boethius is addressing the Creator):

> Quem non externae pepulerunt fingere causae
> Materiae fluitantis opus, verum insita summi
> Forma boni, livore carens.

(No external causes impelled You to make this work from chaotic matter.   Rather it was the form of the highest good, existing within You without envy.)   So *Timaeus*, 29, D, followed by Dionysius and St. Thomas: Gardner, 106–107.

72. To the power of the heavens, which are 'recent things' compared to their Maker.

79. Cf. *Summa Theologiae*, Secunda Secundae, Qu. lxiv, Art. 2, end.

85. Cf. Romans v, 12.

86. Adam.

103. Mercy and Justice.

106–107. *L'ovra ... da l'operante*, 'the workman's work.'

110. Both Mercy and Justice. Cf. l. 103.

120. Cf. Philippians, ii, 8: "and being found in fashion as a man, he humbled himself, and became obedient unto death, even the death of the cross."

130. The 'perfect country' is heaven.

135. The 'created power' is that of the stars.

136. The brute matter of which all these things consist was created directly by God.   The question whether elemental matter was coeternal with God or produced by him had been much discussed before it was authoritatively decided.   It had puzzled even Dante, as he tells us in *Conv.*, IV, i, 8.

139–141. The light and motion of the holy stars draw from a potential complex (of elemental matter) the soul of every brute and plant.

Canto VIII

Argument

The nearer we come to God, the more we appreciate the charm of his Revelation. Thus Beatrice grows in loveliness as she and Dante rise from sphere to sphere; and now a fresh increase of her beauty announces the arrival of the celestial travelers in the heaven of Venus.   The spheres that bear the various stars are transparent hollow globes of light matter, turning all together from east to west, and, in addition, possessing each an independent revolution in another direction and at a different speed.   Moreover, the heaven of Venus — like those of the Moon, Mercury, Mars, Jupiter, and Saturn — has, attached to itself, a little revolving sphere carrying the planet.   The circuit of this smaller ball is called an *epicycle*.   Mathematically, an epicycle is defined as a circle whose center is on the circumference of a greater one.   By means of this device (and others) the Ptolemaic astronomers explained the varying distances of each planet from the earth.   Every heavenly body, except the sun and the fixed stars, has three different revolutions: the general diurnal course, the periodic orbit of the individual sphere, and the accompanying turn of the epicycle. The sun and the fixed stars have the first two. In the heaven of Venus Dante and his guide find the third of the epicycles.

Here, as in the other spheres, they enter the planet itself, where the moving souls appear as lights flitting through the bright substance of the star, the rate of their speed being an indication of their joy and love, which depend on the distinctness of their eternal vision of God. They are perceived as sparks are seen shooting in a flame, or as, in song, a voice passing from note to note is distinguished from other voices holding one tone. Their apparent position in the universe is a symbol of the degree of beatitude enjoyed by those whose love was too much of the flesh. They are the best of the spirits whose excellence is marred by some taint of worldliness; it is therefore appropriate that their heaven should be the highest of those reached by the earth's conical shadow, as it is projected into space.

Among these souls is that of Charles Martel, son of Charles II of Apulia and grandson of Charles of Anjou, heir to the thrones of Naples, Provence, and Hungary, at the age of 24. In 1291 he married Clemence, daughter of Rudolph I. He died in 1295, and the Neapolitan succession was transferred to his brother Robert. His father lived until 1309. The contrast between Robert's niggardliness and his father's lavish expenditures suggests a discussion of heredity. Human dispositions are molded by the stars. God has embodied his providence in these agents — has made it a "power" in the skies. The stars (which constitute "Nature") do their work unerringly: a defect in them would imply a fault in their Maker. But in their operation they are cognizant of no distinction of parentage or rank. Hence, in choosing a vocation for a youth, we should consider, not his family, but the character he has received from Nature. If we do otherwise, we trouble the organism of society by putting its members into the wrong places.

In the spring of 1294 Charles Martel visited Florence with a brilliant retinue, and was received with unprecedented magnificence, as G. Villani relates in his *Croniche*, VIII, xiii. We may infer from the present canto that our poet then made his personal acquaintance. Indeed, we are justified in conjecturing that Charles, on this occasion, heard and applauded Dante's *canzone* (the first in the *Convivio*), *Voi che 'ntendendo il terzo ciel movete*, which was presumably the great literary novelty in Florence at the time of his visit; for he greets Dante in heaven with a reference to this poem. This episode affords, then, a clue to the date of composition of the *canzone* in question. When they met in Santa Maria Novella, Dante won the admiration of Charles by his perfect calligraphy, and was offered the post of *dictator pulcherrimus*. The powers invoked in the opening line of the lyric — those who by their intelligence move the 3rd heaven — are the Principalities, the angels who preside over the sphere of Venus; but when Dante wrote the lyric, he was under the impression that they were the Thrones.

Carlo Martello, the Guelf, of French origin, balances Manfred, the Ghibelline, of German stock, (*Purg.* III).

1. The belief that 'mad love' was sent down from a star by a goddess was a dangerous one.

2. *Ciprigna*, 'Cypriote': Venus, who was born near Cyprus and had a famous temple there.

7. *Dĭōne*, daughter of Oceanus and Thetis, was the mother of Venus.

8. According to Virgil (*Aen.*, I, 657–660, 715–722), Cupid, disguised as Aeneas's son Ascanius, sat on Dido's lap. The ancients foolishly ascribed Dido's 'mad love' to divine instigation.

23. When winds become ignited, they are 'visible' in the form of lightning or meteors: cf. *Purg.* V, 37–39.

26. 'Round,' dance.

27. In the Empyrean, in company with the Seraphim, the highest of the angels.

54. A silkworm.

57. I should have shown thee the fruit of my love.

58–60. Provence, which lies on the left of the Rhone below its confluence with the Sorgue, was the dowry of Beatrice, wife of Charles of Anjou, Charles Martel's grandfather.

61. *Ausonia*: a name for Italy used by the Latin poets. — *S'imborga*, 'is skirted': *borghi* means 'outskirts,' 'suburbs.' The towns of Bari, Gaeta, and Catona mark roughly the northeast, northwest, and southwest confines of the Kingdom of Naples, won by Charles of Anjou.

63. The rivers Tronto, on the east side, and Verde, on the west, separate the Kingdom of Naples from the Papal States at the north.

65. In virtue of a claim on his mother's side, Charles was crowned titular King of Hungary.

67–69. Trinacria is Sicily, conquered by Charles of Anjou. Between the southeasterly and northeasterly capes of Pachȳnus and Pelōrus lies the Bay of Calabria, exposed to the 'vexation' of Eurus, the east wind.

70. The darkness from Etna is not due, as Ovid sang (*Met.*, V, 346–356), to the struggles of the giant Typhoeus, buried under the whole island of Sicily, but is caused by the effect of the sun's heat on 'sulphur in formation.'

72. Sicily would now be awaiting a line of kings descended from Charles of Anjou and Rudolph of Hapsburg (respectively the grandfather and the father-in-law of Charles Martel), if the revolution of 1282, called the Sicilian Vespers, breaking out in Palermo with the cry "Death to the French!" had not driven Charles's people from the island and given the crown to Peter III of Aragon.

76. Charles Martel's brother Robert succeeded his father, Charles II, in 1309; he had been chosen for the succession before 1300. Robert, who had spent some years as a hostage for his father in Spain, is represented as having adopted the traditional miserliness of Catalonia.

82. The 'stingy' Robert descended from the 'lavish' Charles II. The latter, with all his faults, is said to have been liberal in his expenditures.

87. In God, the beginning and end of all good.

90. 'That thou discernest it by looking into God': that thou art one of the blest, who see all things in God.

98–99. The divine goodness 'makes its providence to be a power' in the revolving heavens.

120. *Maestro*: Aristotle, whose *Politics* Dante cites in *Conv.*, IV, iv, 5.

123. The 'roots' are the dispositions of men.

124–126. One is born a legislator, or Solon; another a general, or Xerxes; another a priest, or Melchisedech (Gen. xiv, 18); another a mechanic, or Daedălus (who lost his son Icărus while they were flying through the air: cf. *Inf.* XVII, 109–111).

127. The spheres, which stamp human character.

129. The individual who receives the stellar influence.

130–132. Esau and Jacob, though brothers, were radically different from the start: Gen. xxv, 21–27. Quirīnus, or Romulus, was the son of such a poor father that his paternity was ascribed to the god Mars.

138. 'I will have thee cloak thyself in a corollary.' The corollary is added to the demonstration, as a cloak to a suit of clothes. Cf. *Purg*, XXVIII, 136. See *Cons*., III, Pr. x: "veluti geometrae solent demonstratis propositis aliquid inferre, ... ita ego quoque tibi veluti corollarium dabo." (Then, I will give you a kind of corollary, just as the geometricians infer from their demonstrated propositions things ....)

147. King Robert was addicted to writing sermons.

Canto IX

Argument

There is no repining among the blessed. Each spirit is aware that the stellar influences which shaped its mortal life are directed by the same providence that determined its eternal capacity for happiness, so that there is an exact correspondence between earthly conduct and heavenly reward. All are so full of joy, of love for their Maker, of admiration for his work, and of eagerness to conform to his will, that there is no room for dissatisfaction.

Among those in whom love — the motive power of all good — was abundant, but was ill employed, we find Cunizza da Romano from the March of Treviso in northeastern Italy, the troubadour Foulques, or Folquet, from Marseilles, and the Biblical Rahab of Jericho.

Cunizza, youngest of the six sisters of the cruel tyrant Ezzelino da Romano, is said to have had three husbands and at least one lover. At the instigation of her brothers, she forsook her first spouse, Rizzardo di San Bonifazio, being aided in her escape by Sordello (*Purg*. VI), who was a minstrel at her court. In 1265, the year of Dante's birth, she was in Florence — an elderly lady — at the house of the Cavalcanti, and there granted freedom to her father's and brothers' slaves. She made her will in 1279, leaving her property to the sons of Alessandro da Mangona (*Inf*. XXXII, 55–60), who were related to her through her mother.

Folquet de Marselha, the son of a wealthy Genoese merchant, became a noted amatory poet in southern France, and addressed impassioned verse to the wives of two of his protectors — as well as to his first patron's sister, whom he used as a screen. He was imitated by several Italian rimesters, and is mentioned with praise in *Vulg. El*., II, vi, 6. Subsequently, repenting of his worldly life, he entered the Cistercian order, was made head of a rich abbey, became in 1205 Bishop of Toulouse, and later took a mercilessly active part in the suppression of the Albigensian heresy and the extermination of its adherents. Marvelous tales were told of his sanctity.   Much of his present bad reputation was acquired after Dante's time.

The story of Rahab is related in Joshua ii.   When Joshua was trying to take Jericho, he sent to the city two spies, who lodged in the house of a "harlot named Rahab."   Their presence becoming known to the enemy, their hostess saved them by sending the pursuers on a false clue, hiding her guests on the roof of the house, and, when the coast was clear, letting them "down by a cord through the window, for her house was upon the town wall."   In return, they promised safety for her and her relatives when Jericho should fall; as a token, she was to "bind" a "line of scarlet thread in the window."   Her service resulted in the victory of the Children of Israel; and when the city was cursed, Joshua proclaimed (vi, 17): "Only Rahab the harlot shall live, she and all that are with her in the house, because she hid the messengers that we sent."   Thus, too, she won salvation, and, according to Dante, was the first soul "assumed" by the heaven of Venus, when the Hebrew spirits were liberated from Limbus. "Likewise also was not Rahab the harlot justified by works," says James ii, 25, "when she had received the messengers and had sent them out another way?" And in Hebrews xi, 31, we read: "By faith the harlot Rahab perished not with them that believed not."   In the allegorical exposition of the Scriptures, Joshua often figures as a symbol of Christ, while Rahab is sometimes interpreted as the Church, which he saved by the "scarlet thread" of his blood.

1. The Clemence addressed may be Charles's daughter, who in 1315 married Louis X of France; but Charles's wife, also named Clemence, who died in 1295, could be intended.

3. Shortly after Charles's death, his son, Charles Robert, was deprived, by his uncle Robert, of the right of succession to the throne of Naples.

4–6. Here, as in all cases where Dante forecasts events subsequent to the time of writing, the prophecy is vague.

25–27. The March of Treviso, in the northeast corner of Italy, lies between the Alps, where the rivers Brenta and Piave have their source, and Venice, the most important of whose islands is called Rialto.

28–30. The 'torch,' or scourge of mankind, is Ezzelino (or Azzolino) III da Romano, the most infamous and bloodthirsty of the petty tyrants of medieval Italy: cf. *Inf.* XII, 110. He was born in 1194, in the little hill town of Romano, and died in 1259.   Cunizza was his sister.

34. *A me medesma indulgo*, 'I grant myself,' i.e., 'I accept.'

35. The influence of Venus, which, in accordance with divine providence, shaped her character.

40. 'This centennial year shall yet be fived' — shall return five times: five centuries shall pass.   Dante probably thought the world would come to an end at about that time.

44. The rivers Tagliamento and Adige, on the east and west, bound the March of Treviso.

46–47. 'But soon it shall come to pass that the Paduans, at the swamp, shall alter (i.e., stain with their blood) the water (the river Bacchiglione) which bathes Vicenza.'   In 1314 the Paduans, who were attacking Vicenza, were suddenly set upon, and defeated with great loss, by a small force under Can Grande of Verona.

48. 'Because the people are stubborn against duty' which is owed to the Imperial authority.

49. The clear river Sile and the turbid Cagnano unite at Treviso, but for some distance beyond the confluence their waters can be distinguished.

50. Rizzardo da Camino, a powerful lord, son of the 'good Gherardo' of *Purg.* XVI, 124.

51. In 1312 Rizzardo was murdered by a hired assassin while playing chess.

53. Alessandro Novello of Treviso, bishop of Feltre. In 1314 four gentlemen of Ferrara took refuge with him, to escape the wrath of Pino della Tosa, who governed Ferrara in behalf of King Robert, Vicar of the Church. Alessandro, yielding to pressure from Treviso, surrendered them to Pino, who put them to death.

54. Malta is the name of several different prisons. On an island in Lake Bolsena was a dungeon of that name, for guilty prelates.

59. 'Party': Guelf.

61. The Thrones are the angels that direct the 7th sphere, the heaven of Saturn.

62. These angels are executors of God's judgments. Cf. *Summa Theologiae*, Prima, Qu. cviii, Art. 6: "Throni dicuntur, secundum Gregorium, per quos Deus sua judicia exercet." (For the *Thrones*, according to Gregory, are so called because through them God accomplishes His judgments.)

63. We see mirrored in the Thrones the punishment that God has in store for the sinners, and therefore we can speak with satisfaction of their misdeeds.

75. Thou canst see my wish in God.

77. The Seraphim, ministers of divine love.

78. Cf. Isaiah vi, 2: "Above it stood the seraphim: each one had six wings."

81. 'If I could *thou* me, as thou *meest* thee': the verbs are constructed, in the same fashion as that in l. 73, from *tu* and *mi*.

82. The Mediterranean, which was thought to extend from west to east 90°, or a quarter of the earth's circumference.

84. The great Ocean, which surrounds all the land.

85. As the opening of the sea is at the west end, it is thought of as stretching from west to east.

86-87. The meridian of any place is a great circle passing through its zenith and nadir and the two celestial poles. The horizon of a place is a great heavenly circle midway between its zenith and its nadir, the plane of the circle being at right angles to that of the meridian. The two circles are, then, 90° apart. When the water enters the Mediterranean, at the Strait, its zenith is that of Gibraltar and its horizon traverses the zenith of Jerusalem: but when it reaches the eastern end of the sea, its meridian is that of Jerusalem and its horizon passes through the zenith of Gibraltar.

89. Between the Spanish river Ebro and the Italian Magra or Macra.

92. Buggea, or Bougie, on the north coast of Africa, was an important town in the Middle Ages. — 'City': Marseilles, which is almost under the same meridian as Bougie.

93. In 49 B.C. there was a fierce naval battle, in the harbor of Marseilles, between Caesar's fleet and the local supporters of Pompey: cf. *Purg.* XVIII, 101-102. See *Phars.*, III, 572-573:

> Cruor altus in unda
> Spumat, et obducti concreto sanguine fluctus.

(Their blood foamed deep upon the wave, and a crust of gore covered the sea.)

97. Belus's daughter, Dido, by her passion for Aeneas, wronged her dead husband, Sichaeus and Aeneas's dead wife, Creusa.

99. 'Than I did, as long as it befitted my hair': until I turned gray.

100. The Thracian princess Phyllis, thinking herself forsaken by her lover Demophoön, son of Theseus, hanged herself.· Cf. Ovid, *Heroides*, II. Rhodŏpe is the name of a mountain range on the edge of Thrace.

101. Alcĭdes, or Hercules, lost his life in consequence of his infatuation for the Thessalian princess Iŏle. Cf. Ovid, *Heroides*, IX.

104. The memory of sin is removed by Lethe, although the souls, seeing all things in God, have an objective knowledge of their past wickedness and recognize the eternal fitness of the dispositions originally given them by the stars. See *Summa Theologiae*, Tertia, Suppl., Qu. lxxxvii. Cf. St Augustine, *De Civitate Dei*, XXII, 30: Gardner, 73.

108. 'By reason of which the world below (mankind) again becomes the world above.' A difficult and very obscure line.

117. 'It (the order) is sealed with her in the highest degree.' Rahab is the supreme representative of our order of beatitude.

118. The earth's conical shadow reaches the sphere of Venus and touches the planet when Venus is at its least, but not when it is at its greatest, distance from our globe. The shadow, according to Ptolemy and Alfraganus, is 871,000 miles long.

123. Which was won by the one and the other palm. i.e., by the nailing of Christ's two hands to the Cross, i.e., which was won through the Crucifixion.

127. Florence is a 'plant' of the devil. Cf. Mat. xv, 13: "Every plant, which my heavenly Father hath not planted, shall be rooted up."

129. Wisdom ii, 24: "Through envy of the devil came death into the world." Cf. *Inf.* I, 111.

130. The florin, bearing the figure of the lily.

134. The Decretals (Canon Law) are studied for financial profit.

142. The unholy union of a corrupt Papacy and the Church. Cf. the prophecy in *Purg.* XXXIII, 37–45.

Canto X

Argument

Leaving behind us the spheres reached by the earth's shadow, we enter upon a new realm of the celestial world and a second division of the *Paradiso*, which is introduced by a prelude comprising the first 27 lines of this canto. Here we are bidden, fixing our minds on the intersection of the equator and the ecliptic and the angle at which they meet, to reflect upon the marvelous Providence that shaped the courses of the stars exactly to meet the needs of man. Contemplating the system of the universe, we cannot fail to form some conception of its triune Maker. Divine Power (the Father, "lo primo valore"), moved by Love (the Holy Ghost), and guided by Wisdom (the Son), created the world of spirit and of matter. "Looking upon his Son with the Love which both of them endlessly breathe forth, the primal and ineffable Power produced — with a plan such that one who considers it cannot be without a taste of Him — all that revolves through mind or through space."

In Dante's allegory the number and the sequence of the orders of beatitude necessarily depend in some measure on the Ptolemaic arrangement of the heavenly bodies and their fitness to symbolize various kinds of goodness. The "essential reward" (to use St. Thomas's phrase) depends on the intensity of love, which is a result of Grace; but the "accidental reward" is determined by the nature of the service done by the individual soul, and this is largely a matter of planetary influence. From the confused mass of stellar powers formulated by astrologers, the poet selected those which were obviously appropriate and harmonious with his ethical scheme. The cold and remote Saturn evidently must represent the monastic type, the life of contemplation; and it is proper that this order should be the highest. Jupiter must stand for Empire, and to its sphere are assigned those who maintained justice. Mars, emblem of war, harbors the Crusaders, who were willing to give their lives for the Faith. And the Sun, the image of enlightenment, eminently suits the theologians. Their souls are conspicuous for exceeding brightness. It may be noted that several of those now sainted had not been canonized in the poet's time, and consequently their station below the warriors was then less striking than it is today.

The one who speaks in our canto is Dante's great master in theology, the Angelic Doctor, St. Thomas Aquinas. Born in 1226 of the princely family of Aquino, he early entered the Dominican order. After studying at Cologne under Albertus Magnus, he taught at the University of Naples. When he died in 1274, on his way to a council at Lyons, it was reported that he had been poisoned to please Charles of Anjou, whom his kinsmen opposed: cf. *Purg.* XX, 69; also G. Villani, *Croniche*, IX, ccxviii. His huge *Summa Theologiae*, a precise and formal discussion, in scholastic style, of questions of Christian doctrine, has remained the principal Catholic authority on dogmatic theology. Very important also are his commentary on Aristotle and his treatise *De Veritate Catholicae Fidei contra Gentiles*, sometimes called *Summa contra Gentiles* or *Contra Gentes*. His mode of thought was strongly influenced by his teacher, Albertus Magnus, and, through him, by Aristotle. The final amalgamation of Christian and Aristotelian philosophy was achieved by him.

In the interpretation of stellar influence, Dante, while far simpler and clearer, is partially in accord with St. Thomas. The latter, in his Commentary on Aristotle's *Metaphysics*, XII, ix, ascribes to the various planets certain dominant effects, which to some extent correspond to the attributes selected by Dante. Stability, for instance, is characteristic of Saturn; mutability, of the moon. — For the double influence of Grace and the stars, see *Purg.* XXX, 109–117. — Attempts to connect Dante's heavens with the moral virtues enumerated by St. Thomas, and with the gifts of the Holy Spirit (correlated by St. Thomas with the virtues), have not resulted very satisfactorily.

2. According to orthodox Catholic faith, the Holy Ghost (or Divine Love) emanates from both Father and Son and consists in their eternal love for each other. Cf. *Summa Theologiae*, Prima, Qu. xxxvi, and xxxvii.

9. The 'two motions' are the diurnal and the annual revolutions of the sun, represented by the celestial equator and the celestial ecliptic. They 'strike,' or cross, each other at Aries, in which constellation the sun is at the time of Dante's journey.

13. At Aries the ecliptic slants across the equator.

14. The seven planets move through the signs of the zodiac, and thus their influence is properly distributed and modified.

16. If the ecliptic, or zodiac, were not thus slanting, the solar and stellar influence could not operate as it does. There would be no seasons, and hence no generation.

19. If the obliquity of the ecliptic were greater or less, the succession of the seasons would not be so effective on the part of the globe where there is land.

32-33. The sun's apparent course around the earth, from day to day, is spiral.   In the spring season it rises every day farther north and earlier than the day before.   Cf. Ristoro d'Arezzo, I, xxiii.

35-36. A disconnected thought, without associations, may be contrasted with the thought of *Inf.* XXIII, 10 ("E come l'un pensier de l'altro scoppia").

39. Revelation enlightens us instantaneously.

41-42. The souls of the great theologians are brighter than the sun.   Daniel xii, 3: "And they that be wise shall shine as the brightness of the firmament; and they that turn many to righteousness as the stars for ever and ever."   Mat. xiii, 43: "Then shall the righteous shine forth as the sun in the kingdom of their Father."

45. Let them make themselves fit for Heaven.

48. Cf. *Summa Theologiae*, Tertia, Suppl., Qu. lxxxv, Art. 2: "oculus non gloriosus non potest inspicere solem in rota sua propter magnitudinem claritatis."   (Now a nonglorified eye is unable to gaze on the very orb of the sun on account of the greatness of its clarity.)

49. The '4th family' is the 4th order of the blessed, the *sapienti*.

50. Cf. Ps. xvii (Vulg. xvi), 15: "I shall be satisfied (*satiabor*), when I awake, with thy likeness."

51. God 'satisfies' the blessed by revealing to them the mystery of the Trinity: they see how the Holy Ghost and the Son exist in him.   Cf. Dante's profession of faith: *Par.* XXIV, 130.

63. 'Divided among many things my mind, which was concentrated on one.'   The blessed souls are revealed again.

67. Latona's daughter is Diana, the moon.   Sometimes, in moist weather, we see the moon 'girdled' with a shining halo.   Cf. *Purg.* XXIX, 78.

69. Moisture is 'the thread of which the belt is made.'

74. Cf. Isaiah xl, 31: "But they that wait upon the Lord shall renew their strength; they shall mount up with wings as eagles."

75. To expect, on earth, to conceive of that song is as hopeless as expecting news from the dumb.

83. Since the original sin, man has needed grace to kindle his natural love of God: *Summa Theologiae*, Prima Secundae, Qu. cix, Art. 3.

87. Here is a distinct promise of Dante's ultimate salvation.   Cf. *Purg.* II, 91-92.

90. It would be as unnatural for one of these souls to refuse to satisfy Dante, as it would be for water not to run downhill.

92. The 'garland' is the ring of shining spirits.

96. The speaker, St. Thomas Aquinas, who belonged to the Dominican order, declares that St. Dominic led his flock over a road where the sheep 'fatten well, if they do not stray,' i.e., they have abundance of spiritual food, as long as they adhere to his rule.   This expression calls for an explanation in the next canto.   Cf. Pr. xi, 25: "The liberal soul shall be made fat (*impinguabitur*)."

97 ff. For the companions of St. Thomas, see Gardner, 257-258, 261: first comes his master; the next nine are all cited in his *Summa Theologiae*, and on three of them (Peter Lombard, Dionysius, and Boethius) he wrote special commentaries; on his left is Sigier of Brabant, his opponent, whom he confuted.

99. The Swabian known as Albertus Magnus, Albert of Cologne, and "Doctor Universalis," who lived from 1193 to 1280, and taught for some time at Cologne, was one of the most erudite men of the Middle Ages and one of the greatest scholars of all time.   His most important work was the reconciliation of Aristotelian philosophy and Christian theology.   St. Thomas was his principal follower.

104. Gratian, in the first half of the 12th century, composed the *Decretum*, a collection of sacred and ecclesiastical utterances, which became the leading textbook of Canon Law. This work did much to establish an agreement between religious and civil law and thus 'helped the one and the other court.'   He marked the jurisdictions of Church and State, and may therefore be called a representation of "Prudentia legislativa."

107. Peter Lombard, the "Magister Sententiarum," professor in Bologna and Paris, and Bishop of Paris, made four volumes of doctrinal excerpts from the Church Fathers, called the *Sententiae*, which were used in the schools as a manual of theology. In his preface he compares his work to the widow's mite (Luke xxi, 2). He lived in the 12th century. He was called *Jedidiah*, or "Beloved."

109–110. The '5th light,' that of Solomon, is the 'most beautiful' of all the circle, since it comes from the love which phrased the Song of Songs, the epithalamium of Christ and Church. He revealed truth in Proverbs and Ecclesiastes.

111. Some theologians (as St. Jerome) maintained that Solomon was saved, others (as St. Augustine) that he was damned. See 1 Kings, xi, 4–12.

112–114. See 1 Kings iii, 12: "Lo, I have given thee a wise and an understanding heart; so that there was none like thee before thee, neither after thee shall any arise like unto thee." It is apparent that the phrase "no second ever rose," in l. 114, has raised in Dante's mind a question which is answered in Canto XIII.

115. The 'candle' is Dionysius the Areopagite, St. Paul's convert in Athens (Acts xvii, 34), to whom was ascribed a Neoplatonic work of the 5th or 6th century, called *De Caelesti Hierarchia*, the great authority on the orders of the angels, their nature, their functions, and their relation to the heavens. Cf. XXVIII, 130–139; also Letter to Can Grande, xxi, 60–61.

118–120. At the beginning of the 5th century Paulus Orosius, a Lusitanian priest, composed the first compendium of universal history, entitled *Historia adversus Paganos*, showing the hand of God in the direction of human affairs, and refuting the pagan attribution of present troubles to the baleful influence of Christianity. This work, which was widely read, was one of Dante's chief sources of information. It was undertaken at the suggestion of St. Augustine, whose *De Civitate Dei* it supplements.

125. 'The blessed soul that exposes the deceptive world' is Anicius Manlius Severinus Boethius, author of *Consolatio Philosophiae*, a beautiful treatise in prose interspersed with poetry, much admired in the Middle Ages. It was one of the two books with which Dante began the serious study of philosophy.

127–129. Boethius, who was an important statesman as well as an author, was imprisoned, under false charges, and finally put to death by Theodoric in 525. He is known in the Church as St. Severinus, being regarded as a martyr to Christianity: cf. G. Villani, *Croniche*, II, v. After the "exile" from Rome, his body was buried in the church of S. Pietro in Cielo d' Oro (St. Peter's of the Golden Ceiling) in Pavia.

131. St. Isidore, Bishop of Seville, who died in 636, wrote a very useful encyclopedia, called *Origines* or *Etymologiae*. — The Venerable Bede, an English monk who died in 735, was the author of an important historical work, the *Historia Ecclesiastica Gentis Anglorum*. — Richard, prior of the Monastery of St. Victor in Paris, composed, among other things, a treatise *De Contemplatione*: cf. Letter to Can Grande, xxviii, 80. He died in 1173. According to St. Bonaventure, Dionysius and Richard especially taught the anagogical sense of the Scriptures.

132. Richard of St. Victor was called the 'Great Contemplator.'

134–135. He was eager to reach Heaven, where his questions might be answered.

136. Sigier of Brabant, a brilliant and daring philosopher, was a professor at the University of Paris in the third quarter of the 13th century. After two condemnations for heresy, he went to Orvieto, and was there (it would seem) murdered by a half-crazy cleric. We may infer that Dante knew nothing of his heresy nor of his tragic end, or perhaps Dante assumed that he repented. His unorthodox theory of intelligence was refuted by St. Thomas, who now presents him.

137. Sigier lectured in the Latin Quarter, in the *rue du Fouarre* (Straw St.), which in Latin is *Vicus Straminis* or *Straminum*. It is now called *rue Dante*.

138. 'Demonstrated enviable truths.'

140. The Church.

Canto XI

Argument

The learned St. Dominic and the loving St. Francis were sent into the world by God to enable his worshipers to follow Christ more fearlessly, guided by Dominican wisdom, and more steadfastly, moved by the seraphic ardor of the Franciscans. The two great brotherhoods established by these holy men were to be the two wheels of the chariot of the Church. Unhappily the members of both orders soon fell away from the example of their teachers, and strife and degeneracy prevailed. The sheep, straying from the fold and seeking strange pastures, ceased to fatten on the word of God.

The lives of the two founders are briefly summarized in this canto and the next — that of St. Francis being told by St. Thomas, a Dominican, that of St. Dominic by a Franciscan, St. Bonaventure. In Heaven we find the harmony and courtesy that should have existed on earth. It was an established rule of the two orders that a Franciscan should preach in a Dominican church, a Dominican in a Franciscan, exalting the two founders on their respective feasts. Two such sermons are extant, one attributed to St. Thomas, one to St. Bonaventure. The latter compares the two orders to the "two milch kine" that drew the Ark from the country of the Philistines (1 Kings vi, 12).

In his portrayal of the sweet, Christlike figure of St. Francis, Dante follows in the main the *Legenda Beati Francisci* of St. Bonaventure (or Bonaventura), a 13th century mystic, who, after having been a professor in Paris, became general of the Franciscans, bishop, and cardinal. Dante probably drew also from Ubertino da Casale, *Arbor Vitae Crucifixae*, V. The life of St. Francis had from the beginning a striking resemblance to that of Christ, and his legend tended to emphasize the similarity. Of the many miracles attributed to St. Francis, our poet mentions only that of the Stigmata, the divine attestation of his conformity to Jesus; and of the rules of his order, Dante singles out the one most important, in his eyes, for the reformation of both clergy and laymen — the rule of poverty.

St. Francis was born in 1182 in the Umbrian town of Assisi, the son of a well-to-do merchant. Alert and merry, he was a leader among the gay youth of his city until a series of mishaps — imprisonment in Perugia, a severe illness, disappointment over a projected military adventure in Apulia — followed by two startling religious experiences, turned his mind to sacred things. Forswearing ownership of property, he devoted the rest of his days to the propagation of his doctrine of pure and simple living and universal love. Neither asceticism nor care ever quite subdued his natural cheerfulness, his playful fancy, his keen interest in the doings of his fellowmen. He died in 1226, and two years later was canonized by Gregory IX.

The sight of celestial spirits and eternal joys brings home to Dante the pettiness of all that is deemed most important on earth. Compared with the pursuit of heavenly gladness, even the gravest of worldly occupations are but empty trifling. "The child's play of grown people," says St. Augustine (*Confessiones*, I, ix), "is called business" — "maiorum nugae negotia vocabantur, puerorum autem talia cum sint, puniuntur a maioribus." (Elder folks' idleness, must, forsooth be called business, and when children do the like, the same men must punish them.)

4. The *Aphorisms* of Hippocrates served as a textbook of medicine.

16. The 'light' emanating from the soul of St. Thomas.

21. 'I apprehend whence thou derivest thy thoughts,' i.e., what is the occasion of them.

25–26. See X, 96, 114.

31. The 'Beloved' is Christ.

32. "And about the ninth hour Jesus cried with a loud voice, saying, ... My God, my God, why hast thou forsaken me?" (Mat. xxvii, 46).

33. Christ 'wedded' the Church with his blood on the cross.

37. The Seraphim, the highest order of angels, represent heavenly love.

38. The Cherubim, the next order, represent celestial wisdom.

43. Assisi is situated between the river Topino and the Chiascio, which runs into it below. The Topino empties into the Tiber.

44. On the hill, in the vicinity of Gubbio, from which the Chiascio river flows, St. Ubald had his hermitage, before he became bishop of Gubbio. He died in 1160.

45. The west slope of Mt. Subasio, facing Perugia, is less steep than the other side. From Porta Sole, the upper part is brown; the lower part, less steep, is green.

46–48. The gate called Porta Sole is on the side of Perugia nearest to Subasio. The town feels the effect of the summer sun and the winter snow on the mountain. East of the range to which Subasio belongs are the little towns of Nocera and Gualdo, which 'weep because of the heavy mountain chain' of the Apennines on their east. The Monte di Nocera may be seen, from Porta Sole, covered with snow in mid-April.

50. Assisi lies on a spur of the mountain. — Even before Dante, St. Francis had been called a Sun, a traditional appellation with the Franciscans.

51. This real sun, where Dante now is. — The sun rises from the Ganges, due east from Jerusalem, at the vernal equinox.

52–54. The spot from which the new Sun rose should be called Orient or Dayspring. Luke i, 78: "the dayspring from on high hath visited us." Cf. Zechariah iii, 8, "adducam servum meum Orientem" (I will bring my servant the Orient), and vi, 12, "ecce vir Oriens nomen ejus" (behold a man, the Orient is his name) (the English Bible has a different rendering of both passages). The usual form of the name Assisi, in the Tuscan of Dante's day, was *Ascesi*, which may be interpreted as meaning 'I have risen.' While this is suggestive of dayspring, it is inadequate (*corto*): 'Orient' is the only fit word. Ubertino da Casale, *Arbor Vitae Crucifixae*, V, cites Bonaventure as an authority for identifying Francis with the angel of Rev. vii, 2, "ascending from the east, having the seal of the living God": Gardner, 218, 232.

58–59. While still a youth, he espoused Lady Poverty, against his father's will. The marriage of St. Francis and Poverty has repeatedly been depicted in art, notably by Giotto in a fresco in the church of S. Francesco in Assisi.

61–62. Summoned by his father before the episcopal court of Assisi, St. Francis stripped off his clothes and gave them to him, keeping nothing he had received from his family. Thus did he wed Poverty. — *Coram patre* is a Biblical phrase: Mat. x, 33, "before my Father." — This mystic wedlock is only slightly indicated by Tomaso da Celano and St. Bonaventure: Gardner, 253.

65–66. From Christ to St. Francis (who was born in 1182), no one had cared for Poverty.

67–69. 'And it availed not that men heard how he who terrified the whole world (Caesar) found her, with Amỹclas (a poor fisherman), fearless at the sound of his voice.' See *Phars.*, V, 515–531. Amyclas, who had nothing to lose, was not afraid when Caesar knocked on his door; he was "securus belli" — fearless of war. But even this example of the advantages of indigence — upon which Lucan moralizes — did not make Poverty seem desirable.

71–72. When even Mary had to remain at the foot of the cross, Poverty accompanied her Spouse: Christ's raiment was taken from him, and "they parted his garments, casting lots upon them" (Mark, xv, 24). Cf. Ubertino da Casale, V, iii: Gardner, 255.

76–78. 'Love, wonder, and sweet gaze made their concord and their glad looks to be a source of holy thoughts' in the beholders.

79. His first disciple was a rich citizen of Assisi named Bernard.

80. St. Francis and his followers went barefoot.

83–84. Egidius, a simple-minded mystic, and Sylvester, a priest, followed the Bridegroom for love of the Bride.

87. St. Francis substituted a rope for the usual belt.

89. His father, Pietro Bernardone, was a tradesman of Assisi. Before his conversion, Francis had associated with youths of higher station.

90. When he first visited the Papal court, his appearance excited derision.

93. In 1210, Innocent III verbally, and with some reluctance, sanctioned St. Francis's Rule, which seemed to him harsh and dangerous.

96. 'Would more fitly be sung (by the Seraphim) in praise of Heaven' than thus related by me.

97–99. 'The holy purpose of this Arch-shepherd was rounded with a second crown by the Eternal Breath (the Holy Ghost) through Honorius.' — In 1223 St. Francis obtained a definite, official sanction of his Rule from Honorius III. — *Archimandrita*, 'head of the fold,' a term of the Greek Church, is one of the words that Dante got from the *Magnae Derivationes* of Uguccione da Pisa. It is used of the Pope in Ep. XI, vi, 13; of St. Peter in *Mon.*, III, ix, 17.

100–102. In 1219 St. Francis and some of his disciples accompanied the crusaders to Egypt, where he preached before the Sultan.

106. St. Francis retired to a shelter built by his followers on the wild and rugged Mt. Alvernia (called "la Vernia" and "la Verna"), between the upper Arno and the source of the Tiber.

107. There, in 1224, Christ appeared to him and imprinted on his hands, feet, and side the Stigmata, or marks of his five wounds. This miracle, attested by contemporary evidence, was confirmed by three Papal bulls.

108. These marks he bore until his death in 1226. He died in Porziuncola, where is now the Church of Santa Maria degli Angeli, in the plain below Assisi.

115–117. St. Francis, desiring to rise to Heaven 'from the lap' of Poverty, commanded his followers to strip his body, after his death, and let it lie for some time on the bare ground.

136. Only one of Dante's two questions (ll. 25–26) has been answered.

137–139. 'For thou shalt see from what source (the Rule of St. Dominic) the shoot (the degenerate mass of Dominicans) is torn, and thou shalt see what my correction means.'

Canto XII

Argument

St. Dominic, whose eulogy is pronounced by the Franciscan St. Bonaventure, was born in Calaruega in Old Castile circa 1170. He studied at the University of Palencia, became a canon in the cathedral of Osma in 1194, and in 1204 went to Languedoc, to combat the Albigensian heresy, which was widespread and firmly entrenched in southern France. There he was associated with Folquet (IX, 94), Bishop of Marseilles. In 1216 the order of preachers which he had founded obtained Papal sanction. He died in Bologna in 1221, renowned for his learning, his austere and holy life, and his vigor in defending the orthodox faith. He had received the office of *magister sacri palatii*, or Papal theologian, which has ever since been held by a Dominican. Dante's biographical data agree with the incidents recorded in the *Legenda Aurea* (ed. T. Graesse, chap. cxiii), a 13th century compilation by Jacobus de Varagine, or Jacopo da Varaggio. There are told the two prophetic dreams and the anecdote of the nurse finding the child seated on the bare ground. The ultimate source of the Legend is probably a life by a Spanish friar, Petrus Ferrandi, about 1238.

As St. Thomas had deplored the decline of the Dominicans, so St. Bonaventure denounces the quarrels of the Franciscans and their distortion of their master's simple code. Two hostile factions divided the order: the Conventuales, who favored a lax interpretation of the Rule, and the Spirituales, who declared that it should be observed to the letter, and tended to exaggerate its severity. The leader of the former party was Matteo Bentivenga of Acquasparta, near Todi, general (1287–1289) of the Franciscans, cardinal, and on several occasions Papal legate. In 1300 and 1301 he was sent to Florence by Boniface VIII to restore peace; after his second unsuccessful attempt he excommunicated the city. The Spirituales had for their champion (after 1300) the fervid preacher Ubertino da Casale, from Monferrato, who, incurring the disapproval of his superiors, retired to Mt. Alvernia (XI, 106), and there composed the *Arbor Vitae Crucifixae*. He finally joined the Benedictines. He died in 1338.

For the companions of St. Bonaventure, see Gardner, 257–261.

There were in Dante's time two schools of Christian philosophy: the Platonic-Augustinian, dominant in the first half of the 13th century, which maintained the primacy of the will, the preeminence of the idea of the good over the idea of the true, generally followed by the Franciscans; the Aristotelian-Thomistic, more influential after 1245, when Albertus Magnus began teaching in Paris, maintaining the primacy of intellect, the doctrine that blessedness depends on vision. The first of Dante's rings is essentially Thomistic, the second Augustinian. Dante supports the Thomistic side.

3. 'Millstone': the ring of spirits. In a mill, the two grindstones operate concurrently, and both are necessary.

8. 'Pipes': the singing souls.

9. 'As a direct ray surpasses its reflection' — 'the one it has reflected.'

12. Iris, the rainbow.

13. The outer arc of a double rainbow is called the reflection, or echo, of the inner one. It was formerly thought to be really a reflection. — The two bows may represent two schools of thought.

14. 'Wanderer': the nymph Echo, who for love of Narcissus wasted away to a voice. Cf. *Met.*, III, 395–401.

27. The two circles operate simultaneously, like a pair of eyes. Dante seems here to confuse the *turning* of the eyes, which must affect both at once, with shutting and opening, which may affect one without the other.

29. The North Star, or north.

33. 'For whose sake there is such fair speech here concerning mine.' St. Thomas, for love of his own leader, St. Dominic, has been praising St. Francis.

37–38. 'The Christian army,' made helpless by sin, had been 'rearmed' by Christ's atonement.

43. Cf. XI, 38–46.

47. Spain is the country nearest the source of Zephyr, the west wind. Cf. *Met.*, I, 63–64:

> vesper et occiduo quae litora sole tepescunt,
> proxima sunt Zephyro.

(The western shores which glow with the setting sun are the place of Zephyrus). Petrus Ferrandi compares St. Dominic to Hesperus, rising from the west: Gardner, 245.

49–51. Compared with Italy, Calaruega (in Old Castile) is 'not very far' from the Atlantic. Spain lying due west of the Italian peninsula, the sun sets behind its Atlantic shore at the time of the vernal equinox (in the summer the direction is northwest: cf. XI, 51). When the sun sinks over the Atlantic, it 'hides itself from every man,' because there is no land beyond. — Cf. *Aen.*, XI, 913–914:

> ni roseus fessos iam gurgite Phoebus Hibero
> tinguat equos noctemque die labente reducat.

(But ruddy Phoebus now laves his weary team in the Iberian flood, and, as day ebbs, brings back the night.)

54. The shield of Castile has two lions and two castles quartered, one lion above the castle and one below.

58–60. Before his birth, his mother dreamed that she brought forth a black and white dog with a burning torch in its mouth. Black and white are the Dominican colors; the torch signifies zeal; the word *Dominicani* suggests *Domini canes*, 'dogs of the Lord.'

61–63. His baptism is conceived as a wedding. He espoused Faith, as Francis (in ll. 61–63 of XI) espoused Poverty. Dominic and Faith 'dowered each other with mutual health.' Dante evidently plotted out cantos XI and XII, to make them parallel, line by line. Francis and Dominic are the symmetrical 'two wheels' of the Chariot of the Church.

64–66. His godmother dreamed that he bore on his forehead a star which illumined the world.

67. 'And that he might be in syntax what he was in reality.'

69. 'With the possessive of him to whom he wholly belonged.' *Dominicus*, 'the Lord's,' is a possessive of *Dominus*. Cf. *Summa Theologiae*, Tertia, Qu. xvi, Art. 3.

71. Among the interpretations of the name *Dominicus* in the *Legenda Aurea* is 'keeper of the vineyard of the Lord.' — Note that in ll. 71, 73, 75 *Cristo* is in rhyme with itself. The same thing occurs in XIV, 104, XIX, 104, XXXII, 83. In the *Commedia* Dante will not allow *Cristo* to rhyme with any other word.

75. The 'counsels' of Christ are poverty, continence, and obedience, and the first of these is poverty: "Sell that thou hast, and give to the poor" (Mat. xix, 21). Dante insists that St. Dominic, as well as St. Francis, was a lover of Poverty. Their love is declared in ll. 73–75 of XI and XII.

79–81. His father's name was Felix, which means 'happy.' His mother's name, Joan, signifies in Hebrew 'the grace of the Lord,' an interpretation cited by several of Dante's authorities.

83. Enrico da Susa, professor in Bologna and Paris, bishop of *Ostia* and cardinal, was a great authority on canon law. *Taddeo* di Alderotto of Florence, also a professor in Bologna, was a famous medical authority. Both lived in the 13th century.

84. The 'true manna' is true knowledge, the 'bread of the angels' (II, 11).

88. The Papal chair, 'which once was kinder' than it is now.

89. The difference in its disposition is 'not because of itself' (the Papal office has not changed), but because of the degeneracy of its latterday occupants.

91–93. Permission to dole out in charity only a third or a half of the money on hand, 'the income of the first vacancy,' 'the tithes which belong to God's poor' — he asked for none of these things.

95. The Faith, the seed from which sprang the bright souls which 'enfold' Dante.

98. St. Dominic went to Rome with Folquet of Marseilles (IX, 94) and asked permission to found a new order; official sanction was given in 1216.

106. The two-wheeled 'chariot' of the Church. Cf. *Purg.* XXIX, 107.

112–113. 'But the rut which the outside of its circumference made is forsaken.' The wheel is St. Francis. His track is deserted by the Franciscans.

114. 'So that there is mold where the crust was.' Good wine makes a crust, bad wine makes mold. — There is an abrupt change of metaphor from ll. 112–113 to l. 114.

117. This line is very puzzling. It may mean: 'That the one in front throws at the one behind'; those who set out to follow in St. Francis's footsteps are now facing in opposite directions. The order is split into two hostile factions.

120. The tare 'shall complain that the bin is taken from it.' Cf. Mat. xiii, 30: "Gather ye together first the tares, and bind them in bundles to burn them: but gather the wheat into my barn." — There may be here a reference to the condemnation of a group of the Spirituales by the Pope in 1318.

124. The faithful follower of St. Francis — if one is to be found — shall come neither from Casale nor from Acquasparta, the homes of the leaders of the two factions: Casale, home of Ubertino; Acquasparta, home of Matteo Bentivenga.

125. The Rule of St. Francis.

127. For St. Bonaventure, the "Seraphic Doctor," see the Argument to Canto XI.

129. 'Always sacrificed the left hand care,' i.e., temporal interests. Cf. Pr. iii, 16: "in her (Wisdom's) left hand riches and honour" — "in *sinistra* illius divitiae et gloria." Dante believed that the Church should discard all temporal interests.

130. Illuminato and Augustino were two of the early followers of St. Francis. They are praised by St. Bonaventure in his *Legenda*.

133. Hugo (or Hugh) of St. Victor, a famous theologian who died in 1141, was the teacher of Richard (X, 131) and Peter Lombard (X, 107). He was exalted by St. Bonaventure above all other medieval authors.

134. Petrus Comestor, or Peter the Devourer (of books), also of the abbey of St. Victor, was the author of a commentary on the Bible as a narrative of revelations from the beginning to the time of the Apostles. He died in 1179. — Peter of Spain, a great logician, became Pope John XXI, and was killed soon after, in 1277, by the fall of a ceiling. He balances Paulus Orosius. He is the only contemporary Pope met by Dante in Paradise.

135. 'Twelve books': his *Summae Logicales*.

136. Nathan: see 2 Samuel vii and xii; 1 Kings i, 34.

137. St. John Chrysostom ("Golden Mouth"), Metropolitan or Patriarch of Constantinople,

a vigorous and eloquent defender of Christianity, died in 407. — St. Anselm of Piedmont, Archbishop of Canterbury, a keen theologian, the author of *Cur Deus Homo*, died in 1109. These two were kindred spirits to Bonaventure in the fight against corruption. Bonaventure often quotes Chrysostom. Both Bonaventure and Thomas used Anselm as a source. — Among the prophets and ecclesiastics is a grammarian, Donatus, who taught in Rome in the 4th century, and wrote a work which long remained the standard textbook of Latin grammar. A prophet must be trained in the arts of discourse (hence Donatus), with understanding of words and the gift of tongues (hence Isidore), in logic (hence Peter of Spain), in rhetoric.

138. Grammar is the first of the seven liberal arts of the Trivium and Quadrivium.

139. Rabānus Maurus, Archbishop of Mainz, an encyclopedic writer and Biblical commentator of the 8th and 9th centuries, one of Bonaventure's sources.

140. Joachim, Abbot of Flora in Calabria, founder of a new branch of the Cistercians, died in 1202. Freely interpreting the Apocalypse, he proclaimed the impending age of the Holy Ghost, to follow the dispensations of the Father and the Son, contained in the Old and the New Testament. His prophecies — and many others falsely ascribed to him — had a great vogue in the 13th century. Joachim, in a way, balances Sigier; for his doctrines had been condemned by Bonaventure as Sigier's *De Unitate Intellectus* had been attacked by Thomas. Thus each is introduced in Heaven by his earthly adversary. Dante, who doubtless was not familiar with Joachim's works, regards him as a prophet of the two orders, for which he had both Dominican and Franciscan authority.

142. *Inveggiare*, 'to envy,' can also mean *inveggiare in buona parte*, 'to envy in a good sense,' hence 'to eulogize,' which would seem to be the meaning here.

143–145. 'Brother Thomas's ardent courtesy and respectful style moved me to praise that great paladin (St. Dominic), and moved this company with me': I was constrained to admire and covet the excellence of St. Dominic, which had produced such a disciple as St. Thomas, and therefore I was impelled to praise him. *Palatini* was a title given to counts of the royal palace; St. Dominic was *magister sacri palatii* in Rome, — The interpretation of these lines is still far from certain. It is noteworthy that of the two parallel cantos, XI and XII, each ends with a puzzle.

Canto XIII

Argument

Once again Dante touches on the puzzling question of the imperfection of our earth. The real and complete universe exists only in the mind of God. What we call the world is only a shadow of the divine Idea. It is the product of the skies working upon matter. Now, as we have been told before, matter, for some unexplained reason, is faulty; and the skies are continually changing. If matter were perfect, and if the heavens were always in their most effective conjunction, the physical universe would exactly represent the Lord's conception. This divine plan is transmitted as a pattern and a creative force to the nine orders of angels, and by them is embodied in the numberless formative powers of sky and earth, from the highest to those whose work lasts but a moment; yet at all stages the result is inferior, in greater or less, degree, to the ideal model.

If, however, the triune God creates directly, with his absolute Power, Wisdom, and Love, the product is without flaw. Thus Adam and Christ (in his human aspect) came into the world as perfect examples of mankind, endowed with all the wisdom that men may possess. For wisdom is inborn, a gift of Grace. Experience and knowledge grow with years, but not wisdom. According to the Old French *Image du Monde*, of the first half of the 13th century, Adam knew everything. When, therefore, it was said that Solomon never had an equal in understanding, it is evident that Adam and Christ must be excluded from the comparison. In fact, as it turns out, the only competitors are kings; for the gift which Solomon craved and obtained was not general intelligence but "kingly prudence." The story is told in 1 Kings iii, 5–12: "In Gibeon the Lord appeared to Solomon in a dream by night: and God said, Ask what I shall give thee. And Solomon said ..., Give ... thy servant an understanding heart to judge thy people, that I may discern between good and bad. ... And the speech pleased the Lord, that Solomon had asked this thing. And God said unto him, Because thou hast asked this thing ... Behold, I have done according to thy words: lo, I have given thee a wise and an understanding heart; so that there was none like thee before thee, neither after thee shall any arise like unto thee."

All this is explained to Dante while he stands in the midst of the twenty-four doctors, who, like blazing orbs, surround him in two concentric rings. The better to visualize the scene, the reader is asked to pick out twenty-four of the brightest fixed stars and imagine them arranged in the shape of a double Ariadne's Crown. Fifteen miscellaneous ones are selected first, there being, according to Ptolemaic astronomy, fifteen stars of the first magnitude in the whole sky. Next are added the seven conspicuous members of the Wain (the Great Bear or Dipper), a constellation which in our climate never sinks below the horizon: cf. Canzone C, 28–29. The remaining two of the twenty-four are from the hornlike Little Bear (or Little Dipper) whose peak is the North Star; the two chosen — those which, at the other extremity, form the mouth of the horn — are, according to Alfraganus, of the second magnitude.

12. The daily rotation of the heavens.
14. The daughter of King Minos (*Inf.* V, 4) was Ariadne. Ariadne was carried to heaven by Bacchus, and her crown was turned into a constellation: *Met.*, VIII, 174–182.
18. That one should start at the word 'First!' and the other at the word 'Next!'
23. The Chiana is a sluggish stream in Tuscany.
24. The Primum Mobile, swiftest of the heavens.
25. *Paean* (accusative *Paeana*) is a name given to Apollo, and also a hymn in his honor. As celebrants of old sang hymns to heathen deities, so the Heavenly chorus sings of the threefold God and the twofold Christ, perhaps in the words of the Athanasian Creed.
37. The 'breast' of Adam, whence was taken the 'rib' to form Eve.
41. Christ's death 'atoned' for original sin in past and future generations.
48. The light that envelops the soul of Solomon.

51. A circle has but one point as its center. The truth is as a mathematical point, in which the two opinions coincide.

52–54. "In the beginning was the Word" (John i, 1). The Word, or *idea*, is the conception of the universe which the Lord brings forth by his love. The whole immortal and mortal world is only the manifestation of this *idea*, which in its reality exists in God.

55–57. 'For that living Light (the Son, Wisdom) which so streams from its Lamp (the Father, Power) that it is never divided therefrom, nor from the Love (the Holy Ghost) which is their third part.'

59. The 'nine subsistences' are the nine orders of angels, reflecting the Divine Wisdom which contains the plan of the universe.

60. "And the Word was with God, and the Word was God" (John i, 1).

61. 'Thence (from the angels) it descends to the ultimate potentialities,' i.e., to the elements, from which all other mortal things may be made.

62–63. 'Coming, step by step, so far down that it finally produces only brief contingencies,' i.e., perishable things of short and dependent existence.

67. 'Their wax' is matter; 'that which directs it' is Nature, 'the revolving sky.'

68–69. 'Are not always the same; and therefore it (the light of the divine idea — cf. ll. 53, 55) afterward shines through (sc., through Nature's work) more or less beneath the ideal pattern.' The material world is inferior to God's conception, and manifests it with more or less imperfection. Cf. *Mon.*, II, ii, 2: "Sciendum est igitur quod, quemadmodum ars in triplici gradu invenitur, in mente scilicet artificis, in organo et in materia formata per artem, sic et naturam in triplici gradu possumus intueri. Est enim natura in mente primi motoris, qui Deus est; deinde in celo, tanquam in organo quo mediante similitudo bonitatis eterne in fluitantem materiam explicatur." (Be it known then that like as art exists in three grades — in the mind of the artificer, in the instrument, and in the material informed by art — so too we may regard nature in three grades. For nature is in the mind of the first mover, which is God, and further in the heaven as in the instrument by means of which the likeness of the external excellence is spread over fluctuating matter.)

79–80. 'However, if the hot Love prepares and stamps the clear Sight of the primal Power' — if Divine Love directs Divine Wisdom in its creative Power: i.e., if the three Persons of the Trinity collaborate in direct creation. Cf. X, 1–3.

82–84. This happened when "God formed man of the dust of the ground" (Gen. ii, 7), and when Christ was conceived.

97–98. The question of the number of the heavenly motors, or angels, had been treated by Plato and Aristotle, and is discussed by Dante in *Conv.* II, iv, v. The angels are almost countless.

98–99. 'Or whether an absolute premise with a conditional premise have ever produced an absolute conclusion': a scholastic problem in logic, also touched upon by Plato and Aristotle. The answer is "no."

100. 'Not, whether a prime motion is to be admitted,' i.e., a motion independent of any cause: see Aristotle, *Physics*, VIII, i, ii. All motion is dependent on God: *Mon.*, I, ix, 2.

102. 'Right angle': Euclid, III, 31. Note that here again the answer is "no."

103–105. 'Wherefore — if thou notest what I said, and this — that peerless vision which the arrow of my intention hits is kingly prudence.'

117. 'In the one case as well as in the other': whether he affirms or denies.

119. Cf. Pr. xxix, 20: "Seest thou a man that is hasty in his words? There is more hope of a fool than of him."

125. Parmenĭdes, Melissus, and Bryson are Greek philosophers criticized by Aristotle.

127. Sabellius and Arius are heretical theologians. The first denied the Trinity; the second, founder of the Arians, denied the Consubstantiality of Father and Son.

128–129. Instead of reflecting the Scriptures accurately, like a glass, they gave a distorted image of them, similar to faces mirrored in sword blades.

139. *Berta* and *Martino* were equivalent to our 'Tom, Dick, and Harry.'

Canto XIV

Argument

The nearer we are to God, the more beatitude we are capable of receiving. Now, inasmuch as man was made to consist of both spirit and matter, it follows that the blessed will be more perfect after the resurrection than before and therefore more like to God, who is absolute perfection. As St. Thomas says (*Summa Theologiae*, Tertia, Suppl., Qu. xciii, Art. 1): "Anima conjuncta corpori glorioso est magis Deo similis quam ab eo separata, inquantum conjuncta habet esse perfectius: quanto enim est aliquid perfectius, tanto est Deo similius." (The soul united to a glorified body is more like to God than when separated therefrom, insofar as when united it has more perfect being. For the more perfect a thing is the more it is like to God.) The bodiless soul in Heaven has full spiritual happiness; but when clad again in the flesh, it will possess bodily happiness as well: its joy will be increased "extensively." Therefore the blessed, while feeling no sorrow, look forward with pleasure to the Judgment Day, when, as they know, they will be complete, more akin to their Maker, and endowed with an additional capacity for blessedness. "Omne autem imperfectum," says St. Thomas (*loc. cit.*), "appetit suam perfectionem. Et ideo anima separata naturaliter appetit corporis conjunctionem." (Now every imperfect thing desires its perfection. Hence the separated soul naturally desires reunion with the body.)

The effulgence that clothes the soul will remain after the restoration of the flesh, but it will not dazzle the bodily eyes; for the glorified body can suffer nothing except through the spirit. This "claritas" is discussed by St. Thomas in the *Summa Theologiae*, Tertia, Suppl., Qu. lxxxv, Art. 2-3. In Article 2 he says: "Sicut corpus gloriosum non potest pati aliquid passione naturae, sed solum passione animae; ita ex proprietate gloriae non agit nisi actione animae. Claritas autem intensa non offendit visum, inquantum agit actione animae, sed secundum hoc magis delectat; offendit autem, inquantum agit actione naturae. ... Et ideo claritas corporis gloriosi, quamvis excedat claritatem solis, tamen de sua natura non offendit visum, sed demulcet." (Just as a glorified body is not passible [*sic*] to a passion of nature but only to a passion of the soul, so in virtue of its property of glory it acts only by the action of the soul. Now intense clarity does not disturb the sight, insofar as it acts by the action of the soul, for thus it rather gives delight, but it disturbs it insofar as it acts by the action of nature. ... Hence, though the clarity of a glorified body surpasses the clarity of the sun, it does not by its nature disturb the sight but soothes it.)

This doctrine is appropriately imparted to Dante in the solar sphere. Thence he is uplifted to Mars, and is made aware of his rise by a difference in the light that surrounds him, the white sheen of the sun being changed suddenly to the glow of the ruddy planet.   Here a grand spectacle confronts him, more startling than the rings of bright spirits he has just seen.   The star is traversed by two immense shining bands — each like a milky way — which, intersecting, form a huge Cross, composed of the souls of warriors of the Faith.   Through the glittering mass sparklike figures continually dart to and fro.   We shall see presently that the two remaining planets are adorned by the poet's fancy with similar majestic images: in Jupiter we shall find the vast Imperial Eagle, also made up of gleaming spirits; in Saturn, Jacob's Ladder, the token of contemplation. In these three emblems — Cross, Eagle, Ladder — is summed up all that the Middle Ages held dearest.   With such glorious symbols our author — using no materials but light, motion, and music — contrives to enrich and diversify his portrayal of the upper heavens.

7–9. The sound waves proceeding from St. Thomas, in the ring of bright spirits, and from Beatrice, in the center, remind Dante of the circular ripples in a round vessel, when the water is stirred at the edge or in the middle.

27. The 'rain' of Grace.

28–30. Once more the souls celebrate the mystery of the Trinity.   Cf. XIII, 26.

34. The 'light' is that of Solomon: X, 109.   The Song of Solomon celebrates the union of the divine with the human, the resurrection of the body.

36. Gabriel.   Cf. Luke i, 28.

40–42. The brightness of the 'garment' of light shall be proportionate to the fervency of love in each soul, the love shall be proportionate to the distinctness of its vision of God, and that vision is a gift of Grace, or predestination, not dependent on merit.

45. Man is composed of both flesh and spirit, and is incomplete if either element is lacking.

53. The coal glows through the flame that envelops it.

68. Cf. Acts xxvi, 13: "I saw in the way a light from heaven, above the brightness of the sun, shining round about me and those which journeyed with me." — Just as Dante is about to leave this sphere, a new host of loving spirits begins to appear, like a gleaming horizon, around the two rings of shining souls.   Why this army of the Holy Ghost — the throng of those who were wise in the things of the Spirit — thus momentarily and mysteriously reveals itself, we are not told.

96. 'Sun': God, the source of light.   According to the *Magnae Derivationes* of Uguccione da Pisa, ἥλιος, the Greek word for 'sun,' comes from the Hebrew *Eli*, 'God.'

99. The Galaxy, or Milky Way, was differently explained by different authorities.

102. Two diameters of a circle, intersecting at right angles, form a cross and divide the circle into four quadrants.

104. Once more *Cristo* occurs in the rhyme: cf. XII, 71.

106. Cf. Mat. x, 38; xvi, 24.

109. Arm of the cross.

112. The moving lights in the cross are compared to bits of dust dancing in a ray of sunshine in a dark room.   Cf. Lucretius, II, 114–120.

117. In warm countries the house is regarded primarily as a shelter from the heat.

125. The song which Dante cannot entirely catch is evidently a triumphal hymn to Christ, sung by the knights of the Cross.

131. Dante seems to be rating the song above those 'beauteous eyes'; but, as he presently explains, he is not really doing so, since he has not yet looked upon them in this sphere.

133. 'The living stamps of all beauty' are Beatrice's eyes, which become more potent from sphere to sphere, as she approaches God.

136–137. 'May excuse me for that (i.e., l. 131) of which I accuse myself in order to excuse myself' — i.e., for the accusation which I bring against myself merely in order to have an opportunity to deny it — 'and may see that I am telling the truth.'

138. 'For that holy delight (the eyes) is not cast out (set aside, as of less account than the song) here.'

Canto XV

Argument

> Isque ubi tendentem adversum per gramina vidit
> Aenean, alacris palmas utrasque tetendit,
> effusaeque genis lacrimae et vox excidit ore:
> "venisti tandem, tuaque exspectata parenti
> vicit iter durum pietas?"

(And he, as he saw Aeneas coming toward him over the sward, eagerly stretched forth both hands, while tears streamed from his eyes and a cry fell from his lips: "Art thou come at last, and hath the love thy father looked for vanquished the toilsome way?")

Thus Virgil in the 6th book of the *Aeneid* (ll. 684–688) describes the meeting of Aeneas and the shade of his father, Anchises, in the Elysian Fields. Dante, too, in the realm of the blessed, finds the spirit of an ancestor who has long been awaiting him — his great-great-grandfather, Cacciaguida, a crusader, knighted by the Emperor. A person of that name appears in a document of 1131. Aside from what is told us in the *Paradiso*, we know nothing of Cacciaguida, nor of his wife, Alagheria, who came from somewhere in the Po valley, nor of his two brothers, Moronto and Eliseo. There was in Florence an Elisei family from Rome, but there is no evidence of a connection between them and the Alighieri. Cacciaguida had a son Alighiero, father of Bellincione, who likewise had a son Alighiero, father of Dante.

In the first rapture of fatherly welcome, the old warrior forgets to adapt his speech to mortal comprehension, and pours forth his love in words "so deep" that Dante cannot fathom his meaning. When the fire of his affection has subsided to a steady glow, and his language no longer passes earthly understanding, he proceeds to tell his descendant of the good old Florence of the first half of the 12th century. A strikingly similar picture is to be found in G. Villani's *Croniche*, VI, lxix. Those were the days of plain living and domestic peace.

Women were sure they would not have to end their days in exile, nor were they left alone while their husbands went to France on business. In one of those sweet scenes of home life which our poet sketches from time to time, we see a woman watching over the cradle, soothing her child with the baby talk "which first amuses fathers and mothers"; another matron, while she "draws the tresses from her distaff," retails to her little ones the folklore of her day, the legends of the founding of Fiesole, Troy, and Rome — stories happily preserved for us in the first book of Villani and in other chronicles.

4. The spirits in the Cross.

14. Meteors were explained as dry vapors which had risen so high as to take fire and then had plunged back in the direction of the earth.

22. 'The gem did not leave its ribbon': the bright spirit did not go outside the Cross. Silk ribbons studded with pearls were common in Dante's time.

28–30. 'O blood of mine, O lavish grace of God! To whom was Heaven's gate ever twice opened, as to thee?' Heaven receives Dante now, and will receive him again after his death; such a thing has never happened since the days of St. Paul. — The use of Latin — the language of Church and school — adds dignity to this celestial greeting. It is made more appropriate by the reminiscence of Anchises, to whom, indeed, the phrase *sanguis meus* (meaning 'my child') belongs: "Proice tela manu, sanguis meus" (cast from thy hand the sword, thou blood of mine!) in *Aen.*, VI, 835, where Anchises is addressing Julius Caesar.

34–36. Until now, Dante has not looked into the eyes of Beatrice in this sphere.

50. 'Derived' from reading of Dante's visit in the Book of Fate, 'where white and black are never altered.'

56. Unity is the beginning of number, as God is the beginning of thought; from the conception of unity is derived the conception of all numbers, and in the divine mind all thought is contained.

73–75. 'As soon as the primal Equality (God, in whom all powers are perfect and therefore equal) revealed himself to you, desire and faculty in each one of you became equal in weight': the blessed have no wish which they have not intelligence to fulfill.

86. 'Jewel': the Cross.

88. Cf. Mat. iii, 17: "This is my beloved Son, in whom I am well pleased."

92. 'Family name': Alighieri. Alighiero (or Allagherius), son of Cacciaguida, was the first male member of the family to bear this name, which, as we learn presently, he derived from his mother. His name occurs in documents of 1189 (where it is joined with that of his brother Preitenitto) and 1201.

93. The circle of Pride, in Purgatory. Dante apparently regarded pride as a family failing.

97. The old city walls: the *first* medieval walls, which were virtually identical with the Roman walls.

98. Beside these walls stood the ancient Abbey, the *Badia*, whose bell continued, in Dante's day, to mark the hours for the Florentines. 'Tierce' is the period from 6 to 9 A.M.; 'nones,' that from noon to 3 P.M.

104–105. The marriageable age had not yet become absurdly low, nor the dowry ruinously high.

106. There were no houses built on too large a scale for their occupants.

107–108. Sardanapālus, king of Assyria, was notorious in antiquity for his luxury and effeminacy. He is mentioned by Paulus Orosius and Egidio Colonna. Cf. Juvenal, *Satires*, X, 362:

> et venere et cenis et pluma Sardanapalli.

(... the loves and the banquets and the downy cushions of Sardanapalus.)

109–111. Rome was not yet surpassed in splendor by Florence, which has been swifter in its rise and will be swifter in its fall. Montemalo (or Montemallo), now Montemario, is a hill that affords the approaching traveler a view of Rome; similarly the height called Uccellatoio offers the stranger, as he draws near on the north, an outlook on Florence.

112. Bellincion Berti, father of the 'good Gualdrada' of *Inf.* XVI, 37, was a worthy and distinguished Florentine citizen of the second half of the 12th century.

115. Of the Nerli and del Vecchio families it seems that virtually nothing is known.

117. Cf. Pr. xxxi, 19: "She layeth her hands to the spindle, and her hands hold the distaff."

128. Cianghella, of the della Tosa family, a contemporary of Dante, seems to have been notorious for her immodesty. Boccaccio speaks of her in the *Corbaccio*, 228–230, — Lapo Salterello, also of Dante's time and one of his fellow exiles, a jurist and versifier, was in general a man of good renown; but Dino Compagni, in his *Cronica*, II, xxii, enumerates him among the "malvagi cittadini," and accuses him of corrupt practices.

129. For Cincinnatus, the plowman dictator, cf. VI, 46; for Cornelia, mother of the Gracchi, *Inf.* IV, 128.

133. Invoked in the pains of childbirth.

139. Conrad III, of Swabia, leader of the crusade of 1147. As Conrad III never came to Italy, possibly Dante has confounded him with Conrad II.

143. Mohammedanism.

144. The Popes, who are no longer interested in the reconquest of the Holy Land.

Canto XVI

Argument

"Iam vero quam sit inane, quam futtile nobilitatis nomen, quis non videat?" (Likewise, who sees not what a vain and idle thing it is to be called noble?) says Boethius, in *Consolatio Philosophiae*, III, Pr. vi. Other authors known to our poet, in Latin, Provençal, and Italian, disparage the glory of birth, and exalt the true nobility of character. Dante himself devotes the 3rd Canzone of the *Convivio* to the development of this theme, and touches upon it in *Monarchia*, II, iii, 4. Yet in the presence of his belted ancestor he cannot check a feeling of family pride, which betrays itself by the use of the respectful "voi." Amid the mortifications of exile, he must have taken real satisfaction in the thought of the knighthood won by old Cacciaguida; and in the *Paradiso* he makes the most of this distinguished forbear. To him he assigns a minute description of ancient Florence, and into his mouth he puts — in the next canto — a touching account of Dante's own banishment. In answer to the poet's questions concerning his people, the time of his boyhood, the size of Florence in his day, and the prominent men of the city, Cacciaguida furnishes us with a few precious biographical facts and an abundance of antiquarian information. In the long list of families illustrious two centuries before, but for the most part insignificant in 1300, we note a great many Germanic names, representing the old feudal aristocracy. Others, such as Caponsacco and Infangato, were evidently, at the start, humorous nicknames, handed down to descendants.

10. According to tradition, the plural *vos* was first used, in addressing one person, when Julius Caesar made himself Emperor. Cf. *Phars.*, V, 381–386.

11. Rome, the seat of the Papacy, is now the place where the Emperor is least honored. And in the environs of Rome *tu* is employed much more freely than it is in the more northerly parts of Italy.

13–15. Beatrice, 'who stood a little apart,' smiled indulgently at Dante's weakness, just as, in the Old French romance of *Lancelot du Lac* (cf. *Inf.* V, 127–138), the Dame de Malehaut, watching the first clandestine interview of Guinever and 'Lancelot, coughed on hearing the impassioned speech of the Queen. — The Lady of Malehaut, in whose castle Lancelot had for some time secretly lived unrecognized, was secretly in love with him. — Guinever, after having drawn from Lancelot the avowal of his love, asks: 'Whence comes this love of yours for me?' Then it is that (in some manuscripts but not in all) the Lady of Malehaut coughs.

25. John the Baptist is the patron saint of Florence.

28–29. Cf. *Met.*, VII, 79–81.

33. Dante cannot reproduce the old fashioned speech of Cacciaguida, but he suggests it with this line. He was aware that the vulgar tongue changes from generation to generation.

34. From the Annunciation (Luke i, 28). The Florentine year began with the Conception, March 25.

37–39. 'This fire (Mars) came 580 times to its Lion, to be rekindled under its paw.' Between the Conception — the beginning of the year 1 — and the birth of Cacciaguida, Mars returned 580 times to the constellation of Leo, which, being of like disposition to Mars, reinforces the influence of that planet. As Mars completes its revolution in 687 days, we shall get the year of Cacciaguida's birth by multiplying 687 by 580 and dividing by 365: 1091. He was therefore 56 when he followed the crusade, having lived from 1091 to 1147.

41–42. 'Where the last ward (the part of the city called Porta S. Piero) is first reached by the runner in your annual sports.' The races were run on June 24 (St. John's day) along the Corso, which enters the 'last ward' near the Mercato Vecchio; now Via degli Speziali.

43–45. With this sentence, presumably, Dante veils his lack of further information.

47. 'Fit for arms, between Mars and the Baptist' — between the old statue of Mars, on the river, and the Baptistery, on the north side (cf. *Inf.* XIII, 146–147; *Par.* XV, 134): the ancient city lay between these two monuments.

50. Towns near and belonging to Florence, which received many immigrants from them.

53–54. Galluzzo and Trespiano are villages a few miles south and north of Florence. Today they mark the city limits.

56. Aguglione was in Val di Pesa; Signa is on the Arno, west of Florence. The 'farmers' from these country towns, who in Florence have become prominent lawyers and politicians, are probably Baldo d'Aguglione and Fazio Morubaldini.

58. The clergy.

61. This is perhaps Lippo Velluti, a man of importance in Florence in the second half of the 13th century.

62. Semifonte, a stronghold in Val d' Elsa, was reduced by Florence in 1202. The acquisition of this and other places was facilitated by the position of Florence as head of a Tuscan league organized, under the patronage of the Church, for the purpose of resisting the encroachments of the Emperors, after the death of Henry VI.

63. Lippo's father and grandfather were soldiers. If the reference in these lines is not to him, the phrase may have its commoner sense of 'went begging.'

64. Montemurlo, a fortified place beyond Prato, was ceded by the Counts Guidi to Florence.

65. The Cerchi, from 'the parish of Acone' in Val di Sieve, became leaders of the White party in Florence.

66. Montebuono, a strong castle of the Buondelmonti in Val di Greve, was taken by Florence in 1135.

67–68. Cf. Aristotle, *Politics*, III, iii.

69. The human body is born pure and wholesome, but begins to lose its purity as soon as superfluous food is taken.

73. Luni, in Tuscany, and Urbisaglia, in the March of Ancona, were fallen cities. In Lucian's *Charon or the Spectators*, cities perish like men.

75. Chiusi, in Val di Chiana, and Sinigaglia, in the March of Ancona, were in decay, the first wasted by malaria, the second by bloodshed.

82–83. St. Thomas and Brunetto Latini, following the common opinion, attribute tides to the influence of the moon.

88–93. Old families that have declined or disappeared.

94. In 1280 the Cerchi bought the palace of the Counts Guidi, near the Porta S. Piero.

95. The Cerchi became leaders in party strife. Cf. note to l. 65.

96. The exile of the Whites, including many of the Cerchi, in 1302.

97. Ravignani: a great family of Porta S. Piero, from whom the Counts Guidi descended.

98–99. For Bellincione Berti, cf. XV, 112. A branch of his family took the name Bellincioni.

101. It would seem that the della Pressa family held public offices.

102. The Galigai, a Ghibelline family, 'had hilt and pummel gilded,' a sign of nobility.

103. A 'stripe of vair' (fur) traversed the scutcheon of the Pigli family.

104. The Sacchetti were an old Guelf clan. The other three had sunk into poverty in the 14th century.

105. The Galli had lost everything. — 'Those who blush for the bushel' are the Chiaramontesi, disgraced by one of their kin, who, when salt commissioner, used a false measure. Cf. *Purg.* XII, 105.

106. The 'stock' is that of the Donati. The Calfucci died out.

108. These families had almost vanished in the 14th century.

109. The Uberti, who in the latter part of the 12th century rebelled against the Florentine government and for a while gained control of the city. For Farinata degli Uberti, see *Inf.* X.

110–111. The Lamberti had golden balls on their shield. Both they and the Uberti were of German origin.

112–114. The Visdomini and the Tosinghi, 'keepers and defenders' of the Bishopric of Florence, administered the episcopal revenues, whenever the see was vacant, until a successor was chosen.

115. The 'arrogant race' is probably the Adimari family. Filippo Argenti (*Inf.* VIII, 61) belonged to this clan.

119–120. Ubertino Donati, who had married one daughter of Bellincione Berti, was displeased when another daughter was given in marriage to one of the Adimari.

121–122. The Caponsacchi, a great family of Fiesole, settled in Florence near the Mercato Vecchio.

123. The Giudi and Infangati declined in wealth and numbers.

125. The Porta Peruzza, named after the Peruzzi family, who lived near by.

126. In Dante's time the Peruzzi, or de la Pera, had apparently become insignificant.

127–130. Those who now wear any of the insignia of the Imperial Vicar, Hugh of Brandenburg, received their knighthood from him. Hugh the Great took up his abode in Florence, where he founded seven abbeys and created many knights. He died in 1001, on St. Thomas's day; and therefore the festival of the apostle renews every year the memory of the 'great baron.'

131–132. One, however, of the knights whose nobility goes back to Hugh, is now 'siding with the people.' This is Giano della Bella, who introduced, in 1293, severe reform measures directed against the nobles, and was banished in 1295. His family has somewhat changed the scutcheon of the 'great baron,' 'bordering' it with a 'fringe.'

133. These families also fell from their high estate.

134. *Borgo*: the quarter called Borgo Santi Apostoli, where the Gualterotti and Importuni lived.

135. The undesirable new neighbors are the Buondelmonti (cf. 1. 66), who, after the destruction of their castle of Montebuono in 1135, returned to take up their abode in Florence.

136. The Amidei. — The bloody feud between the Amidei and the Buondelmonti divided all Florence for a long time. Cf. G. Villani, *Croniche*, V, xxxviii.

137. The indignation of the Amidei against Buondelmonte dei Buondelmonti, who, on his wedding day, in 1215, forsook his betrothed — one of the Amidei — for a daughter of the Donati. To avenge this insult, the Amidei murdered him; and this was the beginning of the feud. Cf. *Inf.* XXVIII, 103-111.

141. The suggestion came from a certain Gualdrada Donati.

143. The Ema is a little stream that has to be crossed on the way from Montebuono to Florence.

145-147. 'But it was fitting that Florence, in her last peace, should offer a victim to that mutilated stone which guards the bridge' — the old, broken statue supposed to be of Mars (the first patron of Florence) at the end of the Ponte Vecchio. Cf. *Inf.* XIII, 143-150. The victim was Buondelmonte, who was killed on Easter morning at the foot of the statue.

153. The Florentine banner was, in those days, never 'turned upside-down,' in derision, by victorious enemies.

154. In 1251, after the expulsion of the Ghibellines, the Guelfs altered the Florentine standard from a white lily in a red field to a red lily in a white field. The Ghibellines kept the old colors.

Canto XVII

Argument

The younger Scipio, in the sixth book of Cicero's *De Re Publica*, is lifted to the skies in a dream, and there meets his great ancestor, who predicts to him the future course of his life. So it fares with Dante, who learns what is in store for him, not from the lips of Beatrice, as Virgil had led him to expect (*Inf.* X, 130-132), but from Cacciaguida. The picture of Dante's exile, as drawn here and in the *Convivio* I, iii, 3-6, is the more effective for its manly reticence, and for the author's habitual silence regarding the events of his external experience. The loss of reputation, of cherished family and friends, and of personal dignity is set forth in these brief passages of concentrated pathos, which no reader can ever forget, and which are in need of no commentary.

Less clear is the reference to the poet's fellow outcasts of the White party, whose companionship he describes as the worst affliction of all. In this large band of exiles, whose energies were bent on forcing their way back into the city and regaining the supremacy they had just lost, Dante was surely the man of most note and the natural leader. We have evidence of his activity in June, 1302, when they were in Pisa; in June, 1303, he was apparently not with them; but in March, 1304, when Cardinal Niccolò da Prato came to Florence as a peacemaker, Dante, appealing to him in a Latin letter (Epistola 1), made himself spokesman for the Whites. In the ill-fated military adventure of July, 1304, he had no part, nor did he share in the disastrous operations of 1306–1307. It was doubtless early in 1303 or in the spring of 1304 that he turned his back on his "wicked, foolish" comrades and "made a party by himself." There was obviously a violent difference of opinion on some matter of policy; Dante's advice was not followed, he left the party in disgust, and his opponents came to grief. Torraca suggests that the quarrel may have occurred in May, 1304, when the Whites chose twelve delegates to represent them in a parley with the Cardinal, and Dante was not one of the number.

Involved in this problem is the question of the date of Dante's residence in Verona, his "first refuge" after his banishment. Alberto della Scala, lord of Verona, died in 1301; his oldest son, Bartolommeo, on March 7, 1304; the next son, Alboino, in 1311; the third, Can Grande, outlived Dante. The "great Lombard" who received our poet so hospitably must have been either Bartolommeo or Alboino. Of the latter Dante speaks slightingly in the *Convivio*, IV, xvi, 6. If, however, Alighieri remained with the exiles until after the arrival of Niccolò da Prato, Alboino must have been his host, since Bartolommeo was dead. In the present state of our knowledge, the question reduces itself to a balance of the weight attached, on the one hand, to the epistle to the Cardinal, as an indication that Dante was still, in March, 1304, in active collaboration with the Whites, and, on the other, to the disrespectful allusion to Alboino in the latter part of the *Convivio*, as being inconsistent with the praise bestowed on the head of the house of the Scaligeri in our canto. Most commentators, following the poet's son Pietro, have identified the "great Lombard" with Bartolommeo. Some, as Torraca and I. Del Lungo (*Il Canto XVII del Paradiso*, 1910), have favored Alboino.

At the court of Verona, destined to become a great general and ruler and friend of learning, appears Dante's future patron, Can Grande della Scala, the man upon whom the exile's political hopes were to center after the untimely death of Henry VII. Cacciaguida's eulogy of this promising lad (a boy of nine in 1300) ends with one of those veiled prophecies which deal with the really unknown. With it we may compare the Hound of *Inferno* I, 100–111, and the Eagle of *Purgatorio* XXXIII, 37–51.

1–3. Eager to learn from his heavenly ancestor something about his kin, Dante compares himself to Phaëthon, the son of Apollo and Clȳmĕne, who, having been told that the god was not really his father, went to his mother to find out the truth: *Met.*, I, 748–756. For the accentuation of *Climenè*, cf. *Inf.* V, 4, and XXX, 2. — The example of Phaëthon still makes fathers cautious in granting their sons' requests, because of the tragic results of Apollo's indulgence, when he allowed Phaëthon to drive the chariot of the sun: *Met.*, II, 31–328.

5. The light of Cacciaguida.

14–16. The blessed see even 'contingent,' or casual, things — whether they be past, present, or future — as clearly as 'earthly minds' can grasp an eternal, concrete, elementary fact — as for instance the geometrical proposition that 'two obtuse angles cannot be contained in a triangle.' Cf. Aristotle, *Metaphysics*, IX, x.

17–18. Cf. *Summa Theologiae*, Prima, Qu. xiv, Art. 13.

27. 'An arrow foreseen comes slower' — i.e., strikes us with a less violent shock. Cf. *Summa Theologiae*, Secunda Secundae, Qu. cxxiii, Art. 9: "jacula quae praevidentur minus feriunt" (the blows that are foreseen strike with less force) (quoted from Gregory).

31. 'In no ambiguous terms,' such as heathen prophets used in order to ensnare the 'foolish folk.' Cf. *Aen.*, VI, 99: "Horrendas canit ambages." (She chants her dread enigmas.)

33. John i, 29: "Behold the Lamb of God, which taketh away the sin of the world."

37. 'Contingency' is the whole sequence of casual events, as distinguished from the eternal and inevitable. — Contingency, or casualty, is confined to the world of matter.

40–42. 'But it [contingency] does not derive inevitability therefrom (from being foreseen by God), any more than a boat going downstream derives inevitability from the eye in which it is mirrored.' Casual things are no more necessary from being anticipated by omniscience than they would be if there were no power to see them coming. Cf. *Summa Theologiae*, Prima, Qu. xxii. Art. 4.

46–47. Hippolȳtus was driven from Athens by the false accusation of his stepmother, Phaedra. Cf. *Met.*, XV, 493–505, l. 498: "sceleratae fraude novercae" (the wiles of his accursed stepmother).

50. Apparently the exile of Dante and other opponents of the Papal policy was planned in Rome in April, 1300, two months before Dante's priorate.

51. The place 'where Christ is bought and sold every day' is Rome.

52. Cf. *Cons.*, I, Pr. iv, end: "Quo fit ut existimatio bona prima omnium deserat infelices." (By which means it cometh to pass that the first loss that miserable men suffer is their estimation and the good opinion that was had of them.)

53. *Vendetta*: many regarded the disgrace and death of Boniface VIII as a divine punishment for his cruelty and ambition.

62. The Whites, Dante's fellow exiles. — Cf. Ecclus. viii, 18–20.

63. Vale of tears, misery.

71. *Gran Lombardo*: the head of the great house of the Scaligeri, or della Scala family, of Verona.

72. The Scaligeri had as their armorial bearings a ladder, to which was added, at the top, an Imperial eagle.

77. Mars.

82. Before 1312, when the Gascon Pope, Clement V, after promising to support the Emperor, Henry VII, in his expedition to Italy, promoted opposition to it. Cf. *Inf.* XIX, 83; *Par.* XXX, 133–148.

84. Indifference to wealth and to peril is a characteristic of 'magnanimity': *Summa Theologiae*, Secunda Secundae, Qu. cxxix, Art. 8, end.

97–99. Dante's life extended long beyond the miserable end of Boniface and of Corso Donati (*Purg.* XXIV, 82–87). The latter was a 'neighbor' in the strictest sense of the word. It may be, however, that l. 98 refers to Dante's enduring fame, rather than to his bodily existence.

100–102. 'When, by its silence, the blessed soul showed that it had finished putting the woof upon the web which I had given it warped.' Cacciaguida had embroidered his answer upon the canvas of Dante's question.

110. Florence.

129. Dante chose to write his poem in the 'comic' rather than the 'tragic' style, that he might, when occasion required, sacrifice elegance to vigor.

130–132. Cf. *Cons.*, III, Pr. i: "Talia sunt quippe quae restant, ut degustata quidem mordeant, interius autem recepta dulcescant." (For the remedies which remain are of that sort that they are bitter to the taste, but being inwardly received wax sweet.)

135. 'Proof': because it requires exceptional courage to 'strike the highest peaks.'

138. The statement was perhaps approximately true for Dante's first readers.

139–142. The listener is never satisfied nor convinced by an unknown example or an obscure argument.

Canto XVIII

Argument

After noting, in the Cross of Mars, various champions of the Faith (among whom are two Old Testament heroes), Dante finds himself transferred to the next planet and once more is made aware of his uplifting by the increased beauty of his guide and by the changed color of the light that envelops him. Human justice, according to our poet, is a product of the heaven of Jupiter, and in this star appear the souls of the just. They reveal their nature by arranging themselves successively in the shapes of the letters that spell the first verse of the Book of Wisdom: "Love righteousness, ye that be judges of the earth." "*Diligite justitiam*" are "the first verb and noun" of the text, and "*qui judicatis terram*" are "the last." — in all, "thirty-five vowels and consonants." First the bright spirits flutter and sing; then, arraying themselves in the form of one of these letters, they are silent for a little while, after which they break ranks and resume their tuneful flight until the next letter is fashioned. Like the cranes which Lucan describes in *Pharsalia*, V, 711–716:

> Effingunt varias casu monstrante figuras;
> . . . .
> Et turbata perit dispersis littera pinnis.

(They describe various chance-taught figures ... until the letter is broken and disappears as the birds are scattered.)

Having reached the end of the sentence, they remain in the shape of the final M, symbol of Monarchy, the embodiment of justice. Presently a fresh swarm

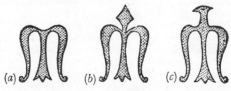

(a)   (b)   (c)

Figures illustrating the successive changes of the shape assumed by the Spirits of the Just, from M to the Florentine Lily and Imperial Eagle. (From the design of the Duke of Sermoneta.)

of lights descends upon the top of the figure, and more than a thousand rise like sparks from its lower parts, transforming it into the Imperial Eagle — the eagle of heraldry.   Monarchy is the earthly representative of Justice, and the ultimate form of Monarchy is the Empire.

1. Cf. *Summa Theologiae*, Prima, Qu. xxxiv, Art. 1: "Id enim quod intellectus concipiendo format est verbum." (Therefore it follows that the interior concept of the mind is called a word.)

2. Cacciaguida is called a 'mirror' because he reflects God's mind.

6. Cf. Deut. xxxii, 35: "To me belongeth vengeance, and recompence."

21. Beatitude consists not only in acceptance of the demonstration of divine truth but also in the companionship of the blessed and the comprehension of their state as a manifestation of divine grace.   This idea is conveyed by Beatrice in a figure as appropriate as it is sweet and modest.

25. Cacciaguida.

28. The 'tree' of the heavens, which derives all its sustenance from above, is conceived as a fir, whose branches grow in rings or 'tiers' around the trunk.   The fifth ring is the heaven of Mars.

36. The soul, when named, will flash over the cross as lightning flashes across a cloud.

38. Joshua. successor of Moses and conqueror of the Promised Land.

40. Judas Maccabaeus, the Hebrew champion who delivered his people from the tyranny of the Syrians.   See 1 Macc. ii–ix.

42. 'And joy was the whip of the top,' i.e., it was joy that made it (the light) spin.   Several times in the *Paradiso* Dante makes a swift rotary motion the symbol of keen delight.

43. Charlemagne and Roland are characters in the Old French *Chanson de Roland*, which was a favorite romance in western Europe.

46. William, count of Orange, is the hero of a group of Old French epics, of which the best known is the *Aliscans*.   He combatted the Saracens in southern France, as Charlemagne and Roland fought against them in Spain.   Associated with him is the gigantic Renoart, of Saracen birth but baptized.

47. Godfrey of Bouillon, leader of the first crusade (1096), battled with the Saracens in the Holy Land and became first Christian king of Jerusalem.

48. Robert Guiscard, a Norman conqueror of the second half of the 11th century, took a large part of southern Italy and Sicily from the Saracens.

58–60. Cf. Aristotle, *Ethics*, II, iii, 1.

61–63. Thus from an increase of Beatrice's loveliness I inferred that I had risen to a greater and swifter sphere.   Since all the heavens revolve together from east to west, the outer must move faster than the inner, just as the tire of a wheel moves quicker than the hub; and as Dante proceeds from the center to one heaven after another, each successive sphere he reaches must, in a given time, cover a greater arc than its predecessor.   As long as Dante remains in a sphere, he of course revolves with it.

64–66. The change from the red light of Mars to the whiteness of Jupiter is compared to the change in a pale lady's face when a blush suddenly passes from it.

68. The 'temperate sixth star.' Jupiter, is between hot Mars and cold Saturn.

70. 'Torch of Jove': the planet Jupiter.

82. The Muses are associated with the winged horse, Pegasus.   It is not clear whether Dante had in mind any special Muse, nor, if so, whether the one invoked is Calliope (*Purg.* I, 9), Urania (*Purg.* XXIX, 41), or Euterpe (who presided over the sphere of Jupiter).

94. The Italian name of the letter is *emme*.   For this whole passage see illustration, in Argument above.

96. The planet looked like a silver background with a golden M embroidered on it.

109–111. 'He (God) who paints there has no one to direct him, but he himself directs; and from him we recognize that power which is the essence of nest building.' The instinct of the little bird, which is able to build its nest without having any need of a pattern, comes directly from God, and, in its own small way, serves as an image of the creative activity of God, who constructs solely from his inner conception. Cf. *Summa Theologiae*, Prima, Qu. xix, Art. 4, end.

112. The rest of the blessed souls, those that had not yet left their places in the M.

113. The Florentine lily is very similar in shape to a capital M of the type Dante has in mind. (See illustration above.) These lines may indicate that the Guelf souls, though seemingly reluctant at first to give up their own standard, readily conform to the Imperial design.

122. Mat. xxi, 12.

123. Cf. Acts xx, 28: "the church of God, which he hath purchased with his own blood."

124. Cf. Luke ii, 13: "militia caelestis" — "heavenly host."

126. Cf. Romans iii, 12: "they are all gone out of the way."

129. Nowadays wars are waged by means of excommunications and interdicts.

130. John XXII, who was Pope when Dante was writing, issued and revoked many excommunications. He amassed a large fortune. In 1317 he excommunicated Can Grande della Scala, who remained under the ban until his death.

132. Cf. Isaiah iii, 14: "for ye have eaten up the vineyard."

133–136. My heart is so set on John the Baptist (i.e., on the gold florin bearing his image) that I have forgotten Peter and Paul. — Soon after Dante's death John XXII caused a scandal by having minted in Avignon a gold coin almost exactly like the florin of Florence.

Canto XIX

Argument

The doctrine emphasized in this canto is that Heaven can be won only through faith in Christ. "Neither is there salvation in any other: for there is none other name under heaven given among men, whereby we must be saved" (Acts iv, 12). "Quod nemo, quantumcunque moralibus et intellectualibus virtutibus, et secundum habitum et secundum operationem perfectus, absque fide salvari potest, dato quod nunquam aliquid de Christo audiverit. Nam hoc ratio humana per se iustum intueri non potest, fide tamen adiuta potest. Scriptum est enim ad Hebraeos: 'Impossibile est sine fide placere Deo'" (That no one, however perfect in the moral and intellectual virtues, both as to disposition and practice, may be saved without faith, if he have never heard aught of Christ. For human reason of itself cannot see that this is just, but helped by faith it may. For it is written *ad Hebraeos*, "Without faith it is impossible to please God.") (*Mon.*, II, vii, 4–5.) That a pagan on the banks of the Indus, who has never heard of Christ, should be lost for lack of faith seems to mere human reason unjust. But to attribute injustice to God is a contradiction of terms; for we derive our notion of right and wrong from him, and what we call justice is simply his will. "Ex hiis iam liquet quod ius, cum sit bonum, per prius in mente Dei est; et, cum omne quod in mente Dei est sit Deus (iuxta illud: 'Quod factum est in ipso vita erat'), et Deus maxime se ipsum velit, sequitur quod ius a Deo, prout in eo est, sit volitum. Et cum voluntas et volitum in Deo sit idem, sequitur ulterius quod divina voluntas sit ipsum ius. Et iterum ex hoc sequitur quod ius in rebus nichil est aliud quam similitudo divine voluntatis; unde fit quod quicquid divine voluntati non consonat, ipsum ius esse non possit, et quicquid divine voluntati est consonum, ius ipsum sit. Quapropter querere utrum de iure factum sit aliquid, licet alia verba sint, nichil tamen aliud queritur quam utrum factum sit secundum quod Deus vult" (Hence it is clear that right, since it is good, exists primarily in the mind of God. And since everything that is in the mind of God is God — according to that word "What was made was life in him" — and since God supremely wills himself, it follows that right is willed by God, inasmuch as it is in him. And since in God the will and what is willed are identical, it follows further that the divine will is right itself, and hence it follows again that right as manifested in things is nought else than the similitude of the divine will. Whence it comes to pass that whatever is not consonant with the divine will cannot be right, and whatever is consonant with the divine will is right. Wherefore to ask whether anything takes place by right, though the words differ, is yet nought else than to inquire whether it takes place according to what God wills.) (*Mon.*, II, ii, 4–6.) When Dante propounds to the Eagle, in the heaven of Jupiter, the problem of the justice of the fate of the virtuous heathen, he is rebuked with two solemn warnings, one before and one after the statement of the question. Man must not presume to fathom the unfathomable purpose of his Maker. "What shall we say then? Is there unrighteousness with God? God forbid. For he saith to Moses, I will have mercy on whom I will have mercy, and I will have compassion on whom I will have compassion ... Shall the thing formed say to him that formed it, Why hast thou made me thus? Hath not the potter power over the clay, of the same lump to make one vessel unto honour, and another unto dishonour?" (Romans ix, 14–21). Only in the following canto do we find the solution, which proves to be not inconsistent with the human idea of right.

On earth justice is possible only under a universal monarchy: this is shown by the strife among kings, when there is no Emperor to control them. Cf. *Convivio*, IV, iv, 1–4. It is fitting, then, that a fearful arraignment of the sovereigns ruling in 1300 should be uttered by the Imperial Eagle. "Et vidi, et audivi vocem unius aquilae volantis per medium caeli, dicentis voce magna: Vae, vae, vae habitantibus in terra" (And I beheld, and heard an eagle flying through the midst of heaven, saying with a loud voice, Woe, woe, woe, to the inhabiters of the earth) (Rev. viii, 13). The passage reminds one of Sordello's famous poem on the death of Blacatz, and also of the series of portraits in the Valley of the Princes, in

Purgatorio VII. "And another book was opened, which is the book of life: and the dead were judged out of those things which were written in the books, according to their works" (Rev. xx, 12). Thus the living kings are judged by the Eagle — those Christian kings whose record is such as to deserve rebuke even from the heathen. Contrasted with them is the Eagle itself, whose single voice — a compound of all the voices of all the just — symbolizes the unity of justice and the perfect harmony of the righteous. Such concord no pen ever described before.

9. Cf. 1 Cor. ii, 9: "Eye hath not seen, nor ear heard, neither have entered into the heart of man ..."

28-29. The angelic order of the Thrones, which reflects God's judgments, presides over the sphere of Saturn. Cf. IX, 61-62.

35. Cf. *Met.*, VIII, 238 ("plausit pennis" — clapped her wings) and XIV, 507 ("plausis circumvolat alis" — he circled round with flapping wings).

40. Cf. Pr. viii, 27: "he set a compass upon the face of the depth."

44. Cf. XVIII, 1. See *Summa Theologiae*, Prima, Qu, xxxii, Art 1: "per verbum intelligitur ratio idealis, per quam Deus omnia condidit" (the word as meaning the ideal type whereby God made all things).

45. Cf. XIII, 52-78. God's ideal conception is infinite, while the created universe is finite.

46. 'And a proof of this (the inferiority of every created thing to the creative mind) is that the first proud one (Lucifer) ...'

48. 'Fell unripe, because he would not wait for light.' Without special grace (the "light of glory") it is impossible for any created mind to see God in his essence (cf. XIV, 48); but Lucifer and his companions in pride, did not wait to be given the light of glory but tried by their own powers to penetrate God and to become like him. Cf. *Vulg. El.*, I, ii, 4: "divinam curam perversi expectare noluerunt." (They perversely refused to wait for the divine care.) See *Summa Theologiae*, Prima, Qu. lxii-lxiii.

58-60. Earthly intelligence, then, can no more penetrate eternal justice than a human eye can penetrate the ocean. Cf. Ps. xxxvi, 6: "thy judgments are a great deep."

66. Without grace, all that we take to be light is darkness, either the shadow or the poison of the flesh — either ignorance or vice.

72. Cf. Romans x, 14.

79. Cf. Romans ix, 20: "Nay but, O man, who art thou that repliest against God?"

82. 'Surely, for him who sophisticates with me ...' Dante is putting subtle questions about justice to the Eagle, who is its embodiment.

83. If you mortals had not the Bible and its clear utterances to guide you, there would be no end to your sophistries, since even with the Bible you enter into such discussions.

85. Cf. *Cons.*, III, Pr. iii: "Vos quoque, O terrena animalia" (you also, O earthly creatures).

87. Cf. Malachi iii, 6: "For I am the Lord, I change not."

89. 'No created goodness draws it (the divine will) to itself.'

104. For the third time we have *Cristo* in rhyme with itself: cf. XII, 71. See also XIV, where the rhyming lines are the same as in this canto: 104, 106, 108.

106. Mat. vii, 22-23.

110. Mat. xxv, 31-46.

115. Albert of Austria. Cf. *Purg.* VI, 97.

116. The devastation of Bohemia in 1304. — The pen of the recording angel.

118. 'On the Seine': in France.

119. Philip the Fair, to supply himself with money after the battle of Courtray in 1302, debased the coinage of the realm, causing great misery.

120. Philip died in 1314 from a fall occasioned by a wild boar which ran between his horse's legs. *Colpo di cotenna,* 'boarskin blow,' is an odd phrase: the king's death was due, not to the tusks of the boar, but to its bristly hide brushing against the horse.

123. The first part of the 14th century saw the wars of Edward I and Edward II against the Scots under Wallace and Bruce.

125. Ferdinand IV of Castile and Wenceslaus IV (*Purg.* VII, 101).

127. Charles II of Naples, titular King of Jerusalem, was called 'the Cripple' on account of his lameness.

128-129. His goodness will be marked 1, his wickedness 1000. He seems to have had no virtue except liberality: cf. VIII, 82; *Purg.* XX, 79.

131. Frederick of Aragon, King of Sicily: cf. *Purg.* VII, 119; *Conv.*, IV, vi, 20; *Vulg. El.*, I, xii, 5. After warring for some years with Charles of Naples, he made peace with him and married his daughter. Upon the death of Emperor Henry VII, he abandoned the Ghibelline cause.

132. *Aen.*, III, 707-715.

133-135. To indicate at the same time his insignificance and his wickedness, his many misdeeds shall be recorded in shorthand.

137. James, King of Majorca and Minorca. — James II of Aragon. Cf. *Purg.* VII, 119.

139. Concerning Dionysius of Portugal and Hakon of Norway, Dante probably knew little.

140. Rascia was a state made up of parts of Servia, Bosnia, Croatia, and Dalmatia. Its king in 1300 was a certain Stephen Ouros, who counterfeited the Venetian ducat.

142. The throne of Hungary, which belonged to Charles Martel (VIII, 64-66), was usurped by Andrew III.

144. Navarre would be happy if she could protect herself with the mountain chains that enfold her — that is, if she could make the Pyrenees a bulwark against France, which is destined to annex her on the death of her queen, Joanna, married to Philip the Fair.

145-147. We may regard as a 'foretaste' and a warning of these great disasters the misfortunes of a couple of towns in Cyprus, which are already bewailing and scolding about their 'beast,' the dissolute King of Cyprus, Henry II of Lusignan.

148. This little beast trots along beside the big ones on the path of crime.

Canto XX

Argument

By way of answer to Dante's question in the preceding canto, we now find illustrated the possibility of salvation for a virtuous man living in pagan times. "Invincible" (that is, insuperable, inevitable) ignorance is not an absolute bar: cf. *Summa Theologiae*, Prima Secundae, Qu. lxxvi, Art. 2. Often, says St. Thomas, has grace been extended to the worthy but otherwise unenlightened: "multis gentilium facta fuit revelatio de Christo ... Sibylla etiam praenuntiavit quaedam de Christo ... Si qui tamen salvati fuerunt quibus revelatio non fuit facta, non fuerunt salvati absque fide Mediatoris; quia etsi non habuerunt fidem explicitam, habuerunt tamen fidem implicitam in divina providentia, credentes Deum esse liberatorem hominum secundum modos sibi placitos, et secundum quod aliquibus veritatem cognoscentibus Spiritus revelasset" (Many of the gentiles received revelations of Christ ... The Sibyl too foretold certain things about Christ ... If, however, some were saved without receiving any revelation, they were not saved without faith in a Mediator, for, though they did not believe in Him explicitly, they did, nevertheless, have implicit faith through believing in Divine providence, since they believed that God would deliver mankind in whatever way was pleasing to Him, and according to the revelation of the Spirit to those who knew the truth) (*Summa Theologiae*, Secunda Secundae, Qu. ii, Art. 7). The *Commedia*, however, affords only two individual examples: that of Cato in *Purgatorio* I, and, in the present canto, that of Ripheus, an inconspicuous character in the *Aeneid*. Nowhere, before Dante, do we find any suggestion that this Trojan prince attained Heaven, nor that he was of particular importance. Virgil mentions his name, with those of other Trojans, in *Aen.*, II, 339 and 394. In *Aen.*, II, 426–427, he adds a brief description:

> Cadit et Ripheus, iustissimus unus
> Qui fuit in Teucris, et servantissimus aequi.

(Ripheus, too, falls, foremost in justice among the Trojans, and most zealous for the right.)

Nothing more. But these words evidently made a profound impression on Dante and led him to conjecture that such devotion to justice must have been a result of grace — of that divine plan which no created mind can penetrate. The upright heathen, who has made the most of his natural endowments, is met by grace, which moves him to love good above everything else and finally reveals to him the essential truth of salvation through Christ. The choice of such a minor personage as Ripheus emphasizes the mystery of God's predestination. On the other hand, Ripheus was a Trojan, a representative of that noble stock from which the Romans sprang. And among the Trojans he was "the most righteous of all, and the strictest observer of justice."

Quite different is the case of the just Emperor Trajan, who, in Christian times, died a pagan, but, in response to the prayer of St. Gregory the Great, was allowed to emerge from the lower world (where conversion is impossible) and resume his body for a little while — long enough to embrace the true faith and secure a place in Heaven. A reference to this widely current legend occurs in *Purgatorio* X, 73–76: Trajan's redemption is an example of the efficacy of saintly intercession. The effect of petition in one's own behalf is illustrated by a Biblical character, King Hezekiah. We are to understand, however, that in all such instances God's will is not altered, the prayer itself being foreordained.

Grouped with the three princes already mentioned are David, chosen by God to be ruler over his people, William the Good, the just king of Sicily, and the Emperor Constantine, who exemplifies the doctrine that the evil consequences of a well meant act do not constitute guilt for the doer. Of these six foremost champions of justice, two are ancient Hebrews, three belong to classical antiquity, and one is a modern. These spirits form the Eagle's eye: cf. illustration, p. 268.

David is the pupil, and the other five make up the eyebrow. The curve in which the latter are arranged is evidently a semicircle, although the poet calls it *cerchio* and *tondo*. In the description of this company we find a sort of formal symmetry that reminds us of the architectural structure of lines 25–63 in *Purgatorio* XII, where are pictured the carvings on the floor of the terrace of Pride: in our canto lines 37–72 fall into six sections of six verses each, and the second tiercet of every section begins with "Ora conosce." Thus the number six is made conspicuous in the sixth heaven.

Eye and eyebrow of the Eagle formed by:
1. David, 2. Trajan, 3. Hezekiah, 4. Constantine,
5. William of Sicily, and 6. Ripheus.

The Eagle, in this canto, is responsible for three very striking figures: the murmur of countless voices rising from the bird's body up through the neck, like the sound of many waters, until it takes the form of speech in the beak; the silence of the single voice of the bird, followed by a chorus of the individual souls that compose it, even as the disappearance of the sun introduces the great host of stars, which shine with its light; the satisfaction of the Eagle in the completion of its divine message — a satisfaction compared to that of the lark, which flies singing into the sky and then suddenly stops, sated with the sweetness of its own note. This last simile goes back to the Provençal poet Bernart de Ventadorn.

3. Cf. *Aen.*, II, 795: "consumpta nocte" (when night is spent).

6. Dante thought of all the stars as deriving their light from the sun.

19. Cf. Ezekiel xliii, 2: "his voice was like a noise of many waters."

22–24. In the cittern, or lute, 'the sound is shaped at the neck,' where the fingering is done; in the reed, at the holes.

38. David.

39. See 2 Samuel vi, 2–17. — The Ark of the Covenant.

45. For the story of Trajan's justice to the poor widow for the death of her son, see *Purg*. X, 73–93.

48. The life of the souls in Limbus.

51. King Hezekiah being "sick unto death," Isaiah announced to him his impending fate. "Then he turned his face to the wall, and prayed unto the Lord," and "wept sore." Whereupon the Lord sent word through Isaiah that he had heard Hezekiah's prayer and seen his tears. "I will heal thee," he said. "And I will add unto thy days fifteen years." See 2 Kings xx, 1–6; also Isaiah xxxviii, 1–5. There is no mention here of penitence.

54. 'Turns today's into tomorrow's down on earth.' In such cases the 'prayer' and its result are a part of the divine plan.

55–57. Constantine, ceding Rome to the Pope and transferring the capital to Byzantium, made himself, the Eagle, and the laws Greek. Cf. *Inf*. XIX, 115–117; *Inf*. XXVII, 94–97; *Purg*. XXXII, 124–129; *Par*. VI, 1–3.

58–59. Cf. *Summa Theologiae*, Prima Secundae, Qu. xx, Art. 5.

62. William II, called 'the Good,' king of Sicily in the second half of the 12th century.

63. The kings of Naples and Sicily who were rebuked in XIX, 127–135.

76. 'Thus the image appeared to me, (satisfied) with the stamp' of God's will.

79–80. My doubt showed through me, as a coat of paint shows through glass.

94. Mat. xi, 12: "the kingdom of heaven suffereth violence."

100. The first and fifth are Trajan and Ripheus. (See figure in Argument above.)

105. The one (Ripheus) had faith in the feet (of Christ) that were to suffer (being nailed to the cross), the other (Trajan) had faith in the feet that had suffered. *Passuri* and *passi* are Latin future and perfect participles. Both Ripheus and Trajan had faith in Christ, one before and one after the crucifixion.

106. The soul of Trajan.

108. The hopefulness of St. Gregory.

111. Trajan's will.

116. 'Second death'—when Trajan died for the second time. The phrase is not used in its theological sense (as in *Inf.* I, 117).

118. The inclination of the will to good is a result of grace: *Summa Theologiae*, Prima Secundae, Qu. cxi, Art. 2.

120. The 'first wave' of a fountain is the water that is gushing into it from the bottom.

122–123. Cf. St. Thomas, *Summa Theologiae*, Prima Secundae, Qu. cix, Art. 5.

127–128. *Purg.* XXIX, 121–129. The three theological virtues (Faith, Hope, and Charity, whom Dante had seen beside the right wheel of the chariot of the Church) were Ripheus's baptism.

137–138. 'For our good is perfected by this good, namely, that we will what God wills.' Our happiness is made perfect by the complete surrender of our will to God.

142–148. While the Eagle speaks, the lights of Trajan and Ripheus flash together (like the twinkling of a pair of eyes) at the two ends of the semicircle, — just as a lute player accompanies a singer by touching the strings.

Canto XXI

Argument

The sphere of the cold planet, Saturn, symbolizes the spiritual state of contemplative minds. Here Dante encounters an atmosphere of monastic discipline. His eagerness to penetrate the secret of predestination is kindly but firmly checked. No song is heard. His beauteous guide refrains from smiling. According to the Pseudo-Dionysius, the highest contemplation ends in silence, without words or concepts. The Rule of St. Benedict admonishes us to rise to glory by the Jacob's Ladder of humility, two of whose twelve steps are silence and the mortification of laughter (Busnelli, II, 92–93). The silence of the souls and the seriousness of Beatrice are, it is true, artistically turned to double account by the author, who wishes to create a suggestion of loveliness beyond anything hitherto conceived. We have seen the brightness and swiftness of the lights increase from sphere to sphere; at this point the absence of description serves to convey the impression of a still higher degree of intensity.

Corresponding to the Cross in Mars and the Eagle in Jupiter, we find in Saturn a Ladder of golden light, the emblem of Contemplation, stretching upward farther than the eye can follow — such a ladder as Jacob once saw. "And he dreamed, and behold a ladder set upon the earth, and the top of it reached to heaven: and behold the angels of God ascending and descending on it" (Gen. xxviii, 12). A similar ladder adorns the gown of Lady Philosophy in the *Consolatio Philosophiae* of Boethius (I, Pr. i). In the fragmentary Old Provençal *Boeci* — probably through an error in reading the Latin text — the figures climbing the rungs are called birds; and by an odd coincidence Dante likens to birds the bright spirits that come swarming down the steps to meet him. Foremost among them is the stern reformer and famous doctor of the Church, Peter Damian.

This Peter, born in Ravenna in 1007, came of a family so poor that he was abandoned by his mother. As a child he tended pigs until he was rescued and sent to school by his brother Damian, then Archdeacon of Ravenna. In gratitude he afterward named himself "Damiani," or Damian's. Having made good use of his opportunities, he won fame and wealth as a teacher in his native city. But he soon sickened of the corruption of the world, especially of the clergy, and withdrew in 1037 to the Benedictine monastery of Santa Croce di Fonte Avellana on a mountainside in Umbria. There he preached and practised the strictest asceticism. Some twenty years later he reluctantly became Cardinal and Bishop of Ostia, and was sent on several important missions; as soon as possible, however, he returned to his cloister. He died in 1072. Among his writings — the most important of which are concerned with the reform of Church discipline — is one entitled *De Quadragesima sive de Quadraginta duabus Hebraeorum Mansionibus*, an allegorical treatise which Dante may have known.

Another saintly Peter of Ravenna was Pietro degli Onesti, who called himself and was universally called "Petrus Peccans," or Peter the Sinner. He founded in 1096 the monastery of Santa Maria in Porto, where his grave is still to be seen. Apparently there was in Dante's time some confusion of these two Peters, and scholars and editors have continued to debate the proper punctuation of the verb in l. 122, whether to understand it as *fu* (third person) or *fu'* (first person), in which matter the manuscripts are of little help, since the apostrophe would not be there in any case. Petrocchi's decision to give the form as in the first person is therefore a matter of interpretation, which has been followed here as being the meaning more probably intended. Pier Damiano did indeed commonly sign his name *Petrus peccans* (as did also Pietro degli Onesti, however!).

6. Sěmělě, daughter of Cadmus and mother of Bacchus, having insisted on beholding her lover, Jupiter, in all his heavenly majesty, was burned to ashes by his splendor: *Met.*, III, 253–315; cf. *Inf.* XXX, 2.

13-15. Saturn ,'the seventh brightness,' being in line with the constellation of Leo, its cold influence 'now radiates downward' mitigated by the heat of the Lion.

18. Saturn.

24. 'By balancing the one side with the other': i.e., by weighing in the scales my desire to see Beatrice against my desire to obey her.

25-27. The cold, crystal planet 'bears the name' of Saturn, that 'dear governor' of the world who ruled in the Golden Age.

40-42. When the sparkling host of souls, in its descent, reaches a 'certain round' of the ladder (probably the one nearest Dante), it breaks up into groups that hover and flit like birds.

59. The hymns sung by the spirits in the preceding spheres.

76. Why does God choose one soul for a particular office, rather than another? Once more Dante is confronted with the inscrutable mystery of predestination, which perturbs and baffles him. And once more his curiosity is curbed. Cf. XIX, 52-66, 79-90; XX, 130-138.

90. 'I match the clearness of my flame.' Again the doctrine that happiness depends on clearness of spiritual vision, which is a gift of grace.

92. The Seraphim are the angels who are closest to God, and who represent divine love.

101-102. 'Consider, then, how it can do on earth' (where it 'is smoky') 'that which it cannot do' in Heaven (where it 'shines').

106. The northern part of the Apennines.

109. Catria is a high eastern spur of the Apennines, between Urbino and Gubbio.

110. 'Hermitage' (cf. *Purg.* V, 96): the monastery of Santa Croce di Fonte Avellana.

122. The monastery of Santa Maria in Porto, 'on the Adriatic shore,' near Ravenna.

125. The cardinal's hat.

126. 'Which is shifted' (literally 'poured') 'only from bad to worse': each successive cardinal is worse than the one before.

127. St. Peter. See John i, 42: "And when Jesus beheld him, he said, Thou art Simon the son of Jona: thou shalt be called Cephas, which is by interpretation, A stone." *Petrus* is a translation of the Aramaic *cephas.* — St. Paul, the 'chosen vessel.' See Acts ix, 15. Cf. *Inf.* II, 28. — Cf. *Par* XVIII, 131.

Canto XXII

Argument

The deafening cry of reprobation and prophecy of punishment, with which the preceding canto ends, leaves us in startled and wondering suspense, much as we were left at the close of the 20th canto of the *Purgatorio*, when the mountain shook and all the souls raised a shout of thanksgiving at the release of Statius. Dante and his readers are, however, soon reassured; and presently more shining spirits appear, brightest among them the great founder of the Benedictine order. St. Benedict's career is related by Gregory the Great in his *Dialogi*, II. He lived from 480 to 543. Born in Nursia, he was educated in Rome, but at the age of fourteen withdrew to the wilderness, where he dwelt for three years in a cave. His mature life was devoted to the conversion of pagans and the direction of his busy and scholarly order.

Between Saturn and the fixed stars is a distance greater than any hitherto traversed by Dante.   The long, swift ascent symbolizes the uplifting of the soul by contemplation.   In the 8th sphere, which contains countless heavenly bodies, the poet enters the constellation of Gemini, under whose influence he was born. Thus, in a spiritual sense, he returns, like Plato's departed, to his native star: cf. *Par.* IV, 52–57.   Beneath him are the sun, the moon, and all the planets, and, lowest, our little earth, so tiny that its pettiness makes him smile.   Once St. Benedict, standing at a window, had a similar vision, suddenly beholding the whole world collected, as it were, under one sunbeam (Gregory the Great, *Dialogi*, II, xxxv).

A closer parallel to Dante's experience, however, is to be found in Cicero's *De Re Publica*, VI, where Scipio, in a dream, is lifted to the skies.   "Erant autem eae stellae, quas numquam ex hoc loco vidimus, et eae magnitudines omnium, quas esse numquam suspicati sumus, ex quibus erat ea minima, quae ultima a caelo, citima terris, luce lucebat aliena.   Stellarum autem globi terrae magnitudinem facile vincebant.   Iam ipsa terra ita mihi parva visa est, ut me imperii nostri ... paeniteret" (There were stars which we never see from the earth, and they were all larger than we have ever imagined.   The smallest of them was that farthest from heaven and nearest the earth which shone with a borrowed light. The starry spheres were much larger than the earth; indeed the earth itself seemed to me so small that I was scornful of our empire) (*De Re Publica*, VI, xvi). He sees the starry sphere, the seven planets (including sun and moon), and the earth.   The shade of his ancestor says: "Omnis enim terra, quae colitur a vobis, angustata verticibus, lateribus latior, parva quaedam insula est circumfusa illo mari, quod Atlanticum, quod magnum, quem Oceanum appellatis in terris, qui tamen tanto nomine quam sit parvus, vides.   Ex his ipsis cultis notisque terris num aut tuum aut cuiusquam nostrum nomen vel Caucasum hunc, quem cernis, transcendere potuit vel illum Gangen tranatare?" (For that whole territory which you hold, being narrow from North to South, and broader from East to West, is really only a small island surrounded by that sea which you on the earth call the Atlantic, the Great Sea, or the Ocean.   Now you see how small it is in spite of its proud name!   Do you suppose that your fame or that of any of us could ever go beyond those settled and explored regions by climbing the Caucasus, which you see there, or by swimming the Ganges?) (*De Re Publica*, VI, xx).   So Dante sees the whole inhabited continent — short from north to south, but broad from east to west — exposed "from hills to river mouths," from Caucasus to Ganges and Ebro.   This, then, is "the little threshing floor that makes us so ferocious"!   Like a threshing floor our earth appeared to Alexander the Great, when, according to an ancient legend, he had himself carried up to the sky by eagles or griffins.   Equally insignificant it seemed to Boethius (*Cons.*, II, Metr. vii, 1–6):

Quicumque solam mente praecipiti petit,
 Summumque credit gloriam,
 Late patentes aetheris cernat plagas,
 Artumque terrarum situm:
 Brevem replere non valentis ambitum
 Pudebit aucti nominis.

(The man who recklessly strives for glory and counts it his highest goal should consider the far-reaching shores of heaven and the narrow confines of earth. He will be ashamed of a growing reputation which still cannot fill so small a space.)

In Canto XXVII, ll. 76–87, Dante describes a second downward look from the same constellation, with which he has been revolving. It would appear from this passage that during his first observation he reached the meridian of Jerusalem, the center of the inhabited earth. The phrase "while I was circling with the eternal Twins" indicates that this first gaze lasts a considerable length of time. When it began, he was presumably in line with central Asia, and saw the whole of that region, as far east as the mouth of the Ganges; when it ended, he was on the meridian of the Holy City, and could see the entire westerly stretch of land to the Atlantic. If the sun, too, had been in Gemini, he could have taken in the whole continent (which is 180° broad) at one sweep, from a position on the line of Jerusalem; but inasmuch as the sun was in Aries, some 40° west of the observer, the part of the earth illumined by its light did not coincide with Dante's field of vision.

37–39. On the summit of Monte Cassino, in the Kingdom of Naples, St. Benedict in 528 erected two chapels in a temple of Apollo and converted the heathen; there arose the first and most famous monastery of his order. Cf. St. Gregory the Great, *Dialogi*, II, viii.

49. Probably St. Macarius of Alexandria, a disciple of St. Antony and a promoter of monasticism in the East. He died in 405. — St. Romualdus of Ravenna, dissatisfied with the laxity into which the Benedictines had fallen, founded in 1012 the order of Camaldoli. Cf. the *Ermo* of *Purg.* V, 96. His life was written by St. Peter Damian (XXI, 121).

62. The Empyrean, or real Heaven.

67. It does not revolve, like the material heavens.

71. Gen. xxviii, 12.

77. Cf. Isaiah vii, 11: "Is this house, which is called by my name, become a den of robbers (*spelunca latronum*) in your eyes?" Mat. xxi, 13: "My house shall be called the house of prayer, but ye have made it a den of thieves."

83. 'Belongs to the people who ask in God's name' — to the worthy poor.

88. Acts iii, 6: "Then Peter said, Silver and gold have I none."

90. St. Francis of Assisi (XI).

94. 'Jordan turned back': Joshua, iii, 14–17.

96. The turning back of the Jordan and the parting of the Red Sea were examples of divine intervention 'more wonderful to behold than succor here.' Therefore we must not despair. Cf. Ps. cxiv (Vulg. cxiii), 3 and 5: "The sea saw it, and fled: Jordan was driven back." "What ailed thee, O thou sea, that thou fleddest? thou Jordan, that thou wast driven back?"

106. Scartazzini notes that this is the last of Dante's sixteen apostrophes to the "reader."

109–110. 'Thou wouldst not have drawn out and put thy finger in the fire so quickly as I saw the sign.' The order of the two acts is inverted (as in II, 23-24) to give the impression of simultaneousness. — Gemini (the Twins), the sign that follows Taurus (the Bull) in the zodiac. Dante has risen to the heaven of the fixed stars.

113. Gemini, the house of Mercury, bestows a taste for learning.

115-117. The sun was rising and setting with Gemini when Dante first breathed 'the Tuscan air': he was born, then, between May 21 and June 21.

121-123. Entering upon the third stage of his celestial journey, Dante invokes the aid of his native constellation for the 'difficult pass' that is drawing him on — namely, the description of the higher heavens. This appeal, one of Dante's most charming inventions, stands in line with the preludes in I, 1-36, and X, 1-27. Here, however, he calls, not on Apollo, but on his own stars.

142. Hyperion is often called by ancient poets the father of the sun. See *Met.*, IV, 192: "Hyperione nate" — son of Hyperion (cf. 241).

144. *Maia* and *Dïone* are invoked, because, like Hyperion, they are parents of gods whose names are borne by heavenly bodies: Maia is the mother of Mercury; Dione, the mother of Venus. Cf. *Theb.*, II, 1 ("Maia satus" — the son of Maia) and *Aen.*, I, 297 ("Maia genitum" — the son of Maia); *Par.* VIII, 7.

146. *Padre*: Saturn. — *Figlio*: Mars.

151. 'Little threshing floor': the inhabited part of the earth. Cf. *area* in *Cons.*, II, Pr. ii.

Canto XXIII

Argument

As the pilgrim approaches the confines of the material universe, he begins to catch glimpses of reality — of the true life of the world of spirit. In the 8th heaven Dante has a beautiful vision of the triumph of Christ and Mary, in the midst of the whole army of the blessed, "all the fruit harvested from the revolution of these spheres." Their appearance is eagerly awaited by Beatrice and greeted by her with a cry of rapture. The starry sphere is a traditional symbol of the Church; here all the elect are gathered, in company with the Apostles and the Evangelists, to whom, perhaps, this heaven especially belongs. In this borderland between the visible and the invisible universe, Jesus, the Man-God, comes to meet the upward-faring soul. The rising of Christ and Mary to the Empyrean, before the waiting host, symbolizes the Ascension and the Assumption. The triumph here depicted is a counterpart of the pageant of the Church Militant in the Terrestrial Paradise. In this scene the angels have no share. The canto ends with the triumph of St. Peter, who does not as yet rise to the Empyrean, but remains with his flock, in the place of Christ.

For the traditional identification of the 8th heaven with the Church, see G. Busnelli, *Il concetto e l' ordine del 'Paradiso' dantesco*, I, 1911, 118–119. The same author cites (pp. 114–116) from a commentary on the Transfiguration, by Innocent III, a passage in which Christ is described as possessing the four characteristics of the sun: brightness, impassibility, subtlety, agility. The same passage throws some light on the appropriateness of Dante's ensuing examination, by the Apostles, in the three Christian virtues. The inability of the unaided human eye to see Christ is discussed by Rabanus Maurus, St. Gregory, and others: Busnelli, I, 110–113. Christ is compared to sun, moon, and star in Rev. xxi, 23, xxii, 16. — The superiority of the Apostles to other men is declared by St. Thomas in his Commentary on Romans viii, 5, and Ephesians i, 3. While others may have done greater things, the Apostles did what they did with greater love, and so achieved greater merit. In Mat. xix, 28, Jesus promises his followers that they "shall sit on twelve thrones, judging the twelve tribes of Israel"; and St. Thomas, in his Commentary, points out that judges must be elevated above the rest of the world. It is therefore not unlikely that Dante meant to assign to the Apostles a sphere higher than those allotted to other men. This 8th heaven, with its ecclesiastical traditions, would be a fit place for them. Here St. Peter triumphs, and here Dante is judged by Peter, James, and John. With the Apostles are probably associated the Evangelists, and also, it would seem, Adam, the man shaped by God's own hand.

5. Cf. *Aen.*, XII, 475: "Pabula parva legens nidisque loquacibus escas" (gleaning for her chirping nestlings tiny crumbs and scraps of food).

12. In the middle of the sky the sun seems to move slower than it does near the horizon.

19–21. The blessed were predisposed to virtue by the heavens which influenced them at birth; and salvation was made possible by Christ.

26. Trivia is one of the names of Diana: the moon.

30. Christ illumines all the blessed, just as our material sun illumines all the stars — 'the phenomena on high' (cf. II, 115).

37. See 1 Cor. i, 24: "Christ the power of God, and the wisdom of God." Usually Christ is identified with Wisdom.

38. See Hebrews x, 20: "a new and living way, which he hath consecrated for us."

55–57. 'Polyhymnia and her sisters' are the Muses, who nourish (or 'fatten') the tongues of poets.

70. Cf. XVIII, 21.

73. Mary, the 'Mystic Rose.' Series of prayers to the Virgin were named *rosaria*. — The Word: cf. John i, 14: "And the Word was made flesh."

74. Gigli: the Apostles. In his unfinished commentary on Isaiah, St. Thomas discusses the resemblance of saints to lilies.

75. See 2 Cor. ii, 14: "Now thanks be unto God, which always causeth us to triumph in Christ, and maketh manifest the *savour* of his knowledge by us in every place" — "*odorem notitiae suae manifestat per nos.*"

79–81. 'As ere now my eyes, covered by a shadow, have seen a flowery meadow under a sunbeam that streams clear through a rifted cloud': an exceedingly beautiful simile used to describe the vast throngs of flowerlike souls illumined from above by the dazzling light of Christ, who has risen once again to the Empyrean, in order that Dante's own eyes may not be entirely blinded by his brightness.

88. The mention of Mary in l. 73. Among the bright lights, hers is now the greatest (l. 90).

94. The 'torch' is perhaps the Archangel Gabriel, the messenger of the Annunciation. He now forms a circling halo around the head of the Virgin.

99. Cf. *Met.*, XII, 51–52:

> qualemve sonum, cum Iuppiter atras
> Increpuit nubes, extrema tonitrua reddunt.

(Or like the last rumblings of thunder when Jove has made the dark clouds crash together.)

101. The 'sapphire' is Mary. This gem, besides being precious and beautiful, possesses a beneficent power.

106. Until Mary shall rise to the Empyrean, following Christ.

112. 'The royal cloak of all the revolutions of the world' is the 9th sphere, the Primum Mobile which surrounds the other eight revolving spheres.

115. Even the lower or inner edge of the Primum Mobile is far beyond the reach of Dante's eye.

120. Christ, the 'seed' or child of Mary.

123. 'Because of the spirit (of grateful love) which breaks even into external flame' — which, in default of words, finds expression in a gesture. — This figure reveals the same tender recollection of family life that we find in Dante's other references to children.

124. All the bright souls — the 'whitenesses' — extend their flames upward after Mary.

128. *Regina celi*: an antiphon sung in the office of the Virgin after Easter. "O Queen of Heaven, rejoice, for he whom thou wert worthy to bear rose as he promised; pray to God for us. Hallelujah!"

131. The blessed souls.

132. They are now filled with the good which they sowed on earth. Cf. Galatians vi, 7: "whatsoever a man soweth, that shall he also reap."

134-135. The 'exile of Babylon' is the earthly life. Cf. Ps. cxxxvii (Vulg. cxxxvi), 1: "By the rivers of Babylon, there we sat down, yea, we wept, when we remembered Zion." — On earth 'they forsook gold,' following the precept of Jesus in Mat. xix, 21: "If thou wilt be perfect, go and sell that thou hast, and give to the poor, and thou shalt have treasure in heaven."

138. In company with the souls of the Old and the New Convenant. Prophets and Apostles preached the same faith.

139. Cf. Mat. xvi, 19: "And I will give unto thee the keys of the kingdom of heaven."

Canto XXIV

Argument

In the course of the celestial journey, God is revealed through his works, through Christian doctrine, and finally through immediate contemplation of himself. "For now we see through a glass, darkly; but then face to face: now I know in part; but then I shall know even as also I am known. And now abideth faith, hope, charity, these three" (1 Cor. xiii, 12–13). The full comprehension of these fundamental Christian virtues precedes the direct vision of God; and therefore the poet represents himself as passing an examination in them, in the 8th sphere, before seeing, in the ninth, the Lord in his relation to the angels, and, in the Empyrean, the triune Divinity in his essence. It is fitting that the glorification of these virtues should proceed from a living man, inasmuch as they are essentially human qualities: the blessed retain Love, intensified and purified; but with them Faith has become knowledge, and Hope has been exchanged for fulfillment. St. Bonaventure, *Itinerarium Mentis in Deum*, says we must enter Paradise and the fruition of truth, by means of faith, hope, and charity: Gardner, 308–309. Dante, in his *Convivio*, III, xiv, 15, tells us: "by these virtues we ascend to philosophize in that celestial Athens."

Dante's examiners are St. Peter, St. James, and St. John, the disciples most closely associated with Jesus, and the traditional representatives of the virtues he preached. The fitness of Peter and John to stand for Faith and Love is obvious; less clear is the special appropriateness of the assignment of Hope to James, which will be discussed in connection with Canto XXV. After his colloquy, in this sphere, with the Apostles and Adam, Dante converses only with those who serve as his guides, Beatrice and St. Bernard.

Throughout the exposition of Faith, in this canto, question and answer follow one another as in a catechism, and Dante compares himself to a candidate undergoing the test required for a doctor's degree. He offers as a description of Faith the statement of St. Paul in Hebrews xi, 1: "Now faith is the substance of things hoped for, the evidence of things not seen." This formula, says St. Thomas, although some say that it is not a definition, contains all the elements of one: "licet quidam dicant praedicta Apostoli verba non esse fidei definitionem, tamen, si quis recte consideret, omnia ex quibus fides potest definiri in praedicta descriptione tanguntur" (Though some say that the above words of the Apostle are not a definition of faith, yet if we consider the matter aright, this definition overlooks none of the points in reference to which faith can be defined) (*Summa Theologiae*, Secunda Secundae, Qu. iv, Art. 1). And he adds: "Si quis ergo in formam definitionis huiusmodi verba reducere velit, potest dicere quod *fides est habitus mentis, qua inchoatur vita aeterna in nobis, faciens intellectum assentire non apparentibus.*" (Accordingly if anyone would reduce the foregoing words to the form of a definition, he may say that *faith is a habit of the mind, whereby eternal life is begun in us, making the intellect assent to what is nonapparent.*)

But why, demands St. Peter, did St. Paul call Faith first a "substance" (*sustanza*) and then an "evidence" (*argomento*)? The eternal Heavenly life, replies Dante, is beyond the perception of mortals and, for them, exists only in their belief; hence Faith, from the human point of view, is the material, or substance, of which the hoped-for joys consist. Moreover, while in ordinary matters we argue from proved facts, in religion we use as our basis for further reasoning a belief; and so Faith, in theological questions, takes the place which in worldly syllogisms is taken by evidence.

1. Cf. Luke xiv, 16, and Mat. xxii, 14: "A certain man made a great supper, and bade many" —"many are called, but few are chosen."
2. Cf. Rev. xix, 9: "Blessed are they which are called unto the marriage supper of the Lamb." The Paschal Lamb of the Hebrews, slain and eaten at Easter time, became a symbol of Christ.
8. 'Bedew him'; give him a few drops from the fount of Truth, upon which his thought is bent.
11. It is evident from l. 30 and from XXV, 14, that *spere* means 'circles,' rings of spirits dancing in a round, or carol.
16–18. The pace of the circling rings of dancers is a measure of their 'wealth' of gladness.

26-27. 'For our imagination — not to say our speech — is too bright a color for such folds.' Human speech and even human memory are not profound enough to describe or retain an impression of such depth of holiness.   The metaphor is taken from the technique of painting (in *V. N.*, XXXV, Dante appears as an artist): pictures, in our poet's day, consisted mainly of faces and garments, the latter falling in folds, and these folds presented the deepest shades; skill was required to find a color dark enough to portray them, while preserving the purity of tone the Tuscans loved.

31. First (ll. 22-23) the shining spirit circles about Beatrice and sings, 'then' it stops and speaks the words just cited.

39. Through faith Peter "walked on the water, to go to Jesus": Mat. xiv, 25-29.

46. In an examination or *disputatio* leading to the degree of Doctor of Theology, a first time was set aside for the discussion of a given question. The Master would first state the question; then the "bachelor" would adduce "proofs" (*approvare*) both *pro* and *contra* but would not presume to give the final definition or terminate the question. This was done only by the Master.

48. The candidate 'arms himself to argue' the question, 'not to decide it.'

59. 'By the high commander': St. Peter, the first commander of the Church.   Note that *primipilus* is the title of a Roman military officer.

62. Cf. 2 Peter iii, 15: "our beloved brother Paul."

63. 'Who, with thee, brought Rome into the right line' — into the path of Christianity.

75. 'It assumes the concept': it falls into the category. *Intenza* is the scholastic Latin *intentio*, 'notion' or 'concept'; English *intention* has often been used in this sense.

90. Romans xiv, 23: "for whatsoever is not of faith is sin." Cf. Hebrews xi, 6: "But without faith it is impossible to please him: for he that cometh to God must believe that he is."

91. 'Rain': inspiration.

93. 'Parchments': Testaments.

98. The two Testaments are the premises from which the conclusion is deduced.

101. The miracles, which cannot be explained as products of nature.

104-105. 'The very thing that is to be proved (the revealed Truth), and naught else, is thy voucher for it.' St. Peter, wishing, as examiner, to draw out Dante more fully, tells him that he is arguing in a circle.

106-108. If the world was converted to Christianity without the miracles related in the Bible, this conversion was itself a far greater miracle, and quite sufficient proof of divine intervention. The argument is taken from St. Augustine, *De Civitate Dei*, XXII, v: "hoc nobis unum grande miraculum sufficit, quod ... terrarum orbis sine ullis miraculis credidit." (This one grand miracle suffices for us, that the whole world has believed without any miracles.) St. Thomas also, *De Veritate Catholicae Fidei*, I, vi, discourses on the miracle of the conversion of the world to Christianity.

115. St. Peter.

124-126. St. Peter now sees in God that which on earth he accepted through faith. This faith was so strong that it impelled him to enter the Sepulchre before John, although the younger disciple reached it first: John xx, 3-8.

134. St. Thomas, *Summa Theologiae*, Prima, Qu. ii, Art. 3, gives five physical and metaphysical proofs of the existence of God: the impossibility of explaining the world without the assumption of a first motor, of a first efficient cause, of a first necessity, of a first goodness, of a first governing intelligence. In Prima, Qu. 1, Art. 5, he tells us that theology makes use of philosophy.

136. Luke xxiv, 44: "These are the words which I spake unto you, ... that all things must be fulfilled, which were written in the law of Moses, and in the prophets, and in the psalms, concerning me."

137. The Apostles.

141. We may use with 'Trinity' the verb 'are' or the verb 'is.'

144. Various passages in the Bible are cited in support of the doctrine of the Trinity: Mat. xxviii, 19; 2 Cor. xiii, 14; 1 Peter i, 2; 1 John v, 7 ("For there are three that bear record in heaven, the Father, the Word, and the Holy Ghost: and these three are one").

Canto XXV

Argument

Until the very end of his life Dante cherished, at the bottom of his heart, a hope that he might be called back to his city, to that Florence which he so loved and so reviled. Pathetic indeed is the yearning expressed in the opening lines of this canto. Some day, he thinks, his great poem may win such fame as to "overcome the cruelty that locks him out" — "la crudeltà che fuor mi serra." The longing to return is voiced in the *Convivio*, I, iii, 4; and the same sentiment is treated half playfully, half sadly, in the first Eclogue, 39–50.

It is fitting that a disclosure of the poet's one earthly hope should serve as prelude to a canto in which Hope is the principal theme. In this virtue he is tested by St. James, as he was tried in Faith by St. Peter; but the examination is less searching. The definition of Hope recited by Dante is that of Peter Lombard in the *Sententiae*, III, xxvi: "Est enim spes certa expectatio futurae beatitudinis veniens ex Dei gratia et ex meritis praecedentibus." (Now hope is a certain expectation of future beatitude proceeding from God's grace and antecedent merits.) "Sine meritis," he adds, "aliquid sperare non spes sed praesumptio dici potest." (Without merits, to hope for something is not hope but presumption.) When we say that Hope comes from Grace and from antecedent merits, we must remember that these two sources are not of the same kind: the impulse to hope springs from Grace alone, while our merits are, as we know, a necessary condition of the fulfillment of our assurance of salvation. This is explained by St. Thomas in the *Summa Theologiae*, Secunda Secundae, Qu. xvii, Art. 1.

St. James is the only Apostle whose death is recorded in the Bible. The "certain expectation" of Heaven led him to martyrdom and made him a suitable exponent of Hope. So says Chrysostom, quoted in the *Summa Theologiae*, Tertia, Qu. xlv, Art. 3. It should be noted also that James the Apostle, son of Zebedee and brother of John, and James, "the Lord's brother," author of the Epistle, were in Dante's time regarded as the same person. In the Epistle of James i, 12, we read: "Blessed is the man that endureth temptation: for when he is tried, he shall receive the crown of life, which the Lord hath promised to them that love him" — words of hopeful message. And in v, 8: "Be ye also patient; stablish your hearts: for the coming of the Lord draweth nigh."

The end of the canto once more leaves us startled and curious; for the poet, as he gazes into the effulgence of St. John — who now appears on the scene — is stricken with sudden blindness.   Love is blind; and it is during his brief period of sightlessness that Dante undergoes, in the next canto, his examination in that virtue.   Furthermore, the celestial pilgrim cannot see God until his earthly sight is quenched and replaced by a spiritual sense.   In Canto XXIII, 33 — and again in l. 87, after his eyes were fortified (ll. 47-48) by the vision of enlightenment — Dante was unable to bear the light of Christ.   Even when his new sight comes, it must be trained and purified and strengthened by degrees.   A similar blindness came upon St. Paul at the time of his conversion.   Acts ix, 3-9: "And as he jouneyed, he came near Damascus: and suddenly there shined round about him a light from heaven: and he fell to the earth, and heard a voice. ...   And Saul arose from the earth; and when his eyes were opened, he saw no man: but they led him by the hand, and brought him to Damascus.   And he was there three days without sight, and neither did eat nor drink."   To these three days is generally assigned the rapture of St. Paul (2 Cor. xii), when "he was caught up into paradise, and heard unspeakable words, which it is not lawful for a man to utter."

5. Cf. Jeremiah xi, 19: "But I was like a lamb ... that is brought to the slaughter; and I knew not that they had devised devices against me."

7. *Vello*, 'fleece,' carrying out the figure of the *agnello*: I shall then be a full-grown poet, no longer a bleating lamb.

8. In the church of S. Giovanni, where he was baptized.   Cf. *Inf.* XIX, 17.

10-12. In San Giovanni I was admitted to the Faith, and for my proficiency in that Faith I was applauded in Heaven by St. Peter; it is therefore appropriate that I receive the laurel crown, the earthly reward for my Faith, in the place where I first embraced it.

13. St. James, who comes from the same ring as St. Peter.

14-15. 'The first fruit which Christ left of his vicars' is Peter.

18. The grave of St. James at Compostela in Galicia (the northwestern corner of Spain) was for several centuries a favorite place of pilgrimage.

26. *Coram me* (Latin), 'before me'.

30. The 'court' of Heaven. — In the Epistle of James there are some references to divine liberality.   See i, 5 ("God, that giveth to all men liberally") and 17 ("Every good gift and every perfect gift is from above, and cometh down from the Father of lights"); ii, 5 ("Hath not God chosen the poor of this world rich in faith, and heirs of the kingdom which he hath promised to them that loved him?")

32-33. 'Thou knowest that thou dost personify it (Hope) as many times as Jesus bestowed most honor on the three.'   Three of the disciples (Peter, James, John) were chosen by Jesus to be present and to receive the clearest revelation of his character on three different occasions: at the Transfiguration (Mat. xvii, 1-8), in the Garden of Gethsemane (Mat. xxvi, 36-38), and at the raising of the daughter of Jairus (Luke viii, 50-56).   On these three occasions Peter, James, and John stand respectively for Faith, Hope, and Love.

38. Ps. cxxi (Vulg. cxx), 1: "I will lift up mine eyes unto the hills, from whence cometh my help."   The 'hills' are the two Apostles, who have bent Dante's eyes beneath the weight of their light.

40. The counts in the Imperial court of Heaven are the Saints.

46–47. Three questions are asked: what is Hope, to what degree dost thou possess it ('how does thy mind blossom with it'), and from what source dost thou derive it? Beatrice (l. 51) forestalls Dante's response to the second question, since his affirmative answer would imply that he thought himself worthy of salvation, and hence might smack of vainglory; to the other two he replies.

55. By 'Egypt' is meant life on earth. See Ps. cxiv (Vulg. cxiii), 1.

56. Cf. Hebrews xii, 22: "ye are come ... unto the city of the living God, the heavenly Jerusalem, and to an innumerable company of angels."

57. Cf. Job vii, 1: "militia est vita hominis super terram" (the life of man on earth is a warfare). The English version is quite different.

60. Souls in Heaven have no further use for Hope, but St. James loves it still.

70. Cf. Daniel xii, 3: "And they that be wise shall shine as the brightness of the firmament; and they that turn many to righteousness as the *stars* for ever and ever."

73–74. Ps. ix, 10: "And they that know thy name will put their trust in thee" — "sperent in te." — 'Theody,' sacred song.

78. 'I shower in turn': I communicate to others the hope I have derived from David and thee.

81. James and John, the sons of Zebedee, were surnamed by Jesus "Boanerges, which is, The sons of thunder": Mark iii, 17.

84. The victory of martyrdom. He was put to death by Herod Agrippa. — The 'battle-field' of life. James was a strenuous and rigid ascetic.

89. 'The token' set up by the Old and the New Testament is indicated in ll. 91–96. — *Ed esso* etc., 'and it (the token) points it out to me,' i.e., points out what blessedness in Heaven means — perfect joy of the body and the spirit.

91–93. Isaiah lxi, 7 and 10: "therefore in their land shall they possess the double: ever-lasting joy shall be unto them"; "he hath clothed me with the garments of salvation." The 'double garment' is the effulgence of the soul and the clarified body.

94. John.

95. St. John 'treats of the white robes' of the elect in Rev. iii, 5, and vii, 9–17. The 'white robes' symbolize the brightness or glory of "the souls that God has made his friends." The body, after the Resurrection, will become bright and pure like the spirit, and will share in its happiness. According to St. Bonaventure, *Breviloquium*, VII, vii, the body is called the "second robe."

100. The 'light' of St. John.

101–102. In mid-winter the constellation of Cancer, for a month, shines all night long. If it contained a star as bright as this newly appeared 'crystal,' night, during that month, would be as light as day. In other words, the effulgence of St. John is as bright as the sun.

103–111. The three representatives of the Christian virtues dance before Beatrice, as the Virtues themselves did (in allegorical form) in *Purg.* XXIX, 121–129.

112. John xxiii, 23: "Now there was leaning on Jesus' bosom one of his disciples, whom Jesus loved."

113. Ps. cii (Vulg. ci), 6: "I am like a pelican of the wilderness." It was generally believed that the pelican brings its young back to life with its own blood; hence this bird was taken as a symbol of Christ.

114. John was entrusted with the care of Mary. John xix, 27: "Then saith he to the disciple, Behold thy mother! and from that hour that disciple took her unto his own home."

119. Dante had an opportunity to see seven eclipses of the sun, two of them total in Italy.

123. Dante is trying to see, through the effulgence, the body of St. John, believing, according to an old legend, that John was taken up to Heaven in the flesh. John xxi, 22–23: "Jesus saith unto him (Peter), If I will that he (John) tarry till I come, what is that to thee? follow thou me. Then went this saying abroad among the brethren, that that disciple should not die: yet Jesus said not unto him, He shall not die; but, if I will that he tarry till I come, what is that to thee?" In a fresco, attributed to Giotto, in Santa Croce, John is rising in body, obliquely, from the grave to God.

126. Ephesians i, 4: "According as he hath chosen us in him before the foundation of the world."   In *Conv.*, II, v, 12, Dante tells us that the elect are to fill the places of the fallen angels, who were "perhaps a tenth part" of all the angelic orders.

127. The 'two robes' are the effulgence of the spirit and the clarified body.

128. 'The two lights that have ascended' are Christ and Mary, who have returned to the Empyrean: XXIII, 86, 120.   Theirs are the only human bodies now in Heaven.   This is the opinion which was expressed by St. Thomas in *Summa Theologiae*, Tertia, Qu. liii, Art. 3; previously he had been inclined to have a different one.

132. The 'threefold breath' of Peter, James, and John.

134. The vigorous simile is taken from Statius, *Theb.*, VI, 779–781.

Canto XXVI

Argument

In the course of the examination in Love, conducted by St. John, no definition of that virtue is given, perhaps because Dante could find none to his liking.   The candidate for admission to the mysteries of Paradise is asked merely what he loves, and why.   God is naturally the first and greatest object of his affection; then the rest of the universe insofar as it is in the likeness of its Creator.

After a somewhat brief colloquy — brief, no doubt, because Dante's whole life has shown him to be an adept in Love — the traveler's sight is restored, and he finds that Adam has joined the group.   To him the poet mentally addresses four questions, which are all answered, though not in the order in which they are put.   First comes the reply to number three: What was the real nature of Adam's sin?   Number one follows: How long ago was he created?   Question four, which is next taken up, is concerned with the language which the first man invented and spoke.   And last we have the answer to number two: How long did Adam stay in the Garden of Eden?   The author of original sin, which led to ultimate Redemption by Christ, is a figure that is really necessary to the completeness of a scene devoted to the triumph of the Savior.

12. Ananias cured St. Paul of his blindness by "putting his hands on him."   Acts ix, 17–18.

16. Dante answers St. John's query (ll. 7–8): What is the object of thy love?

17. Rev. i, 8: "I am Alpha and Omega, the beginning and the ending, saith the Lord." Dante knew the name *alpha*, possibly not *omega*.   The Vulgate in the 13th century read "alpha et ω" or "α et ω."

28–30. 'For good, as such, kindles love in proportion as it is understood, and kindles the greater love, the more goodness it contains within it.'

31. Since love is attracted by goodness, and all goodness is in God, he must be the primal object of love.

38. Aristotle, who in his *Metaphysics*, XI, vii, discusses the existence, the unity, and the perfection of the First Mover, and in viii the nature of the First Substance.

42. Exod. xxxiii, 19: "I will make all my goodness pass before thee."

44. 'Proclamation': probably the Gospel of John, which opens solemnly and mysteriously with the announcement of the Incarnation ("In the beginning was the Word," etc.), God's great sacrifice to man; cf. John iii, 16. Some critics, however, think that the reference is to the Revelation, and particularly to the verse cited in the note to l. 17.

49–51. An odd combination of metaphors. Such mixing is not uncommon in Dante.

53. 'Christ's Eagle' is John. The "four beasts" of Rev. iv, 7, are traditionally identified with the four Evangelists; St. John is the "flying eagle."

64–66. I love the various creatures of God that make up the world, in proportion to the grace which their Maker, in his predestination, has bestowed upon them.

69. Isaiah vi, 3, and Rev. iv, 8.

70–71. 'And as one is awakened by a keen light because of the spirit (or sense) of sight running to meet ...' Cf. *Conv.*, III, ix, 7–10, where the act of sight is described scientifically.

72. 'Coat': membrane of the eye.

97. It is not evident to us just what kind of a creature Dante had in mind, but it is quite possible that he may have been thinking of a falcon.

107–108. 'Which makes itself a [complete or perfect] image of other things, while nothing makes of itself a [perfect] image of it (the mirror).' God reflects everything, but nothing can wholly reflect God. Cf. *Summa Theologiae*, Prima, Qu. lvii, Art. 2: "Deus per essentiam suam, per quam omnia causat, est similitudo omnium." (Therefore as by His essence, by which he causes all things, God is the likeness of all things.)

110. Beatrice, who in the Garden of Eden prepared Dante for the ascent to Heaven.

113. The 'wrath' of God.

117. Adam's sin was not gluttony but disobedience, caused by pride. Cf. St. Augustine, *De Civitate Dei*, XIV, xii–xiv.

118. 'Therefore, in the place whence thy lady drew Virgil': in the Limbus. Cf. *Inf.* II, 52 ff.

120. The 'assembly' of the blessed, for which Adam yearned before his release from Limbus by Christ.

121. The signs of the zodiac.

122. Gen. v, 5: "And all the days that Adam lived were nine hundred and thirty years."

123. The two numbers added make 5232 years between the creation of Adam and the Crucifixion. Cf. *Purg.* XXXIII, 62. — Eusebius of Caesarea puts the birth of Christ in the year 5200 of the world.

125. The 'unaccomplishable task' which Nimrod's people attempted was the building of the Tower of Babel: Gen. xi, 4–9. Cf. *Inf.* XXXI, 77–78; *Purg.* XII, 34. — Dante evidently changed his opinion on this subject, for in *Vulg. El.*, I, vi, 5–7, he had said that Adam's language was spoken by all men until the confusion of tongues, and by the Hebrews after that event. His study of human speech doubtless led him to the conclusion that an unwritten language could not last without change through many generations.

130. 'It is a natural operation for man to speak': hence he always does speak, in some fashion.

134. We do not know where Dante got the idea that the first name of God was *I*. This letter is the initial of *Jehovah*, and also of *Jah*: cf. Ps. lxviii (Vulg. lxvii), 5 ("extol him ... by his name Jah "). Moreover, standing for the number 1, it is the symbol of unity.

136. *El* is the Hebrew name. St. Isidore, *Etymologiae*, VII, i: "Primum apud Hebraeos Dei nomen El dicitur." (The first name of God for the Hebrews is *El*.) Cf. *Vulg. El.*, I, iv, 4.

137–138. Cf. Horace, *Ars Poetica*, 60–61.

139–142. Adam lived in the Garden of Eden, on the mountaintop, before and after his sin, only about six hours — 'from the first hour to the one that follows the sixth, when the sun changes quadrant' (passes from the first quadrant, or 90°, to the second), i.e., from sunrise until the hour that follows noon. Among the various estimates of theologians, Dante chose one of the shortest, that of Petrus Comestor (cf. XII, 134).

Canto XXVII

Argument

When Dante once more gazes down at the earth, he finds that during the interval since the end of his previous observation (XXII, 133–153) he has traversed 90°, or a quarter of the whole circumference. Six hours, then, have elapsed. At the close of the first look, he was on the meridian of Jerusalem; he is now in line with the Strait of Gibraltar, having covered the whole length of the Mediterranean, whose extent was curiously exaggerated by the ancients (cf. IX, 82–87). Had the sun been under Gemini (but so placed as not to obstruct his sight), he could have beheld, from his present viewpoint, the whole western hemisphere, from Jerusalem to the Island of Purgatory; but, as he tells us (ll. 86–87), "the sun was ahead of me, distant a sign and more beneath my feet." The signs of the zodiac are, of course, all in the eighth heaven. Dante is in Gemini; and the sun is "in," or under, Aries. Between Gemini and Aries is Taurus. We may suppose that the poet is at or near the western extremity of Gemini, and we know that the sun is in line with a point something less than a third of the way from the eastern end of Aries. Each of the twelve signs is 30° long. A line drawn from Dante to the center of the earth, and a line drawn from the sun to the same point, would then be separated by an arc of not more than 40°. It follows that some 40° of Dante's field of vision, on the eastern side, is in the dark, or at least in the twilight. Instead, therefore, of seeing clearly to the Phoenician coast, at the eastern end of the Mediterranean, he sees "almost the shore" (l. 83) — perhaps as far as Greece. It should be remembered that all this Mediterranean region was observed by him at the time of his first inspection.

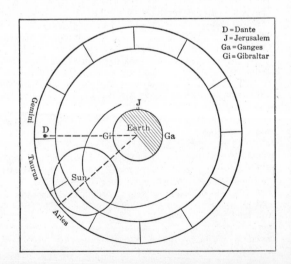

D = Dante
J = Jerusalem
Ga = Ganges
Gi = Gibraltar

See Moore, III, 62–71.

1-6. The splendor of the host, as it sings the hymn *Gloria Patri*, seems to the enraptured spectator 'a smile of the universe!'

10. The 'four torches' are the lights of Peter, James, John, and Adam.

11. The flame of St. Peter.

13-15. If the planets Jupiter and Mars were birds, and each should molt and exchange feathers with the other, Jupiter would turn red and Mars white: thus St. Peter's effulgence reddens. A whimsical figure.

22. In 1300 Boniface VIII was Pope; but his election, corruptly procured during the lifetime of his predecessor (Celestine V), is condemned as invalid by St. Peter, first of the Popes. The discordant wrath of Peter and the whole heavenly host is rendered the more terrific by its incongruity with the peaceful joy of Paradise.

23. For the repetition, cf. Jeremiah vii, 4, where "the temple of the Lord" occurs three times.

25. St. Peter's 'burial place' is Rome, where he suffered martyrdom.

28. Cf. *Met.*, III, 183-185:

> Qui color infectis adversi solis ab ictu
> Nubibus esse solet aut purpureae Aurorae,
> Is fuit in vultu visae sine veste Dianae.

(And red as the clouds which flush beneath the sun's slant rays, red as the rosy dawn, were the cheeks of Diana as she stood there in view without her robes.)

34. Cf. Daniel iii, 19: "Then was Nebuchadnezzar full of fury, and the form of his visage was changed."

36. *Mat.* xxvii, 45: "Now from the sixth hour there was darkness all over the land unto the ninth hour."

41. Linus and Cletus were Bishops of Rome in the 1st century.

42. Cf. 1 Peter v, 1-2.

44. Sixtus, Pius, Calixtus, and Urban, Bishops of Rome in the 2nd and 3rd centuries, were all martyrs.

46-48. We never intended that our successors should treat the Guelfs as sheep, the Ghibellines as goats: cf. Mat. xxv, 33.

50. The Papal troops sent against Frederick II in 1229 wore this token on their shoulders, and were called *chiavisegnati*. In Dante's own time the Pope was again warring against Christians: see *Inf.* XXVII, 85-90.

52. The Papal seal bears the image of St. Peter.

55. Mat. vii, 15: "Beware of false prophets, which come to you in sheep's clothing, but inwardly they are ravening wolves."

58. Cahors, the old capital of Quercy in southwestern France, was a nest of usury: see *Inf.* XI, 50. John XXII, Pope from 1316 to 1334, came from that town: cf. XVIII, 130-136. His predecessor, Clement V, was a Gascon; he is mentioned in *Inf.* XIX, 82-87, *Purg.* XXXII, 148-160, *Par.* XVII, 82.

61. Scipio the younger, who conquered Hannibal and thus saved Rome. Cf. Conv., IV, v, 19.

67-72. These lines present the strange and lovely picture of an inverted snowstorm. Dante sees 'the ether grow beautiful, flaked with triumphant vapors' (the swarm of bright spirits returning to the Empyrean), 'just as our air flakes downward with frozen vapors' in midwinter, when the sun is in Capricorn—'when the horn of the Sky Goat and the Sun touch each other.' It must be remembered that 'wet vapors' produce rain, snow, and hail, while wind, lightning, and meteors are caused by 'dry vapors.'

79. See XXII, 133-153.

80-81. The ancients divided the habitable part of the earth into seven strips, or 'climates,' stretching east and west. In the middle of the first, or most southerly, of these zones is the meridian of Jerusalem; the westerly end is at the meridian of Gibraltar. The distance between the middle and the end, according to Dante's geography, is 90°, or six hours' revolution. See Moore, III, 101 and 132.

82–84. Beyond Cadiz the poet sees the 'mad track' of Ulysses out in the unknown Ocean; cf. *Inf.* XXVI, 90–142, where the voyage is described as a *folle volo* (l. 125). On the hither side of Cadiz he sees 'nearly' (*presso*) the Phoenician shore, where Europa mounted on the back of Jupiter disguised as a bull; cf. *Met.*, II, 833–875, especially 868–869.

98. 'Leda's nest' is the constellation of Gemini, so called because the Twins (Castor and Pollux) were the children of Leda by Jupiter in the form of a swan.

99. The ninth heaven, or Primum Mobile, which contains no visible bodies.

100. While in other spheres the lower part is less bright than the upper and otherwise differentiated, in the Primum Mobile all parts are alike, and, of the nine heavens, it turns the fastest in all its parts.

107. 'The middle' is the earth, a motionless globe surrounded by the revolving heavens.

111. 'The power which it (the ninth heaven) showers' — transmits to the rest of the world.

112–114. 'Light and love envelop it round about, as it envelops the other heavens; and that belt (the Empyrean, or Heaven of light and love) is governed only by him (God) who girds it.' Every sphere except the ninth is surrounded by another sphere; but the ninth, the outermost sphere of the material universe, is surrounded only by the world of spirit, the Heaven of light and love, the Empyrean, which is the Mind of God. Moreover, every material heaven is directed by an order of angelic Intelligences; but in the Empyrean the only governing Intelligence is the Lord, in whom it exists.

115. The unit of time is the day, which is determined by the revolution of the Primum Mobile.

117. Just as 10 is determined by 5 (its 'half') and 2 (its 'fifth').

118. In this metaphor the ninth sphere is a pot in which Time has its roots, while its leaves and flowers appear in the others.

121. Greed is likened to a flood. — This apostrophe is suggested by the contrast between Time and Eternity, on the one hand, and, on the other, the pettiness and brief duration of the goods coveted by men.

124. Cf. Romans vii, 18: "to will is present with me; but how to perform that which is good I find not."

136–138. 'He who brings morning and leaves evening' (l. 138) is obviously the sun. Now Circe was the daughter of the sun and, according to the familiar story, had the power to change men into beasts. It is also possible that the "old witch" seen in the second dream of Purgatory (XIX, 7–24) represents Circe, since she declares that she turned Ulysses from his way, and she certainly symbolizes the sins of upper Purgatory, among which is avarice, or cupidity, the keynote of Beatrice's present discourse. Thus Circe, daughter of the sun, would represent worldly goods generally, viewed as tempting man and turning him from heavenly things. *Aspetto* (l. 137) can here bear the meaning of 'sight.' On the basis of these several possible meanings in the detail, Beatrice is saying that the white skin of human nature (the innocent child) turns "black" (i.e., is corrupted by sinful desire) as soon as it looks upon worldly goods, that is, at the first sight of them (*primo aspetto*), in their power to tempt. Thus Circe is called *bella* in precisely the sense of having this power as temptress. Such an interpretation of this notoriously difficult terzina has the merit of fitting perfectly into the line of Beatrice's discourse, from l. 121 on. Many other views have been held.

142. 'Be unwintered,' become a spring instead of a winter month. Through an inaccuracy in the Julian calendar, which made the year of 365 days and 6 hours, the solar year gained over the standard year about one day in a century; in the course of something less than 90 centuries then, January would have been pushed into the spring, if the error had not been corrected (as it was in 1582 under Gregory XIII, when the present calendar was adopted). The line means: 'But before 9000 years have gone by,' i.e., 'within a little while.'

143. The Julian year was really about $\frac{1}{130}$ of a day too long; but the error was sometimes estimated at a figure not far from $\frac{1}{100}$. See Moore, III, 96–97.

147. Once more we have a vague prophecy of violent reformation.

148. The poet returns to the metaphor of l. 126.

Canto XXVIII

Argument

In the Crystalline Heaven, on the confines of the world of matter, the poet beholds a symbolic picture of God, not in his divine essence, but in his relation to the nine orders of angels that govern the spheres. First Dante catches sight of the image reflected in the eyes of Beatrice; then he turns to gaze on the splendid spectacle itself. His initial perception of the truth comes, then, from Revelation. Once before, the lady's eyes have served a like purpose: in *Purg.* XXXI, 118–126. In Dante's new vision God appears as a microscopic point of exceeding brightness. The center of a circle is like the Almighty in its immobility and its lack of extension. Minuteness is a token of indivisible unity; and the one Indivisible Unit is the center and source of all light. See *Summa Theologiae*, Prima, Qu. xi, Art. 2–4. Encircling the point, about as far away as a halo is from the star it surrounds, a bright ring revolves; and, one after another, eight more concentric girdles of fire are turning, the outermost being of inconceivable magnitude. Their light and speed are proportionate to their proximity to the Point; thus the tiniest circle — the one closest to the center — is the swiftest and brightest, whereas in the material universe the smallest and nearest sphere is the slowest in its revolution. In the world of spirit, space signifies nothing, and vicinity to God is everything; in the physical universe, moreover, the center is the earth, while the center of the spiritual world is God.

The nine rings represent the heavenly Intelligences, which fall into three hierarchies, each composed of three orders: Seraphim, Cherubim, Thrones; Dominations, Virtues, Powers; Principalities, Archangels, Angels. They preside respectively over: the Primum Mobile, the Starry Heaven, the sphere of Saturn; the spheres of Jupiter, Mars, the sun; the spheres of Venus, Mercury, the moon. All these names of angels occur in one place or another in the Bible, but with no suggestion of system; five of them are mentioned by St. Paul (Ephesians, i, 21, and Colossians i, 16), who had visited Paradise. St. Ambrose, *Apologia Prophetae David*, V, 21, enumerates nine angelic choirs; but for an exact designation and classification of the orders — with a lengthy but confused account of their functions — we must look to a fifth or sixth century Neoplatonic Greek treatise, *De Caelesti Hierarchia*, sometimes called the Pseudo-Dionysius. This work, attributed to St. Paul's disciple, "Dionysius the Areopagite," was translated into Latin in the 9th century by the Irish monk and mystic, Johannes Scotus Erigena; in the first half of the 12th century an elaborate commentary on this version was composed by Hugh of St. Victor; and in the second half of the 12th century there was a new translation by Johannes Sarracenus, a friend of John of Salisbury. St. Thomas, in his *Summa Theologiae*, uses both versions and also, apparently, the original text; in his commentary on Dionysius's *De Divinis Nominibus* he uses always the Sarracenus version: see Gardner, 86.

The matter is discussed by St. Thomas in the *Summa Theologiae*, Prima, Qu. cviii, and by Dante in the *Convivio*, II, v. The present canto corrects an error of arrangement made by the author (and others) in his previous description — a shifting of Thrones, Dominations, Powers, and Principalities. In this chapter of the *Convivio*, 7–11, Dante informs us that the three hierarchies contemplate respectively the three persons of the Trinity — Power, Wisdom, and Love, embodied in the Father, the Son, and the Holy Ghost. And inasmuch as each person can be regarded in three ways — in itself, and in its relation to each of the other two — every hierarchy is divided into three orders. St. Thomas ascribes to the nine orders the following functions: Seraphim, love; Cherubim, sight; Thrones, taking and holding; Dominations, command; Virtues, execution; Powers, judgment; Principalities, direction of nations; Archangels, direction of leaders; Angels, direction of individuals.

15. Contemplation of the Primum Mobile suggests the image of the angels and the universe in their relation to God.

27. The motion of the Primum Mobile itself.

32. 'Juno's messenger' is Iris, the rainbow: cf. *Met.*, I, 270–271.

54. Cf. XXVII, 112.

55. The angelic circles are an 'example,' or pattern, of the material spheres.

60. Few philosophers attempt to solve the problem of the relation of the spiritual to the physical world.

70. The Primum Mobile.

76. 'Correspondence' of each heaven to its governing Intelligence, or order of angels.

77. 'Of greater (size) to more (intelligence) and of smaller (size) to less (intelligence).'

81. The wind-gods were sometimes represented as heads blowing a threefold blast from the middle and the two corners of their mouths. See Ristoro d'Arezzo, *Composizione del mondo*, VII, iii. Thus Boreas blows not only the north wind, but also the northwest and northeast. The last is, for Italy, the 'mildest' and clearest. — For the whole image, cf. *Aen.*, XII, 365–367.

90. The sparks into which the fiery rings resolve themselves represent the individual angels that compose the orders. Every angel constitutes a species by itself, but nevertheless it belongs to one of the nine orders, and never leaves it (cf. l. 91).

93. According to an old story, the inventor of the game of chess asked of the King of Persia, as a reward, one grain of corn for the first square, two for the second, four for the third, eight for the fourth, and so on, with successive 'doubling,' through the 64 squares of the chessboard. The result is a number of 20 figures.

105. The Thrones, like the Cherubim and the Seraphim, receive God within them. The line is very obscure; but the idea seems to be that the designation 'Thrones' is appropriate because these angels form the bottom of the highest set, the sovereign angels being (so to speak) seated upon them. According to Dionysius (*De Caelesti Hierarchia*, VII, I, end), the Thrones are so called because they are remote from everything earthly, are close to the highest, receive the divine advent without matter and without motion, carry God, and are fit for divine offices.

114. These are the 'steps': Grace begets good will, Grace and good will constitute desert, desert determines the degree of sight, and sight is the source of love.

117. 'Nocturnal Aries' means 'autumn,' because in that season Aries is the constellation opposite the sun.

130. The great authority for the names, orders, and functions of the angels is a Neoplatonic work, not earlier than the 5th century, *De Caelesti Hierarchia*, attributed to Dionysius the Areopagite, St. Paul's convert in Athens (mentioned in Acts xvii, 34). He was thought to have derived his information from St. Paul, who had visited Paradise.

133. St. Gregory, in his *Moralia in Librum Beati Job*, arranges the angelic orders thus: Seraphim, Cherubim, Powers; Principalities, Virtues, Dominations; Thrones, Archangels, Angels. This sequence is followed by Brunetto Latini in the *Trésor*, and by Dante in *Conv.*, II, v. Elsewhere Gregory has a still different arrangement.

137. Dionysius.

138. St. Paul. — Cf. 2 Cor. xii, 2–4.

Canto XXIX

Argument

A medieval poet could scarcely close a discussion of angels without giving his opinion on certain moot questions concerning them. In this canto, then, we are enlightened as to the date of their creation, the nature of the meritorious act which saved the good ones, the time and character of the sin which damned the bad ones, and the faculties which heavenly Intelligences may possess. To the modern reader such speculations seem otiose; and we are perhaps justified in believing that they did not appear very important to Dante. At any rate, he bitterly denounces those preachers who entertain their congregations with idle guesses, instead of feeding them on the Word of God. It is noteworthy that Dante holds no converse with the angels. He evidently thought of them as exalted, divine, nearer to God than to man. Even those which appear in Hell and Purgatory, although their duties bring them close to the traveler, preserve a certain air of austerity and remoteness.

1. At the vernal equinox, when, at dawn and at sunset, the sun and the moon are opposite each other on the horizon, one rising and the other setting. — 'Latona's children' are Apollo and Diana, the sun and the moon.

2. The sun is in Aries (the Ram, *Montone*), the moon is in Libra (the Scales).

3. The two luminaries 'belt' themselves with the horizon': the horizon line bisects them both.

4. 'As long as is the time between the moment when the horizon runs through the middle of the moon and the moment when the horizon no longer touches the moon' — i.e., about a minute. The sun and moon, exactly balanced for an instant on opposite sides of the horizon, suggest to the poet the figure of a gigantic pair of scales, suspended from the zenith. And just as, in a balance, one scale immediately goes down, and the other up, so one of the two luminaries rises above the horizon and the other sinks below it.

7. The simile of the sun and moon in balance is used to convey the idea of one instant of intermediate stillness and suspense — the silence that intervenes between Beatrice's speech at the end of the last canto and her discourse that begins in l. 10.

12. God is the center of all our conceptions of space and time. — *Ubi* ... *quando* (Latin), 'where ... when.'

13. God was impelled to create the angels, not by a desire to increase his own weal, but by a wish to share his goodness with other beings. This is the doctrine of St. Thomas in *De Veritate Catholicae Fidei*, II, xlvi, and St. Augustine in *De Civitate Dei*, XI, xxiv. Cf. *Par.* VII, 64–66, XIII, 52–55.

15· *Subsisto* (Latin), 'I am.'

19. Time has reference only to created things; for God all time is present, and 'before' and 'after' have no significance. Therefore we may not say that God was inactive 'before' the creation. Cf. St. Augustine, *Confessions*, VII, xv, xvii; XI, xiii: Gardner, 16–68.

21. 'The moving of God' etc. means the creation. Gen. i, 2: "And the spirit of God moved upon the face of the waters." The figure is particularly appropriate here, because the 9th sphere was often called the "aqueous heaven."

22. The line means 'pure form (i.e., character without matter: the angels), pure matter (i.e., matter without spirit: the stuff of which the earth was made), and form and matter conjoined (i.e., the heavens).'

23. 'Came into an existence that had no lack,' i.e., came into independent being (*substantia*). God created the heavens, the angels, and brute matter all together on the first day. Cf. Ecclus. xviii, 1: "Qui vivit in aeternum creavit omnia simul." (He who lives forever created the whole universe at the same time.) So Gen. i, 1: "In principio creavit Deus caelum et terram." (In the beginning God created the heaven and the earth.)

32–33.   The three kinds of beings above named were arranged in due order. At the top (*cima*) were 'those in which pure activity was produced,' i.e., the angels, which, having no body, are pure intelligence, or 'form'; and form, or character, begins to operate as soon as it exists, and continues to operate completely and incessantly. The angels have no powers that are not in constant and full activity. Cf. *Summa Theologiae*, Prima, Qu. l, Art 2.

34. 'Pure potentiality' is characteristic of brute matter, which is capable of no independent activity.

36. Spirit and matter are always united in the spheres.

37–38. A curious Latinizing construction: 'Jerome (in his commentary on the Epistle of Paul to Titus) wrote you down a long lapse of ages from the creation of the angels.' St. Jerome's opinion — that the angels existed countless ages before the creation of the world — is recorded and refuted by St. Thomas in *Summa Theologiae*, Prima, Qu. lxi, Art. 3.

41. Cf. *Mon.*, III, iv, 11: "Nam quamquam scribae divini eloquii multi sint, unicus tamen dictator est Deus, qui beneplacitum suum nobis per multorum calamos explicare dignatus est." (For though the scribes of the divine utterance be many, one is he who dictates to them, even God, who has deigned to set forth his will to us by the pens of many writers.)

44. The angels, who move the heavens.

45. 'Their perfection', i.e., the opportunity for their proper work: 'movers' whose essence is pure activity (cf. note to ll. 32–33) must have something to move.

49. 'One would reach' the number 20, in counting. The rebellious angels fell before one could count 20. The beatitude or damnation of the angels depended on the first act of their will after creation — assuming that they were created in grace and in the exercise of their free will: so St. Thomas in *Summa Theologiae*, Prima, Qu. lxii, Art. 5. Satan and his companions, moved by pride, immediately rejected grace, and fell; the others accepted grace, and thereby enjoyed complete vision of God, which made sin impossible (*loc. cit.*, Art. 8).

51. The lost angels in their fall disturbed brute matter, the 'stuff' of the physical elements.

56. *Inf.* XXXIV, 19–69.

62. Grace revealed the right course to them, and their merit consisted in choosing it.

66. The degree of openness depends on love (*caritas*), which is a result of foreordained disposition.

71. 'It is taught' in the lectures of doctors of theology.

76. The angels.

79. Nothing ever intervenes between their mind and the image of all things in God.

80–81. Forgetfulness is the intervention of a new concept between the former one and the consciousness. With the angels, no concept, or perception, is ever interrupted by another. — St. Thomas inclines to the opinion that angels do not need — and therefore do not possess — memory, but he admits the possibility of their possessing it in a certain sense, if memory be considered as a faculty of the mind: *Summa Theologiae*, Prima, Qu. liv, Art. 5. Cf. St. Augustine, *De Trinitate*, IX, ii, and X, xi. Dante is more positive than his masters. Angels have only intelligence and will. See Moore, IV, 154. St. Thomas, *Summa Theologiae*, uses the term *dividendo* in describing forgetfulness.

97–102. Mat. xxvii, 45: "Now from the sixth hour there was darkness over all the land until the ninth hour." To explain this darkness at the Crucifixion, some said that the moon left its course to make an eclipse, others that the sun hid its own rays. Dionysius (XXVIII, 130) favored the first explanation, St. Jerome the second. Both are recorded by St. Thomas in *Summa Theologiae*, Tertia, Qu. xliv, Art. 2. The second theory has the advantage of accounting for an obscuration "over all the land," whereas an ordinary eclipse would darken only a part of it. The miraculous eclipse recorded in the Bible 'answered for the Spaniards and the Indians' — at the two extremes of the habitable world — 'as well as for the Hebrews.'

103. Lapo and Bindo seem to have been common names in Florence. They were originally nicknames respectively for Jacopo and Ildebrando.

111. Cf. 1 Cor. iii, 10–11: "I have laid the foundation ... For other foundation can no man lay."

117 'The cowl puffs up' with self-satisfaction.

118. The devil is nestling 'in the tail of the hood,' waiting for the preacher's soul.

124. 'On this (credulity) St. Antony fattens his pig.' St. Antony, the founder of monasticism, is generally represented with a hog under his feet, the symbol of his subjugation of the flesh. The monks of his order kept herds of swine, which were regarded as sacred and allowed to roam anywhere, even into private houses. The degenerate Antonians were the most shameless and importunate of the mendicant preachers and pardoners, and Dante compares them to their own pigs.

134. Daniel vii, 10: "thousand thousands ministered unto him, and ten thousand times ten thousand stood before him." Cf. note to XXVIII, 92.

135. This ambiguous line must mean: 'No definite number is apparent.'

137. Every angel constituting a species by itself, no two perceive God alike.

139. 'The act of conception' is the vision of God, which depends on Grace.

Canto XXX

Argument

We now cross the boundary of the world of matter and enter the realm of pure spirit. As the stars, at dawn, gradually fade away before the sunshine, so the bright angelic rings disappear, leaving only the light that emanates from the Point. This light — when the traveler passes from Primum Mobile to Empyrean — becomes so overpowering that he once more, for an instant, loses his sight, to have it restored more fit for the experiences to come. So it fares with all the souls that reach Paradise: they are blinded "to make the candle ready for its flame." Again and again Dante's vision, accustomed to physical cognition, must be purified, strengthened, and adapted to a new kind of perception. Thus, in these closing cantos, one glorious symbol succeeds another.   The first impression he receives is an overwhelming consciousness of Grace, which appears as a vast, inexhaustible river of light.   Next he becomes aware of the souls that Grace sustains — beautiful flowers covering the banks of the stream, visited by ministering angels which flit like sparks between the current and the shores.   Thus far his view of Heaven has been wholly abstract and symbolic.   To behold it in a semblance of concrete reality, his eyes must be touched by Grace, so that they may see the World of the Blessed as it shall be after the Resurrection, when the souls shall be reclothed in the flesh.   He stoops over the bank until his lashes dip in the flood.   Suddenly all is transformed.   The river gathers into a round sea of light, and all about it the banks rise up "in more than a thousand tiers," whereon, as though in their glorified bodies (ll. 44-45), are seated the Elect.   The whole cup-shaped amphitheater presents the figure of a rose, the emblem of love.

I Cor. xiii, 12, "For now we see through a glass, darkly; but then face to face," reads in the Vulgate: "Videmus nunc per speculum in aenigmate, tunc facie ad faciem"; and St. Thomas, in his Commentary on the passage, is led by the Latin phraseology to distinguish three different kinds of sight.   The highest grade of sight, he tells us elsewhere, is the direct intuition of essence; this kind of sight is enjoyed by angels contemplating themselves and by angels and blessed contemplating God: *Summa Theologiae*, Prima, Qu. xii, Art. 4; Qu. lvi, Art. 3.   By a special grace, this intuition was accorded, for one instant, to St. Paul (Secunda Secundae, Qu. clxxv, Art. 3); his contemplation was of the highest type ever granted to man in the first life (Secunda Secundae, Qu. clxxx, Art. 5).

1-3. Dante is about to describe the aspect of the sky, with the stars gradually fading, a little before dawn.   'The sixth hour (i.e., noon) is glowing' some '6000 miles away from us.'   Noon is separated from sunrise by a quarter of the earth's circumference — that is, according to our author's geography (*Conv.*, III, v, 11), by 5100, a quarter of 20,400.   If noon, then, is 6000 miles off, sunrise must still be 900 miles (or about an hour) away.   The sun is below our horizon on one side, and the earth's conical shadow, projected into space, is correspondingly above our horizon on the other.   As the sun rises, the shadow sinks; and when the middle of the sun shall be on the horizon line, the apex of the shadow will be on the same plane in the opposite quarter.   An hour before dawn, therefore, 'this earth is already bowing its shadow down almost to the level bed' of the horizon.   Cf. Moore, III, 58-59.

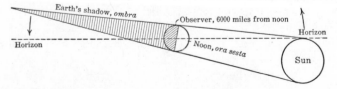

7. Aurora, the dawn.
9. 'From sight to sight': i.e., star by star.   Cf. II, 115.

12. In the allegorical vision which Dante has beheld, the Point seems to be encompassed by the rings of light, whereas in reality God encompasses everything.

24. A 'comic poet' is one who writes in familiar, a 'tragic poet' one who writes in exalted style.

33. Now that Beatrice has reached her own home, the Empyrean, she is seen in her full beauty, which defies description.

39. 'The biggest body' is the Primum Mobile, which surrounds all the rest of the material world.

43. In the Empyrean are two victorious armies, the 'soldiery' of blessed souls that resisted temptation, and the host of good angels that triumphed over the bad.

44–45. The spirits of the elect will be seen by Dante 'in that aspect' in which they are to appear at the Last Judgment: i.e., in their bodily form.

49. Cf. Acts xxii, 6: "suddenly there shone from heaven a great light round about me."

51. Cf. Acts xxii, 11: "I could not see for the glory of that light."

61. See Daniel vii, 10: "A fiery stream issued and came forth before him." Also Rev. xxii, 1: "And he shewed me a pure river of water of life, clear as crystal, proceeding out of the throne of God and of the Lamb." Cf. Isaiah lxvi, 12. In the apocryphal Book of Enoch, rivers of flaming fire issue from under the throne. St. Bernard, *Sermones de Diversis*, XLII, vii, says: "torrente voluptatis potantur justi." Dante makes of this traditional river a symbol of Grace, or, more specifically, of the "Light of Glory." See Singleton (1958), pp. 15–23.

63. The spring flowers that cover the banks are the souls of the just.

64–66. The 'living sparks' that emerge from the flood and nestle in the flowers, 'like rubies set in gold,' are the angels, whose function it is to assist in the transmission of grace.

88–89. 'The eaves of my eyelids' are the lashes.

100. We find that the light still represents Grace, or more specifically, the "light of glory." See Singleton (1958), pp. 15–38.

102. Cf. St. Augustine, *Confessions*, I, i: "Fecisti nos ad te, et inquietum est cor nostrum, donec requiescat in te." (Thou hast created us for thyself, and our heart cannot be quieted till it find repose in thee.)

106–108. The whole material universe forms a globe, whose exterior is that of the Primum Mobile. One ray of God's grace descends upon this sphere, and gives it life and motion; then, reflected from its smooth, round surface, is transformed into the circular ocean of light that appears as the floor of Paradise.

117. The vast, cuplike theater is called a 'rose,' and its sections 'petals.'

124. The 'yellow of the rose' is the sea of light that forms the bottom of the arena. Cf. Rev. iv, 6: "And before the throne there was a sea of glass like unto crystal."

129. See Rev. iii, 5: "He that overcometh, the same shall be clothed in white raiment"; and vii, 13: "What are these which are arrayed in white robes?" Cf. *Par.* XXV, 88–96.

131–132. Men are so wicked, and the end of the world is so near, that only a few more souls are expected in Paradise.

133. The impressive episode of a vacant chair in Heaven is found in several medieval legends: in the Syriac version of the *Visio S. Pauli*, in the vision of Tundal, and in the *Dialogus Miraculorum* of Caesarius of Heisterbach.

134. The homage which Dante, in these lines, pays to his worshiped Henry acquires tremendous force from the unfitness of a symbol of mundane sovereignty in Paradise.

137. Henry of Luxembourg, elected Emperor (Henry VII) in 1308, crowned at Milan in 1311, attempted to restore the balance of power and the Imperial authority in Italy, but met with determined opposition and died at Buonconvento in 1313.

142. The Pope, or 'prefect in the sacred court,' is Clement V, who died in 1314, eight months after Henry.

144. Clement, after encouraging Henry to undertake the Italian expedition, underhandedly worked against him, and finally opposed him without disguise. Cf. *Inf.* XIX, 82–87; *Par.* XXVII, 82.

146–147. For Simon Magus, cf. *Inf.* XIX, 1. — Clement shall fall into the 3rd pouch of the 8th circle of Hell, where simonists are planted upside down in fiery holes. In the hole of the simoniacal Popes, each new arrival pushes his predecessors farther down: *Inf.* XIX, 73–75.

147. Clement's predecessor in simony is Boniface VIII: *Inf.* XIX, 51–57. He is called 'the man of Anagni' because he was born in that town, and in 1303 was assaulted and taken prisoner there: *Purg.* XX, 85–90. Anagni was known also as *Alagna* and *Anagna.* — These fearful words are the last spoken by Beatrice.

Canto XXXI

Argument

Through all Dante's *Paradiso* there has been little thought of matter. Sound and light have been the main ingredients of his marvelous effects, even in the physical heavens. And now, in the last four cantos, he achieves what no other poet, before or since, has attempted with so much as a shadow of success: the presentation of a world beyond the perceptions of sense. Discreet omission and subtle suggestion, insistence on a progressive sharpening of spiritual insight, repeated warning that the increasingly exalted vision can be expressed only in ever more inadequate symbols — these are the elements from which the master creates an atmosphere of supersensual grandeur, love, and joy. A well-contrived gradation leads from the first comprehension of Grace to the immediate view of God, the climax of the poem. No incongruous didactic theme is allowed to disturb our tenuous but distinct impression of actual presence. Questions physical and metaphysical have been disposed of ere we reach the Empyrean. The only doctrines formulated here are the appropriate ones of predestination and the salvation of infants; these are set forth in Canto XXXII.

To afford some support for the imagination, to lend to the ethereal conception some of the solid substance of personal identity, the poet fancies himself permitted by a special grace to gaze on the assembly of the Blessed as they shall appear after the Judgment Day. "For our conversation is in heaven, from whence also we look for the Saviour ...: who shall change our vile body, that it may be fashioned like unto his glorious body" (Philippians iii, 20–21). The vast amphitheater (whose floor is a sea of glory) is thronged with faces, all of them clearly visible, in spite of incalculable distance. Between them and their Maker, who shines from above, hovers a thick swarm of angels, messengers between God and man; and even these purely spiritual beings now show themselves to Dante in a bodily form. Their presence, however, in no wise obstructs the direct vision of the Lord; in other words, the Just receive grace not only through angelic transmission, but straight from the Creator himself.

While Dante is wondering at this scene, Beatrice slips away, just as Virgil, his mission ended, silently took his departure from the Garden of Eden (*Purg.*

XXX, 46–54). This time, however, there is no sadness in the parting, for the "Gentilissima" has simply returned to her high seat in Heaven; whereas the earlier companion went back to eternal captivity below.   Now that the pilgrim is in the actual presence of God, he has no further need of Revelation for a guide; and Beatrice, who was chosen from all the souls in Paradise to perform this office for him, now resumes her own personality and her own place.   In her stead, at Dante's side, is St. Bernard, the type of Intuition.   Reason, Revelation, Intuition represent the three stages of approach to God.

The verses of the present canto offer an unusual abundance of examples of hiatus and diaeresis, which would seem to indicate a slow, thoughtful, impressive delivery.   In such cases as *cominciò | elli* and *farà | ogni* (where a final vowel is stressed) hiatus is the rule in our poet.   Also, in words like *ardüa, fïata, gaudïoso* (contrasted with *gaudio*), *glorïose, orïental, regïon, rïaccesa, süadi* — mostly Latinisms — diaeresis is rather to be expected in the *Commedia,* although the number of such forms is uncommonly large in this canto.   Very rare indeed, on the other hand, are lines comparable to 37, 47, and 53:

> ï/o che | al divino da l' umano,
> menava | ï/o li occhi per li gradi,
> già tutta mï/o sguardo avea compresa.

Curiously enough, the name Beatrice, which in the *Paradiso* very frequently shows separation of the *e* and the *a* (as is always the case with *bëato*), here in every instance combines the two vowels into one syllable.   Is this because the Bestower of Blessings has now become once more Beatrice Portinari?   It is to be noted that in ll. 79–90 Dante addresses her as *tu;* up to this time he has always used the respectful *voi.*

The power of angels to assume aerial bodies is admitted by St. Gregory, *Moralia,* XXVIII, i (commentary on Job xxxviii, 7).

1. The figure of the rose seems to be Dante's own, although Paradise is sometimes represented in roselike form in early Italian art.   The rose, too, was sometimes used as a symbol of the Passion.   On the fourth Sunday of Lent, the Pope blesses a gold rose ("rosa aurea mixta cum balsamo et musco"), with a ceremonial that indicates an association of this flower with Christ and Heaven.   The Old French *Roman de la Rose,* the great literary success of the 13th century, made all western Europe familiar with the rose as a symbol of earthly love; Dante's white flower is the rose of Heavenly love.   The figure of the rose is also an homage to Mary, who presides in the assembly.

13. Cf. Ezekiel i, 13: "their appearance was like living coals of fire."

14. Cf. Daniel x, 5 ("whose loins were girded with fine gold") and vii, 9 ("whose garment was white as snow"); also Song of Solomon v, 10 and 11: "My beloved is white and ruddy" and "His head is as the most fine gold."   The angels embody love, purity, and faith.   Cf. the figure of the Griffin in *Purg.* xxix, 113–114.

26. Members of the Old (Hebrew) and the New (Christian) Church.

31–33. The 'zone' that is always 'covered by Helice' is the North. The nymph Helĭce or Callisto was transformed into the constellation of the Great Bear, and her son Arcas or Boötes into the Little Bear: *Met.*, II, 496–530, especially 515–517; cf. *Purg.* XXV, 131. The Bears, or Dippers, are close to the North Star.

35. The 'Lateran' is the old Papal palace in Rome: cf. *Inf.* XXVII, 86. According to tradition, it was given to St. Sylvester by Emperor Constantine (cf. *Inf.* XXVII, 94–95), and became the seat of Christian dominion. Less than a century later, the barbarians invaded Rome.

39. This phrase, the climax of the tiercet, is Dante's last and bitterest fling at Florence.

59. For the characteristics of *senio*, or old age, see *Conv.*, IV, xxiv, 4. This elder is St. Bernard, founder of the Abbey of Clairvaux in Champagne, a great preacher and mystic of the first half of the 12th century, famous for his ardent devotion to the Blessed Virgin. It was he who preached the second crusade. One of his works is cited in Epistola XIII, xxviii, 80.

67–68. Beatrice's own seat is 'in the third row from the top tier.' The 1st row is that of Mary, the 2nd that of Eve, the 3rd that of Rachel, beside whom Beatrice sits: see *Inf.* II, 102; *Par.* XXXII, 8–9. Contemplation and Revelation sit side by side. The number 3 (as well as the number 9) has always been mysteriously associated with Beatrice: see *V. N.*, XXIX.

73–75. An 'eye' at the very bottom of the sea 'is not so far away' from the top of the earth's atmosphere — the 'region that thunders highest up' (cf. *Purg.* XXI, 43–57, and XXXII, 111).

81. See *Inf.* II, 52–93; *Purg.* XXX, 139–141.

85. Cf. *Summa Theologiae*, Secunda Secundae, Qu. clxxxiii, Art. 4: "Libertas a peccato … vera libertas … vera servitus est servitus peccati." (Freedom from sin is true freedom … true servitude is the servitude of sin.)

96. The 'prayer and holy love' are Beatrice's.

104. The Veronica is the true image of the Savior, left on a kerchief which a holy woman had handed him, on his way to Calvary, to wipe the sweat from his face. It was shown at St. Peter's in Rome on certain days. Hosts of pilgrims went from afar to see it, as Dante tells us in *V. N.*, XL, 1–7.

111. St. Bernard in his meditations had a foretaste of the peace of Heaven. In the *Meditationes Piissimae* (ascribed to him), i, we find a rhapsody on the joys of contemplation. Cf. *Sermones in Cantica Canticorum*, XXIII, 15–16, and lxxiv.

125. For Phaëthon and his luckless attempt to drive the chariot of the sun, cf. *Inf.* XVII, 106–108; *Purg.* XXIX, 118–120; *Par.* XVII, 3.

127. The streak of light on Mary's side of the uppermost tier of the arena is called an oriflamme of peace.' The real oriflamme — a red pennant on a gilded staff, given by the Archangel Gabriel to the kings of France — was a standard of war.

132. Every angel, as has been said before, forms a species by itself, with its own degree of brightness and its own ministry.

Canto XXXII

Argument

On one side of the rim of the great cup of Paradise sits Mary; on her right is St. Peter, and beyond him St. John; on her left is Adam, then Moses. Opposite Mary, on the other side of the rim, sits John the Baptist, with St. Anna on his right and St. Lucia on his left. The Virgin is in the midst of four men, the Baptist is between two women. From Mary to the bottom of the cup extends a straight row of Old Testament women, the first of whom (after Mary) are Eve, Rachel,

ROSA CELESTIALE

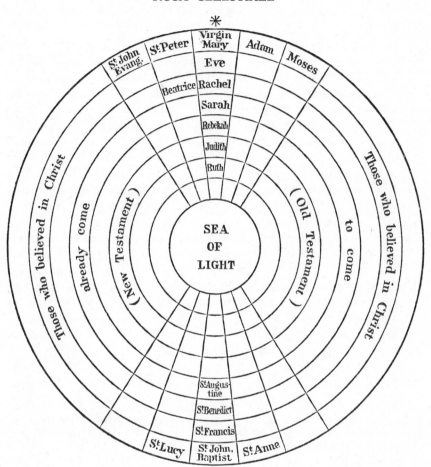

Sarah, Rebecca, Judith, and Ruth; on the right of Rachel is Beatrice.   Across the
cup from this row, a line of holy men stretches from John the Baptist to the
bottom — the second, third, and fourth being St. Francis, St. Benedict, and St.
Augustine.   The half of the amphitheater which lies at the right of the line of
men and at the left of the row of women is filled with the souls of virtuous
Hebrews who died before the Redemption.   The other half — at the right of
Mary's line and at the left of John's — belongs to the souls of Christians; here
some of the seats are still empty.   The lower part of both halves, from the
middle down, is occupied by the spirits of children who died before the age of

moral responsibility.   They are here because their parents had faith in Christ, either before or after his coming; on the Christian side, baptism is an indispensable prerequisite.

The children are mentioned here for the first time; no sphere offers an appropriate place for them, unless we are to understand that they are included in the army of the blessed which assembles in the eighth heaven.   Like the adults, they enjoy various degrees of beatitude, in proportion to the grace accorded them at birth.   Our poet here departs from St. Thomas (*Summa Theologiae*, Tertia, Qu. lxix, Art. 8), who declares that all children admitted to baptism receive the same amount of grace; St. Bonaventure, however, admits the possibility of difference for them.   Their presence serves to emphasize the mystery of predestination, in accordance with which all the seats in the Rose are allotted. Dante's insistence on this doctrine renders futile any attempt at general classification of the souls in the Empyrean.   In Hell and Purgatory the topography is systematically described for us.   No such exposition is given us in Paradise. In the journey through the spheres, we are introduced to certain types of merit and reward, which may or may not correspond in a way to the gradations of the amphitheater.   In the Rose itself we are informed of the great vertical and horizontal divisions, and the position of a few of the souls; and we may infer that proximity to Mary or to John the Baptist is a sign of honor.   Beyond, that all is mystery.

Gazing upon this vast assembly, Dante finds satisfaction of the desire expressed in Canto XXII, ll. 58–60, to behold the Elect uncovered.

In the mosaic representation of Paradise in the Florentine Baptistery, the shape is circular and Mary is opposite John the Baptist.

4–6. The 'wound' of orginal sin (inflicted by Eve and healed by Mary) is discussed in *Summa Theologiae*, Prima Secundae, Qu. lxxxv, Art. 3.   Mary is often represented as the counterpart of Eve.   The word *Ave*, with which she is greeted, is the reverse of *Eva*; so says, among others, Dante's son Pietro.   St. Bernard, *Sermo de Beata Maria Virgine*, compares Mary to a rose, Eve to a thorn.

7–9. Cf. *Inf.* II, 102; *Par.* XXXI, 67–69.

11. Ruth. — David.

12. *Miserere mei*, 'have mercy upon me.' Ps. li (Vulg. I), 1.

18. The 'locks of the flower' are its petals, and the petals of the rose are presumably the sections of seats in the amphitheater. — The line of Hebrew women cuts through all the rows from top to bottom.   The first seven have been named; the rest are not.

19–20. 'According to the look which Faith turned on Christ': i.e., according as the Faith of the Hebrews and of certain pagans looked forward to Christ to come, or the Faith of the Christians looked back to Christ crucified.   On one side of the partition (made by the line of Jewesses) are the Hebrews, on the other the Christians.

25–26. 'Where the semicircles are broken by empty space': where some seats, here and there, are still vacant.

31. Mat. xi, 11: "Among them that are born of women there hath not risen a greater than John the Baptist." Cf. *Purg.* XXII, 153.

32. "He shall be filled with the Holy Ghost, even from his mother's womb" (Luke i, 15).

33. The Limbus, where John, after his death, had to wait some two years for the descent of Christ to rescue the souls of the just.

35. St. Augustine, the founder of Theology, and St. Benedict (XXII, 28) and St. Francis (XI, 43), the great founders of orders, may be regarded as successors of John the Baptist. Cf. Luke i, 17.

38–39. After the Last Judgment, the souls from the Old Church will be exactly equal in number to those from the New.

46–48. According to the usual opinion, the bodies of all the elect will rise, at the Resurrection, in the aspect of the prime of life. Cf. *Summa Theologiae*, Suppl., Qu. lxxxi, Art. 1–2. So they are commonly pictured in medieval art. In his striking departure from current belief, Dante was influenced certainly by a desire for significant visible contrast and also, we may conjecture, by that love of little children which he has more than once revealed. The sweet conception of an encircling sea of baby faces, all twittering with baby voices, must have charmed him as it charms us.

49. Dante is silently wondering why, if these children never won merit by the exercise of their free will, some have higher seats than others. He learns presently that the degree of beatitude (symbolized by the height of the seat) is determined by predestination, not by one's own acts: cf. *Summa Theologiae*, Prima Secundae, Qu. cxii.

53. Everything has a definite cause.

58–59. 'And therefore this company, hurried to the true life, is not *sine causa*' (Latin: 'without cause').

67–69. Jacob and Esau 'struggled together' in their mother's womb: Gen. xxv, 22–25. Cf. Malachi, i, 2–3: "I have loved you, saith the Lord. Yet ye say, wherein hast thou loved us? Was not Esau Jacob's brother? saith the Lord: yet I loved Jacob. `And I hated Esau." So Romans ix, 10–15: "And not only this; but when Rebecca also had conceived ...: (For the children being not yet born, neither having done any good or evil, that the purpose of God according to election might stand, not of works, but of him that calleth;) It was said unto her, The elder shall serve the younger. As it is written, Jacob have I loved, but Esau have I hated. What shall we say then? Is there unrighteousness with God? God forbid. For he saith to Moses, I will have mercy on whom I will have mercy." See *Summa Theologiae*, Prima, Qu. xxiii, Art. 3.

70–72. 'Therefore the heavenly light must crown us fitly, according to the complexion of that grace.' Our halo, or reward, in Heaven is proportionate to the grace bestowed on us at birth. The odd expression, 'the color of the hair of that grace,' was evidently suggested by Esau's red hair: Gen. xxv, 25. Esau, without apparent reason, differed in looks from Jacob, just as he differed from him in character and in divine favor.

75. 'Primal keenness' of spiritual sight, which is bestowed by Grace.

76. 'New,' fresh from creation: before Abraham. 'New' is the original meaning of *recens*.

80–81. 'It was requisite for the males to win strength for the wings of innocence by circumcision.' Cf. *Summa Theologiae*, Tertia, Qu. lxx, Art. 2: "Circumcisio instituta est ut signum fidei Abrahae, qui credidit se patrem futurum Christi sibi repromissi; et ideo convenienter solis maribus competebat. Peccatum etiam originale, contra quod specialiter circumcisio ordinabatur, a patre trahitur, non a matre." (The institution of circumcision is as a sign of Abraham's faith, who believed that he himself would be the father of Christ, who was promised to him: and for this reason it was suitable that it should be for males only. Again, original sin, against which circumcision was specially ordained, is contracted from the father, not from the mother.) See Prima Secundae, Qu. lxxxi, Art. 5. Cf. *Inf.* IV, 37–38.

82–84. After the Crucifixion, the unbaptized innocent children were 'confined below' in the Limbus: cf. *Inf.* IV, 30, 34–36. Since the Redemption, there has been no salvation without baptism in Christ. See *Summa Theologiae*, Tertia, Qu. lxx, Art. 2: "Baptismus in se continet perfectionem salutis, ad quam Deus omnes homines vocat ... Circumcisio autem non continebat perfectionem salutis, sed figurabat ipsam ut fiendam per Christum." (Baptism contains in itself the perfection of salvation, to which God calls all men ... On the other hand, circumcision did not contain the perfection of salvation, but signified it as to be achieved by Christ.) Cf. Tertia, Qu. lxii. — For the fourth and last time, we have a series of rhymes in *Cristo*.

89. The heavenly Intelligences, or angels.

94. The angel Gabriel. Cf. XXIII, 94–96.

95. Luke i, 28: "Hail, thou that art highly favoured."

114. The 'burden' of human sin.

119. 'The Empress': Mary. Augusta was an established title for the wife of the Emperor. Cf. XXX, 136.

125. Mat. xvi, 19. Cf. *Inf.* XIX, 91–92.

127. St. John, the author of the Apocalypse.

128. The Church.

129. John xix, 34.

130. Peter. — Adam.

131. 'Leader': Moses. See Exod. xvi, 14–35.

133. St. Anna, mother of Mary.

137. St. Lucia, the type of Illumining Grace, who has twice come to Dante's aid: *Inf.* II, 97–108; *Purg.* IX, 55–63.

138. 'When thou wast bending thy brows to fall': *Inf.* I, 61. Lucia sent Beatrice to save Dante at the time when the wolf was driving him back into the wooded valley.

139. Since, within the poem, this journey to the afterlife has never been termed a *dream*, but has always been presented as *real*, it is not possible to understand this verse, with the verb *assonnare*, to contradict this fundamental postulate of the experience. Many differing views have been held of the meaning. The view that seems most persuasive in the total context would see in the phrase *che t'assonna*, modifying *tempo*, a clear reference to the accepted fact that the experience of rising so high, all the way to God, on the part of a man who is still mortal, must of necessity be of the briefest duration. (Cf. "mortal weight," *Par.* XXVII, 64). The blessed and the angels are privileged to gaze upon God through all eternity, but a mortal man can have the experience through the *light of glory* only momentarily. Thus St. Thomas, under the standard heading "Of Rapture" (*Summa Theologiae*, Secunda Secundae, Qu. clxxv, Art. 3 ad 2), states: "The Divine Essence cannot be seen by a created intellect save through the light of glory, of which it is written (Psalm xxxv, 10): *In Thy light we shall see light*. But this light can be shared in two ways. First by way of an abiding form, and thus it beatifies the saints in heaven. Secondly, by way of a *transitory* passion [italics added] ..." which was the experience of St. Paul when rapt to the third heaven.

Thus St. Bernard, with his phrase *il tempo che t'assonna*, is (given the moment and the context) referring to the fundamental difference between the pilgrim's mortal condition (his mortal weight that will pull him down) and the condition of the blessed, which is his own. "Your experience here," he means, "is necessarily *transitory* and can last only for the briefest time." Accordingly, the following simile of the tailor suggests, "Let us make the most of the time that is left to you." *Assonnare* is thus not literal in its meaning but bears an allusion that makes it metaphorical. "Sleep" is a falling away from the final experience, which must happen soon, for the mortal man's experience of the light of glory is most transitory. (On the *light of glory* see Singleton (1958), pp. 15–23.)

Canto XXXIII

Argument

The *Commedia* differs from most narratives in the abruptness of its beginning and end. No prelude is suffered to retard the entrance of the theme, and no epilogue dispels the stupendous exaltation of the climax. Isolated, complete in itself, the story of repentance, reform, and regeneration pursues its steady march from the opening line of the poem to its grand culmination — admission to the actual presence of God. Such an experience as this final one far transcends the powers both of speech and of recollection. Cautiously, laboriously, the poet feels his way through the dim chambers of memory, evoking evanescent glimpses of unspeakable vanished impressions, which, in the cruel lack of every means of direct conveyance, he can express only in the form of unsubstantial images. No tinsel royalty belittles Dante's Paradise, no pitiful attempt to describe the indescribable. First of all, we are made conscious of the unity and the universality of the Almighty: indivisible and undiversified, he contains the entire multiform world, whose true existence is in him alone. Next his threefold oneness is disclosed to us by the symbol of three mysterious rings — three distinct circles of three different colors, but occupying exactly the same place. One of these rings, depicting in itself, with its own color, the figure of mankind, reveals the human nature in Christ and its absolute union with the divine. At this point a sudden flash of Grace for one instant illumines the beholder with full understanding, and his individual will is merged in the World Will of the Creator.

A purely intuitive, intellectual vision is devoid of physical images; but after the experience is over, the memory may retain impressions capable of expression in concrete form. Thus St. Paul's memory, at the close of his vision of Paradise, kept certain "likenesses of visible things." St. Thomas, *Quaestiones de Veritate*, Qu. xiii, Art. 3; *Summa Theologiae*, Secunda Secundae, Qu. clxxv, Art. 4.

Although the persons of the Trinity are very often described by Church writers as of exceeding brightness, the conception of the three rings of light seems, in the main, to be of Dante's invention. In Rev. iv, 3, we read: "And he that sat was to look upon like a jasper and a sardine stone: and there was a rainbow round about the throne, in sight like unto an emerald." Commentators indulged in much speculation on this verse, attempting to determine the colors of the three precious stones. St. Thomas makes them white, green, and red, the colors chosen by Dante to designate the three virtues. Furthermore, the image of the rainbow was used to symbolize the Trinity (particularly by St. Basil in *Epistolae*, Classis I, Ep. xxxviii); the figure was not inappropriate, because, according to Aristotle and others, the rainbow consists of three colors, which blend into one another.

1. The beautiful prayer to the Blessed Virgin, with which this canto opens, is quite in the style of St. Bernard.   Such an intercession is wholly in accordance with Catholic practice.

22. The lake of ice at the center of the earth or, more probably, the whole cavity of Hell.

65–66. The Cumaean Sibyl was accustomed to write her prophecies on loose tree leaves, which, whenever a wind arose, were scattered about and lost: Aen., III, 441–451.

76–78. When we turn from gazing on a very bright light, our eyes are blurred for everything else: cf. XXV, 118–120.   So the sight of God makes all other vision seem confused and meaningless.

82. To behold the divine essence, our human sight must be fortified by divine enlightenment: St. Thomas, De Veritate Catholicae Fidei contra Gentiles, III, liv.

86. God is the Book of the Universe.   Cf. Purg. III, 126.

88. Nothing being accidental in God, the distinction between substance and accident does not exist in him: Summa Theologiae, Prima, Qu. iii, Art. 6. — Costume, ' habit.'

89–90. God, containing all things, is a perfect unit: see Summa Theologiae, Prima, Qu. iv, Art. 2. Cf. Par. XXVIII, 16–21.

91–93. Painfully groping in his memory, the poet is encouraged by a sense of satisfaction with his statement — a reminiscence of the glow of contentment (the "passione impressa") which came over him when he first comprehended the union of everything in God.   This feeling leads him to believe that his report thus far has been correct. — By ' the universal form of this knot' is meant the absolute principle of this union — the fusion of all things temporal and eternal in the Creator.

94–96. The expedition of the Argonauts, under Jason, in search of the golden fleece (Inf. XVIII, 86–87; Par. II, 16–18) was thought to have occurred in the 13th century B.C.   The Argo was the first ship ever built: hence Neptune's surprise.

100–102. Cf. Summa Theologiae, Prima Secundae, Qu. v, Art. 4: "Perfecta beatitudo hominis in visione divinae essentiae consistit.   Est autem impossibile quod aliquis videns divinam essentiam velit eam non videre. ... Visio autem divinae essentiae replet animam omnibus bonis, cum conjungat fonti totius bonitatis. ... Sic ergo patet quod propria voluntate beatus non potest beatitudinem deserere." (Man's perfect happiness consists in the vision of the divine essence.   Now it is impossible for anyone seeing the divine essence, to wish not to see it. ... But the vision of the divine essence fills the soul with all good things, since it unites it to the source of all goodness. ... It is thus evident that the happy man cannot forsake happiness of his own accord.)

118. The circle representing the Son seemed reflected from the circle symbolizing the Father, just as one arch of a double rainbow is reflected by the other (cf. XII, 10–13) — ' Iris by Iris.'

119. The Holy Ghost emanates equally from Father and Son. Cf. X, 1–2.

125–126. Mat. xi, 27: "no man knoweth the Son, but the Father; neither knoweth any man the Father, save the Son."   Cf. Summa Theologiae, Prima, Qu. xxxiv, Art. 1: "Pater enim intelligendo se et Filium et Spiritum Sanctum ... concipit Verbum." (For the Father, by understanding Himself, the Son, and the Holy Ghost, conceives the Word.)

133–135. Cf. Mon., III, iii, 2: "geometra circuli quadraturam ignorat." (The geometrician knows not how to square the circle.)

143. St. Thomas, in De Veritate Catholicae Fidei contra Gentiles, III, xxv, tells us that, inasmuch as the knowledge of God is the natural goal of man's desire, no other knowledge can suffice for human happiness.

144. The circle, being the perfect figure, is an emblem of perfection; and circular motion symbolizes full and faultless activity.   St. Thomas, In Librum B. Dionysii De Divinis Nominibus, Caput iv, Lectio 7: "Et ideo circularitas motus animae completur in hoc quod ad Deum manuducit." (And therefore the circularity of the movement of the soul is completed in that it leads to God.)   At the end of his journey, in the presence of his Maker, Dante's love is made perfect, ' like a wheel in even revolution.'

145. The stars, at which the poet has gazed wistfully from below, are now beneath him. Their conformity to God's plan is not more complete than his, nor is their rotation more perfect than the movement of his desire and will.

Index

This list is intended to include the names of persons and places mentioned in the poem. All names are given in their conventional English form wherever possible. Even though a name may occur more than once in a single passage or a given canto, only its first occurrence there is listed. Italicized numbers of cantos and verses indicate that the reference to the person or place in question is indirect, without the actual name appearing there. For a more complete index, or rather, for a work that can serve such a purpose in the most minute detail, see Paget Toynbee, *A Dictionary of Proper Names and Notable Matters in the Works of Dante*, revised by Charles S. Singleton, Oxford, Clarendon Press, 1968.